Young Men in Uncertain Times

YOUNG MEN IN UNCERTAIN TIMES

Edited by
Vered Amit and Noel Dyck

berghahn
NEW YORK • OXFORD
www.berghahnbooks.com

Published in 2012 by
Berghahn Books
www.berghahnbooks.com

©2012, 2013 Vered Amit and Noel Dyck
First paperback edition published in 2013

Library of Congress Cataloging-in-Publication Data
Young men in uncertain times / edited by Vered Amit and Noel Dyck.
    p. cm.
  Includes bibliographical references and index.
   ISBN 978-0-85745-249-8 (hardback : alk. paper) ~ ISBN 978-0-85745-250-4 (institutional
ebook) ~ ISBN 978-1-78238-312-3 (paperback) ~ ISBN 978-1-78238-313-0 (retail ebook)
   1. Young men~Cross-cultural studies. 2. Young men~Attitudes. 3. Young men~Social conditions. I. Amit, Vered, 1955- II. Dyck, Noel.
  GN483.Y675 2012
  305.242'1~dc22
                                                                        2011014593

British Library Cataloguing in Publication Data

A catalogue record for this book is available from the British Library

Printed in the United States on acid-free paper.

ISBN 978-1-78238-312-3 paperback
ISBN 978-1-78238-313-0 retail ebook

We dedicate this volume to the memory of Eduardo P. Archetti,
a much missed friend and colleague.

Contents

Acknowledgments

We would like to thank Marion Berghahn for first suggesting this project and for her encouragement and insight throughout its development. We also thank our contributors for their participation in this volume.

Pursuing Respectable Adulthood
Social Reproduction in Times of Uncertainty

Vered Amit and Noel Dyck

In 2009, in the midst of a severe global economic downturn, a number of columns appeared in North American and British newspapers pondering the fate of youths and the implications of this downturn for them, especially for young men. Among these essays could be found an extended piece by Doug Saunders, the London-based columnist for the Canadian newspaper *The Globe and Mail*, ruminating on the circumstances of the half dozen or so young men who, day after day, hung around outside his house "wearing hoodies and white sneakers and doing not much of anything except smoking skunk, drinking lager from cans and trying to get their bull terriers to fight" (2009: F1). Saunders explained that these young men formed part of the one million Britons between the ages of eighteen and twenty-four who had become known by the bureaucratic tag of NEETs (Not in Employment, Education, or Training). While their situation had been exacerbated by the recession of 2008/09, it did not altogether have its genesis therein. Even in the previous boom years, unskilled youths such as these had a high level of unemployment and dependency; yet in spite of a decade of youth training programs, social mobility had declined rather than improved. These deepening disparities reflected the transformation of the British economy from manufacturing to finance, services, and knowledge based industries, a shift that had left behind the unskilled offspring of generations of blue-collar industrial workers. Furthermore Saunders argued that the scope and persistence of the NEET population represented the failure of the British educational system to guide this transition and the tendency for government programs to focus on trying to attract employers to declining industrial areas rather than changing the way in which people worked. And he cautioned that "in places where the economy is moving fast into a post-industrial mode, it is worth watching the British example: When you shift from brawn to brains, you need to do something for the guys left standing out in the street" (2009: F6).

Writing along similar lines in the British newspaper *The Guardian*, Polly Toynbee (2009) pointed out that the income gap had grown during the 1980s and 1990s. The failure to help a previous generation of disenfranchised youths in the 1980s downturn had devastated "post-industrial regions" of Britain. It was therefore imperative, Toynbee argued, to increase the number of spaces available in British universities and ensure an even greater government commitment to youth training and job subsidies, in order to avert "an entirely predictable social calamity."

Bob Herbert, a *New York Times* op-ed columnist, noted strikingly similar unemployment trends in the United States, especially among young men. Citing statistics provided by the Center for Labor Market Studies at Northeastern University, Herbert (2009) noted that only 65 out of every 100 men aged twenty to twenty-four and 81 of every 100 men aged twenty-five to thirty-four were working, while the numbers among male teenagers were "disastrous" and among minority teenagers "catastrophic." But while Saunders and Toynbee identified persistent employment problems with a particularly marginalized population, Herbert seemed to feel that the problem had become more pervasive because the American economy is simply no longer able to produce sufficient "good jobs" to meet the needs and lifestyle expectations of the American population:

> The unemployment that has wrought such devastation in black communities for decades is now being experienced by a much wider swathe of the population. We've been in deep denial about this. Way back in March 2007, when the official unemployment rate was a wildly deceptive 4.5 percent and the Bush crowd was crowing about the alleged strength of the economy, I [Herbert] wrote:

> "People can howl all they want about how well the economy is doing. The simple truth is that millions of ordinary American workers are in an employment bind. Steady jobs with good benefits are going the way of Ozzie and Harriet. Young workers, especially, are hurting, which diminishes the prospects for the American family. And blacks, particularly black males, are in a deep danger zone."

These columns thus focus on the circumstances of particular segments of youth populations as a lightning rod for assessing the social impacts of politico-economic changes which are exacerbated by but actually preceded the recent global economic recession. In these and many other similar media reports, there appears to be an increasing recognition that economic restructuring has had fundamental consequences for certain young men as members of an identifiable and identified social category, not to mention as individuals. Furthermore, the ways in which young men are affected by these processes are seen as posing broader social issues. In particular, the idleness of youths, especially of male youths, is represented as highlighting the deepening inequalities associated with post-industrial shifts in the structure of the labor market and economy.

But there is an important distinction between, on the one hand, a concern with the serious problems that are confronting many young men and, on the other, the notion of young men themselves constituting a distinctive and increasingly worrisome type of "problem." Even if the particular columnists we have cited are largely sympathetic to the plight of these socially excluded youths, nevertheless, as Doug Saunders noted in his own piece, other popular observers are as likely to depict them as posing a dangerous menace to social order, a "feral youth peril."

Moral panics about one category or another of youths in general and of young men in particular are hardly new. As Saunders has also noted, they have many earlier parallels in British popular representations at different historical moments. And indeed for youth studies researchers, there is likely to be a strong sense of déjà vu since over three decades ago the researchers of the Centre for Contemporary Cultural Studies (the Birmingham School) noted the tendency by self-proclaimed moral guardians to scapegoat youths as agents of social breakdown (Clarke et al. 1976).

But these newspaper columns also reveal an equally familiar proclivity to resort to shopworn political interpretations of and "solutions" to the problems facing youths. As Saunders's and Toynbee's articles illustrate, there is an easy slide into assumptions about the play of class, resulting in a tendency to explain the problems of young men as largely restricted to the most marginalized and uneducated sections of the working class. In turn, there is a quick resort to asserting the capacity of education to serve as a panacea for all economic and social ills, even when the limited impacts of previous educational initiatives are acknowledged.

These kinds of diagnoses and prescriptions are hardly restricted to popular media accounts. As we shall try to illustrate in this opening chapter, a wide cross-section of scholarly literature reiterates them in one form or another, often with little more in the way of critical interrogation and, if anything, an even greater penchant for sweeping ideological homilies.

The result has all too often been less a thorough investigation of the various circumstances in which young men are situated than an assertion of superficial stereotypes.[1] Curiously, there is an implicit tendency in these approaches to depict young men as though, in certain vital respects, they exist almost apart from and perhaps even in opposition to the rest of society. Yet when assumptions such as these seem not only to waft through newspaper columnists' explanations but also to appear unannounced within academic treatments of young men, we are obliged to take account of the ways in which they are being depicted and conceptualized by those who would purport to understand and explain them.

Envisioning Young Men

Within academic writings there is a frequently encountered but seldom acknowledged tendency to envision young people in general and young men in particular in terms of certain underlying assumptions and approaches drawn from developmental psychology. The notion of "socialization" is a key part of this schema for defining and charting how children and youths—with requisite supervision and direction from parents, institutions, and adult society in general—proceed along and through a set of defined stages towards maturity. It is assumed that universal stages of transition and development will, when successfully negotiated, lead from birth to "normal" adulthood along a reasonably predictable trajectory. Viewed thus, the trope of "socialization" demarcates and constructs an allocated zone and period of development that proceeds under the purview of adults and socializing institutions, not to mention "natural" processes of growth. Young persons are expected to move through this developmental chain and eventually emerge as more or less completely formed and functioning adults, although allowance is made for "abnormal" outcomes that can be accounted for in terms of either "under-socialization," "over-socialization," deprived environments, or some other factor (Stainton-Rogers and Stainton-Rogers 1992: 46).

During the last two decades socialization theory has been increasingly criticized—not least in anthropology and sociology—for its tendency to gloss childhood and youth almost exclusively as preparatory stages for the eventual incorporation of young persons into the society of adults (Amit-Talai 1995: 224; Bucholtz 2002: 529; Thorne 1993: 3). Critics of socialization theory assert that more is to be gained by addressing young people not solely as a future generation of adults but as fully engaged social actors who are already immersed within more or less complicated and uncertain settings. Youths, like full-fledged adults, live in the present, in concretely historical and open-ended time. Their interactions are not "preparation for life; they are life itself" (Thorne 1993: 3). The trouble with demarcating youth primarily as a developmental stage is that this inclines adults, including social commentators, to classify young people's experiences and complaints as being largely the products of inexperience and, thereby, intrinsically ephemeral concerns that are likely to be "outgrown" as they move towards maturity and adulthood. Newman et al. (2004: 173) have documented how parents' and other adults' predispositions "not to take kids' stories too seriously" have contributed directly to school shootings in the United States.

A second limitation that afflicts much of the writing on youths and young men derives from depending too often upon stylized and stereotypical anecdotal sources of information rather than the varied and complicated types of findings that emerge from systematic and detailed empirical and ethnographic investigations of particular subjects and settings.[2] Reworked versions of apocryphal acts that are attributed to one or another boy or set of young men can be marshaled not only to capture a reader's attention but also to stand for and "reveal" the underlying nature of young men as members of a broader category. Top-down ways of portraying and outwardly explaining young men—as if they comprise fundamentally transparent figures that belong to a unitary category—serve to accommodate speculation and pronouncements that too readily drift towards superficiality and the stereotypical. Notwithstanding sporadic nods that briefly acknowledge the possibility of some variation among and between young men, ruminations about youthful masculinity too often career along without much, if any, regard for nuance or specificity.

Discourses that unfold within these coordinates can rapidly descend into ideological free-fire zones within which young men may be casually rendered not as knowing, agentive subjects but rather as problematic objects or persons who need to be controlled and disciplined. The breathtaking ease with which sweeping accusations—including their alleged propensity to violence, indolence, sexism, selfishness, or irresponsibility (e.g., Beneke 1997; Connell 2000; Swain 2005)—can be leveled at young men in general without undue concern for adducing empirical evidence or scrutinizing the circumstances of alleged wrongdoings is deeply unsettling. Speaking of young males categorically as though they exist outside of and opposed to the rest of 'society' creates an insidious but recurring form of conceptual segregation that distorts reality. Approaches such as these are unable to tell us enough about young men as individuals operating within given contexts or as members of families, communities, and other social entities. Connell's contention that while the ethnographic moment might once have brought "a much-needed gust of realism to discussions of men and masculinity" (Connell 2000: 32) this methodological approach now needs to give way to analytical deduction mounted at a more universal level strikes us as being both representative of this line of reckoning and fundamentally wrong-headed.

Indeed, ethnographic studies of boys and young men have delineated in valuable ways a set of far too frequently overlooked issues. For instance, the physical maturation of boys into larger and more powerful bodies is readily visible and can be viewed variously as a potentially threatening development or as a useful resource. Burgeoning physical strength may prompt alarm about young men's capacities to commit violent acts and pose danger, but states, armies, and other entities have also long recognized how the physical capacities of young men may be deployed as pliable means for exercising power and control. But far from simply exercising their so-called "innate" physicality, young men need to be trained and disciplined to become effective, if not always politically legitimate, instruments of force. Vigh (2006) and Utas (2008) have detailed the ways that male youths have been recruited and exploited by militias during civil wars in, respectively, Guinea-Bissau and Liberia.

Other locales have hosted forms of "spectacular" violence, such as the sectarian fighting that raged in Northern Ireland during the time of the "Troubles" (Jenkins 1983) or the stylized lynchings that occur in urban barrios in Bolivia (Goldstein 2004). Any lingering presumption that these practices might be attributed simply or primarily to the proclivities of young men has been corrected by detailed ethnographic accounts. Indeed scholars (e.g., Anderson 1999; Hart 2008; Schostak and Walter 2002) have noted just how frequently boys and young men tend to be the most likely and numerous victims of violence, whether at the hands of peers or, as in rural Senegal, of gendarmes "hired" instrumentally by fathers to beat, but not to formally charge, their "rebellious" sons (Perry 2009). Stereotypical depictions of young males as perpetrators of violence thus blithely overlook the fact that boys and young men are so often themselves targets and victims of violence.

The visibility of young males in public places can be problematic in a number of respects, not least when they convene in larger and smaller groups to engage in staged and dramatic play. In the process of expressing or "styling" themselves—even if just walking down the street, standing on a corner, fooling around, or "having a giggle"—boys and young men open themselves and their bodies to social scrutiny and judgment by a wide range of individual and institutional observers. Boys and young men who lack workplaces in which to spend their days gainfully, as well as accommodations of their own to which they might return whenever they wish, become highly noticeable figures on streets where there may not be many, if any, entirely appropriate places for them to pass the time.[3] In western

Kenya young men who are unable to become breadwinners nonetheless imitate the example of a previous generation of labor migrants. But the movement of these youths back and forth along potholed roads in search of paid work that does not exist, has come to be termed as "tarmaccing,"a form of empty wandering that makes their futility and "failure" evident to all whom they encounter (Prince 2006).

The strongest contribution that these kinds of ethnographic approaches can make toward understanding young people, including young men, is to shift our attention from category to context. Instead of pondering the essential nature and characteristics of young males as representatives of their gender and age category or of how they might be "improved" or "saved," our focus turns to the social contexts in which young men are living today. Viewed thus, the ways in which young men respond to shifting and varied circumstances become important vantage points for better understanding the uncertain times in which they and we live.

Social Reproduction Revisited

We started this chapter with reference to recent newspaper columns that treated the idleness of many youths, young men especially, as iconic of the uneven social impact of deindustrialization in affluent countries of the global North. If these themes appear familiar to scholars of youth studies, it may be because, over three decades ago, a seminal body of work that examined the interaction between class, youth, and social change was preoccupied with very similar questions and material. In opening the theoretical overview that formed the centerpiece for the 1976 volume *Resistance through Rituals*, published by the University of Birmingham's Centre for Contemporary Cultural Studies (CCCS), John Clarke, Stuart Hall, Tony Jefferson, and Brian Roberts observed that the subject of youth cultures had received a "massive" amount of attention, above all in the popular media:

> "Youth" appeared as an emergent category in post-war Britain, one of the most striking and visible manifestations of social change in the period. "Youth" provided the focus for official reports, pieces of legislation, official interventions. It was signified as a social problem by the moral guardians of the society—something we "ought to do something about" (Clarke et al. 1976: 9).

Clarke et al. argued that youth had emerged as a metaphor for social change. They noted that there were elements in the British populist and media treatment of young people that exhibited continuity with similar depictions circulated in earlier historical periods. Nonetheless, they also posited that there were some important political and social changes in the post-World War II period which had come to be identified with an emergent "youth culture." The notion of a distinct youth culture arose, they argued, out of a broader debate concerning the extent to which the importance of class was being eroded by post-war affluence. Processes of "bourgeoisification" were supposedly producing new social types and arrangements such as the "affluent worker" and a new type of teenager engaged in changing forms of consumption and leisure (Clarke et al. 1976: 21). Clarke et al. contended that this myth of affluence obscured the persistence of significant class inequalities and poverty even while this dominant ideology had its compromising political effects, for example, on the state incorporation of the Labor Party and trade unions. To critically situate youths within the social landscape reshaped by post-World War II shifts in production, housing, and uneven regional developments, CCCS scholars advocated the adoption of a Gramscian conception of hegemony. Hegemony works by winning and shaping consent "so that the granting of legitimacy to the dominant classes appears not only 'spontaneous' but natural and normal" (Clarke et al. 1976: 38). But hegemony, Clarke et al. noted, cannot be taken for granted: "it has to be *won*, worked for, reproduced, sustained" (emphasis in the original, 1976: 40).

In some important senses, the Birmingham School's insistence during the mid-1970s on the continued importance of class inequalities and poverty in the face of post-World War II "affluence" was prescient both in the short and longer term. Subsequently, the 1980s downturn resulted in a massive increase of joblessness in Britain, permanently blighting the employment opportunities of many young school leavers. And as our opening columnists as well as academic observers (McDowell 2003; Nayak 2003) have noted, the subsequent workings of labor market restructuring continued to polarize workforce inequalities even before the unemployment fallout of the most recent recession.

But the gaps in the Birmingham School's rather particular focus on youth subcultures have also been well noted. Indeed, as Helena Wulff (1995) has pointed out, in the decades following the launch of this body of work, a veritable industry of criticism of CCCS publications was mustered, backhandedly affirming their importance. Criticisms included the tendency of the CCCS scholars to treat youth culture as a working-class "male preserve" (Bucholtz, 2002: 537; Lave et al. 1992). In spite of their affirmation of ethnographic modes of investigation, the CCCS researchers often relied heavily on textual analysis of media (Nayak, 2003: 26; Bucholtz, 2002: 536). It has also been repeatedly noted that the Birmingham School's self-conscious focus on highly stylized spectacular forms of youth subcultures anchored in leisure pursuits provided at best an incomplete account of youthful cultural expressions (Bucholtz 2002; Amit 2001). In fact, the CCCS scholars were quite explicit about the partiality of their subcultural focus: "It is important to stress again that sub-cultures are only one of the many different responses which the young can make to the situations in which they find themselves" (Clarke et al. 1976: 57).

But there is also a sense in which the CCCS researchers' focus on spectacular subcultures as forms of resistance that strive to "*win space* for the young" through stylized forms of consumption and leisure (Clarke et al., 1976: 45, emphasis in the original) was inconsistent with their *own* expressed theoretical focus on hegemony. If hegemony works by winning *consent*, then should not greater attention have been paid to the modalities and implications of consent whether in terms of extending attention to more willingly compliant youths or activities and locations in which youths participate but are less likely to be associated with stylized resistance? In short, why investigate consent through a primary focus on resistance?

This inconsistency is perhaps best illustrated in one of the most famous and ethnographically developed studies carried out by a member of the CCCS, Paul Willis's *Learning to Labor* (1977).[4] Willis's study focused primarily on a group of 12 working-class "lads" attending a boys-only, non-selective secondary school in the British Midlands district. But he drew attention to the distinction between the "oppositional culture" of the "lads" and the conformity of their "ear'ole" schoolmates: "The most basic, obvious and explicit dimension of the counter-school culture is entrenched general and personalized opposition to 'authority'" (Willis 1977: 11). In rejecting school, the lads also delivered themselves into a future of manual labor, but this element of "self damnation" involved a partial penetration of the contradictions vested in the official school paradigm (Willis 1977: 3). This educational paradigm celebrated the social mobility achieved by some working-class individuals without admitting that "not all can succeed, and that there is no point for the unsuccessful in following prescriptions for success—hard work, diligence, conformism, accepting knowledge as an equivalent of real value" (Willis 1977: 129). In other words, while the lads' counter-school culture damned them to the subordination of manual labor, it was also in many ways an accurate assessment of the odds of social mobility for most working-class kids. But what of the "ear'oles" who had vested their hopes in the promises offered by the school and conformed to its rules and protocols? What happened when, for many of them, these aspirations were more or less disappointed? Were they angry, resigned, bewildered, determined to seek even further qualifications, resolutely hopeful that somehow down the road better prospects would manifest themselves, or did they finally themselves become rebellious? Surely a study that insists on viewing young people as active agents[5] in the social and cultural reproduction of labor ought to be as interested in the contradictions and disjunctions vested in conformity as in resistance to dominant institutional and ideological paradigms.

Some thirty years later, the conformity that received little direct attention in Paul Willis's study as well as those of his other CCCS colleagues is, we suggest, still posing some critical questions about the situations, orientations, and prospects of young people worldwide. Like the "ear'oles," why do so many young people strive to conform to the expectations and promises of one or another of various interlocutors: their families, neighbors, employers, educators, state authorities, or even multilateral agencies such as the World Bank? What happens if, in spite of their efforts, these aspirations are not realizable wholly or even in part? In short, what happens when young people accept and try to adapt to the premises entailed in prevailing but often conflicting orthodoxies about the appropriate pathways to adult respectability but find themselves knocking up against the very types of contradictions that Willis had earlier noted in the British educational system?

More than three decades after the Birmingham School launched its investigations in the name of understanding hegemony, youth studies have still provided too little comprehensive reflection upon the workings and implications of youth conformity. In substantial measure both popular and scholarly attention to youths remains firmly trained on what are taken to be actual or potential forms of resistance[6] and opposition. In part, the continuity of this focus reflects some longstanding Western stereotypes of adolescence as a phase of "storm and stress" (Arnett 1999). Many observers thus expect fleeting and hence largely inconsequential, if sometimes troubling, rebellion from youths. In part, the emphasis on resistance reflects the moral panics that, as previously noted, have repeatedly attended populist discourse about youths. But in part, this focus reflects the continuing influence of the Birmingham School's pioneering work. While youth cultural studies have expanded to fill the initial gender gap in the Birmingham School's corpus by including numerous studies of girls and women (e.g., Harris 2004; McRobbie 2000; Mirza 1992; Pomerantz 2008), a very substantial part of this field continues to be shaped by the CCCS's focus on consumption, leisure activities, and stylized resistance, although often without the same priority given to questions of social reproduction and historical changes (Amit 2001).

Diverging from this orientation has been another influential strand of youth studies which has focused on attempts to define the markers and pathways associated with "youth transitions." But the reliance of much of this type of research on broad survey or demographic approaches has resulted in criticisms that it is too mechanistic and does not sufficiently take into account the views and experiences of young people themselves (Nayak 2003: 32). In other words, this focus on transitions does not necessarily privilege youth resistance, but neither is it any more likely to problematize conformity.

Today, in the midst of the largest cohort of young people the world has ever seen or—given declining fertility—is ever likely to see again (Barker 2005: 11), the unwillingness of scholars to view conformity as every bit as puzzling—and therefore requiring interrogation—as resistance is, if anything, even more telling on this global scale than it was in the more localized Midland setting investigated by Paul Willis. But ironically this is to a large extent because many of the structural as well as ideological forces that Willis noted as shaping the choices available to the "lads" are also implicated in the lives—albeit often in much harsher terms—of both their generational successors in Britain as well as of their counterparts elsewhere in the world. If during the 1970s Willis was already noticing unprecedented high levels of unemployment among young British workers, by the twenty-first century this pattern had extended across *all* world labor markets: "the youth unemployment rate is two to three times higher than the adult unemployment rate, regardless of the level of aggregate unemployment" (World Development Report 2007: 99). In the World Bank Report from which this unemployment statistic is drawn, what Willis termed "the common educational fallacy that opportunities can be *made* by education, that upward mobility is basically a matter of individual push, that qualifications make their own openings" (1977: 127) is adamantly upheld:

> Contrary to what might be expected, the greater availability of skilled and educated workers in a more integrated global economy may not necessarily lead to falling returns to skills. It may actually boost the demand for skills even further by inducing faster skill-intensive technological change…The private returns to secondary and higher education have been rising, especially in countries that have close to universal primary education (World Development Report 2007: 3).

But on the margins of the very same page on which this quote appears, a young person in Buenos Aires is cited as complaining that even low-skill jobs now require a secondary school or university education when there is no need for it. In a footnote, the report cites Janice Perlman's longitudinal study of Rio de Janeiro's favelas, which revealed that youths had achieved higher education than their parents without acquiring discernibly better jobs (Perlman 2005 as cited in World Development Report 2007: 229):

> In the late 1960s, people would warn their children that if they did not stay in school they would end up as garbage collectors. In July 2003, the city opened competition for 400 garbage collector jobs and 12,000 people applied. A high school diploma was the prerequisite (World Development Report 2007: 229).

And various other bits of "evidence" are sprinkled throughout the remainder of this report which suggest that in many parts of the world, increased educational qualifications have yielded uncertain or limited rewards even though they have necessitated substantial investments by students and their families.

In a multi-site international study of young men—conducted in the United States, Brazil, the Caribbean and Nigeria—Gary Barker (2005) noted that increased schooling did not always ameliorate the effects of working-class background. In Brazil, he found that "educational attainment for socially marginal young people does not lead as directly to higher income as it does for middle-class youth" (2005: 97). In Nigeria, young people complained that without the right network connections or money to pay bribes it was not possible to find a good job, and even a university education did not necessarily guarantee employment (Barker 2005: 44–46). In Jamaica, he found that young men were dropping out of school because they had accurately worked out that acquiring a university education or completing secondary school did not necessarily yield greater job options (Barker 2005). But across the four settings in which Barker conducted research he also found that, as opposed to intermittent odd jobs, only reasonably stable employment that paid benefits and a secure income was construed as sufficient to achieve a "socially recognized manhood" (Barker 2005: 107), i.e., a respectable adulthood as a young man.

Barker's findings have been echoed in anthropological studies of youths situated in various parts of the world over the last 15 years. In a phenomenon occurring also in many other parts of Africa, Trond Waage (2006) reports that thousands of young men and women in hope of eventually securing a civil service job have flocked to the institutions of higher education, including a recently founded university in the Cameroonian city of Ngaoundéré, but have found that a formal education does not necessarily provide access to the labor market or a role repertoire that ensures adult respectability. In Iran, one of the most youthful nations in the world, the majority of unemployed are aged between fifteen and twenty-four (Khosravi 2008: 5–7). With very low university acceptance rates, most young people find it impossible to access higher education. Yet even successfully attaining a university degree does not guarantee employment. Over 8 percent of unemployed Iranians—or one out of every twelve—holds a university degree, and much of the emigration from the country is comprised of unemployed, university educated people (Khosravi 2008: 7–8). Between 1983 and 1993, the number of educational institutions in Kathmandu (Nepal) almost tripled (Liechty 2003: 57). Since access to jobs at the "officer" level of the civil service or in corporations now requires a bachelor's degree while employment in business, management, or nongovernmental associations increasingly requires at least some college training, an increasing number of young middle-class people are spending long periods in education. But most of these young people will not find it possible to find "acceptable employment." In Kathmandu, for example, "middle-class youth are almost by definition educated and un- or under-employed" (Liechty 2003: 211). Similarly, since its emergence, Honiara, the capital city of the Solomon Islands, has attracted young men from the various islands of the archipelago who have often found it difficult to secure jobs and thereby earn the cash and cargo necessary to secure honor and respect in their home villages. By the 1990s, Christine Jourdan found that many of these young migrants had previously attended school before arriving in Honiara. Their parents had enrolled them in school with the expectation that this education would provide their children jobs with good salaries. But completion of primary school or the first year of secondary school did not go very far in the urban environment and most ended up as unemployed *Masta liu* in the city, unwilling to go home with little or nothing to show for their time away (Jourdan 1995).

Forty years ago, Pierre Bourdieu and Jean-Claude Passeron (1990)[7] argued that schools are more likely to reproduce and legitimate the existing structure of class relations than to challenge its basis, while Paul Willis contended that education in and of itself can neither resolve class inequalities nor create jobs: "No conceivable number of certificates among the working class will make for a classless society, or convince industrialists and employers—even if they were able—that they should create more jobs" (Willis 1977: 127). Nonetheless, the belief in the capacity of education to deliver social mobility and respectability at the level of individuals and economic growth at the level of the state has been powerfully propagated around the globe, and education levels have indeed been rising worldwide (World Education Report 2007: 36).

Not surprisingly, the successful dissemination of a belief in education's capacity to deliver modernization and social mobility has raised aspirations and expectations not only for young people themselves but also for their families and local communities. After all, in most cases family members have made investments and sacrifices to enable the education of their children. But as a result the hopes that are vested in young people's schooling are usually collective or at the very least familial rather than solely individual. In Kathmandu, Mark Liechty found that:

> Members of the middle class are those who have staked their very identities and values in a modern future whose contours lie in a grey zone of uncertainty. It is precisely within this space of anxiety and hope that education lodges—an abstract, almost mystical commodity that represents the only avenue to a modern future that middle-class parents can imagine for their children (2003: 215).

But it is not only members of the urban middle class who can hold onto the promises that have been identified with education even when it does not seem able to deliver on them. The efforts of the Ugandan government and its international donors to shift the orientation of primary education programs towards outfitting rural children with the skills to pursue a future in agriculture have foundered on the stubborn insistence of these students, their parents, and teachers that schooling should instead equip them for urban white collar jobs:

> In the conflict between rural and urban ambitions, the primary school becomes an ambiguous place because it is intended to prepare pupils for rural futures, but rural teachers and parents do not appear to support these intentions. Instead they keep promoting schooling as a place that prepares children for white-collar jobs, upward mobility and thus in effect, urban futures (Meinert 2003: 193).

It is a view of schooling that has remained tenacious even though few of these rural families actually include members who have achieved this kind of urban success (Meinert 2003: 179). And as Lotte Meinert explains, it is a set of aspirations that especially shaped boys' hopes for the future. While both boys and girls aspired to achieve more schooling, for girls the hope of subsequent mobility tended to be vested in achieving a good marriage. For boys, education offered the hope of being able to escape rural poverty through an urban future. But, by the same token, it could also work to make them feel like failures when they were unable to achieve the aspirations raised by their schooling.[8]

For many young people, efforts to conform to dominant and pervasive orthodoxies about the appropriate pathways to a respectable adulthood offer a double-edged sword: on the one hand, if they do not acquire any or much formal schooling, they risk being viewed as failures; on the other hand, if they do attend school but do not succeed in achieving the kind of "good jobs" that this education is assumed to enable, then they are also likely to be viewed as failing. And in contexts, such as that described by Meinert, where families are still likely to vest particular hopes for their collective futures in the success of their sons, young men are all the more likely to feel the effects of the Catch-22 that lies at the heart of this paradigm of modernity and social mobility.

Moral Panics

If young men only had to contend with the disappointment of parents, teachers, politicians, officials, and planners, this would be bad enough. But the unrealizable expectations that have been provoked amidst persisting severe inequalities—within states, across regions, and around the globe—can also elicit far more severe threats to young men's standing. This is so because marginalized young men are also often portrayed as being dangerous.

Moral panics about young men have been a recurrent feature of different historical periods. John Schostak and Barbara Walter have pointed out that boys, and especially lower class boys, have often been the foci of panics in Britain and Europe (2002: 195). And as we also noted earlier, the members of the Birmingham School remarked on this tendency in Britain during the 1970s, while today many observers have pointed out similar depictions of working-class young men as the "feral young peril." But Britain is hardly unusual in this regard. As Gary Barker has pointed out: "in many parts of the world, it has become something of a national sport to demonize young men, particularly low-income young men" (2005: 4). As Barker further notes, this kind of demonization has been associated with "punitive, unjust and ineffective policies," in particular the widespread increase in the incarceration of young men in Latin America, the English speaking Caribbean, the United States, and Europe (Barker 2005: 4; Wacquant 2008: 278). In the United States, the incarceration rates of young black men in particular, rose at a dramatic pace during the 1990s (Holzer and Offner 2006: 17). Their resulting prison records have subsequently served as a kind of negative state "credentialing" announcing the stigma of incarceration to anyone who cares to inquire (Pager 2008: 73). Rising incarceration rates can in turn further ratchet up alarmist media coverage by appearing to substantiate the dangers posed by young men. Thus in France in 2002 changes made to the penal code led to a dramatic rise in prosecutions of public order violations, further boosting moral panics by the media, particularly about young men of Maghrebian origins (Ossman and Terrio 2006: 9–10).

But the depiction of youths and young men in particular as embodying a potential menace to social order is also a frequent subtext in more sympathetic accounts. Analyses that spotlight high levels of youth unemployment frequently include warnings about the potential for danger if this situation is not remedied. Citing the risks of persisting youth unemployment in some regions, the 2007 World Development Report thus warned: "When productive options are not available for jobless youth, there is a greater likelihood that they will enter activities damaging to themselves and society" (2006: 101). The report then goes onto blame "youth difficulties in the labor market" for rising crime rates in France, increased incarceration rates in the United States, and the involvement of Sinhalese youths in civil unrest in Sri Lanka (2006). Similarly, several recent newspaper reports have cited Martina Milburn, CEO of the Prince's Trust, a British non-profit organization, as warning that youth unemployment could be "just the start of a long and downward spiral, which all too often leads to crime, homelessness, or worse" (Olive 2009; Seager 2009). As in most moral panics, the line between victims—who need to be protected—and perpetrators—against whom protection is required—is often very thin. In other words, the very marginalization and exclusion of certain categories of youths is viewed as rendering them as a potential threat. Barriers to meeting expectations of social respectability can thus not only deny young men employment, independence, or marriage; it can also make them a scapegoat for their own marginalization.

Why aren't they angrier?

Underlying warnings about the potential systemic dangers embedded in youth marginalization is the assumption that the persisting socioeconomic barriers faced by many youths are likely to elicit disaffection, which will be acted out in "damaging activities." And indeed a number of studies report just this kind of alienation and consequence. In his comparative study of urban marginality, Loïc Wacquant cites the "mingling despondency and rage of youths shut out from gainful employment who cannot move out of their parents' house and get their own life and family started" as a critical factor in the pandemic violence he observed in a Chicago "hyper ghetto" (2008: 262). In his own comparative study of young men in four different regions, Gary Barker argued that low-income young men were being attracted to violent gangs and armed groups as a means to cope with their sense of social exclusion (2005: 2).

Given the contradictory brew of marginalization, moral panic, and unrealizable expectations with which many young men in so many parts of the world must contend, most observers, whether more or less sympathetic, seem to assume and fear an angry, violent response. But there is enough material at hand about young men who do not display this expected response that we could pose the question somewhat differently. Why, indeed, aren't *more* young men angrier or *more violent?*

While noting the involvement of some marginalized young men in gangs, Gary Barker also acknowledged that the majority of young men in impoverished and violent settings did *not* become involved in gang-related violence (2005: 3). Similarly James Vigil (2007) observed that in the impoverished neighborhoods of East Los Angeles some youths joined gangs while others did not and, even of those who did join, the majority eventually found their way out of these groups.

Linda McDowell conducted a study of young British working-class men in Sheffield and Cambridge who had completed their compulsory schooling in the summer of 1999. While most of these young men had not been particularly successful at school and had not been able to achieve more than low-level entry jobs—"the sorts of McJobs that are regarded as dead end by the majority of the population" (McDowell 2003: 236)—they remained committed to mainstream values about the value of work, domestic respectability, and adult independence. Their low wages notwithstanding, most made regular financial contributions to their parental household and, while they frequented pubs and clubs on weekends, they emphasized that they seldom got drunk and tried to stay out of trouble (2003: 202–203). In spite of an increasing gulf between rich and poor, a more polarized labor market and an awareness of their own limited opportunities, most of these young men remained surprisingly "confident that they would be able to find work and re-establish the type of working class household that most of them had grown up in" (2003: 18).

McDowell's findings are echoed in a study conducted by Anoop Nayak (2003) of sixteen-year-old white working-class men in the northeast of England. While they had in the main rejected higher education or white-collar employment, they were not "work shy" or lazy and regarded themselves as would-be workers. In spite of the collapse of traditional apprentice schemes and an extremely unstable local employment market, they continued to see themselves as heirs to a proud tradition of working-class respectability, "the eternal 'backbone of the nation'—salt of the earth natives who had failed to inherit an industrial heritage that was rightfully theirs" (Nayak 2003: 70). So why were they not angrier or more despondent about the prospects of downward social mobility which they were facing?

The answer may in part lie in the very flexibility of notions of conformity. Thus when they could not achieve their working-class heritage in the old occupational sense, the young men observed by Anoop Nayak enacted their identity as "Real Geordies" through their allegiance to football, drinking, and going out. Similarly, both McDowell and Nayak found that in spite of their own limited prospects these young men sustained their sense of continuity by drawing a sharp distinction between their (and their families') respectability and the roughness of other segments of the working class. In other words, these young men deflected the probability of their own downward social mobility by asserting their superior placement within a working-class hierarchy. They were continuing to conform to the values of working-class "domestic respectability" held by their parents even if others were not (McDowell 2003: 213; Nayak 2003: 170).

In situations elsewhere, where this kind of sharp distinction between a respectable working class and a more sullied underclass cannot be sustained, other researchers have reported the importance of "code-switching." According to Elijah Anderson (1999), in poor inner city districts in the United States, residents often employ the dichotomies of the "decent" and the "street" to draw evaluative distinctions between themselves and other individuals and families in their neighborhoods. While there are extremes, most residents are trying to be decent and the same family can include members who are oriented more towards decency and civility while others are drawn to the "street." There is also, Anderson reports, a good deal of code-switching in which people move between one or the other of these value orientations depending on the situation.

Code-switching has also been reported in other kinds of situations of violence and confrontation. Mats Utas (2008: 129–130) argues that in Liberia a similar process of "masking" and de-masking has made it possible for some youths who have been engaged as combatants in the civil war to assume and then discard a warrior role, avoiding responsibility for what has happened in battle and making it easier for persons to enter and re-enter "moral" society. In other words, code-switching or masking/de-masking can be used to sustain claims for respect and respectability even in the face of involvement in socially sullied activities and/or circumstances.

The salient question may therefore be not whether youths are "lads" or "ear'oles," "street" or "decent," warriors or non combatants, "respectable" or "rough," but rather the degree to which these kinds of evaluative dichotomies can serve to gloss over broader shifts in the structure of opportunities available to young people. Marginalization and declining opportunities can thus be partially or wholly deflected towards another category of persons or to particular situations rather than to more pervasive and enduring generational shifts. Under the cover of apparently persisting adherence to longstanding conventions of adulthood, practices may be changing without necessarily challenging the relevance of these standards.

The impact of these contradictions can also be blunted by the very notion of youth. If available opportunities fall well short of the standards of adult respectability to which young people aspire, they can still be asserted as part of an *eventual* future. So displacement can be as much temporal as categorical. But in the here and now, when opportunities are more meager, the impact of these contradictions can also be blunted by support from the very same personal networks that may heighten these conflicting pressures in the first place. To the extent that families and friends may continue to insist that youths be held to standards of achievement that are no longer realistically attainable, they can pose part of the Catch-22 that entraps young men. But at the same time these intimate links might also provide critical support that can cushion some of the impact of diminished prospects in the future.[9] The young British men studied respectively by Linda McDowell and Anoop Nayak expected to stay in their parental homes for an extended period. In the United States, 40 percent of young adults return to live with their parents for a time and sons are more likely to do so than daughters (Mitchell 2006: 75). Now residing in the city of Bissau, the former members of a youth militia that had been mobilized during the civil war in Guinea-Bissau were, like many of their contemporaries, unemployed, dependent, and marginalized (Vigh 2006). While they might have been "stuck," they were still managing to survive by "living at the mercy and expense of fathers, mothers, uncles or aunts or others from the older generations" (Vigh 2006: 37).

So the contradictions that ensnare young people may also to a certain extent sustain them. Young men may continue to espouse familiar conventions of adulthood while beginning, on an ad hoc and pragmatic basis, to organize their lives around other kinds of realities. Families, friends, and communal networks may, on the one hand, insist on unattainable benchmarks of adult respectability and, on the other, provide a level of support—what Vigh (2006) calls an "economy of affection"—that cushions the resulting shortfalls faced by youths. To situate and understand this dialectic and the structures, relationships, and endeavours to which it gives rise, it is critical that we venture beyond highly paradigmatic and ideological representations of youth and masculinity and systematically explore the specific contexts within which young men are located today.

An Overview of the Volume

This volume is organized into three sections that not only present detailed accounts of the complex circumstances of young men in different parts of the contemporary world but that also bring into focus underlying analytical similarities and differences that emerge from comparative and cross-cultural approaches. The chapters in the first section examine situations where young men, as prospective members of given categories, classes, and institutions, stand as "new boys" who are obliged to fit themselves into exacting and often rapidly shifting social arrangements. Ritty Lukose's chapter explores the cultural politics of globalization among young non-elite male college students in the south Indian state of Kerala. Drawing her account against a backdrop of recent media depictions of globalizing India that celebrate the newly consumerist and globally-oriented middle-class youth category, Lukose shows that globalization does more than simply exclude non-metropolitan youths from its sphere of influence or include them by "trickling down" to benefit them. Adopting an anthropological approach to consumer citizenship, Lukose interrogates commodified modes of masculinity among non-elite young men, treating their world as a window into new forms of lower-caste/class assertion within the public life of Kerala. Thus, young men's practices of "shining" in public are not set apart from social life but instead marshaled by Lukose to explicate the broader dynamics of gender, caste, and class. Public renderings of "shining" underscore escalating inequalities and intertwined anxieties that shape the lives of these young non-elite men as they strive to claim a stake in globalizing India.

Anne Irwin's chapter questions the commonly held perception that military service in general and combat experience in particular constitute established rites of passage into manhood. Accompanying a Canadian infantry company during part of its tour of duty in southern Afghanistan—a tour which, except for a few days, was spent far "outside the wire" of Kandahar Air Field—Irwin itemizes the types of operations, emotions, and experiences that make up a combat tour. Her observations show that, while combat service is transformative, it does not completely or unproblematically turn boys into men. Instead, they become physically and emotionally rather like old men who nonetheless have neither passed fully through adulthood nor left behind other characteristics of youths. For young and inexperienced soldiers in their late teens and early twenties, combat can forcefully invert normative forms of masculinity, stripping them of strength and control over their bodies while leaving them unashamed to display signs of genuine affection for one another, including grief over the loss of comrades.

William Jankowiak, Robert Moore, and Tianshu Pan's chapter traces the institutionalization of an extended youth phase in China, a development that has accompanied the single child policy. Males have traditionally been the preferred social category in China, yet by the end of the twentieth century this pattern was rapidly reversing. With daughters increasingly replacing sons as the preferred gender, the symbolic system that defines contemporary China has altered fundamentally. Jankowiak, Moore, and Pan survey the emergence of extended youth as a distinctly new type of generational phenomenon that affects young Chinese men and women rather differently. Marriage in urban China is no longer considered the final marker of complete adulthood. Moreover, young men continue to shoulder a strong responsibility to uphold the cultural image of being a successful man. Many young singleton males have, in consequence, adopted an image of coolness (*ku*) that speaks less about performance of social roles and thus duty and more about possessing self-independence and mastery of one's social position, a posture that may also conceal an unvoiced fear of failure.

The chapters in the second section look into the ways in which young men struggle to make do and get by in situations where the demands placed upon individual youths who seek to achieve adult male status have become increasingly demanding and oppressive, if not utterly impossible. Daniel Mains's chapter elucidates the linkages between unemployment, masculinity, and migration for young men in urban Ethiopia who have since childhood been encouraged to conceive of the transition from youth to adult in terms of progressive movement but who now cannot find employment that makes this possible. A conjunction of urbanization, expanded access to education, and contracting economic activities strands many of these young men in a space where they are viewed as neither children nor adults, with little likelihood of this changing for them in the future. Unable to take on the social responsibilities of adulthood, particularly with respect to economic independence, marriage, and fatherhood, they are depicted alternately as sources of explosive destruction as well as emasculated dependents who continue to rely upon their parents. Migrating within Ethiopia in order to access work on development projects enables some of them to shift their position within social relationships temporarily. Mains shows that these young men's conceptions of youth and adulthood contribute to shaping the challenges they face within the life course as well as their attempts to negotiate these challenges.

Deborah Elliston's investigation of masculinity and nationalism in the Society Islands seeks to shift our understanding of the linkages between these two fields out of the realm of "commonsense" and into that of the sociological. Starting with an ethnographic moment in the mid-1990s when young Polynesian men faced off against the French military with rocks and Molotov cocktails, she asks why it was young males who responded disproportionately to nationalist leaders' calls for action in response to resumed French nuclear testing in the region. In a society that has had no substantial gender hierarchy and within which gender tends to be minimized and discounted rather than employed as an axis of social difference, assumptions about any naturalized relationship between masculinity and revolutionary violence, between men and nationalist projects, become acutely problematic. In recounting how young men have become situated at the apex of local discourses about nationalism, while women tend to reject these, Elliston explains the emergent conflict between French colonial and Polynesian systems of value that have been shaped through and by gender and labor practices.

Martin Demant Frederiksen's chapter spells out how and why images of masculinity and notions of *dzmak'atsoba* (or brotherhood) have come to loom large in the lives of young men in the Republic of Georgia. A deepening economic crisis has inflicted staggering levels of poverty and unemployment upon post-Soviet Georgia, not least since the 2008 war against Russia. Aspirations of masculinity become complicated when so few men are able to exhibit traditional capacities of "good men," let alone achieve newer indexes of "success" fashioned by post-Soviet *biznes-men*. Living with the prospect that their economic circumstances are unlikely to improve in the future, many young Georgian men engage in stylized forms of drinking and petty crime. Yet, by doing so, argues Frederiksen, they gamely struggle to create a valid moral and social world that offers not only momentary respite but also some sense of permanency. Despite *doing* bad things, they strive to *be* good by attending closely to stylized practices of *dzmak'atsoba* intended to mark them out not only as reliable friends but also as future husbands and fathers.

Rosellen Roche's chapter on masculine "hardening" in Northern Ireland elaborates the dynamics of the enculturation of young males into everyday "low-level" routines of violence that tend to be discounted in the contemporary post-Agreement period. In comparison with more dramatic forms of violence practiced during the height of the "Troubles," youthful instances of threatening looks and words, pushing and shoving, fist fights, kicking, and the aggressive use of sticks, bricks, or knives receive relatively scant attention from higher level social actors, including the police. Nevertheless, youths in Northern Ireland report high levels of personal experience with these practices, which they are inclined to accept as inescapable aspects of their lives. The skilled deduction of external cues of sectarian status that are probed for and displayed through performances of these truculent behaviors can literally "make" or "break" young men.

Thus, young people in Northern Ireland must address not only issues that youths in any urban area might face, but also an entrenched tradition among younger and older men of being ready to be subjected to a variety of types of ethno-national violence.

The chapters in the third section investigate various social, political, and legal binds that young men may find themselves caught up in when dealing with the social and personal consequences of being formally or informally deemed by others to be "trouble." Susan Terrio's chapter reflects upon the nature and implications of recent changes to the French system of juvenile law that effectively target a "new" category of delinquents, namely, young, disadvantaged Muslim males who are identified as being from an "immigrant background" even though most of them are born in France. This development, which deviates so fundamentally from established judicial practice in France, serves to separate French children from "immigrant" youths and to hold the latter more accountable before the law. How, Terrio asks, do young men who are subjected to such measures regard the legal system in a context increasingly marked by tension, mistrust, and growing violence? Her observations of penal proceedings in the Paris juvenile courts indicate that judges have for the most part already formed opinions about the nature of youths accused of wrongdoing on the basis of reports gathered from school counselors, social workers, and child psychologists for court files. Yet as Terrio demonstrates poignantly, young men who do attempt to speak to the charges and presumptions leveled against them tell stories that need to be heard.

Victor Rios and César Rodriquez's chapter examines the mechanisms that serve to designate working-class black and Latino male youths as likely candidates to become "incarcerable" subjects within California's expanding "prison-industrial complex." The dismantling of the welfare state and the rise of a punitive approach in the U.S. during the past forty years has generated a crisis for poor racialized young men, leaving black boys born in 2001 with a one in three chance of ending up in prison. Rios and Rodriguez specify the means by which poor black and Latino schoolboys can be assigned "negative" credentials that, once recorded in their school records, thereafter serve to constrain their opportunities and, thereby, redirect them from "learning to labor" to "preparing for prison." Providing ethnographic examples of this education-to-incarceration "pipeline," the authors conclude that the trouble faced by these young black and Latino men in post-industrial California during an era of mass incarceration is that issues that revolve around factors of social class, economic precariousness, and human dignity end up being prosecuted as criminal matters.

Gary Armstrong and James Rosbrook-Thompson's chapter delves into the ways in which the management of urban disorder in contemporary

Britain has inexorably led to the demonization of boys and young men who inhabit contested urban zones. The implementation of a system of Anti-Social Behaviour Orders (ASBOs) that can be employed to dictate to individuals over the age of ten how they must *not* behave in public has been accompanied by powers granted to police to disperse groups of two or more persons from public places if their presence has resulted, or is likely to result, in any members of the public being intimidated, harassed, alarmed, or distressed. Armstrong and Rosbrook-Thompson detail how these methods of exclusion along with other everyday processes and economies of disorder figure within the life stories of four young men living in the London Borough of Camden. The authors show that in this context the discredited young male provides a convenient "fall-guy" for a period once mooted by certain pundits as one of political progress and economic expansion.

Gillian Evans's chapter investigates the "big man system" and "short life culture" that underpin a spate of knife and gun crimes—including murders—committed by boys and young men in Bermondsey and other areas of London. Although characterized by former British Prime Minister Tony Blair as incidents provoked not by poverty but by a distinctive "black culture," Evans disagrees, contending instead that this is an issue driven by social class and by what it means for black, white, and Asian young men to grow up in working-class areas of British cities. She focuses upon the processes by which underfunded schools serve to accommodate disruptive behavior on the part of some children despite the wishes of most parents and the efforts of teachers in these poorly funded institutions to forestall this. What needs to be understood, Evans suggests, is how certain types of boys use their time at school as an opportunity to practice competing for power and influence in ways that may not be readily permitted in their homes but which they are almost certain to encounter on the "street."

The situations explored by the contributors to this volume thus run a wide gamut, from young men trying to pursue aspirations for social mobility raised by the expansion of emerging economies to others dealing with turbulent transitions and the attendant extinguishment of previously available opportunities for social advancement and adult respectability to yet others dealing with the effects of their consignment to stigmatized social categories. But in all of these varied circumstances, young men are often caught in the vortex of structural and cultural contradictions that they have not created but for whose effects they are somehow being held accountable. To borrow a phrase employed by Gary Armstrong and James Rosbrook-Thompson in their account in this volume of Camden (London) youths, young men are all too often the "fall-guys" for the disappointed aspirations and fears harbored amid larger social formations. But our aim in this volume is not to portray these young men as hapless victims; rather, we wish to draw attention to the ways in which their varied efforts to deal with bewilderingly conflicting expectations and demands often reveal the fracture lines in the contemporary organization of local, national, and global systems.

We commence the volume with three case studies in which at first glance young men seem to be the likely beneficiaries of cultural celebrations of youth as the iconic frontline for, respectively, the new opportunities or the risks presented by globalization. But on further reading, it becomes clearer that while the emerging market economies, consumerism, and urbanization of India and China have indeed produced new opportunities and aspirations, non-elite young men can find themselves caught between their own heightened expectations as well as those of their families, prospective spouses, and peers, on the one side, and limitations in the capacity of these economies to generate the kinds of jobs and incomes they are hoping for, on the other. In Kerala, the gap between educational expansion and the more limited local job market has ensured a steady supply of educated young transmigrants. In China, young men who have migrated to the growing cities find that they do not have the credentials for white collar employment while women are often preferred for less skilled service jobs. But at the same time, shifting gender norms have heightened expectations of male responsibility for generating household income. In both cases, male anxieties about finding the "right" kind of jobs is born out of a complex interaction between new patterns of consumption, style, the reach of localized job markets, and family investments in upward mobility.

The homecoming of Canadian soldiers returning from Afghanistan—escorted by fighter pilots and motorcycle police along a route decorated with yellow ribbons—probably constitutes the most explicit public celebration of young men in this volume. But neither this applause nor the experience of combat have prepared these young soldiers for many aspects of adult civilian life back in Canada. In all three cases in this section, young men are contending with a significant gap between the roles and lifestyles for which they have prepared and the actual facts on the ground. And this gap is not simply a function of youthful miscalculation but of the institutional cultivation of much more broadly held presumptions and desires.

Like many of their counterparts in the cases featured in the first section of this volume, the young men described in the four chapters of the second section are trying to contend with gaps between what is expected of them and what they can realistically accomplish. But if the cases being described for India and China describe the gap created by *rising* expectations, the essays in the second section are largely dealing with circumstances entailing *compromised* norms of adulthood. In these circumstances, young men can find themselves caught between conflicting pressures to uphold traditional norms of adult respectability, meet new standards and expectations, and accommodate volatile political and economic circumstances that are rapidly redefining what is deemed possible or desirable. They comprise a set of contradictory pressures that virtually ensures that these young men will be judged as wanting on one count or another.

Education was once the most reliable avenue in Ethiopia towards social mobility and white-collar government positions. But the structural adjustment programs imposed by the International Monetary Fund have reduced the number of government positions available even as the number of students seeking an education has increased. Consequently, as in Kerala, many young Ethiopian men have joined the ranks of the "educated unemployed," limiting their capacity to assume financial independence and adult responsibilities. Young Polynesian men in the Society Islands are contending with competing discourses of "moral adult masculinity"—a traditional valorization of their capacity to feed their households through involvement in subsistence labor and kin-based exchange relations on the one hand and an emerging emphasis on an ability to generate cash on the other. But, as in China, women are the preferred employees for many of the jobs being produced in the emerging cash economy of the Society Islands. Meanwhile, the aftermath of independence from the Soviet Union and civil war have created a situation of chronic political and economic instability in Georgia. As a result, for many young Georgian men, there are few legitimate avenues left for employment. In all three of these cases, young men are often being condemned as dangerously "lazy" and unreliable, thereby providing a convenient public scapegoat for the broader socioeconomic setbacks entailed in these transitions.

In contrast the "low-level" routine violence that has been a fundamental aspect of growing up "hard" in the midst of the sectarian divides of Northern Ireland has often been obscured by a tendency to focus on the "high-level" violence perpetrated by paramilitary figures and /or security personnel. Yet despite the signing of a peace agreement, the persistence of high levels of communal segregation in Northern Ireland has been associated with enduring expectations of proper masculine "hardness." As a result, many young Northern Irish men are facing a double whammy of poverty and violence.

If the chapters in the second section are concerned with situations in which young men are being held responsible for their inability to overcome broader processes of social destabilization, the chapters in the third section all deal with even more youthful experiences of institutionalized denunciation. These essays recount the way in which judicial, policing, and surveillance systems in the UK, United States, and France have been restructured to systematically demarcate particular categories of boys and young men as targets for intervention and restraint. In France, a view of immigrant minors as different from other children in their propensity to offend has been institutionalized in both national legislation and court practice. In the United States, young working-class black and Latino boys and men are criminalized through punitive systems at school and on the street. In the UK, a system of ASBOs has been disproportionately directed against young working-class boys and men in contested urban zones. These forms of punitive intervention construct the subjects they are supposedly protecting against, through a system of negative credentialing that haunt the futures of certain categories of male youths before they have barely had a chance to exit childhood. The essays in this section do not minimize the poignancy and injustice of these circumstances but they portray the variable ways in which boys and young men may question and react to these forms of vilification. They may not be able to evade but neither are these youths passively accepting the pre-judgments of school officials, police, judges, or politicians.

This volume provides telling revelations of the challenging circumstances facing many young men in different locales around the world. The nature of these challenges and responses to them differ between regions, historical periods, and politico-economic conditions. But these essays remind us that the hopes, fears, and disappointments projected onto young men are often more revealing of the broader social contexts in which they are coming of age than of the young men themselves. This is therefore less a volume about how young men deploy paradigms of masculinity than it is about how they read and respond to their implication in processes of social mobility, inequality, conflict, and historical transformation.

Notes

1. As Lloyd (2005: 2-3) notes, the very different circumstances that appear across— and, we would argue, within—regions mean that the experiences of today's young people may vary enormously.
2. Some recent examples of richer and more nuanced ethnographic studies within or pertaining to this field include: Olwig and Gulløv, eds. (2003), Katz (2004), Cole and Durham, eds. (2008), and Jeffrey and Dyson, eds. (2008).
3. In a similar vein, see also Jeffrey (2010) concerning the dynamics of "timepass" in India.

4. To sidestep the confusion associated with hegemony as a term, Willis avoids using this term but allows that it would be useful if employed to denote aspects of his analysis. In other words, Willis's study is still very much in line with the theoretical focus outlined earlier by Clarke et al. (1976).
5. See Durham (2008) for a thoughtful discussion of the limitations of scholarly assumptions in the field of youth studies about the nature of young people's agency.
6. Katz (2004: 240–258) provides a refreshing critique of the presumed exercise of "resistance" on part of young people that has figured almost automatically in scholarly work during the last few decades.
7. This work was originally published in a 1970 French version: *La Reproduction: Éléments pour une théorie du système d'enseignement.*
8. See Jeffrey, Jeffrey, and Jeffrey (2008) for an examination of the interplay of education, masculinities, and unemployment in north India.
9. The importance of taking account of the social significance of links such as these figures prominently in the generational approach to childhood and youth demonstrated by the contributors to Olwig and Gulløv, eds. (2003); see especially Olwig and Gulløv (2003) and Amit (2003).

Bibliography

Amit, Vered. 2001. "The Study of Youth Culture: Why it's marginal but doesn't need to be so." *Europaea*. 1/2: 145–54.
———. 2003. "Epilogue: Children's Places." In *Children's Places: Cross-Cultural Approaches*, eds. Karen Fog Olwig and Eva Gulløv. London and New York: Routledge.
Amit-Talai, Vered. 1995. "The 'multi' cultural of youth." In *Youth Cultures: A cross-cultural perspective*, eds. Vered Amit-Talai and Helena Wulff. London and New York: Routledge.
Anderson, Elijah. 1999. *Code of the Street: Decency, Violence and the Moral Life of the Inner City*. New York and London: W.W. Norton.
Arnett, Jeffrey Jensen. 1999. "Adolescent storm and stress, reconsidered." *American Psychologist*, 54(5): 317–26.
Barker, Gary T. 2005. *Dying to be Men: Youth, Masculinity and Social Exclusion*. London and New York: Routledge.
Beneke, Timothy. 1997. *Proving Manhood: Reflections on Men and Sexism*. Berkeley and London: University of California Press.
Bucholtz, Mary. 2002. "Youth and Cultural Practice." *Annual Review of Anthropology*, 31: 525–52.
Bourdieu, Pierre and Jean-Claude Passeron. 1970. *La Reproduction: Éléments pour une théorie du système d'enseignement*. Paris: Éditions de Minuit.
———. 1990. *Reproduction in education, society and culture*. Translated from the French by Richard Nice with a foreword by Tom Bottomore and preface by Pierre Bourdieu. London and Newbury Park: Sage.
Clarke, John, et al. 1976. "Subcultures, Cultures and Class: A theoretical overview." In *Resistance through Rituals: Youth subcultures in post-war Britain*, eds. Stuart Hall and Tony Jefferson. London: Hutchinson & Co. Ltd.
Cole, Jennifer and Deborah Durham, eds. 2008. *Figuring the Future: Globalization and the Temporalities of Children and Youth*. Santa Fe: School for Advanced Research Press.
Connell, R.W. 2000. *The Men and the Boys*. Cambridge: Polity.

Durham, Deborah. 2008. "Apathy and Agency: The Romance of Agency and Youth in Botswana." In *Figuring the Future: Globalization and the Temporalities of Children and Youth*, eds. Jennifer Cole and Deborah Durham. Santa Fe: School for Advanced Research Press.

Goldstein, Daniel M. 2004. *Spectacular City: Violence and Performance in Urban Bolivia*. Durham: Duke University Press.

Harris, Anita, ed. 2004. *All about the girl: culture, power and identity*. New York: Routledge.

Hart, Jason. 2008. "Dislocated Masculinity: Adolescence and the Palestinian Nation-in-exile." In *Years of Conflict: Adolescence, Political Violence and Displacement*, ed. Jason Hart. New York and Oxford: Berghahn Books.

Herbert, Bob. 2009. "A Scary Reality." *The New York Times*, August 11. Available from: www.nytimes.com/2009/08/11/opinion/11herbert.html?_r=1&hp=&pagewanted=print [Accessed 11 August 2009].

Holzer, Harry J. and Paul Offner. 2006. "Trends in the Employment Outcomes of Young Black Men, 1979-2000." In *Black Males Left Behind*, ed. Ronald B. Mincy. Washington, D.C.: The Urban Institute Press.

Jeffrey, Craig. 2010. *Timepass: Youth, Class, and the Politics of Waiting in India*. Stanford: Stanford University Press.

Jeffrey, Craig and Jan Dyson, eds. 2008. *Telling Young Lives: Portraits of Global Youth*. Philadelphia: Temple University Press.

Jeffrey, Craig, Patricia Jeffrey, and Roger Jeffrey. 2008. *Degrees Without Freedom? Education, Masculinities, and Unemployment in North India*. Stanford: Stanford University Press.

Jenkins, Richard. 1983. *Lads and Ordinary Citizens: Working-Class Youth Life-Styles in Belfast*. London, Boston, Melbourne, and Henley: Routledge and Kegan Paul.

Jourdan, Christine. 1995. "Masta Liu." In *Youth Cultures: A cross-cultural perspective*, eds. Vered Amit-Talai and Helena Wulff. London and New York: Routledge.

Katz, Cindi. 2004. *Growing Up Global: Economic Restructuring and Children's Everyday Lives*. Minneapolis and London: University of Minnesota Press.

Khosravi, Shahram. 2008. *Young and Defiant in Tehran*. Philadelphia: University of Pennsylvania Press.

Lave, Jean, Paul Duguid, and Nadine Fernandez. 1992. "Coming of Age in Birmingham: Cultural Studies and Conceptions of Subjectivity." *Annual Review of Anthropology*, 21: 257–82.

Liechty, Mark. 2003. *Suitably Modern: Making Middle-Class Culture in a New Consumer Society*. Princeton and Oxford: Princeton University Press.

Lloyd, Cynthia B. 2005. "Executive Summary." In *Growing Up Global: The Changing Transitions to Adulthood in Developing Countries*, ed. Cynthia B. Lloyd. Washington, D.C.: National Academies Press.

McDowell, Linda. 2003. *Redundant Masculinities? Employment Change and White Working Class Youth*. Malden, Oxford, Carleton, and Victoria: Blackwell Publishing.

McRobbie, Angela. 2000. *Feminism and youth culture*. 2nd ed. New York: Routledge.

Meinert, Lotte. 2003. "Sweet and bitter places: the politics of schoolchildren's orientation in rural Uganda." In *Children's places: cross-cultural perspectives*, eds. Karen Fog Olwig and Eva Gulløv. New York: Routledge.

Mirza, Heidi. 1992. *Young, Female and Black*. London and New York: Routledge.

Mitchell, Barbara. 2006. *The Boomerang Age: Transitions to Adulthood in Families*. New Brunswick and London: Aldine Transaction.

Nayak, Anoop. 2003. *Race, Place and Globalization: Youth Cultures in a Changing World.* Oxford and New York: Berg.

Newman, Katherine S. et al. 2004. *Rampage: The Social Roots of School Shootings.* New York: Basic Books.

Olive, David. 2009. "The young and the unemployed." *thestar.com*, August 30. Available from: www.thestar.com/printArticle/688419 [Accessed 30 August 2009].

Olwig, Karen Fog and Eva Gulløv. 2003. "Towards an Anthropology of Children and Place." In *Children's Places: Cross-Cultural Approaches.* eds. Karen Fog Olwig and Eva Gulløv. London and New York: Routledge.

Olwig, Karen Fog and Eva Gulløv, eds. 2003. *Children's Places: Cross-Cultural Approaches.* London and New York: Routledge.

Ossman, Susan and Susan Terrio. 2006. "The French Riots: Questioning Spaces of Surveillance and Sovereignty." *International Migration*, 44 (2): 5–21.

Pager, Devah. 2008. "Blacklisted: Hiring Discrimination in an Era of Mass Incarceration." In *Against the Wall: Poor, Black and Male*, ed. Elijah Anderson. Philadelphia: University of Pennsylvania Press.

Perry, Donna L. 2009. "Fathers, Sons and the State: Discipline and Punishment in a Wolof Hinterland." *Cultural Anthropology* 24(1): 33–67.

Pomerantz, Shauna. 2008. *Girls, Style and School Identities: Dressing the Part.* New York: Palgrave Macmillan.

Prince, Ruth. 2006. "Popular Music and Luo Youth in Western Kenya: Ambiguities of Modernity, Morality and Gender Relations in the Era of AIDS." In *Navigating Youth, Generating Adulthood: Social Becoming in an African Context*, eds. C. Christiansen, M. Utas, and H.E. Vigh.Uppsala: Nordiska Africakaininstitutet.

Saunders, Doug. 2009. "How Britain is falling down on the yob." *Globe and Mail*, 8 August 8: F1 and F6.

Schostak, John and Barbara Walter. 2002. "Young Men Growing Up: Is There a New Crisis?" In *Children's Understanding in the New Europe*, ed. Elisabet Nasman. Stoke-on-Trent: Trentham.

Seager, Ashley. 2009. "Unemployment jumps 220,000 to 2.4 m." *Guardian.co.uk*, 12 August. Available from: www.guardian.co.uk/business/2009/aug12/unemployment-jobless-rise/print [Accessed 12 August 2009].

Stainton-Rogers, Rex and Wendy Stainton-Rogers. 1992. *Stories of Childhood: Shifting Agendas of Child Concern.* New York: Harvester Wheatsheaf.

Swain, Jon. 2005. "Masculinities in Education." In *Handbook of Studies on Men and Masculinities*, eds. Michael Kimmel, Jeff Hearn, and R.W. Connell. Thousand Oaks: Sage.

The World Bank. 2006. *World Development Report 2007: Development and the Next Generation.* Washington, DC: The World Bank.

Thorne, Barrie. 1993. *Gender Play: Girls and Boys in School.* New Brunswick: Rutgers University Press.

Toynbee, Polly. 2009. "Last time we abandoned the young, bits of Britain broke." *Guardian.co.uk*, 21 August. Available from: www.guardian.co.uk/commentis free/2009/aug/21/youth-unemployment-broken-britain/print [Accessed 22 August 2009].

Utas, Mats. 2008. "Abject Heroes: Marginalised Youth, Modernity and Violent Pathways of the Liberian Civil War." In *Years of Conflict: Adolescence, Political Violence and Displacement*, ed. Jason Hart. New York: Berghahn.

Vigh, Henrik E. 2006. "Social Death and Violent Life Chances." In *Navigating Youth, Generating Adulthood: Social Becoming in an African Context*, eds. C. Christiansen, M.Utas, and H.E. Vigh. Uppsala: Nordiska Africaikaininstitutet.

Vigil, James Diego. 2007. *The Projects: Gang and Non-Gang Families in East Los Angeles*. Austin: University of Texas Press.

Waage, Trond. 2006. "Coping with Unpredictability: 'Preparing for Life' in Ngaoundéré, Cameroon." In *Navigating Youth, Generating Adulthood: Social Becoming in an African Context*, eds. C. Christiansen et al. Uppsala: Nordiska Africaikaininstitutet.

Wacquant, Loïc. 2008. *Urban Outcasts: A Comparative Sociology of Urban Marginality*. Cambridge and Malden: Polity.

Willis, Paul. 1977. *Learning to labor: how working class kids get working class jobs*. Farnborough: Saxon House.

Wulff, Helena. 1995. "Introducing youth culture in its own right: the state of the art and new possibilities." In *Youth Cultures: A cross-cultural perspective*, eds. Vered Amit-Talai and Helena Wulff. London and New York: Routledge.

Part I

JUST TRYING TO FIT IN

Chapter 1

"Shining" in Public
Masculine Assertion and Anxiety in Globalizing Kerala

Ritty A. Lukose

A wide-ranging contemporary set of conceptions tout India's place in a globalizing world, particularly images and discourses increasingly popular since the early 1990s that proclaim India as an emerging global power. This is "India Rising," as a recent magazine article puts it (Zakaria 2006). Reform policies that opened up the Indian economy to global market forces—colloquially known as "liberalization"—have significantly transformed the political, economic, and cultural landscape of India. Media representations of Third-World poverty, an uneducated, rural, and traditional society, and an inefficient and corrupt bureaucratic state—all backward or underdeveloped in comparison to the "modern" West—jostle with images of a world-class information technology industry, a robust economy, and a media-saturated, highly educated, urban, affluent, and globally oriented consumer middle class.

This discourse is, of course, a contested one. Vigorous counter-discourses and mobilizations and movements—of slum dwellers, landless laborers, tribals, environmental activists, peasants and women—all challenge the triumphalist claims of "India Rising" in ways that make policies associated with globalization an object of a contested political struggle. In this chapter, moving beyond such explicit discourse and struggle, I explore the everyday cultural politics of globalization among young, non-elite men in the state/region of Kerala. Through an examination of a form of commodified, youthful masculinity that I gloss as "shining" in public, I elucidate the dynamics of gender, caste, and class at the intersection of region, nation, and globe, as these young men struggle to stake a claim in globalizing India.

The discourse of "India Rising" celebrates the categorical role of youth as a key instantiation of globalized India. Media discussions of liberalization often highlight statistics showing that 54 percent of Indians are below the age of twenty-five, making India one of the youngest nations in the world.[1] In the south Indian state of Kerala, people between the ages of fifteen and twenty-five are said to make up 45 percent of the total population (*Outlook* 2004: 52). These youths form a potent new market for fashioning India's newly globalized middle class. One major publication has labeled them "zippies":

> A young city or suburban resident, between fifteen and twenty-five years of age, with a zip in the stride. Belongs to Generation Z. Can be male or female, studying or working. Oozes attitude, ambition and aspiration. Cool, confident and creative. Seeks challenges, loves risks and shuns fear. Succeeds Generation X and Generation Y, but carries the social, political, economic, cultural or ideological baggage of neither. Personal and professional life marked by vim, vigour and vitality (origin: Indian) (*Outlook* 2004: 41).

This definition does not name specific commodities, but draws attention to an embodied demeanor, an attitude, and a set of values. Its reference to the "baggage" of previous generations names a shift in generational sensibilities, attitudes, and values, in which "zippies" are an almost evolutionary alternative to their more backward predecessors.

The media has drawn an even sharper contrast between generational sensibilities in characterizing "zippies" as "liberalization's children." Embodying India's newly found confidence and ambition on the global stage, they are urban, hip, and cool. The term is a play on "midnight's children"—the generation named after the Salman Rushdie novel which focused on those born during the first hour of the year 1947, when India gained its independence from British colonial rule.[2] The term intertwines the lives of those born in the immediate aftermath of independence with the life of the nation, a nation shaped by the socialist-inspired understanding of national development represented by Jawaharlal Nehru, India's first prime minister. In contrast to liberalization's children, midnight's children seem mired in the ideological baggage of Nehruvian nationalist development, with its focus on the rural poor and service to the nation, and were consequently characterized as lacking in ambition, being risk averse, "uncool," and fearful.

In a special section on India's newly globalized youths in the magazine *BusinessWeek* (1999), a table entitled "How India's New Generation is Different" elaborates a set of generational contrasts. The "older generation" idealized "Gandhian poverty" and socialism, grew up in the midst of famine, had only one state-run television channel, was technophobic, was thrifty, grew up within a stable single-party system led by upper castes, favored civil service careers, and had low levels of literacy. In contrast, the "new generation" admires capitalism and wants to get rich, has grown up in the era of food surpluses, can watch fifty television channels, is technologically savvy, consumes guiltlessly, has grown up with shaky coalition governments and assertive lower-caste political parties, favors jobs in the private, corporate sector, and has higher literacy rates. This construction of the lifestyle and generational sensibilities of globalized Indian youths encompasses ideology (capitalism versus socialism), the state of agriculture (from famine to surplus), the spread of mass media, technology, and consumption, the breakdown of the post-independence hegemony of the dominant nationalist political party, the Indian National Congress, and the rising political assertion of lower-caste political parties, shifting career choices, and rising literacy rates—all harbingers of India as a modernized, global power rather than a poor Third-World country. The article's mention of "more voice for lower castes" and rising literacy rates and food surpluses amid the more conventional indices of globalization such as media, technology, and consumption is noteworthy and suggests that journalists see globalization "trickling down" to impact the masses. In short, youths are a key site for popular cultural reconfigurations of the Indian nation in the age of liberalization.

It is against the backdrop of these celebrations of globalizing India, heralding a newly consumerist, globally-oriented middle-class youth category, that I examine the cultural politics of globalization among young, non-elite male college students in the south Indian state of Kerala. One way of understanding their relationship to these dominant images and discourses is to point to the disparities between the non-metropolitan, regional, low-caste, semirural social location of these students and the metropolitan, upper-caste elite indexed by the category "zippie." This chapter not only focuses on non-metropolitan youths; it argues that globalization does more than simply exclude them from its sphere of influence or straightforwardly include them by "trickling down" to benefit them. They are liberalization's children in their own right.

Further, while the discourse of generational shift from midnight's to liberalization's children rightly focuses on the eclipsing of the Nehruvian vision of the nation within liberalizing India, it obscures more than it reveals when it simply highlights the triumph of consumerism.[3] For members of societies that are actively being transformed by globalization, consumer practices and discourses become an increasingly important axis of belonging for negotiating citizenship—in other words, for the politics

of social membership, for negotiations of public life, and for an understanding of politics within the nation. I deploy an expansive anthropological understanding of citizenship in order to explore the crucial role
of consumption in the self-fashioning of young people as part and parcel of their negotiations of public life. Moving beyond formal, legal, and
constitutional definitions—or, citizenship understood narrowly as rights
and obligations with respect to a state—anthropological approaches to
citizenship formation have emphasized the everyday practices of belonging through which social membership is negotiated.[4] Through a careful
analysis of *consumer citizenship*, this chapter argues that the breakdown of
the Nehruvian vision connects with ongoing struggles over the meanings
of public life. In other work I have focused on struggles over public life
that encompass lower-caste cultural-political assertion, the ascendancy of
a Hindu nationalism, reconfigurations of upper-caste, middle-class aspirations, and attempts by the middle class to reconfigure understandings of
citizenship in India (Lukose 2005; 2009).

In this chapter, I specifically focus on forms of commodified masculinity among non-elite young men as a window into new forms of lower-
caste/class assertion within the public life of Kerala. In so doing, I draw on
a wide variety of literature that examines the dynamics of youth culture.
However, I do not render this world as a "subculture" with its own logic,
something that has characterized much of cultural studies' literature on
youth.[5] Rather, in order to apprehend these figurations of youth and the
ways that young people inhabit them, I reconceptualize youth as a social category that sits at the crossroads between familial and educational
contexts, a category that is structured by job, marriage, and consumer
markets.[6] It is moreover a category that closely links education and the
possibilities of migration and creates the conditions for a complex mediation between consumption and citizenship. Consumer and state-centric
developmentalist projects seek to turn people in this category into consumers and citizens, and, as a category, youth is receptive to global migration and changing ideas about sex and marriage.

An ethnographic analysis of commodified forms of masculinity reveals
how anxieties about being young, male, and non-elite are mediated within a new global dispensation. I begin by contextualizing Kerala at the
intersection of Third-World development and trajectories of globalization, demonstrating how the space of youth is produced at this nexus.
I then move on to discuss and analyze the congealing of a commodified
masculine style and its spacio-temporal moorings as a way of discussing
the precarious production of masculinity at the intersection of the postcolonial and the global.

Kerala: Between Development and Globalization

One of the interesting dynamics one encounters when trying to understand the cultural politics of globalization in India from the perspective of
Kerala is that this region has, more often than not, been considered exceptional and "different." Multiple tropes of popular and scholarly com-
mentary on Kerala written over decades run the gamut from matrilineal-
ity to the "revolutionary zeal" of this communist "bastion" to its tropical
beauty to its high levels of literacy. When taken together, these tropes
constitute a discourse about Kerala's exceptionalism.[7]

Specifically, one important thread within the construction of Kerala as
exceptional is the trope of development, in which the so-called "Kerala
Model of Development" is held up as an example for other parts of the
world. This literature highlights the fact that, while Kerala exhibits low
per capita income with high levels of unemployment and poverty, typical of poor regions in Third-World countries with a weak industrial base,
it also has high levels of literacy and life expectancy and low levels of
fertility and infant and adult mortality—at rates that are more typical
of highly industrialized regions of the First World (Franke and Chasin
1992; Jeffrey 1993; Parayil 2000). This modeling of Kerala proposed an
exceptional development profile for the state-region, centering on a high
physical quality-of-life index across a wide spectrum of the population,
notably including women and girls. However, it cannot be ignored that
this exceptional developmental profile is coupled with low levels of income and economic growth and high levels of unemployment.

This "development" literature narrates a heroic story of a progressive
march from "tradition" to "modernity." Education is crucial to the idea of
Kerala as a development success story, particularly the education of girls
and women. However, rather than a "black box" that produces various
development indicators like "literacy" or "low maternal mortality," as I
discuss below, education and its gendering are a contested cultural project
where the historical forces of colonial and postcolonial modernity, development, and globalization meet in order to shape the life trajectories of
youth.

Given these discourses of exceptionalism, how can Kerala be a site
through which we can understand Indian and global modernity? It is
not my intention to nest the region within the nation and then within
the world, as standard spatial imaginings of social scales and globalization would have it. As a region, Kerala's experiences of globalization are
powerfully mediated simultaneously by the shifting context of India's
economic liberalization and through a highly regionally specific trajectory of development and migration. For example, Kerala's development

experience must be contextualized at the intersection between a regionally specific history of leftist radicalism that took on an overwhelmingly
developmentalist form because of how this history intersected with a
Nehruvian and nationalist vision of state-centric development; the figure of midnight's children must be understood at the crossroads between
region and nation. Similarly, constructions of liberalization's children as-
sumes a 1990s metropolitan location as the prime example of globalization in India and discussions of the latter have been dominated by studies
of Delhi, Mumbai, and Bangalore. Kerala's experiences of a global flow
in labor, commodities, and capital, primarily to the Persian Gulf but also
to other parts of the world, are long, expansive, and intense, and they
predate the liberalization of the Indian economy in the early 1990s. However, this does not in any straightforward way make Kerala an exception.
The contemporary economic, cultural, and political manifestations of
international migration within Kerala intersect with this national moment of liberalization without being reducible to it. The rise of Hindu
nationalism during the 1990s and its manifestations in Kerala have provided new conditions in which the politics of gender, caste, and class is
tied to transnational migration and its impact. Further, while a regionally
specific trajectory of international migration started in the early 1970s,
the expansion of consumption and mass media that underlies the cultural
politics of globalization I discuss owes much to the nationally driven economic reforms of the early 1990s. Finally, the politics of gender, class, and
caste as it intersects with the largely male and subaltern migration circuit
to the Gulf is linked to the nationally coded figure of the Non-Resident
Indian (NRI), a figuration of consumer identity in the aftermath of a liberalization tied to a more professional, upper-class emigration to the First
World. So, understanding these dynamics requires a flexible articulation
between region, nation, and globe.

Situated as citizens of the Kerala development state, young people are
also now enmeshed in the hopes, aspirations, and trajectories of transnational migration—whether they manage to migrate or not. This migration is not simply people's movement across borders but a complex
transnational circulation of labor, money, and commodities that has a
profound impact within Kerala through the impact of remittances, education, the expansion of commodity culture, and the structuring of families
and intergenerational relations.[8]

The development state in Kerala is thus intertwined with the state
experiences of migration in ways that profoundly affect the life stage of
youth. The years of college student life are structured at the intersection
of the development state and this migration trajectory. As the authors
of a large-scale study indicate, educational expansion, particularly at the

higher educational levels, and the inability of the local economy to generate jobs have created a large category of the "educated unemployed" between the ages of fifteen and twenty-five (Zachariah, Mathew, and Rajan 2001). There is a high correlation between higher levels of education and unemployment: more than 40 percent of those with a Secondary School Leaving Certificate (equivalent of a high school diploma) and more than 35 percent of those with college degrees are unemployed, with young women unemployed at four times the rate of young men. Kerala's educational system generates a large pool of educated young people, but many of them are unemployed for many years after receiving high school and college degrees, until they emigrate, marry, and either enter the labor force or remain unemployed.

Quite apart from houses, land, gold, and consumer durables, migrant families also spend remittances on the education of children. Most migrants to the Gulf do not get family visas, and children often remain in Kerala with one parent, usually the mother or grandparents. Households with migration connections spend more on education than those without, and successful migration is correlated with higher levels of education. More than 40 percent of the migrants abroad and almost 60 percent of the migrants to other parts of India have either a Secondary School Leaving Certificate or a college degree, compared with 23 percent of the general population (Zachariah, Mathew, and Rajan 2001). This often leads to an intergenerational cycle of migration and education as the increased investment in education leads to migration for younger members of the household.

Needless to say, there emerged throughout the 1990s the sense that the heroically progressive Kerala development model was giving way to a crisis-ridden consumer society. The expansion of economic opportunities through migration and globalization generated a new politics of consumption in which this productive, reformist middle class began reorienting itself, and newly upwardly mobile communities and groups (for example, young men from the formerly untouchable Ezhava caste community that is the focus of this chapter) asserted themselves through consumption in ways that far exceed the mid-century productivist domestic paradigm.[9] While I explore these new configurations ethnographically, some initial sense of this reconfiguration is revealed through an exploration of contemporary mass media and cinema and the ways these impact cultural life of youth, in particular in the context of college, in the region.

Until the 1990s, Malayalam cinema was seen as a vibrant, intellectually sophisticated, socially progressive film culture based on an aesthetic that provided "realistic" depictions of ordinary and everyday life, making it "superior" to other regional and national film industries. With its reliance on a strong and modern literary tradition whose themes and stories were tied to social reform and the left, Malayalam cinema participated in the larger discourse of progressivism and modernity in the region (Muraleedharan 2005; Radhakrishnan n.d.; Rowena 2002). Like the larger contours of progressivism and modernity in Kerala, this cinema too was largely situated in a progressive and modernizing respectable Malayalee middle-class family that Jenny Rowena argues "was predicated on the themes of reform and social responsibility almost always shouldered by educated upper-caste male figures" (2002: 33). Heroism in these films centered on a single male protagonist who was more often than not upper caste/class, while men and women of other castes/classes and women of these upper-caste/class families, were impediments and objects of reform, or were tragic and/or peripheral to the main storylines (Rowena 2002).

In an insightful study of the emergence of youth oriented "comedy-films" of the late 1980s and early 1990s, Jenny Rowena links these films to a new consumerist ethos tied to Gulf migration. While most film critics dismiss these films as silly slapstick, a trend that indicates the decline of Malayalam cinema, she demonstrates how these popular films shift the focus from tears, romance, melodrama, and sentiment rooted in the middle-class family home to that of young, unemployed men from a variety of caste/class backgrounds in public spaces—large cities, work places, men's hostels, lodges—anxiously pursuing jobs and financial stability within an expanding commodity culture through jokes, gags, various kinds of fraudulence, and slapstick. They have become such a ubiquitous part of popular culture that cassettes of famous scenes are popular and television programs devoted to comedy allow viewers to request their favorite scenes from these films.

In this cinema, the upper-caste/class responsible reforming hero is replaced by a group of young incompetent men, many of them from lower caste backgrounds—a shift that marks the assertion of non-elite masculinity through consumerism, social mobility, and the opportunities of Gulf migration. The films are framed by fantasies of wealth, success, and the acquisition of commodities, including the upper caste/class woman. While the difficulties of performing masculinity by becoming a productive breadwinner were central to the modern, middle-class nuclear family in Kerala, here, in the context of acute unemployment and consumerism, this struggle generates a crisis and competition between elite and non-elite young men. The struggle to gain a stable foothold, Rowena argues, is mediated through laughter and comedy; it is, however, a struggle that is resolved through competition and rivalry that ultimately re-asserts the values of an upper-caste/class masculinity in ways that "remasculinize" contemporary Kerala society (2002).

Further, a letter to a newspaper titled "Dubai Dreams" provides some sense of the discourse of youth, education, Gulf migration, and globalization from a middle-class male perspective; it also provides some sense of the competitive terrain shared by these different engagements with globalization.

> Throughout our schooling we were an inseparable gang of five… . School days over, we began our search for admission to pre-university… . Narayanan disclosed that he was unlikely to join us at college as he had been offered a job in Dubai… . In Palghat we resumed our mundane lives, the high point being Narayanan's long newsy letters. Very soon we were familiar with Dubai's modern airport, the luxury hotels, the fully carpeted centrally air-conditioned homes, the duty-free electronic stores and the overstocked supermarkets. Dubai became a cherished dream. A year later Narayanan returned home on holiday. We waited several hours at Madras airport… . Once out of the airport he insisted on taking a tourist taxi and retaining it for the whole day. He checked into an expensive hotel and treated us to a lavish meal… . Year after year Narayanan's annual visits were eagerly awaited by all who knew him. Time passed and the four of us graduated and set out in search of jobs. I moved to Bombay and started work in an international bank. Slowly and diligently I worked my way up the corporate ladder. I began traveling abroad on business… . I transited through Dubai International Airport. Never having forgotten Narayanan, I wished I had had his phone number to call him. During my three hour wait, I entered the spotlessly clean washroom and found the toilet attendant busy with his broom and soap water bucket… . The toilet attendant moved away from the door and looked up. Our eyes met. I quickly averted my eyes and he looked down again at the freshly wiped floors. I left without hugging or even speaking to my beloved friend Narayanan (*Times of India*, August 22, 1994).

This letter suggests how young subaltern males migrate to the Gulf, circulating in and out of Kerala in the shadow of the figure of the affluent, consumerist Non-Resident Indian (NRI), so celebrated as a "mythological hero" for a globalizing middle class (Deshpande 2003). It illustrates the ways in which youth, education, trajectories of migration, and visions of global experiences are intertwined. The author of the letter follows a respectable middle-class path into adulthood ("slowly and diligently"), climbing the corporate ladder of an international bank that allows him to globalize ("traveling abroad on business"). Here is the middle-class male globalizing through the opportunities of a newly liberalized Indian economy in which international banks are now allowed to function—liberalization's children taking advantage of new opportunities. The attitude of the letter writer toward his beloved schoolmate moves from envy about

his friend's experiences abroad and his abilities to consume to a self-righ-
teousness about his own slower career trajectory. It ends with pity and
shame as he, finally a member of the globalized, affluent Indian middle
class, encounters his friend cleaning toilets at an international airport. In
particular, he carefully distinguishes between his own respectable and dil-
igent path into adulthood and his friend's trajectory, which he represents
as an illegitimate shortcut (forgoing college) marked by excessive, envi-
able consumerism in India and Kerala—yet it turns out that all the while
his friend is cleaning toilets in Dubai. The symbolic valence of cleaning
toilets—a traditionally coded occupation of untouchable castes—should
not be elided here, as it creates a contrasting set of trajectories marked by
caste and class associations. Here we have a typical representation of the
non-elite Gulf returnee as a transgressive, illegitimate, excessive, and piti-
able nouveau riche—precisely the image that is depicted in many comedy
films of the late 1980s and 1990s (Osella and Osella 2000).

So far, I have discussed how Kerala sits at the crossroads of development
and globalization and region/nation/globe. I have also discussed how the
social space of youth is structured by this nexus. Within the cultural politics of the region, we see a shift away from stable, progressive narratives
of Kerala's development successes to a more ambiguous and fraught sense
of Kerala as a crisis-ridden, consumer society. In the next section, I focus
on the politics of commodified masculinity in the spaces of everyday life
as a window into how young men mediate their assertions and anxieties
in globalizing Kerala.

"Shining" in Public

An important concept for understanding the association between youth,
masculinity, and new forms of consumption in the Malayalam language is
derived from a youth slang word, chethu.[10] While it can refer to the stylish
nature of many commodities and in some sense can refer to the notion
of "being fashionable" in general, it refers most significantly to a kind of
commodified masculinity.[11] If a male is dressed in a new pair of jeans and
fancy sneakers, he is usually called chethu, which literally refers to the activities of slicing, cutting, and slashing and also the traditional low-caste
occupation of toddy-tapping and the tapper's knife, while figuratively it
means "sharp," "cool," "hip," or "shiny"—something like "cutting-edge."[12]
A fancy car, a stylish house, or a new motorbike are all chethu. A store
dedicated to selling fashionable clothes in town was named Chethu. A
fashionable young man is chethu, although it is interesting to note that
women rarely are. If a woman dresses in a particularly fashionable way

(especially if she is wearing a western-style skirt), she is said to have *gema*, a term that connotes arrogance—something between being a "showoff" and being "stuck up." A young man is rarely described as having *gema*.

One of the more fashion-conscious young men in the college interpreted his sense of *chethu* for me during a long, rambling interview. I never saw Devan in anything but jeans or baggy pants, an oversized shirt that went down to his knees, sneakers, and often a baseball cap with *Boss* emblazoned on it.[13] Somewhat the class clown, he was a curious mixture of anxieties. He came from a lower-middle-class Ezhava family in town. As he tells it, he had been a good student in his well-disciplined Christian school. College was a different story. He did not want to study engineering or medicine, as his parents wanted, saying he found the subjects boring. He had an interest in the civil service. According to Devan, that meant studying something like history, English or political science, subjects he surmised would give him the writing skills and knowledge necessary to pass the civil service exams. As history was "just the study of dates," he dismissed it. He stated that if one were to study English for the exams, he would need a very high-quality education in English from extremely elite schools such as the Doons School or Delhi Public School.[14] English seemed risky given where he was coming from: a marginal college, in a backwater town, in southern Kerala. So, from his perspective, that left political science, which was what he was studying.

However, he was not very serious about college. He blamed a bad crowd he fell in with when he first got to college, going to three or four movies a week, hanging out at the beach, and spending time at the public library reading Mills and Boons novels (a popular series of English-language romance novels) for titillation. He was affectionately known by his friends as "Mr. Quote" because, as I found out, he punctuated much of his speech with quotes in English, from books such as Dale Carnegie's *How to Win Friends and Influence People* to figures like Gandhi. Explaining the effect of falling in with the wrong crowd, Devan said, "You are the company you keep." On the importance of friendship, he quoted Gandhi: "True friendship is a rare one. It is the identity of two souls." Caught between his bourgeois aspirations and his desire to have fun, Devan presented a humorous, anxious set of observations on his life and the meaning of being young.

Devan told me that you needed to be *chethu* in order to matter in his college: "It's the *chethu* style: jeans, a Yamaha bike [he had only a bicycle]. You need to have six or seven jeans, Killer jeans [a brand name]. You need four or five cotton shirts, three to four T-shirts, a well-groomed, *chethu*, smart look. A bike. You must have a bike." Having delineated the minimum material requirements for a *chethu* style, Devan went on to describe the masculine persona that signifies and is signified by this style of commodified masculinity by describing some fine nuances. A less common term often used interchangeably with *chethu* is *ash-push*—a term that many say comes from English, or the sound of English as it is heard by Malayalam speakers:

> It's just a matter of intensity. *Ash-push* is much more intense than *chethu*. *Ash-push* ... a life that is in the *chethu* way, you enjoy life. You go to a beer parlor and have beer, that is *ash-push*. A Yamaha bike, money in the hand, a *line* [slang for a relationship with a girl], that's it, in between you go to a beer parlor and you sip two beers, you have plenty of friends, you enjoy life. You enjoy the life. You don't care about what has happened yesterday. You don't care what will happen tomorrow. You are always happy. That is *chethu*.

This notion of *chethu* encompasses within it several aspects of a youthful, commodified masculinity that brings together clothing styles, status, and an attitude about the world based on ephemerality and some notion of fun. Previously, it was under the rubric of the "folk" and the "rural" that the lower-caste body had been configured. Here, we begin to see how globalization and its signifiers attach themselves to the body of the lower-caste, lower-class male.

An important component of the *chethu* style is the consumption of public space itself. Other than the requisite jeans, shirts, sneakers, and the all-important bike, Devan insisted that you needed to have money in your hand. When I asked him why, he said it was to *karangan*. *Karanguga* can be glossed as "to wander about," "to gallivant." One needs money in order to consume in public. But it implies more than the material ability to participate in spaces of public consumption. Key to this notion is the aimless quality of this mobility—aimless in terms of not having a specific place to go to and also not having a specific goal to accomplish. It implies an ephemerality with respect to both space and time. As Devan stated, part of having a certain kind of *chethu* style was an attitude oriented toward the present, not the past or future. When folded into the idea of "wandering about," it implies a kind of aimlessness with regard to not only the past and future but space as well. Therefore, whether the space was the actual college campus or a beer parlor, movie theater, park, beach, restaurant, ice cream parlor, or bus stand, it was fodder for wandering about. And what was the reason for going to any of those places? The answer would invariably be *chumma*—for "no reason."

Often, this past and future that one is trying to hold at bay are related to obligations and aspirations—to study, work hard, succeed. Here is how Devan described his desired future:

> My idea of the good life is that you must have a lot of money. Per month, you must get ten to fifteen thousand rupees per month. You must have that. You will see. Living is not just eating. I do like traveling. Prices are skyrocketing. For example, all want to have one car. On average, you can spend two thousand rupees on maintenance of a car. Then there is food, housing, social gatherings, like that. If you want to live and have some savings, at least ten thousand per month. You see, lots of modern things are coming into our life, like pagers. Life is too short. You must have ten thousand per month. Then, a good woman. If you have money, naturally, all other things will come. Certainly, it will certainly come. If you have a good job and you are drawing this much salary, like that, you can marry from a well-to-do family, I don't mean top-class, but middle-class, like that. You will naturally get a good woman like that. And you can enjoy life.

This movement from the present to the future, in which one is trying to transform the ephemeral enjoyment of consuming in a *chethu* way in the present into an upperwordly mobile and secure form of middle-class consumption in the future, is a precarious journey, something that makes this *chethu* style problematic. Devan goes on to describe what he calls the "positive and negative aspects" of being *chethu*, expressing his worries about making such a transformation:

> You have to speak in a *chethu* style (*chethu rithiyil samsaram*) and you have to have *chethu* relations. You are good company for everyone. Then, you study well. If you have all this, then you can say that you have a positive *chethu* style. But there is also a negative side. You don't care about what has happened yesterday. You don't care what will happen tomorrow. You don't have aim, but you are always happy. That is *chethu*. There is a negative side. You throw away work and you become *chethu*. What I mean is that you will walk in a *chethu* style. But you degrade yourself sometimes. The positive side of *chethu* is that you should know about what you should do—work. But then you use life as if it's sand. You don't care how much sand came here or how much is there. You don't care what will come in the future and what has come in the past. You will just think about how the sands are flowing now. You only care about the present thing.

All this reveals many of Devan's own anxieties about having had a little too much fun in college. Approaching the end of his college days, unsure about what to do next, remembering when he did work hard in school, wondering how he was going to make his ambitions of the good life materialize, he wondered about the limitations of aspiring to be *chethu* as the past, present, and future weighed heavily on his mind.

Devan's aspirations for and anxieties about achieving the good life mediated the many forces that structure his life—his social origins, his education, the space of youth as pleasure and consumption, and the horizon of getting a job, setting up a household, and being a breadwinner. He most immediately aspired to the pleasures of consumption, marked by ephemerality and fun. This present is marked by the pleasures of self-fashioning and the consumption and traversal of public space. While trying to hold past and future at bay, he is plagued by the enormous task of having to turn his educated and aspiring self into a model of middle-class stability, respectability, and consumption in a future that is his imagined adulthood. Here, it is important to note that the masculinity of *chethu* is an assertive and aspiring lower-caste, lower-class masculinity that lays claim to the public through consumption. It is marked by precariousness and vulnerability, both in terms of its lower-caste and lower-class social location and the wider world of acute unemployment in Kerala. In the broader consumer culture of Kerala during the 1990s, this masculinity sat at the intersection between the developmental state that educated students like Devan and globalization that structured his consumer-oriented visions of the good life.

The masculinity of the *chethu* style involves a congealing of certain fashions, an attitude about past, present, and future, and a mode of traversing public space in which one is very self-consciously on display. However, *chethu* is a precarious achievement, one that can fail in any number of ways. I have discussed some of this precariousness in terms of a lower caste/class masculine struggle to turn a presentist enjoyment of consumption into a secure form of the good life in the future. Moving through public spaces, whether it be the street, a bus stop, the actual space of the college, or the stage of a local beauty pageant, involves for both young men and women a complicated mode of self-presentation and traversal. It is here that we begin to see the ways in which the gendering of the youth/fashion nexus structures the participation of young men and women within the public spaces of consumption and education.

In the town where Devan's college is located, nonfamilial, heterosocial spaces for young people to congregate and socialize were increasing, starting in the mid-1990s, but were not plentiful. Often, spaces of sociality were fashioned in and around the spaces of the college, along with the trains, train station, buses, and bus stands that many students used to get to and from college. More adventurous types might congregate at restaurants, ice cream parlors, or the cinema hall; the most adventurous, at a nearby park or the beach. Of course, the sense of these spaces as relatively safe or transgressive is tied to their relative sexualization. These spaces also enable homosocial and heterosocial forms of sociality, full of pleasure and risk. These practices of sociality constitute these spaces as youthful spaces for friendship and romance. It is instructive here to explore humorous stories about the embarrassment (*chammal*) of navigating sociality and public life, stories that reveal something of its enjoyments and dangers.

In the late 1980s and 1990s, comedy films emerged from and reconfigured comedic repertoires and performative traditions within Kerala. For example, Rowena (2002) discusses the ways that a form of stand-up comedy called *mimicry*, in which pairs or groups of young men perform comedic routines about verbal mishaps and everyday blunders and confusions, begins in the 1970s to replace *kathaprasangham*, an oral genre that features a single performer who recites song, poetry, and dramatic narration. Like the fashion show, mimicry routines have become a central element of youth festivals and college events, now intimately tied to cinema. Early stars of comedy films were mimicry artists. Now, performances of mimicry almost exclusively by young men involve enacting comedic scenes—often depicting everyday blunders and confusions in schools, hospitals, police stations, bus stops, and the family home—from popular films and television programs.

A complex everyday mediation of this genre emerges in popular television programs which highlight moments of public embarrassment—indicated by the word *chammal*. For example, on the television show *Chammal in Demand* on the Kairali satellite television channel, viewers are able to request their favorite scenes of embarrassment from comedy films (Rowena 2002: 161). Sometimes, the term can refer to comedy in general. For example, describing a film or a role as *chammal* refers to its comedic elements. (Rowena also links *chammal* to practices of male rivalry called *para*, in which one is trying to cut one's rival down to size.[15])

However, *chammal* (also for women) takes on a particular salience when tied to a *chethu* masculine style, one in which wandering about looking for some fun can often involve embarrassing oneself in a clownish sort of way, laughing at other people's embarrassment, or embarrassing others, thus becoming an aspect of male rivalry and competition. I discussed various forms of *chammal* with Baiju, a student friend of mine, after he came up to me laughing his head off about something he had just seen. He first described what he called "bad *chammal*," a kind of *chammal* in which one is not relating to one's peers but to authority, and the ways in which authority can embarrass you, administering a dressing down that leaves you looking bad in front of your peers, especially girls:

> You're talking in class. The teacher will tell you to stand up. Then he will start a dialogue: "Boy (*eda*), what is this? Who do you think you are? You have no sense (*bodhum*)." He'll go on for a while. After a little while, you will feel *chummy*.

He then went on to describe a more light-hearted situation, like the one he had just seen:

> Rajiv was going on a cycle. A bus went by with a girl in it whom he knew. Just so he would hear, she said out the window, Hey boy (*eda*) move out of the way! He looked up to see who said that. He hit the curb and fell over.... [laughs] At least he didn't hurt himself.

Finally, he described a *chammal* that he thought was a really big one, involving a friend of his who had just gotten a brand new motorbike:

> You know the road that runs alongside the college? There is that road. Sunish had gotten a Kinetic Honda, the kind that you don't need to change the gears for. There is that curve in the road. Me and my friends were there. They saw him coming and he saw them too. He wanted to shine (*chethu*) in front of them. He took both hands off the handle bars and said, "Hey!" The Honda turned and skidded. That's a big *chammal*.

These examples reveal the unpredictability of attempting to present a certain kind of public persona. All of them involve the management of various kinds of public situations—sitting in a classroom, riding a cycle or a motorbike, running to catch a bus. The stories are funny because they reveal a certain incompetence to manage oneself in public, physically or verbally, in a failure of *chethu*. Sometimes it is your transgression or desire to "shine" that gets you into trouble. Other times, it is the fault of a situation beyond your control. And still other times, someone else does something to embarrass you, like a girl calling out to a boy.

What happens when a man tries to produce *chammal* in a woman? It is here that we begin to see the ways in which this form of masculinity asserts itself against the backdrop of women's traversal and occupation of public space. The situation shifts from small incidents of unpredictability in public to a more rigorous policing in which women's sexuality and their containment is at stake. The most pervasive form in which men address women in public is *comment adi*, "hitting" women with sexualized comments on the street, in a bus, or in various other situations. Part of a set of practices labeled "Eve-teasing" in popular discourse, *comment adi* emerges out of masculine practices of fun in public.[16] As indicated earlier, women deploy a demure demeanor to navigate this precarious terrain.

In an interview, Shijo, somewhat notorious for his playboy image, produced his own rationalizations for this practice. He began by saying that he was not as bad as most other guys because he did *comment adi* only as he was walking along the road. He did not stand at the college junction and continuously make comments to all the women that came by. He then went on to say:

> In nature there is this notion, that the opposites always attract. That cannot be realized. Right? To have a conversation about that is why people *comment adi*. Then, you say it to boost up confidence. For example, when I was walking along, I saw a girl. She was a friend. Not very attractive *(resam illa)*. Somebody said something in a way that hurt her. I don't do things like that. You should do it to boost someone's confidence. I will give you another small example. When I was walking along this morning, I saw a girl. Very attractive. She was good to look at. I am walking this way and so is she. So I go up to her and say, without saying anything dirty, I just want to say that you are good to look at. I like you. Do you think you might like me? Then she will laugh. I know I will not see her tomorrow. I know that. It's just a joke, *tamasha*. It works both ways. I get satisfaction, then her confidence is boosted. I tell her she's good-looking. Her confidence is boosted. There is nothing negative here. That's the way I think about it.

However, other than doing a girl a favor by "boosting up her confidence," he also goes on to blame the manner in which girls behave: "When you walk in an unmindful way, you will get comments. Nobody will like it if a girl walks around feeling a little superior *(gema)*. They will try and degrade her. They will say something in order to lower her, bring her back down." This idea of "walking in an unmindful way" points to the ways in which young women's traversals of public space are regulated. Further, when a man tries to embarrass a woman in public, the specific regulation of women's sexuality begins to reveal itself. This regulation requires both the production of women as sexualized and the policing of that sexualization. In other work I have discussed the spatialized terrain of femininities that mediates how young women are enabled and constrained in their negotiation of the public spaces of the college and consumer spaces (Lukose 2009). A young woman's participation in the public spaces of modernity requires her to mediate her sexuality. This mediation happens through embodiments and negotiations of femininities that enact a cultural politics of globalization within Kerala as women participate in globally-inflected consumer culture and spaces of education.

A further illustration of how forms of masculine assertion are pitted against women in public is exemplified by the tensions that arise between a *chethu* masculinity and middle-class forms of femininity. This mediates a classic trope within the popular-cultural politics of the region—the emblematic tension/desire between a lower class/caste male figure and an upper-class/caste female. During my fieldwork within college spaces starting in the mid-1990s and after, for example, the outside of the eight-foot wall surrounding the college compound, the side facing the street, was full of advertisements for Killer jeans, three kinds of local sneaker brands, Vespa scooters, computer training classes, and the like. Once one entered the revolving gate of the college, however, "fashion" was to be kept at bay: not the wearing of jeans or sneakers by men, that is, but women's fashionable dress. Many girls reported being harassed and bullied by male students about the clothes they wore when they first came to college. If they dared to wear a skirt as opposed to a *churidar* or *pavada*, they were told in no uncertain terms that in this college the male students did not like "modern" girls.

In order to illustrate this dynamic, let us return to Shijo with the playboy reputation. He grew a bit defensive during our discussion of his sexualized comments to girls, as he went on to talk about the assertiveness of the "modern" girl who has too much *gema* by recounting a story of when he was the target of sexual comments. He located this story in a more elite college in the capital city, where all the girls are supposedly "modern":

> In Trivandrum, I had to go to [that] college for some reason, you know it? Yes … I had to go see some friend. You have to walk a lot from the main road. I was alone. I had my two hands in my pockets, like that I was walking, kind of smartly. As I was walking along, there were two or three of them, laughing and going. One said to another, "It seems like he's about to break up and fall. He must need his two hands to be in his pockets in order to help him stand up. What does he think, that it's *chethu?* Oh, it's not *chethu*. He's just got on a pair of stupid jeans." I was shocked. I turned around, angry and hot. I pretended not to hear and I just went on. "Can you see how he struts?" [the girls said]. I just turned and said, "Daughter (*mole*), I have a lot of people to see. Can you just let me go?" I'm telling you. These girls say a lot.

Here, Shijo is constructing a narrative in which his marginalized class status as someone from a non-elite small-town college dressed up to go to the city is mediated through gender, a confrontation with the aggressive "modern" girls of the more elite classes. The narrative plays on tropes of conflict and desire between an aspirational lower-class, lower-caste boy and a newly aggressive upper-class, upper-caste girl that have come to dominate youth-oriented films (Rowena 2002).

When asked to explain why and how girls in other colleges sometimes wore skirts (in Kerala's capital city of Thiruvananthapuram, for example),

I was often told it was because those were rich, Gulf-returned girls. But in fact, the great majority of these girls would never have been to the Gulf. Under the highly restrictive labor laws of many Gulf countries, rarely does a work permit include a family visa. Furthermore, noncitizens are not allowed into the Gulf countries' university systems, so children are commonly left behind for schooling. Young women who wore skirts were not recently returned from the Gulf, and their families may or may not have had connections to the Gulf, but their bodies bore the burden of "foreignness." Further, the relationship between the Gulf and the "West" is a complex mediation that is elided in such markings, where the libertine sexuality associated with the "West" is foisted on a woman associated with the Gulf (even though most women who have been there complain of having had to wear a *burqa* for the first time, and point to having been highly restricted in their mobility). Such situations reveal the ways in which class and urban-rural resentments come to be focused on the female body.

If we go back to the idea of *chethu*—understood as a masculine, fun-loving, consumer identity—and compare it to the ways in which the young woman above struggles to articulate her desire for "fun" it becomes clear that the spacio-temporal grids that underlie those two notions are very different. The ephemerality of *chethu*, located as it is in the here and now, marked by its explicit rejection of the future and unburdened by a sense of the past, shapes the roving, fun-loving persona of a young man in his jeans, riding his motorbike, drinking beer. This is a lower-class, lower-caste masculine consumer identity marked by desire and aspiration. The "modern miss" interested in fashion shows, modeling, and beauty pageants, is a middle-class object of desire that must ultimately be tamed and disciplined. Burdened by tradition, preyed upon by modernity, she must learn to navigate these new spaces of consumption respectably and modestly. Her notions of "fun" are situated in and through notions of tradition and modernity, public and private, that make her claim on these new consumer spaces tenuous.

Further, it is important to note the social categories that appear under the sign of "fun" and those that do not. In this iteration, we have the classic and stereotypical contrast between the lower-class, lower-caste aspiring masculine subject and the upper-caste, upper-class feminine object of desire. Analyses of important films of the 1990s such as *Roja* and *Bombay* have demonstrated the ways in which an upper-caste, upper-class masculine subject is reworked through discourses and ideologies of liberalization.[17] What is absent in this structure of representation that marks "fun" in the public spaces of modernity is the lower-class, lower-caste young woman. There is no need to represent her consumer agency and subjectivity, because she is so thoroughly privatized under the sign of tradition through the intersection of her gender and class and caste status that she can make little claim on a modern public, either as a threatening or entitled figure. The lack of a consumer identity linked to her social location in liberalizing India marks the boundaries of exclusion and inclusion through which consumption has become a new axis of belonging and social membership.

Conclusion

In this article, I have highlighted the cultural-political dynamics of everyday forms of commodified masculinity within the spaces of youth cultural life in Kerala. "Shining" in public reveals the contours and dynamics of assertion and anxiety that mark the lives of young, non-elite men at the intersection of the developmental state and trajectories of migration and globalization. Globalization in India has been narrated through a discourse of generational shift from "midnight's" to "liberalization's" children. While this discourse names a key dynamic in globalizing India, namely the cultural-political dynamics of change as India globalizes, it obscures more than it reveals when this discourse creates static visions of opposing generations located in elite, metropolitan locations. Here, I have sought to highlight non-elite, regional trajectories of young men's lives as embedded in their performances of masculinity within the commodified public spaces of youth cultural life. An exploration of their self-fashioning—through discourses and practices of "shining" in public—and their narratives of hope, desire, and aspiration reveal new and precarious assertions into the public culture of the region that challenge caste and class hierarchies that are often rooted in the cultural and political dynamics of gender differences and sexual regulation of young women. In these ways, it becomes possible to contextualize these young men within ongoing struggles over public life in the region while simultaneously recognizing how this terrain becomes a new space for mediating globalization.

Notes

1. For example, the national news magazine *Outlook* devotes its 12, January 2004, issue to the cover story, titled "The World's Youngest Nation," including these statistics (page 41). The business community touts the youthfulness of the Indian labor force, looking favorably on the earnings potential of young workers. A recent JP Morgan Stanley report states that India will be the youngest nation in the world by 2010, a fact that will help generate and sustain an 8 percent growth rate (*Business Standard*,

30 May 2006). The "second demographic transition," as some have called it, with exploding youth populations in many countries of Asia, Africa, and Latin America, has also been noted by key Indian business leaders such as Nandan Nilekani, CEO of Infosys, an information technology firm that is one of the success stories of the new economic dispensation in India (interview on *The Charlie Rose Show*, 1 March 2006).

2. Rushdie's novel, considered a hallmark in postcolonial literature, marked a generation through its invocation of Nehru's famous speech at the midnight hour of India's independence on 15 August 1947 (Rushdie 1981). For an example of how "midnight's children" is invoked against "liberalization's children" in contemporary journalistic usage, see Kripalani 1999.

3. For discussions of Nehruvian nationalism, see Deshpande 2003, Nigam 2005, and Khilnani 1997. In particular, Fernandes's book on how India's middle class is responding to and being transformed by new economic reforms usefully charts the role of the middle class during earlier periods of anticolonial nationalism, during the aftermath of independence in the era of Nehru, and in the wake of liberalization (2006). Her study examines how her middle-class informants in contemporary metropolitan Mumbai lay claim to public space and engage in forms of politics that generate a new discourse of social exclusion from disadvantaged groups, instead of "speaking for" them, as in an earlier Nehruvian articulation.

4. Holston and Appadurai (1996: 200) argue that "Citizenship concerns more than rights to participate in politics. It also includes other kinds of rights in the public sphere, namely civil, socioeconomic, and cultural."

5. See Hall and Jefferson (1976), Hebdige (1981), McRobbie (1991). These early studies, mainly focused on Europe and the U.S., have expanded to include cultural studies of youth, spatiality, and globalization in a variety of contexts, including the non-West (Cole 2004, 2005; Cole and Durham 2006; Skelton and Valentine 1998; Maira and Soep 2005; Bhavani, Kent, and Twine 1998; Nava 1992; Stearns 2005; Manderson and Liamputtong 2001; Dolby and Rizvi 2007).

6. These crossroads produce a highly disjunctive understanding of the life cycle; one that counters standard anthropological approaches in which youth is a transitory stage within a maturational life cycle, often tied to a focus on rites of passage (Van Gennep 1909). Rather than view the life cycle as a preordained movement from one stage to another, recent approaches explore shifting constructions of the life cycle itself (cf. Johnson-Hanks 2002). Osella and Osella discuss constructions of the life cycle in a Kerala context (1999). Cole (2004) and Cole and Durham (2006) explore shifting ideas about the life cycle in the context of globalization, with a focus on Africa.

7. For a wide-ranging discussion of the "modeling" of Kerala, see Lukose (2009).

8. For an exploration of migration within the South Asian region, see Gardner and Osella (2004). Osella and Osella (2000, 2004b) discuss the impact of migration within the Kerala context.

9. J. Devika outlines how discourses and practices of Kerala's emergent modernity, starting in the 1890s, entailed a reform of community-based practices so as to produce, by the middle of the twentieth century, a middle-class family form in which appropriate forms of domestic consumption were tied to the family role as producer for the developmental needs of the community, state, and nation (2007).

10. Osella and Osella briefly mention this term but do not fully examine its gender implications (1999: 997). Though not popular all over Kerala as a form of youth slang, it was prevalent in southern Kerala where this study was located.

11. The expanding literature on masculinity has been helpful in shifting the study of gender beyond that of women and femininity to processes of gender that structure gender relations. Within the South Asian context, the work of Jeganathan (1997, 2000) and Dhareshwar and Niranjana (1996) focus on non-elite forms and practices of masculinity. For an interdisciplinary focus on masculinities in South Asia see Chopra, Osella, and Osella (2004) and Srivastava (2004). For a discussion of different styles of masculinity in the context of migration and the cash economy in Kerala, see Osella and Osella (2000). Radhakrishnan (2005) and Rowena (2002) provide critical discussions of masculinization in Kerala during the 1990s.

12. Toddy *(kallu)* is an alcoholic beverage created from the sap of palm trees such as Palmyra and Coconut. Toddy tapping is the process by which this sap is extracted and was among the most important traditional occupations of the Ezhava caste in Kerala.

13. All names are pseudonyms.

14. These are elite schools of national repute.

15. *Para* refers to a crowbar, used between pieces of wood to move them apart (Rowena 2002: 129). While Rowena attributes the everyday naming of these practices as *para* to the comedy films, it is unclear clear how the circuit of mediation works in this instance.

16. These practices have become increasingly contested by feminist activism through the framework of sexual harassment, for example through the P.E. Usha case during the 1990s. For a discussion of these contestations and reactions to them within the Kerala context see Radhakrishnan (2005). For a discussion of how the law has understood these practices, see Baxi (2001).

17. These are not "youth" films, marked by explicit attention to consumption and fashion in the way *Kaadhalan* is, and in that sense they do not operate through highly elaborated valorizations of consumer agency and "fun." However, discussions of the films have pointed to the ways they mediate the moment of liberalization and middle-class formation through the figure of the upper-caste, upper-class hero and the conjugal family (Niranjana 1991). In *Bombay*, we do see a non-upper-caste, non-upper-class feminine character, Shaila Banu, but her identity as a Muslim mediates her low-class status.

Bibliography

Bhavnani, Kum-Kum, Kathryn Kent, and France Winddance Twine. 1998. *Signs, Special Issue on Feminisms and Youth Cultures*, 23(3).

Business Week. 1999. "How India's New Generation is Different." Available from: http://www.businessweek.com/1999/99_41/b3650015.htm [Accessed 18 August 2011].

Business Standard. 2006. "India Will Be Youngest Nation by '10: Study." 30 May.

Chopra, Radhika, Filippo Osella, and Caroline Osella, eds. 2004. *South Asian Masculinities: Contexts of Change, Sites of Continuity*. New Delhi: Women's Unlimited Press.

Cole, Jennifer. 2004. "Fresh Contact in Tamatave, Madagascar: Sex, Money, and Intergenerational Transformation." *American Ethnologist*, 31(4): 573–588.

Cole, Jennifer and Deborah Durham. 2006. *Generations and Globalization: Youth, Age and Family in the New World Economy*. Bloomington: Indiana University Press.

Deshpande, Satish. 2003. *Contemporary India: A Sociological View*. New Delhi: Penguin Books.

Dhareshwar, Vivek and Tejaswini Niranjana, 1996. "Kaadalan and the Politics of Resignification: Fashion, Violence and the Body." *Journal of Arts and Ideas* 29: 5–26.

Dolby, Nadine and Fazal Rizvi. 2007. *Youth Moves: Identities and Education in Global Perspective*. New York: Routledge.

Durham, Deborah. 2004. "Disappearing Youth: Youth as a Social Shifter in Botswana." *American Ethnologist*, 31 (4): 589–605.

———. 2000. "Youth and the Social Imagination in Africa: Introduction to Parts One and Two." *Anthropological Quarterly*, 73 (3): 113–120.

Fernandes, Leela. 2006. *India's New Middle Class: Democratic Politics in an Era of Economic Reform*. Minneapolis, MN: University of Minnesota Press.

Franke, Richard and Barbara Chasin. 1992. *Kerala: Development through Radical Reform*. Delhi: Promilla, in collaboration with the Institute for Food and Development Policy, San Francisco.

Hall, S. and T. Jefferson, eds. 1976. *Resistance through Rituals: Youth Subcultures in Post-War Britain*. London: Hutchinson Press.

Hebdige, D. 1979. *Subculture: The Meaning of Style*. London: Methuen.

Holston, James and A. Appadurai. 1996. Cities and Citizenship. *Public Culture* 8: 187–204.

Jeffrey, Robin. 1993. *Women, Politics and Well-Being: How Kerala Became a "Model."* Delhi: Oxford University Press.

Jeganathan, Pradeep. 2000. "A Space for Violence: Anthropology, Politics and the Location of a Sinhala Practice of Masculinity." In *Subaltern Studies 11: Writings on South Asian History and Society*, eds., Partha Chatterjee and Pradeep Jeganathan. Oxford: Oxford University Press.

Johnson-Hanks, Jennifer. 2002. "On the Limits of Life Stages in Ethnography: Toward a Theory of Vital Conjunctures." *American Anthropologist*, 104(3): 865–880.

Khilnani, Sunil. 1999[1997]. *The Idea of India*. New York: Farrar, Strauss, and Giroux.

Kripalani, Manjeet. 1999. "India's Youth." *BusinessWeek*, 11 October, http://www.businessweek.com/1999/99_41/b3650015.htm.

Lukose, Ritty. 2005. "Empty Citizenship: Protesting Politics in the Era of Globalization." *Cultural Anthropology*, 20(4): 506–533.

———. 2009. *Liberalization's Children: Gender, Youth and Consumer Citizenship in Globalizing India*. Durham: Duke University Press.

Manderson, L. and P. Liamputtong Rice, eds. 2001. *Coming of Age in South and Southeast Asia: Youth, Courtship and Sexuality*. London: Routledge.

Maira, Sunaina and Elisabeth Soep. 2004. *Youthscapes: The Popular, the National, the Global*. Philadelphia: University of Pennsylvania Press.

McRobbie, Angela. 1991. *Feminism and Youth Culture: From Jackie to Just Seventeen*. Boston: Unwin Hyman.

Muraleedharan, T. 2005. "National Interests, Regional Concerns: Historicizing Malayalam Cinema." *Deep Focus*, Jan-May.

Nigam, Aditya. 2005. *The Insurrection of Little Selves: The Crisis of Secular-Nationalism in India*. New York: Oxford University Press.

Niranjana, T. 1991. Cinema, Femininity, and the Economy of Consumption. *Economic and Political Weekly*, XXVI(43).

Osella, F. and C. Osella. 1999. "From Transience to Immanence: Consumption, Life-Cycle and Social Mobility in Kerala, South India." *Modern Asian Studies*, 33 (4): 989–1020.

———. 2000a. *Social Mobility in Kerala: Modernity and Identity in Conflict*. London: Pluto Press.

————. 2000b. Migration, Money, and Masculinity in Kerala. *Journal of the Royal Anthropological Institute*, 6 (1): 117–133.

Outlook. 2004. "The World's Youngest Nation." *Outlook*, January 21.

Parayil, Govindan.(ed.) 2000. *Kerala: The Development Experience, Reflections on Sustainability and Replicability*. London: Zed Books.

Radhakrishnan, Ratheesh. 2005. "PE Usha, Hegemonic Masculinities and the Public Domain in Kerala: On the Historical Legacies of the Contemporary." *Inter-Asia Cultural Studies*, 6 (2): 187–208.

————. n.d.a. "What is Left of Malayalam Cinema?" Unpublished Manuscript.

Rowena, Jenny. 2002. *Reading Laughter: The Popular Malayalam 'Comedy-Films' of the Late 80s and Early 90s*. Ph.D. diss., Central Institute of English and Foreign Languages, Hyderabad, India.

Rushdie, Salman. 1981. *Midnight's Children*. London: Jonathan Cape.

Skelton, Tracey and Gill Valentine. 1998. *Cool Places: Geographies of Youth Culture*. London: Routledge.

Srivastava, Sanjay. ed. 2004. *Sexual Sites, Seminal Attitudes: Sexualities, Masculinities and Culture*. Delhi: Sage.

Van Gennep, A. 1909. *Rites of Passage*. Chicago: University of Chicago Press.

Zachariah, K.C., E.T. Mathew, and S. Irudaya Rajan. 2001. "Impact of Migration on Kerala's Economy and Society." *International Migration*, 39(1): 63–85.

Zakaria, Fareed. 2006. India Rising. *Newsweek*, 6 March: 34–37.

Chapter 2

"There Will Be a Lot of Old Young Men Going Home"

Combat and Becoming a Man in Afghanistan

Anne Irwin

Introduction

The title of this chapter was inspired by a comment made to me by a key informant during the course of field research with a Canadian infantry rifle company engaged in combat operations in Southern Afghanistan during the summer months of 2006.[1] He was an experienced soldier, a sergeant whom I had known since 1996 when I had studied the same unit during peacetime training in Canada. The company had been "outside the wire," that is, outside the protective confines of the coalition base at Kandahar Air Field, for several weeks, but had returned to the base for two days of preparation for a major offensive operation. We were sitting in the shade of the big tent where we slept while on base, watching some young soldiers as we talked about his fears that he would not be able to accomplish his personal goal for this tour of duty in Afghanistan, "to bring all my boys home." Our conversation veered to the topic of the end of the tour and of adjusting to life at home and he commented, "there will be a lot of old young men going home from this tour." I dutifully recorded the comment in my fieldnotes that evening and forgot it until I began thinking about the notion of combat service as a rite of passage into manhood. I believe his comment captures very eloquently the paradoxes and complexities of the idea of war service as a transition into male adulthood.

There is a widely-held perception in popular culture, within the military as well as within academic studies of the military, that military service in general and combat service in particular constitute rites of passage into manhood. This is expressed in recruiting slogans such as "the Marine Corps builds men" and "we'll make a man of you," and it is also prevalent in motion pictures. One of the most common tropes in war films is the transition from boy to man effected by the experience of combat (Westwell 2006: 23). The academic literature likewise is replete with metaphors of coming of age through military service (see for example Ben-Ari 1998: 115; Gilmore 1990: 70; Hockey 1986; Kaplan 2000; Karner 1998: 206; Karpinski 2008; Morgan 1994; Samuels 2006; Sinclair-Webb 2000; Winslow 1999). One scholar expresses the opinion of many when she writes, "war has been accepted as the great touchstone of manliness since time immemorial" (Oldfield 1989: 237). Yet, with the notable exception of Winslow (1999) and Samuels (2006), none of these scholars analyzes military service or combat service in terms of the classic tripartite structure of the *rite de passage* (Turner 1974; Turner 1977; van Gennep 1977). Winslow's paper is an analysis of an explicit initiation ritual into an elite unit of the Canadian Forces, and Samuels makes a compelling argument that the post-traumatic stress disorder from which many veterans suffer may be caused by an incomplete rite of passage, with soldiers mired in the liminal phase. Although my analysis takes a different turn than Samuels's, I believe our approaches are complementary rather than contradictory.

A case can certainly be made that combat service bears the characteristics of a rite of passage, but I argue in this chapter that combat service, although transformative, is not a rite of passage for it does not permanently or completely alter participants' statuses from youth to adult manhood. War service does not turn boys into men, but rather, it turns them into old men without passing through adulthood, and even that transformation is not complete, as they retain many of the characteristics of youth.

I begin this chapter by presenting the context of the research on which the argument is based, followed by an ethnographic account of the tour of Afghanistan in which I participated as a researcher. I subsequently problematize the idea that there is a one-to-one correspondence between the infantry and a unitary masculinity. I then apply van Gennep's tripartite model of the *rite de passage* (1977) to the combat tour, focusing primarily on the liminal and re-integration phases of the tour to make the argument that soldiers returning from the tour have not been transformed into adult men but are in some respects stuck in youth and in other respects prematurely old, so that their statuses are indeed a hybrid that could be termed "old young men."

Research Context

In February 2006, the First Battalion of the Princess Patricia's Canadian Light Infantry (1PPCLI), an infantry battalion of the regular Canadian Forces (CF), deployed to southern Afghanistan as part of Canada's contribution to the U.S.-led "Operation Enduring Freedom." The battalion constituted the core of Task Force Orion, the battle group that was responsible for security in the province of Kandahar. Task Force Orion was only a small part of the Canadian contingent, which totalled more than 2500 military personnel. As the Canadian combat unit, the Task Force, numbering approximately 450 personnel, was specifically tasked with "conducting aggressive interdiction operations."[2]

I had been studying the First Battalion of the Princess Patricia's Canadian Light Infantry since 1991 when I spent several months in the field with the unit in Alberta, Canada, as it trained for conventional warfare and for peacekeeping (Irwin 1993). In 1995/1996 I spent almost a year with the unit as I tried to understand how soldiers in this peacetime and peacekeeping army made sense of and negotiated their roles as warriors and soldiers (Irwin 2002). In 2006, the unit's role changed dramatically when it deployed to southern Afghanistan, where there was no peace to keep, but where the unit was expected to undertake what the military calls "full-spectrum operations," including combat.[3] Because of my long-standing research relationship with the unit, I had no trouble gaining access when I proposed to accompany them for the second half of their tour. I went to Afghanistan in March 2006 for two weeks to do a pilot research project (or "reconnaissance" in army parlance) and to determine the feasibility of a longer study after the end of the university term. Deeming a longer project both feasible and important, I returned to Afghanistan at the end of May and spent the remainder of the tour with the unit, returning with the soldiers to Canada at the end of August via Cyprus where they stopped for a five day "decompression" tour (see Irwin 2008 for a critical analysis of the decompression tour).[4]

During the period of my research, the battalion's role did not change, but the public in Canada did become more aware of the true nature of the unit's activities as the death toll rose, and by the end of the tour, there was open acknowledgement in the media and among the public that the Canadian Forces were involved in fighting counterinsurgency warfare.

Because I was interested in how soldiers negotiated their identity as war-riors in the context of their changing roles from peacekeepers to war-fighters, I used traditional anthropological methods, primarily participant observation, living in close intimacy with the troops and participating in their experiences, short of combat, as fully as possible.

Ethnographic Account of the Tour

My research was conducted almost exclusively with one of the rifle com-panies, Charlie Company, which consisted of about eighty-five soldiers of all ranks, ranging from private to major and from eighteen years of age to the late forties, among whom only three were women.[5] These three women, it should be noted, could be considered "social males" (Acker 1990: 139)[6] because they formed such a small minority and participated in the same masculine culture.

The primary focus of my research was 8 Platoon, one of the three platoons that along with the headquarters made up the company. Each platoon was commanded by a lieutenant, who was assisted by his sec-ond-in-command, a warrant officer. The platoon was divided into three sections and a headquarters. Each section of the platoon consisted of five to eight infantrymen commanded by a sergeant with a master corporal as his second-in-command. I use the male gender here purposely. While, as I noted earlier, there were three women serving in Charlie Company, 8 Platoon was an entirely male sub-unit, so I was the only woman in the group. Each of the sections and the platoon headquarters was assigned during operations to one Light Armoured Vehicle (LAV), which was the soldier's home during operations outside the wire. The analysis that fol-lows applies only to the youngest and most inexperienced soldiers, the privates and corporals in their late teens and early twenties for whom this was their first tour.

Any analysis of the tour in Afghanistan must take into account the spatial organization of the experience of the soldiers. The central organiz-ing principle, the notion of "the wire" was used to categorize people and to structure all the routine features of social life, including time, social interaction, and experience. The wire referred to the concertina wire sur-rounding the coalition base at Kandahar Air Field (KAF), and the term "outside the wire" was applied to any activity that took place outside of those protective confines. The most basic distinction between categories of people was that between the people who never left the wire, or the base, and those whose duties regularly and routinely took them outside.

For the troops at KAF, life in Afghanistan was uncomfortably hot (averaging in the mid-fifties Celsius in July), involved long hours of work, and entailed facing the risks presented by the occasional rocket and mortar attack on the camp (these attacks have wounded a few soldiers, but so far have not resulted in any fatalities). Soldiers were also subject to certain deprivations: alcohol was not permitted, and sexual relations, even between spouses serving a tour together, were forbidden. Soldiers were also armed at all times except during physical training and going to the showers, although their weapons were not loaded. There were many different militaries present, each with their own distinct uniforms and badges of rank. I remember feeling very strongly on arriving in Kandahar Air Field that this base was an operational base in a war zone, in part because of the constant dust and noise of helicopters coming and going, and the fact that all military personnel were armed at all times, something that is not common on bases in peacetime in Canada. However, after spending a number of weeks outside the wire, when I returned to KAF I found the differences between KAF and any other peacetime military base to be superficial.

Task Force Orion's tactical headquarters were at KAF, as were the permanent accommodations of the members of each of the companies of the Task Force. Each company was assigned an enormous tent that slept two hundred soldiers in double bunk beds. All members of the company, including the Company Commander and the Company Sergeant Major and all the other company officers, shared the same accommodations. Most soldiers screened off their beds with tarps and blankets to achieve a modicum of privacy, but the resulting privacy was at best illusory and was paid for by a decrease in air ventilation. No one knew what the acronym for these tents really stood for, but, because it was BAT, the soldiers all referred to their on-base accommodation as the "Big-Ass Tent." Beside each bed were the soldiers' barracks boxes which held their gear, and soldiers went to a fair bit of trouble to make their "bed-space" as comfortable and as uniquely personal as possible. Much of this was somewhat wasted effort, since they spent so little time at KAF itself.

The unit rarely spent more that a few days at KAF at any one time, spending most of their time "outside the wire," living a nomadic life, traveling by day and night in the LAVs, sleeping when the opportunity presented itself in the sand next to their vehicles. For the troops who spent the whole tour inside KAF, "outside the wire" was an undifferentiated realm, full of danger and risk, whereas for the soldiers who routinely ventured outside the wire the spatial organization was rather more complex. There were large stretches of road and terrain that were considered dangerous, but there were also spaces which, though outside KAF, were considered, to a greater or lesser extent, also to be "inside the wire"—at least inside a different wire than the one surrounding KAF. Spaces outside KAF considered to be inside the wire were places that, at a minimum, were surrounded by enough protection that soldiers were required to unload their weapons upon entry.

The safest of these places were the Forward Operating Bases (FOBs), District Centers, and Afghan National Army compounds, while the riskiest sites, as opposed to the obvious risk of traveling in convoy, were the Artillery Movement Areas, the patrol bases, and the "leaguers"[7]— temporary sites occupied for as little as a few hours or as long as a couple of days. In these riskier spaces, weapons were kept loaded at all times, and soldiers usually wore body armor and helmets unless they were very close to their vehicles. Each of these different types of space entailed different daily routines, different patterns of social relationships, different habits of dress and deportment, and phenomenologically different experiences. But in all cases the threat of enemy action, although not always in the forefront of one's mind, was like a constant background hum, often outside the frequency range of everyday awareness.

Once outside the wire, assigned tasks included cordon and search operations, show of force patrols, provision of security for meetings with local leaders, reconnaissance patrols for Village Medical Outreach missions or humanitarian aid drops, training Afghan National Army and Afghan National Police units, and, increasingly, clearing compounds and villages, and deliberately seeking out Taliban and engaging them in combat.

What was most apparent about daily life outside the wire was that there was very little that was routine about it. Structured time was entirely disrupted outside the wire. There was no day-to-day routine for sleeping and eating, not even predictable shifts. Moving by convoy and other missions were often conducted during nighttime, whether intentionally, or because of unexpected delays and changes of plans, of which there were many. Because of the intensity of the operational tempo, sleep was a rare commodity. Soldiers became adept at sleeping whenever and wherever they had a chance. Often the chance to sleep only came during daylight hours, for a few hours at a time, but even this sleep was constantly interrupted by the bangs of artillery and mortars, the noise of vehicles starting up, and the sound of small arms fire. When vehicles stopped in a "leaguer," whether for hours or days, the thermal sights needed to be manned and observation posts and sentries posted so that what little sleep was to be had was interrupted by shifts at thermal watch or sentry duty, sometimes two in one five- or six-hour sleep period.

Outside the wire, the daily menu of hard rations or individual meal packs, although containing all the necessary nutrients, became tedious.

There was quite a range of different meals, but after a while they all came to taste the same. Soldiers went to great lengths to structure meals in as "normal" a fashion as possible. For example, despite temperatures soaring into the sixties Celsius and the fact that all the meals are edible unheated, if at all possible meals would be heated before being eaten, sometimes in the LAV's boiling vessel, sometimes with chemical packs, sometimes by being placed on the roof of the LAV for half an hour. Wherever feasible meals would be eaten as close as possible to the "normal" time of day: breakfasts in the morning, lunches near midday, and suppers in the evening. Sections would almost always eat together, and while each soldier would have his or her individual meal pack, the accessories, such as coffee, tea, and gum, were usually pooled and shared afterwards, and the desserts and main meals often traded, in accordance with individual preferences. Frequently, meals would be heated and ready to eat when an order to move would come over the radio and the meals were set aside to be eaten hours later, or sometimes not at all if the delay pushed into the next meal period. Issued meals were supplemented with treats received from family and friends back home, and there were very strong social norms enforcing an ethic of sharing. If anyone were to eat a treat that he had received from home without offering to share with section mates, someone would be sure to ask pointedly, "What does that taste like?" Although almost every soldier had a personal MP3 or IPod player, it was rare in the extreme for anyone to use it with earphones as a personal listening device. It was much more common for soldiers to adapt some sort of speaker system through the intercom of the LAV and share their music.

As I have suggested with respect to meals, another stress factor outside the wire was the fact that plans and orders were constantly changing, and it was therefore impossible to plan ahead or to pace oneself. On one occasion 8 Platoon was sent on what was to be a three-day operation, but the platoon was warned to pack for a week because there was a chance that the mission would be extended. In fact the operation lasted twenty-one days, and on any given day the soldiers had no idea how much longer the mission would last, although rumors about imminent return to KAF abounded. Soldiers were therefore always faced with mundane decisions such as whether to change into that one last clean t-shirt, or pair of socks, or to make them last one more day in case they stayed out longer.

The heat during those twenty-one days was so intense, reaching as high as 64 degrees Celsius, that under their body armor soldiers were soaked with sweat through their t-shirts and combat shirts, sometimes down to the knees. This amount of sweating posed very real risks of serious dehydration, and soldiers routinely each drank ten to twelve liters of water a day, mixing Gatorade into every fourth or fifth bottle. The necessity of saving water for drinking meant that it was unusual to waste it on such luxuries as washing and shaving. Pre-moistened wipes were used occasionally, and hand sanitizer was usually available in each LAV for use before meals, but soldiers normally only shaved when they had a break in activity at a Forward Operating Base.

Social relationships outside the wire took on a particular pattern, which I refer to as enforced intimacy. Soldiers slept within an arm's reach of each other and knew the most intimate details of their comrades. The stress engendered by the complete lack of privacy was managed through joking and teasing, a phenomenon observed by other anthropologists of the military (Ben-Ari and Sion 2005: 658–9). Interpersonal conflict was repressed or suppressed outside the wire, only to emerge in the form of petty bickering when soldiers had more than a few days of safety at KAF.

Military Masculinity Problematized

In his seminal work on masculinity, R.W. Connell argued that masculinity is not unitary but is configured differently in different times and places, and he coined the term hegemonic masculinity to refer to "the configuration of gender practice which embodies ... the currently exalted form of masculinity" in a particular culture (Connell 2005: 77). The military and the infantry in particular are frequently considered sites where hegemonic masculinity is produced and reproduced (Anonymous 1974; Connell 2005: 77; Dunivin 1994; Gill 1997; Helman 1997; Karner 1998; Sinclair-Webb 2000). Some scholars have added nuance to these analyses by pointing out that even in the military, the supposedly quintessential site of monolithic masculinity, there are pluralities of forms of masculinity that are called forth in different contexts (Barrett 2001; Hockey 2002; Hockey 2003; Morgan 1994). Morgan argues, for instance, for "the need to see the military as a site for the development of a plurality of masculinities rather than a single, dominant, and highly embodied masculinity" (1994: 180). Even in the military masculinity must be considered contingent, multiple, and fluid, especially in recent years with more women serving in combat or near-combat roles (Morgan 1994: 171). This begs the question, then, about what sort of adult masculinity is the end product of the rite of passage that so many consider combat service to be. Acker argues that "currently, [adult] hegemonic masculinity is typified by the image of the strong, technically competent authoritative leader who is sexually potent and attractive, has a family, and has his emotions under control" (Acker 1990: 153). If this is indeed the model of masculinity into which combat is supposed to transform young men, then as we will see, the experience of combat cannot be considered the rite of passage that accomplishes this.

The Tour as a Rite of Passage

Even as we reject the experience of combat as a rite of passage, however, a tour of duty in Afghanistan can be analyzed in terms of the tripartite structure of a rite of passage, (Turner 1974; Turner 1977; van Gennep 1977) with the deployment phase (the departure from Canada) representing the rite of separation, operations in the country representing the liminal phase, and the redeployment (the return to Canada) representing the reintegration phase. During the deployment phase, soldiers are confronted with many of the classic characteristics of a rite of separation, including the most obvious: the physical separation from pre-existing statuses by means of geographic removal from the country. In preparation for this removal, soldiers participate in mission-specific training and are tested to ensure that there are no medical, psychological, or personal reasons for them to be left behind. Immediately before the deployment they are issued new uniforms because in Afghanistan they wear the "arid Can pat," or Canadian camouflage pattern designed for desert environments, whereas in Canada they wear a green camouflage uniform. They get their hair cut very short and some even shave their heads, and there are official farewell ceremonies as well as unofficial parties. They update their wills and make arrangements in case of being killed or wounded, ensuring that their next of kin notification forms are up-to-date and correct.

One last activity is a formal picture-taking event, organized by the battalion, when each soldier has his or her photograph taken in "full fighting order," wearing a beret with the unit cap-badge rather than a helmet as would be normal during operations. These photos which soldiers call their "death photos" are filed for use in the press release in the event of the soldier's death. There are some superstitions around these photos. One soldier who was sick on the day the photographs were taken had never had a "death photo" shot and took this to mean that he would survive the tour. Another soldier took me aside before a major operation in which he was afraid he would be killed and gave me messages for his wife and asked me to make sure that "they" did not use "the cheesy combat photo" of him in the press release but one of my photographs of him smiling with his soldiers. I promised I would do my best if the occasion necessitated it. All of these activities carried out in preparation for leaving the country and the possibility of death seem to be symbolic of the stripping away of pre-existing statuses. It would appear, then, that the deployment phase looks very much like the separation phase of a rite of passage, but the liminal phase is more difficult to delineate.

Considering the tour itself a liminal phase would suggest that the tour takes place in one undifferentiated realm, but, as mentioned above, the central organizing principle of the tour is the phenomenological difference between life at KAF and life "outside the wire." For the soldiers who spend the entire tour in Kandahar Air Field, the period in Afghanistan certainly has aspects of liminality: physical separation, deprivation, and—as I will explain further below—a certain amount of communitas (Turner 1974; 1977). But for the combat soldiers who spent little time at KAF, the times inside the wire and outside the wire were so fundamentally different from each other that it is difficult to consider the tour as all one phase. It is probably more accurate to consider the periods outside the wire as liminal episodes, so that each trip outside the wire was itself a rite of passage consisting of the three phases nested within a longer liminal phase. What I am suggesting here is that for the combat soldiers time "in-country" is a liminal phase with periods of deeper liminality each framed by their own rites of separation and reintegration.

In this chapter I am not evaluating just any tour as a rite of passage, but specifically the experience of combat. In addressing the question of whether combat transforms youth into men, one of the first steps must surely be to define what I mean by combat, a task that is not as straightforward as one might expect, especially in the Afghan context of counterinsurgency warfare. A minimalist definition would limit the notion of combat to the emic concept of the TIC, the acronym soldiers use to refer to "troops in contact." A TIC refers to a discreet event, bounded in time and space during which soldiers are engaged violently with the enemy. This minimalist definition however would not include a range of activities that are nonetheless experienced as combat or combat-like. An example would be when a vehicle full of troops triggers the explosion of an IED (improvised explosive device) without the immediate presence of the enemy. These occasions, which are far more frequent than actual firefights, pose a danger to life and limb and usually include the threat of a subsequent ambush and actual combat. This first example is an omnipresent danger for any soldier, or indeed civilian, who ventures outside the wire, and is not a danger that is restricted to the members of the combat arms.

Another typical situation which blurs the category of combat would be the fighting patrol during which troops are expecting to encounter the enemy and are prepared physically and psychologically for a fight, but in fact never have an opportunity to engage the enemy. Although in this case troops may not have been in physical contact with the enemy, the emotional and physical labor which is represented by the intent approximates combat. This second example is an activity in which only the combat troops of the Task Force would have been involved.

If we limit the definition of combat to participation in a TIC, not all of the soldiers of 8 Platoon let alone Charlie Company would have been involved, and even for those soldiers who were so involved, TICs were very rare occurrences. And yet, every member of the Company who served outside the wire during the 2006 tour considers him or herself to have "done a combat tour." If we are to respect the soldiers' existential reality, we might define combat as any time outside the wire during which the potential for and threat of combat were ever-present (as was a constant need to prepare), and occasionally manifest. Using this definition, there are certainly some very strong indications that the episodes outside the wire could be considered combat and were also liminal experiences.

The Liminal Experience of Combat

Leaving the wire always entailed much preparation: checking maps, issuing orders, loading equipment into the LAVs, and loading extra ammunition in the LAVs. On a personal level, almost every soldier took the opportunity while at KAF to get his or her hair cut extremely short, and many chose to shave their heads in the interests of hygiene because of the lack of opportunity outside the wire to wash. On the boundary of KAF there was a buffer zone between rows of concertina wire where convoys leaving the camp would stop, soldiers would dismount from the vehicles, load the magazines onto their personal weapons and arm the big cannon on the LAV. This buffer zone included the office of the contractor who provided interpreters to the military, so this was also the place where a unit which had been assigned an interpreter for the period would pick up its assigned interpreter. Soldiers would climb back into the vehicles once more, post air sentries to stand in the open hatches of the vehicles, and head out for anywhere from three days to three weeks of operations.

The combat soldiers experienced each of these episodes outside the wire as an ordeal to endure and survive and as a period of deprivation, both of which are among the characteristics of the liminal phase (Morinis 1985: 151). These periods were also understood and experienced as tests of skill and ability, both at the personal and the group level, during which soldiers struggled to maintain alertness despite fatigue and boredom. The constant fear of injury or death and the necessity to be ready for any eventuality competed with the need for sleep. Of all the deprivations—freshly cooked food, sex, alcohol, washing—lack of sleep was the most debilitating and the most salient feature of life outside the wire.

Along with intense sleep deprivation, life outside the wire was characterized by uncertainty and unpredictability, in part due to the actions of the enemy and in part due to the commands of higher authority. Soldiers were constantly aware that a routine patrol or convoy might lead to walking or driving into an ambush, or an apparently innocent vehicle might hold a suicide bomber. In response to intelligence to which soldiers at the company level were not privy, commanders would issue orders, only to change them hours later. On one occasion, the company received four changes of mission in as many hours. Although plans were made in response to enemy activity or a threat of enemy activity, or requests for assistance from allied forces, to the soldiers these constantly changing plans appeared capricious and contributed to an apathetic attitude and the perception of a lack of agency—in short, these soldiers found themselves at the mercy of those in command, another feature of the liminal phase.

In some respects, and at some moments, normative masculinity was turned upside down.

Certainly, one of the features of adult masculinity is control over one's bodily functions, yet soldiers spoke unashamedly among themselves and in front of me of losing control over their bladders and bowels before, during, and after firefights. A number of them confided in me that they vomited before combat operations, or even operations that might lead to combat. Incontinence can be thought of as a marker of extreme old age and infancy, yet none of these young men was the least bit embarrassed or ashamed to acknowledge this loss of control over bodily functions.

Soldiers were also not ashamed to display signs of affection with each other, and unlike Karner, I do not believe that this "male bonding" was a substitute for intimacy (Karner 1998: 217), since it appeared to consist of genuine affection and even love. The soldiers in the company were also very open and expressive of their grief in the context of the death of comrades in much the same pattern as Morgan has described among British soldiers during the Falklands War (Morgan 1994: 177).

On one occasion, 8 Platoon was supposed to have been sent to an area of high risk, the Panjwaii District. This was a notorious district where the platoon had been involved in fire fights on multiple occasions, and less than a month before, Corporal Tony Boneca had been killed there by enemy fire. At the last moment, presumably because the company commander felt the platoon needed a rest, 9 Platoon was sent instead, and 8 Platoon remained behind in the relative safety and comfort of a Forward Operating Base near the village of Spin Boldak. The next morning, the sergeant major spread the word that there was to be a company parade in the centre of the FOB. The soldiers formed up in a hollow square and the company commander addressed them, telling them that Corporal Chris Reid had been killed in an improvised explosive attack, and that the platoon was still engaged in a TIC (troops in contact). The expressions of grief and dismay were open and genuine and many soldiers wept openly. Only a few hours later, at around midday, the sergeant major called everyone together for another parade and again the company formed up in a hollow square. This time the company commander began with the words, "there's no easy way to tell you this. This morning I told you that 9 Platoon was still involved in a TIC in Panjwaii. There have been three KIA" and as he announced their names, "Sergeant Vaughn Ingram, Corporal Bryce Keller, and Private Kevin Dallaire," I heard moans behind me, and, glancing over my shoulder, saw a number of soldiers dropping to their knees, sobbing. The rest of that day was full of mourning, in part because the members of the platoon, not being involved in combat at that moment, had the luxury of allowing themselves an open expression of grief. Soldiers cried and held each other, and some of them sobbed in my arms, all of it entirely without shame or embarrassment at the time or later.

The shared grief and deprivation, as well as the enforced intimacy, led, during periods outside the wire, to very strong expressions of communitas among the privates and corporals in the platoon. The pre-existing social structure was simplified to those who gave commands and those who obeyed, and, as noted above, among peers everything was shared, including meals and treats sent from home. Although it was clear who was in command at any time, badges of rank and name tags were entirely obscured by body armor, so that although the soldiers were not "divested of outward attributes of structural position" (Turner 1974: 232), the outward attributes were invisible. Turner argues that "communitas is almost always thought of or portrayed by actors as 'a moment in and out of time,' or a state to which the structural view of time is not applicable" (1974: 238). This is certainly the way soldiers describe the experience of true combat, and is very much how I experienced the one occasion when I got caught up unexpectedly on the fringes of a firefight. They described and I experienced time slowing down and everything becoming very clear.

Turner argues further that the liminal phase is one during which neophytes learn ways to "confer some degree of intelligibility on an experience that perpetually outstrips the possibilities of linguistic (and other cultural) expression" (1974: 240). There were myriad ways that soldiers learned from each other to make sense of and express their experiences. One of the most striking and humorous was the day after a firefight when a spontaneous discussion arose about how "our TIC" would be portrayed in a Hollywood movie. Unfortunately I did not have my audio recorder near at hand, but to this day I remember vividly the animated way in which they discussed which Hollywood stars would play which soldier in the company, how rather than walk to the village, they would rappel out of helicopters, they would never run out of ammunition, and every hand grenade would explode with the force of a five hundred pound bomb.

Coming Home: Reintegration

While the episodes outside the wire were arguably experienced as liminal phases, the real test of whether the tour of Afghanistan can be considered a rite of passage into manhood is the reintegration phase during which initiands are reintegrated into society in new statuses with new responsibilities and privileges. I want to consider now how soldiers are reintegrated into society and, especially, in what statuses they are reincorporated. The return to Canada from combat duty in Afghanistan was a protracted process, involving first a return to KAF from outside the wire (Irwin 2008). Several days were spent at KAF returning some equipment, attending briefings, sleeping as much as possible, doing laundry, and passing on "soldier-level tips" for survival to the incoming soldiers who were to replace them. Subsequently there was an air journey to the Canadian Forces support base in the Persian Gulf where soldiers turned in their weapons, ammunition, and body armor. For most of the soldiers this was a moment full of meaning: shedding the more than twenty pounds of ballistic plates encased in Kevlar and handing over the weapon that had been within reach for the entire tour were powerful symbols that the tour was over and that they had survived it.

From the Persian Gulf they flew, unarmed and dressed now in civilian clothes, to Cyprus for the "decompression" which consisted of a few briefings but which was mostly devoted to relaxation in the form of sleep, binge drinking, and sightseeing. After five days in Cyprus they boarded an aircraft yet again, now dressed in clean uniforms, wearing berets instead of helmets, for the final leg home. Fighter planes escorted the returning aircraft into the Edmonton International Airport and, once the soldiers deplaned, motorcycle police escorted their buses to the base. The route from the airport to the base was festooned with yellow ribbons, which have become symbolic in recent years of returning soldiers. At the base a lecture building had been set aside for the reunion with their families. It was a very emotionally charged moment, with mothers and fathers, wives, husbands, and children running to greet the returned soldiers. Many tears were shed on the part of family members and soldiers. It was not an entirely happy homecoming for all of the soldiers. One of the soldiers was expecting his wife to meet him but found on arrival that she had decided to leave him and was not there to greet him. Other soldiers had asked their family members to wait and meet them in private, because they were not certain how their families or they would handle the heightened emotion of the homecoming in such a public setting.

This moment was the ultimate reintegration, the moment when soldiers returned to their families and to their homes. What was particularly striking to me was how many mothers thanked me for having been there with their sons as a surrogate mother and then told me that they hardly recognized their own sons because of the dramatic physical changes that had taken place during the tour.[8] Because I had been with them constantly during the second half of the tour, I had not noticed the changes myself, but when I was shown photographs of soldiers taken before the tour, I was immediately struck by how much they had aged. They did not seem to have aged into adults, however, but into old men.

Gabriela Spector-Mersel has pointed out the near invisibility of old and aging men in the literature on masculinity (2006), and Wainwright and Turner have argued for the analysis of aging to include the notion of the social construction of aging as well as an acknowledgement of the ontological realities of the aging body (2004). In their ethnography of aging dancers, they suggest that the rigors of the dancer's life lead to premature aging of the body so that dancers can be considered to be too old for their work well before middle age (2004: 111). The same phenomenon is true of infantry soldiers, and a forty-year-old infantry corporal is certainly considered "over the hill" by his peers and superiors. Like the veterans of the first Gulf War interviewed by Kilshaw, the veterans of Task Force Orion complained of weakness and loss of muscle tone and felt that their bodies had shrunk during the tour (Kilshaw 2009: 176). At the start of the redeployment phase, as we were about to return to KAF, a number of soldiers complained to me that they had lost from twenty-five to thirty-five pounds of muscle, and that they were worried that they would look like "scrawny old men" in front of their replacements who would look like they did at the beginning of the tour: fit, strong, "buff." Many of the returning soldiers were also marked by scars and permanent disabilities, some severe enough for them to have to leave the service. One of the members of 8 Platoon, for example, suffered two gunshot wounds to his leg, one of which shattered his femur. In his early twenties, he now has a titanium rod from his hip to his ankle and will probably always need a cane to walk. He did not return with his peers because he had been repatriated after receiving his wounds but he was there to greet his platoon comrades on their return.

Others returned with less visible scars, with psychological wounds which made sleep difficult. Several soldiers and I commiserated with each other over the irony of not being able to sleep in the safety of one's own bed whereas we had slept soundly (albeit for only short periods at any one time) lying in the sand next to a Light Armoured Vehicle. All the returning members of 8 Platoon had experienced far more dramatic events than most young adults experience: they had suffered bereavement, having had friends killed beside them; some of them had administered first aid to badly wounded comrades; they had been called upon to make life or death decisions in split seconds; and some of them had killed in the heat of battle.

Thomson and Whearty have suggested that, as men age, they tend to downsize their networks of friends and kin (2004: 4). This was evident among the returning soldiers, who tended to limit their closeness to those who had shared with them the intense experience of combat. Most of them told me that none of their friends, family members, or even other soldiers who had not served in Afghanistan would ever be able to understand what the tour was like. All of these factors combined to give the impression of old age, both physically and emotionally, yet in many ways the returning soldiers also seemed mired in a perpetual adolescence.

This perpetual adolescence was evident in the way their section commanders referred to them always as "the boys." Indeed, they constantly referred to themselves and each other as "the boys." And in many respects, they were still boys. Although on the tour they had experienced an array of dramatic and even traumatic events, many of them had never lived anywhere but with their parents or in barracks, and I was constantly surprised by their naivety especially with respect to financial matters. Most of them had never held a mortgage or taken out a bank loan or, indeed, signed a lease. Living at home or in an institutional setting had in some ways infantilized them; being told what to wear, when to eat, and when to wash had resulted in the tendency to diminish their sense of autonomy and agency, and this was exacerbated by the uncertainty and unpredictability of life during the tour.

Like the squaddies studied by Hockey, these soldiers made up for the deprivations of the tour immediately on arrival in Cyprus through drinking and casual sex (Hockey 2002; 2003). During the decompression in Cyprus, no one was permitted to rent or drive any type of motor vehicle. In North American society today, driving a car is one of the well established markers of adulthood and the soldiers experienced the prohibition against driving as "treating us like kids." The explanation offered by commanders for this policy included the fact that Cypriots drove on the left, so adjustment to driving would be difficult, as well as the risks associated with drinking and driving. There was also some suggestion that risky driving behavior was commonplace among soldiers just returning from deployment. There were, however, many recreational packages available in Cyprus, and among the most popular was the go-cart track with a bar. During the two evenings I spent at the track with some of the soldiers I was reminded again and again how very young they were as they drank beer and played boisterously, racing go-karts around the track and bumping into the rubber tires that formed the perimeter of the track, only days after being involved in a deadly firefight. Additionally, binge drinking and casual sex, both activities commonly associated with young working class men (Canaan 1996; Sabo 2006: 544) continued, at least among the younger privates and corporals who are the focus of this analysis, after their return to Canada.

Two years after the return of the unit to Canada, 8 Platoon's former platoon commander, who had survived the tour with his platoon, volunteered for a second tour of duty, and was killed in action, although not in combat. Captain Jon Snyder fell down a well and drowned during a night patrol in the Panjwaii District, the same area where most of the company's fatalities had taken place. Members of 8 Platoon, his first platoon in Afghanistan, served as his pall bearers at his funeral in Ottawa at the national cemetery. The military funeral was not just a time to grieve, but was also a reunion for the members of the platoon, some of whom had taken their releases from the services and some of whom had been posted to distant bases. One who had since taken his release from the military paid for his own trip to Ottawa from Newfoundland, saying that he still felt a strong connection with his former commander. There were many tears as soldiers wept in each other's arms over the loss of their platoon commander, but there was also a lot of drinking, singing, reminiscing, laughing, and genuine intimacy. As I shared in their grief at Jon's death and their joy at reconnecting, I was forcefully reminded how old and young they were at the same time.

Conclusion

In this chapter I have argued against the popular image of combat service as a rite of passage into manhood. I have tried to show that the traditional form of masculinity that is deemed to be the product of military socialization is more complex and pluralistic than the prevailing stereotypes allow. Although I agree that combat service has some of the features of a rite of passage—specifically, a tripartite structure of separation, liminality, and reintegration—I question the simplistic notion that this rite of passage, if indeed it is a rite of passage, transforms boys into men. I have tried to demonstrate that although combat may be experienced as a transformative liminal phase, young men who go to war return not magically transformed into adult men but rather changed into old young men who are perhaps still liminal or marginal in the sense that they are neither old nor young, neither youth nor adult, but boys with some of the attributes of extreme old age.

In the end, the sergeant whose comment inspired the title of this chapter did "bring all his boys home," although not all of them came home unscathed. Some of them are suffering from psychological wounds that manifest themselves as nightmares, others have physical scars, and he himself has had to leave the infantry because of a disability incurred during the tour. Some of the soldiers in his section have left the army and some have left the infantry, but those who have stayed with the battalion were, at the time of the writing of this chapter, about to embark on the battalion's second tour in Kandahar. May they all come home safe.

Notes

1. I acknowledge with gratitude the support of the University of Calgary Research Grant #1007103 which made this fieldwork possible. I am grateful to the members of the Canadian Forces who were instrumental in facilitating my research and, especially to the members of Charlie Company, 1 PPCLI, who kept me safe during the tour.
2. Lieutenant Colonel Ian Hope, personal communication, June 2006, Kandahar Air Field.
3. Lieutenant Colonel Ian Hope, personal communication, June 2006, Kandahar Air Field.
4. The Department of National Defence provided transportation for me from Canada to Kandahar, as well as accommodations and food during the entire fieldwork period.
5. One of the women, Captain Nichola Goddard was killed in combat in May of 2006 after my first trip and before my second trip. I never had the opportunity to meet her, but I heard her voice many times over the radio during the pilot project. She was the first Canadian woman, and the highest ranking officer at the time, to have been killed. I use the male gender throughout the paper, not just because males were a distinct majority, but in order to ensure anonymity for the women soldiers who were so few in number.
6. Acker uses this expression, based on Sorenson's work, to refer to the exceptional woman working in a male-dominated organization who behaves and is accepted socially as if she were male (Sorenson 1984).
7. The term leaguer is derived from the Boer War when Boers circled their wagons at night in a *laager* (Dutch for "camp"). Whenever the company stopped for more than a few minutes, it would pull into a field and form a square with the armored and heavily armed LAVs on the perimeter, their big cannons, machine guns and thermal

sites trained outside the square, and the headquarters and more vulnerable support vehicles within. This formation was called a leaguer. If a platoon stopped independently it would form a "starburst" leaguer, a circular formation with each of the four vehicles pointing outward.

8. I had not been aware that soldiers had been writing emails home about me to their mothers and wives, nor did I realize the extent to which they thought of me as a surrogate mother. Some of them had jokingly referred to me as the Platoon's mom, but I had not made any effort to "mother" them. The role of mother, however, was one to which they might easily assign me, because of my age and my white hair.

Bibliography

Acker, Joan. 1990. "Hierarchies, Jobs, Bodies: A Theory of Gendered Organizations." *Gender and Society*, 4 (2), March: 139–158.

Anonymous. 1974 "Life in the Military." In *Men and Masculinity*, eds. Joseph H. Pleck and Jack Sawyer. Englewood Cliffs: Prentice-Hall.

Barrett, F.J. 2001. "The Organizational Construction of Hegemonic Masculinity: The Case of the U.S. Navy." In *The Masculinities Reader*, eds. S.M. Whitehead and F.J. Barrett. Cambridge: Polity Press.

Ben-Ari, Eyal. 1998. *Mastering Soldiers: Conflict, Emotions, and the Enemy in an Israeli Military Unit*. New York and Oxford: Berghahn Books.

Ben-Ari, Eyal and Liora Sion. 2005. "'Hungry, Weary and Horny': Joking and Jesting among Israel's Combat Reserves." *Israel Affairs*, 11 (4): 655–671.

Canaan, Joyce E. 1996. "'One thing leads to another': drinking, fighting and working-class masculinities." In *Understanding Masculinities*, ed. Máirtín Mac an Ghaill. Buckingham and Philadelphia: Open University Press.

Connell, R.W. 2005. *Masculinities*. 2nd edition. Cambridge: Polity Press.

Dunivin, Karen O. 1994. "Military Change and Continuity." *Armed Forces and Society*, 20 (4): 531–547.

Gill, Leslie. 1997. "Creating Citizens, Making Men: The Military and Masculinity in Bolivia." *Cultural Anthropology*, 12 (4), Nov: 527–550.

Gilmore, David. 1990. *Manhood in the Making: Cultural Concepts of Masculinity*. New Haven and London: Yale University Press.

Helman, S. 1997. "Militarism and the Construction of Community." *Journal of Political and Military Sociology*, 25 (2): 305–332.

Hockey, John. 1986. *Squaddies: Portrait of a Subculture*. Exeter: University of Exeter Press.

———. 2002. "'Head Down, Bergen On, Mind in Neutral': The Infantry Body." *Journal of Political and Military Sociology* 30(1), Summer: 148–171.

———. 2003. "No More Heroes: Masculinity in the Infantry." In *Military Masculinities: Identity and the State*, ed. Paul Higate. Westport: Praeger.

Irwin, Anne. 1993. "Canadian Infantry Platoon Commanders and the Emergence of Leadership." MA Thesis, University of Calgary.

———.2002. "The Social Organization of Soldiering: A Canadian Infantry Company in the Field." Ph.D. diss., Manchester University.

———. 2008 "Redeployment as a Rite of Passage." Canadian Defence and Foreign Affairs Institute.

Kaplan, Danny. 2000. "The Military as a Second Bar Mitzvah: Combat Service as Initiation to Zionist Masculinity." In *Imagined Masculinities: Male Identity and Culture in the Modern Middle East*, eds. Mai Ghoussoub and Emma Sinclair-Webb. London: Saqi Books.

Karner, Tracy Xavia. 1998. "Engendering Violent Men: Oral Histories of Military Masculinity." In *Masculinities and Violence*, ed. Lee H. Bowker. Thousand Oaks, London, and New Delhi: Sage Publications.

Karpinski, Eva. 2008. "En-trenched Manhood: War and Constructions of Masculinity in George Orwell's *Homage to Catalonia.*" *Men and Masculinities*, 10 (5): 523–537.

Kilshaw, Susie. 2009. *Impotent Warriors: Gulf War Syndrome, Vulnerability and Masculinity.* New York and Oxford: Berghahn Books.

Morgan, David H. J. 1994. "Theater of War: Combat, the Military, and Masculinities." In *Theorizing Masculinities*, eds. Harry Brod and Michael Kaufman. Thousands Oaks and London: Sage.

Morinis, Alan. 1985. "The Ritual Experience: Pain and the Transformation of Consciousness in Ordeals of Initiation." *Ethos*, 13(2), Summer: 150–174.

Oldfield, Sybil. 1989. *Women against the Iron Fist: Alternatives to Militarism 1900–1989.* London: Blackwell.

Sabo, Don. 2006. "Masculinities and Men's Health: Moving Toward Post-Superman Era Prevention." In *Reconstructing Gender: A Multicultural Anthology*, ed. Estelle Disch. Boston: McGraw-Hill Higher Education.

Samuels, Karen. 2006. "Post-traumatic Stress Disorder as a State of Liminality." *Journal of Military and Strategic Studies*, 8 (3): 1–24.

Sinclair-Webb, Emma. 2000. "'Our Bülent Is Now a Commando': Military Service and Manhood in Turkey." In *Imagined Masculinities: Male Identity and Culture in the Modern Middle East*, eds. Mai Ghoussoub and Emma Sinclair-Webb. London: Saqi Books.

Sorenson, Bjorg Aase. 1984. "The organizational woman and the Trojan horse effect." In *Patriarchy in a welfare society*, ed. Harriet Holter. Oslo: Universitetsforlaget.

Spector-Mersel, Gabriela. 2006. "Never-aging Stories: Western Hegemonic Masculinity Scripts." *Journal of Gender Studies*, 15(1), March: 67–82.

Thompson, E.H., Jr. and P.M. Whearty. 2004. "Older Men's Social Participation: The Importance of Masculinity Ideology." *The Journal of Men's Studies*, 13(1): 5–24.

Turner, Victor. 1974. *Dramas, Fields, and Metaphors: Symbolic Action in Human Society.* Ithaca and London: Cornell University Press.

———. 1977. *The Ritual Process: Structure and Anti-Structure.* Ithaca and London: Cornell University Press.

van Gennep, Arnold. 1977. The Rites of Passage. London and Henley: Routledge and Kegan Paul.

Wainwright, Steven P. and Bryan S. Turner. 2004. "Narratives of Embodiment: Body, Aging, and Career in Royal Ballet Dancers." In *Cultural Bodies: Ethnography and Theory*, eds. Helen Thomas and Jamilah Ahmed. Malden, MA: Blackwell Publishing.

Westwell, Gus. 2006. *War Cinema: Hollywood on the Front Line.* London and New York: Wallflower.

Winslow, Donna. 1999. "Rites of Passage and Group Bonding in the Canadian Airborne." *Armed Forces and Society*, 25 (3): 429–57.

Chapter 3

Institutionalizing an Extended Youth Phase in Chinese Society
Social Class and Sex Differences in the Pursuit of the Personal and the Pragmatic

William Jankowiak, Robert Moore, and Tianshu Pan

Introduction

Throughout most of Chinese history, males—and especially sons—have comprised the preferred social category in which parents strove to develop emotional and ethical obligation. This relationship has constituted the fundamental value orientation by which Chinese society has traditionally organized itself. But the 1949 communist transformation of society, especially urban life, profoundly altered the parent-son dyad, and in its place the parent-daughter bond became increasingly paramount. Even in the countryside, where the parent-son relationship and the patrilineal principle remained sociological constants, a transformation took place by the late twentieth century. Increasingly, urbanites and some rural residents (Shi 2009; Yan 2003) began to prefer daughters to sons. In the countryside, the cultural shift in sex preference has little to do with emotions and everything to do with pragmatics. The cost of bride price has increased tenfold, and families have had greater difficulty in raising funds to pay bride price. Interestingly, daughters are perceived to be more economically beneficial. Additionally, daughters are regarded as being more loyal and emotionally involved with their natal families. In this way, daughters are tacitly replacing sons as the preferred gender. The material factors responsible for this shift are undermining the symbolic system that has long legitimated a different set of sex-linked obligations. This transformation is most immediately and acutely experienced among China's youths who have become a new pioneer generation that is completely rewriting Chinese cultural life, much the way the "baby boomers" in the U.S. have done for that culture. The resulting reinterpretation of cultural life has brought with it new economic opportunities that continue to wear several faces based on class position and gender. Now, however, the gender that is prospering the most in China are the females. The remaking of female opportunities is taking place with the creation of something quite new in Chinese society: the creation of a new youth stage of life. For much of Chinese history, individuals moved from childhood through adolescence to adulthood, but today this is starting to change. Economic and social reforms have provided the material, symbolic, and psychological foundations for an extended youth phase.

Youth, that long curving transition from childhood to adulthood, is a phase of life that frequently tests and challenges a culture. Feeling little stake in the status quo of the adult world and armed with access to new sources of power in their young lives, youths often play the role of shock troops for the latest social or political movements, taking little for granted (Moore and Rizor 2008). The experimental propensities of the young, seen against the conservative objections of older generations, reveal facets of cultural systems—their basic values and assumptions—that otherwise often remain invisible. The efforts of youths to test and redefine morality give a glimpse into the social landscapes of the future. This is especially so among wealthier societies where the transformation from adolescence is being delayed and is organized around personal development. In this period of extended youth, individuals are encouraged to explore personal, social, and economic opportunities, if for no other reason than to increase their understanding of themselves and the economic options available to them. In this context, individuals need "more time to develop the emotional maturity, cognitive skills, and social intelligence to navigate the challenges of uneasy transitions, fluid careers, and changing families" (Gerson 2009a). Though not every community sees its adolescents entering into an extended youth phase dedicated to engagement in positive experimental—or even explicitly defiant—behaviors, there is nonetheless a fundamental shift in social understandings that is currently play-ing itself out in contemporary China. Moreover, we believe this shift is affecting young men and women differently. To date, there have been no studies that explicitly examine this social shift or that have examined the sex-linked patterns in economic opportunity. Consequently, we believe that a sustained effort to understand what is happening between genera-tions and among the sexes, both in Greater China at large and within the confines of individual Chinese households, is overdue.

In this chapter, we will explore the emergence of China's youth stage as a distinctly new type of generational phenomenon. After discussing how specific structural and cultural factors have contributed to the delayed ar-rival of adulthood, we will examine the economic, demographic, and cul-tural factors responsible for a youth stage's ability to survive, as well as its ability to thrive, in contemporary China. Finally, we will discuss how the social transformation in the meaning of adulthood has impacted men's and women's perceptions of family, parenthood, marriage, economic op-portunities, and life-orientation.

The Chinese Family: An Overview

Anthropological and historical research on Han Chinese kinship systems has resulted in broad agreement concerning the ideal of the late imperial Chinese family, an ideal that continues to shape parent-child relations. Its most prominent elements were patrilineal descent and inheritance, and patriarchal authority. Families that matched, or nearly matched, the ideal were those in which a respected older-generation male offered firm but benevolent guidance to his wife, sons, daughters-in-law, and other kinsmen and household members. In fact the ultimate ideal, rooted in the Confucian scholarly tradition, envisioned a five-generation household based on these elements. The ideal expresses itself in a cycle of deference: deference of wives to husbands, children to parents, and younger siblings to older siblings. A measure of the interdependence of the parent-child bond in China can also be seen in the countless apocryphal tales of the dynastic period that lavished moral praise on filial children who sacrificed parts of their bodies to produce potent medicine to heal ailing parents (e.g., Ebrey 1988: 78). Contemporary Chinese families, however, do not generally match this ideal—which comes through clearly in historical re-search and fictional accounts of late imperial China.

Still, the prestige of the ideal was real enough, and its force resulted in efforts on the part of family members to adhere to its patriarchal and patrilineal values. As a consequence most Han Chinese families exhibited identifiable patriarchal/patrilineal features in the realm of property management and inheritance as well as in their rituals for weddings, funerals, and the commemoration of ancestors. Furthermore, children were expected to not only honor and obey their parents but also to cherish and care for them in their old age.

Many Chinese families have, in recent decades, experienced change due to the influence of Maoist egalitarianism in the 1950s, 1960s, and 1970s, and, in subsequent decades, due to the introduction of consumerism and new ideas concerning husband-wife relations (Davis and Harrell 1993; Parish and Whyte 1978; Yan 1997). Yunxiang Yan, for example, describes the rural families of Xiajia village, in northeastern China, as being more responsive to and motivated by the husband-wife conjugal tie than the traditional parent-child link. One consequence of this new affective dynamic is the practice of serial divisions of family property whereby a child takes his or her share of the family estate upon marriage rather than waiting for the eventual division of family property among all members of the inheriting generation. Along with this practice comes the emergence of what Yan calls "empty nest families," a common phenomenon of Western culture, wherein older married couples live by themselves after all their children have moved out. All in all, there is a strikingly new emphasis on the conjugal couple.

Accompanying this is the relative increase in the influence of the young vis-à-vis their elders. Yan reports an increase in Xiajia of the number of stem families: those in which a man in the younger generation serves as the family manager. The increased power of youths is derived from a number of factors, including the marriage reform laws of 1950 and the new educational opportunities that tend to benefit the younger generations in particular. In addition, William Parish and Martin King Whyte (1978) have remarked on the relative increase during the 1970s in the power enjoyed by daughters-in-law in their domestic confrontations with their mothers-in-law. Yan (1997; 2003) reports on an extension of this power, noting that in the 1990s young married men in Xiajia tended to side with their wives rather than with their mothers when disagreements occurred. More recently, working in a different northeast village, Lihong Shi (2009) reports a similar shift in preference away from devaluing sons in favor of daughters. Economics are one of the reasons for the shift: in the past thirty years the average salary has increased 15 times, while bride wealth increased over 70 times, reflecting the increasingly heavier burden to finance a son's wedding (Shi 2009: 10). She notes a "fierce competition among rural males for a spouse. Rural women have gained power in the marriage market by having a powerful say in the financial negotiations for the marriage" (2009: 4). Shi adds that rural men have more difficulty in negotiating the marriage market than do urban men due to women's expanded opportunity for upward mobility though marriage (2009: 4). Moreover, men cannot readily remarry and must live with the shame of being like old bachelors if they lose their wives. In contrast, women, unlike in imperial China, can easily and readily remarry. Further evidence of the importance of daughters can be found in Tianshu Pan's ongoing anthropological research conducted in the affluent parts of the lower Yangtze Delta Valley (i.e., Northern Zhejiang, Southern Jiangsu, and Shanghai metropolitan area). In this setting, the elevated status of "filial daughters" has deep roots in the region's cultural history; daughters are expected, if not required, to fulfill their natal responsibilities after they have married out. In other words, married-out daughters (from all social strata) seldom sever their ties with their natal home.

This shift away from the son to the daughter bond is not unique to rural village life, for it had already taken place in urban China. For example, William Jankowiak (1993) found that by 1981 there was a new natal reality in urban China whereby the mother-daughter bond had tacitly replaced the conventional father-son bond. Urbanites continued to speak about the father-son bond, while the primary caretakers of parents were daughters.

The affective nature of the conjugal family described by Yan and Shi parallels the pattern of affections typical of courting couples. It seems that romantic love, which commonly emerges as the primary focus of attention in the leisure activities of unmarried adolescents and young adults, has also made itself felt within contemporary Chinese families—even to the point of disrupting the longstanding ideal that has, until recently, shaped these families. Yan emphasizes, however, that the loss of parental power within these families does not imply a loss of commitment to the family on the part of the young people. It is not the extended family as such, but parental authority in general, which marks the change in the structure of the contemporary conjugal family. Still, the pull of traditional hierarchical kinship relationships has by no means disappeared, even in the PRC. Based on her research in the southern city of Kunming, Susan Blum documents the continuing power of these relationships as prototypical models against which non-kin relationships are often constructed (Blum 1997). The intense commitment to the parent-child relationship in China, and a close adherence to its imperatives, would seem to all but rule out the existence of a youth culture, especially one that might test interpretations of morality, seize opportunities for self-expressiveness, and thus act in conflict with parental interests. Even less likely, it would seem, would be specific institutions that distance and separate the young from their elders. Working in rural north China in 2004, Mette Hansen and Cuiming Pan (2008)found a modified arrangement: young males' discourse is loaded with assertions that value individuality while also signaling men's continued commitment to their natal family.

Thomas Shaw (1994), working in the 1980s in Taibei, the capital of Taiwan, found a fun-oriented group of Taiwanese middle-class adolescents who defined themselves as separate from the family. Shaw argued that Taiwanese youths' distinct values and demonstrated behavior patterns were typical of a youth culture. The youths (in Taiwanese, 'kah-a') sought amusements among themselves at the same kind of places where youths in Western culture tend to cluster: shopping malls, discos, and fast-food restaurants. Their emphasis on popular music and dancing, stylish clothing, and riding motorbikes also parallels Western youth cultures. Taiwan's kah-a possibly exemplified a foreshadowing image of an extended youth culture that could well become widespread in the People's Republic. The Taiwanese kah-a's chief distinguishing feature was their self-indulgent pursuit of amusement and fun. This pursuit marks kah-a youth culture as different from the better known, more serious, and moralistic youth movements that characterized China in the earlier parts of the twentieth century, the best known of which were the May Fourth Movement and the Cultural Revolution.

The May Fourth Movement: 1919–1921

The first appearance of a quasi-Chinese youth culture that sought to free males and females from China's patriarchy occurred during the May Fourth Movement, which emerged most notably among Beijing and Shanghai university students. It was not representative of an early twentieth-century Chinese youth culture, but many of the values articulated during that time eventually entered into the Chinese cultural mainstream and resulted in a blurring of generational distinctions between youth and adult cultures. One consequence was that youthful activities became once again subordinate to adult concerns.

The May Fourth Movement signaled, as no other event in Chinese history previously had, a struggle over the meaning of intergenerational respect, authority, and autonomy. Named after the massive student-led street demonstrations in Beijing on 4 May 1919, the Movement was inspired by an array of dramatically innovative political, cultural, and literary ideas. The sources for these ideas were mainly Western, and they became the basis for more liberal ideas about family and governmental authority structures as well as new literary forms. Some of the most significant of these new ideas dealt with the status of women. In late imperial China, the societal positions of men and women were seriously prescribed, resulting in limited roles within the extended family system. Marriages were arranged, and choice and individual expression were subordinated to the parental generation's intentions and interests. The May Fourth Movement was the first broadly based movement to reject the disadvantaged status of youths in general and women more specifically and, instead, to idealize their potential and importance. In so doing, the Movement also promoted, albeit indirectly, the ideal of individual expression, the value of romantic love, and the centrality of the nuclear family. From the perspective of the Movement's young intellectuals, women were the emblematic icons with which to challenge a social order that had imprisoned everyone. In effect, the freedom of women contained a broader freedom, one that was for everyone.

That the May Fourth Movement glorified youth is evident in the titles of its most prominent journals, i.e., *New Youth*, *Young China*, and Young World. One of the most widely read works of fiction during this time was Ba Jin's *Family*, a novel set in then contemporary China, in which the pure and idealistic young are starkly contrasted with their foolish and decadent elders. In written works and speeches as well as everyday conversations, the idea that China's old ways needed to be abandoned—and that it was the young who would lead this abandonment and forge a strong and modern China—dominated this era. Nor was this ideal idle speculation or romantic fantasy. It proved seminal. The values that came to guide China's leaders and intellectuals in the decades following the May Fourth era issued forth from those who were in their twenties and thirties in May 1919, people like Chen Duxiu, Hu Shi and a youthful Mao Zedong.

Jeffery Wasserstrom (1991) has identified a number of structural features of Chinese student life that can foster a well-organized culture of resistance, a culture that often gives birth to political activism. First among these are the many overlapping clubs, sports teams, academic groups, and student councils common to university campuses; these provide a ready-made network of organized groupings through which political ideas and activities can be promoted. Second is the all-encompassing nature of university life. Most students eat, sleep, study, and socialize on campus and, unlike most Chinese workers, for example, are not distracted on a daily basis by family obligations. Third is the fact that student life itself encourages a kind of national culture, so much so that the activities of students at Fudan University in Shanghai resemble closely those of students at Qinghua University in Beijing or Zhongshan University in Guangzhou. In addition, students tend toward cosmopolitanism and thus are less likely than workers to be drawn into debilitating rivalries based on native place associations (though such associations do exist on many campuses). The physical nature of campuses also encourages rapid organization in that the university offers the student a number of public arenas such as dining halls and sports areas. A longstanding organizational practice, for example, was the calling of students to a rally by ringing a bell, a campus feature that lasted throughout the Warlord and Republican eras and continued into the 1980s. Finally, students are in contact with intellectuals who present and discuss new ideas and, therefore, are more likely than workers to first promote such ideas through political action. Factors like these encourage student organization and political activism, even though it is typically workers rather than students who suffer from the worst forms of oppression (Wasserstrom 1991: 131–145).

The Cultural Revolution: 1966–1976

The second appearance of a "youth culture" arose entirely due to the state's encouragement and support of politically mobilized youths who were encouraged to pursue group actions aimed at identifying and punishing unworthy classmates and teachers. The mass mobilization or Cultural Revolution (CR) arose out of Chairman Mao Zedong's efforts and teachings, supported by other Communist Party leaders, to regain control over the government. Its effects were felt not only on campuses but also in factories, neighborhoods, and rural communities throughout the PRC. Mao believed that young people were more pure and capable of promoting revolution than their elders, and many young students took his sentiment to heart. One effect was to virtually eliminate the authority of the teachers. The CR carried with it a variety of unique and intense, though largely temporary, features including the deification of Mao and, in everyday life, punitive physical assaults on high school and college teachers. Its net effect was to reduce a previously powerful and respected social class into silence and, in some cases, driven to suicide.

The aggressive behavior carried out by Red Guard youths against each other and against targeted adults was remarkable in the extent and degree of its violence. Chinese history does not offer other examples where masses of young people carried out prolonged assaults against their elders. Almost as surprising as the attacks themselves is the self-righteous moralizing used to justify them, given the specific Chinese historical context. Confucian tradition does not promote the idea that young people have something to teach their elders about morality any more than it encourages young people to drive the lesson home through physical assault and public humiliation. It promotes, in fact, exactly the opposite behavior.

There are, however, precedents in other societies for adolescents and youths using their voices and their muscle to bring moral pressure against specific members of the adult community. Such have been reported as operating among the Hopi of the American southwest and the Mbuti pygmies of Central Africa (Schlegel and Barry 1991). In early modern Europe, adulterers and others who strayed from the community's standards of decency were liable to be noisily mocked in the middle of the night by groups of boys and young bachelors or, during the day, lampooned with the use of effigies (Schlegel and Barry 1991). However, traditional China did not rely on adolescent peer groups as instruments for social control.

The student "culture" of the Cultural Revolution resembled many youth cultures in that it offered a distinct value system and a status hierarchy according to which members of peer groups could be ranked. Nevertheless, if we compare the CR youth culture with typical Western youth cultures, the uniqueness of the CR culture becomes readily apparent. Consider, for example, the American student-based youth culture that first arose in the 1920s and whose basic features are still found on contemporary high school campuses. Where Chinese youth reflected the interests of specific adults and saw their ideals as highly moralistic, the American youth culture (Bailey 1988; Fass 1977) revolved around entertainment, romantic behavior, and personal pathos. The status hierarchies of the two youth cultures were also distinctly different. To be at the top of the heap in a Red Guard faction usually depended on having a "good" class background (i.e., parents and grandparents who lived or had lived in poverty), an ability to portray oneself as deeply devoted to Chairman Mao's ideology, and apparent courage and leadership abilities.

Besides high school and university Red Guards, there was another category of youths who were active in urban affairs. These "social youths" (i.e., unemployed young people) were composed of former Red Guards who were now unemployed, alienated, and often hostile to adult authority, and who periodically expressed their frustration through petty criminal acts. They were viewed as a new type of hooligan who desired "status, freedom, and power [all qualities] … most youth desired but found lacking in their lives" (Yao 2004: 457).

During the factional fights, the local red rebels victimized cadres from both the street and residents' committees. The key players among the rebels in Five Mile Bridge were not Red Guards from the high schools but those who were officially categorized as "social youths." Our findings support Elizabeth Perry's assertion that the Red Guard movement accounted for only part of the mass activism of the Cultural Revolution; in Shanghai rebel workers remained politically influential for much longer and created a far greater impact than the student Red Guards (see Perry and Li 1997: 2).

The origins of "social youths" as a salient folk category arose in the early 1960s when municipal governments were faced with a rapid rise in unemployment. The aftermath of the Great Leap Forward's (1958–1961) harmful economic policies resulted in the closure of many factories, and thus there was little need for additional workers (Pan 2002). In Shanghai, with its stagnant industrial economy, this meant that most of the city's 180,000 high school graduates would remain jobless and therefore become by default "social youths" (Pan 2002).

Despite the official effort to mobilize high school graduates and dispatch most of them to the countryside, many youths chose to remain at home in the hope that their street officers and neighborhood committee cadres would help them find jobs. Soon many "social youths" became disillusioned with the lack of support.

The Cultural Revolution, as in the case of previous crackdowns on counterrevolutions in the late 1940s and early 1950s, provided an opportunity for revenge, or in the words of the active participants themselves, "to right the wrongs with the support of Chairman Mao." For these restless youths, their motivation to make revolution in the neighborhood did not reflect loyalty to Mao or his party, but rather an urgent need to improve their life chances by "fishing in the troubled water." For example, its members showed little interest in political debates or siding with different factions and were primarily concerned with redressing socioeconomic grievances (Perry and Li 1997: 97). Elizabeth Perry and Xun Li rightly argue that the egalitarian ideal of the Cultural Revolution served only to exacerbate the feelings of injustice among those condemned to low status occupations, such as the transient workers (Perry and Li 1997: 99). Moreover, the political upheavals did not result in the institutionalization of a fully formed vibrant youth culture.

Throughout most of the twentieth century, American youths developed within a milieu that supported increased freedom and a delayed age of marriage. Although different factors were responsible for the development of an American and later a Chinese youth stage, it is significant that the two youth stages shared some similarities. For example, both systems embraced freedom and the individual's right to public expression as positive values. In addition, both systems condoned, albeit often tacitly, engagement in physically stimulating and, thus, exciting activities. Still, there was one essential difference between the two youth systems: the American youth stage flourished, while China's intellectually constructed Red Guard "youth culture" largely disappeared as soon as the political forces behind it withdrew their support.

The Red Guard and unemployed urban social youth activities offer the clearest Chinese case of adolescent social systems that were largely, though not entirely, free of adult control. They also present an array of horrors that, in fact, call to mind the violent and nightmarish scenes from William Golding's (1954) novel *The Lord of the Flies*. The violence that broke out in some Red Guard confrontations and "struggle sessions" is an index of the degree of independence exercised by the young people involved. Quite a few first-hand accounts of these make clear that attacks on victims and enemies were, in many cases, as much personally as politically motivated. Often the difference between being a leader or a target of physical assault depended on one's organizational and rhetorical skills, not one's political ideals or devotion to the Great Helmsman.

Furthermore, autobiographical accounts of Cultural Revolution student life make it clear that romantic and sexual liaisons, though usually surreptitious, were not unknown. Nor was the quest for fun unknown.

Government policies eventually made it possible for students to travel freely, without charge, throughout China, and millions took this opportunity to see parts of the country they had never been able to visit before. It may be that the students of the CR generation were the first Chinese since the revolutionary days of the Yanan era to travel widely and, for some— both male and female—to pursue premarital affairs. Given the extent of the freedoms, the opportunity to express them made the youth cohort, which came of age during the Cultural Revolution, unique in Chinese history. But in the late 1960s, massive numbers of students were suddenly thrust from positions of unprecedented freedom into lives of repression and isolation. At that time the Party began to step up its policy of sending young people down to the country so that they could experience the hardships of peasant life. This policy, which lasted well into the 1970s, eventually sent some sixteen million urban youths to the countryside and brought to a close an era of unprecedented student independence (Gao 1987; Liang and Shapiro 1983; Schoenhals 1996).

The shift in party policies allowed youths to gradually return to their homes and be assigned work in various urban work units. Unmarried youths who were fortunate enough to gain entrance into the university to focus on their studies stayed with their parents, while others who were assigned a clerk or worker position settled into a predictable rhythm of semi-engagement with their work. In every way, China's unintended social experiment—that had enabled the reappearance of a vibrant youth phase organized around freedom and delayed responsibility, all in service of the pursuit of adventure—had ended.

1980s Urban Chinese Social Organization and Its Non-Emerging Adulthood

From 1949 to the beginning of the twenty-first century Chinese urban life was organized around the work unit (*danwei*) and the smaller stem family (i.e., nuclear family with one or two kin living together). This form of social organization was highly restrictive of individual, social, and geographical mobility. Its opportunity structures were quasi-feudal, with an emphasis on political position and bureaucratic rank. The work unit, the local embodiment of the communist state, stressed similar social values to those emphasized in Soviet-dominated Eastern Europe.

China's *danwei* insularity fostered a fortress mentality that de-emphasized the importance of choice, innovation, and change. Given the difficulty of changing one's employment, people seldom left and new people seldom arrived. Life was organized around a succession of non-stimulating events and routine social encounters. The work unit mode of social organization had a profoundly numbing effect on the individual's engagement in the wider social universe. Contrary to contemporary American society (Lane 2000; Putnam 2000), people entertained themselves through an endless cycle of visiting among family members and friends. In this milieu, there was no youth culture per se. Because there was an absence of economic opportunity, there was no need to leave one's natal home. Although in the early 1980s there was said to be no "unemployment" in China, only "youths waiting for a job," the increase in leisure time did not lead to the creation of a youth cohort through which youths sought to separate themselves from their parents and "hang out" with fellow age mates. Most unemployed youths preferred to remain embedded within their respective families and wait for a job, their own one-room apartment, marriage, and parenthood. The Chinese city provided few opportunities for employment, leisure activities, or amusement, and social life remained confined to an endless cycle of visits with friends and family.

Because there were no outside opportunities to do much, youths more or less occupied their time with one another and waited to be assigned to a work unit. Youths for the most part did not form a pool of like-minded individuals who found mutual support and protection among themselves. Rather they sought out a few age mates who were friends for mutual support. Urban youths, associating with their parents and participating in dense friendship networks, were not highly satisfied with their lives. Their dissatisfaction arose from the absence of another aspect essential to the formation of a youth culture: the ability to choose and, thus, become responsible for the direction of one's life. In the early 1980s, there was an absence of opportunities to achieve one's own future goals. Adulthood was defined, as it always had been, through achieving specific social markers: marriage and then parenthood. Maoist urban China, much like rural China, did not have an "emerging adulthood" (see next section) segment. As was typical of life in late imperial China, youths had outlooks and desires that were remarkably similar to their parents' generation. In this way, the junior and senior generations were more or less interchangeable.

William Jankowiak found in his visits to hundreds of families in Hohhot, the capital of Inner Mongolia Autonomous Region, that regardless of age cohort or gender, everyone spoke in one voice: a general lamentation over the lack of choice, and the boredom and ennui of their lives. For most, life had become a dead end. The 1980s social system with its emphasis on rigid egalitarianism, social control, restricted mobility, and conformity undermined many core Chinese cultural values (e.g., achievement, choice, and autonomy). In many ways, Maoist policies were at odds with the Chinese culture. In this setting, young individuals grew increasingly restless and disappointed with their lives (Jankowiak 1993: 96). If life is about process, as much as it is about reaching desired end points, then not being able to choose or seek new avenues heightens the sense of personal frustration and undermines wellbeing. Because people want a sense of responsibility for how they lead their lives, they "are interested in exploring their personal lives in terms of how they have been able to affect them" (Mines 1988: 576). Whatever momentary "flow state" (Csikszentmihalyi 1990) or sense of satisfaction urbanites experienced through attending a wedding celebration, participating in an all-night poker event, or engaging in an evening dance/kissing party (whereby married and unmarried men and women danced with a non-partner, flirted, and, at times, engaged in light kissing on the cheek, neck, or lips), or partaking in a Sunday afternoon family dinner, everyone readily acknowledged that when the subject turned to the pursuit of distant goals, they were, by and large, dissatisfied with their lives.

Economic Reforms, Singletons, Extended Youth, and Emerging Adulthood

Jeffery Arnett (2004) notes that "emerging adulthood" arises whenever there is a material base that enables youths to subsist, if not prosper, independent of family support. For the first fifty years of the People's Republic of China's history the material factors necessary to create a youth stage were absent. Ten years after market reforms, Chinese cities came to resemble in many ways a typical European city: there were more economic opportunities, apartments to rent, and a pronounced change in social norms that enabled males and females to not only hang out but also cohabit with one another. For the first time, the material factors necessary for the creation of a youth culture had appeared. But material factors, in and of themselves, are seldom sufficient; something else is needed. In the case of China, the emergence of a new social category—youth culture— required a political act: the institution of a single child policy.

The single child policy had numerous unintended consequences. First, it altered the way many Chinese looked at the relationship between sex and marriage. If marriage was no longer primarily for reproduction, then it followed that parenthood was no longer a primary marker of adulthood. This fact was not lost on Chinese sociologists who pointed out that the separation of sex from reproduction contributes to making family life associated less with child rearing and more with hedonistic pleasure (Zheng 2009). This redefinition of the meaning of sexuality and marriage is taking place within an emergent economy that provides China's youths with more economic and social opportunities than those available in their parents' generation. For many urban youths, migration to another locale for economic opportunity resulted in the dilution of interaction and thus parental authority. Today's youths live in work sponsored dormitories, share a rented apartment with one or two other roommates who may or may not be their boyfriend/girlfriend, or live alone. These structural changes provided China's singletons with an expanded cognitive horizon in which to explore, change jobs, date, and thus learn from their successes and failures. The new cultural arena further enabled many youths to develop a more refined sense of responsibility and strengthened their resolve to more effectively manage their lives. The new economic opportunities also provided youths with greater financial independence. For example, Jankowiak's Hohhot survey found in 2006 that forty-two out of ninety-eight or 43 percent of youths working in the central business district did not live with their parents. Youths who continued to live with their parents readily noted in interviews that even though their parents continued to treat them as if they were still children (haizi), they felt, at least in their mind's eye, that they were adults. In contrast, under 1980s Chinese work-unit socialism, everyone who was not married would have lived with his or her parents. In the 1980s marriage and parenthood, but not necessarily age, were the more salient cultural markers used to signify the arrival of adulthood.

By the early twenty-first century, marriage in urban China is no longer considered to be the full marker of complete adulthood. The shift to independent residence patterns resulted in the lessening of family loyalty in favor of greater loyalty first to one's self, and then to one's parents, followed by the nation. Further, adulthood in China, much as in the U.S., is increasingly defined through a series of subjective markers that suggest greater autonomy, mastery of self and thus adulthood. Today, China's youths increasingly embrace the values of personal inquiry, self-sufficiency, self-fulfillment, and happiness, all of which carry, albeit implicitly, an additional attribute of adulthood: personal and social responsibility (see Fong 2004; 2007). In this way, identity exploration and not social position constitute the new criteria youths use to assess the presence or absence of adulthood. The search for self-fulfillment is evident in the remarks of many young people interviewed by William Jankowiak, beginning with a twenty-three-year-old youth who moved from a small town in Inner Mongolia to its capital city, Hohhot, who admitted, "I struggle for a better life. It is this struggle to improve that makes life worth living. A kind of faith that I can make it and make life worth living." For him and for most of his friends, success is not so much about obtaining greater material benefits as it is about the fulfillment of personal goals based in an ongoing dialogue with one's self. This desire for personal improvement is evident in a twenty-eight-year-old female sales clerk who said, "There are days when I wonder why I could not make a sale—I get depressed. I work very hard. I always wonder how I might improve." Another twenty-two-year-old college graduate noted that "work is an important source for self-fulfillment." Meanwhile, a twenty-four-year-old elementary school teacher admitted that she gained tremendous reward from teaching her students: "I am often very tired but I feel so fulfilled." Personal fulfillment can also be heard in a thirty-five-year-old mother's reflections on her ten-year-old daughter's future: "I want my child to travel and see the world. I never had the opportunity to travel—I want my child to do this." It can also be found in the remarks of a nineteen-year-old man: "I want to embrace and enjoy life as much as I can. I believe in the beauty of life. [I want] to explore the world and dedicate myself to making a difference every day. I want so much to travel around the world." The thrill of involvement and potential success can be seen in a twenty-year-old woman who said: "I was so excited and felt so fulfilled the day I opened my hairdressing salon… I knew I was going to learn a lot and improve my position."

This ambition to improve oneself, to learn new skills, to be tested in a competitive arena and to succeed—all aspects associated with adulthood—is found similarly in a twenty-four-year-old male who stated: "I could get a good job in Inner Mongolia … but in Beijing life is fast… . I think I can make my fortune in Beijing. I can earn enough to do things, and to get a wife." He then added, "I want a challenge… . Money isn't everything, but it is important these days." For this young man, like so many others who opened up in this series of interviews, it was not money per se but the challenge to test his mettle in a major cosmopolitan arena that made Beijing more attractive than Hohhot. A similar pursuit of self-improvement is found in a twenty-five-year-old man's explanation for quitting his job at a foreign-operated hotel and taking a pay cut in order to take a job that offered better opportunities to learn new tasks and perhaps attain personal growth and happiness: "Before, I thought that money was everything. I now realize that there is more to life than consumption and the drive to earn more and more things or find the most beautiful girl."

Rural migrants in Hohhot readily acknowledged that one of the reasons they wanted to live in the city was to train themselves by facing challenging circumstances (*duanlian ziji*), or, in the words of one individual, "to open my eyes" (*kaikuo yanjin*) and "to change myself" (*gaibian ziji*) (Shanshan Du, email correspondence, 2006; Zheng 2004: 198). If in 1981 Hohhotians spoke of their lost dreams, two decades later migrant youths spoke of dreams they thought could be realized. For them, the future was an array of choices and possibilities. In this way, the differences between rural and urban youths' life orientations had blended together. Moreover, rural youths' rising expectations and changing attitudes toward "eating bitterness" (i.e., onerous tiring labor) resulted in many refusing to take the jobs their fathers and uncles once readily took. By 2000, this new orientation was nicely captured in a twenty-year-old migrant cook's comment about his dream: "[to] have my own restaurant, [so] that I will be able to travel and go places and learn about the world and become successful in marriage and life. I know that with hard work and dedication I can make it." The young cook's tale is similar to the Horatio Alger stories popular in the United States at the turn of the twentieth century. Alger's heroes were poor boys who faced many challenges before being rewarded with success for their character development and diligence.

In contrast to these urban young people who spoke so candidly of their dreams and aspirations, those who remain in rural areas may feel confined and frustrated over their life circumstances. The stigmas of farm labor have negatively impacted youths, and most no longer want that way of life. Similarly, middle-aged rural women may also be re-evaluating their sacrifices for their family's wellbeing; they now wonder whether their sacrifices are worth it. The reflections of the middle-aged women who remained behind resemble urbanites of the early 1980s, who also complained of boredom, frustration, and unfruitful lives. In both eras, the Chinese have yearned for the freedom to choose, to have opportunities to achieve, and thus to gain respect. In this way, Mainland China's rural and urban youths are actively and optimistically engaged with the future and are not like their Russian counterparts who only want "to live for today and not think of tomorrow" (Williams, Chuprov, and Zubok 2003).

The Hohhot findings are consistent with Vanessa Fong's research findings (2004) concerning Dalian youths' attitudes toward the future. Fong discovered that ambitious striving might produce happiness and satisfaction as well as stress and frustration. In effect, achievement and stress are different sides of the same coin (Fong 2007). The dilemma for Chinese youths is to achieve personal advancement, while in the process not losing their support network. Regardless of sex differences, singletons have adopted different values and outlooks and embrace ethics associated with individualism. However, there are gender and class differences that impact men and women differently when it comes to timing (or when to embrace certain roles) as well as the availability of economic opportunities that can enable someone to realize his or her life goals. And it is important to consider these gender and social class differences as well.

Maleness and Femaleness: Shifting Images and Opportunities

Prior to the re-emergence of China's market economy men and women both worked. The Chinese family required both spouses' incomes and labor to survive. Moreover, Chinese communist ideology held it important for both genders to work in order to achieve status and respect. For most, work in the socialist command economy was considered easy and even boring. However, employment held very little opportunity for self-fulfillment. In fact, people often admitted they did not like their job but did like the time to be more engaged in their personal hobbies. In the market economy the conjugal family continues to need both sexes' incomes, but it is now tacitly expected that the husband bear the greater responsibility to support the family. This presents something of a paradox: young females are as ambitious or even more so than young males, yet there is an expectation that the husband will be the more able provider. This assumption that the man holds the greater responsibility has placed a disproportionate burden on urban and rural men working in the city. Not only are women actively competing with them for many jobs, but many women also expect men to shoulder the greater share of financial responsibility for maintaining the family.

These conflicting expectations can be seen in the shift in the way that urbanites perceive gender differences. Compared to Jankowiak's (1993) 1980s survey, there is today more blurring in men's and women's rankings of gender ideal typifications. The distinguishing markers are not as clear-cut as before. This is evident in the increase of traits perceived as being gender neutral.

There have been three significant shifts in the ways young men and women differ from their counterparts in the early 1980s (or their parents' generation). The first involves the recognition that men and women have equal intelligence (*congming*). In contrast to the 1980s when college educated women and men were unanimous in their view that men were smarter than women, urban youths no longer hold to this view. Intelligence is no longer the monopoly of any one gender. The single child policy has resulted in girls being encouraged to achieve at the same level as boys. This is amply demonstrated in daily classroom performance. The end result is that girls are perceived to be just as intelligent as boys. The shift in gender definitions is also manifested in other performance domains. For example, Tianshu Pan has observed in the elite Fudan University that boys are less assertive and confident compared to female students. He recalls that in the 1980s this was not the case; even in the English department where women outnumbered men, men were still assertive. He adds: "In all the courses I taught, the women tended to score higher than men and contributed more to class discussion. Today, 50 percent of China's university students are women compared to 23 percent in 1980" (Hewitt 2009).

This ratio is similar to the U.S. where 57 percent of all college undergraduates are women.

The second shift has to do with life's pressures (*yali*). Although men and women acknowledge that both sexes feel pressure (*yali*), it is understood that men have traditionally felt the greater responsibility for the family's financial wellbeing and thus, in that regard, have experienced more pressure. It was repeatedly pointed out that men have a strong responsibility to their parents and children to uphold the cultural image of being a successful man. For example, they have to get a job, an apartment, maybe a car, and they must support their new family. They are expected to make more money and believe they are looked down upon if they do not accomplish these goals. This heightened pressure on men arose from a shift in the organization of gender and cultural expectations about family life and is reflected in the opinions of women today concerning the pressures they feel. Significantly, women in their early thirties who are married with a child feel both sexes have equal amounts of pressure on them and maintain that women suffer as much as, if not more than, men from depression. Women in their thirties enjoy pointing out that "behind every successful man is a woman." This qualification was absent in the gender discourse of the 1980s. Today, there is an agreement that a good marriage can be mutually supportive in facing life's pressures. This suggests that youths today perceive marriage as a joint partnership in which emotional support is deemed equally important to both sexes.

Jankowiak's 2000 Hohhot survey did find a shift among college students in their preferred images of maleness: gentility and cultivated politeness was no longer the preferred posture. It had been replaced by a persona that was organized around an image of forcefulness, assertion, and aggressive ambition. The ideal male model was no longer the college professor but the chief executive officer businessman. The return of the businessman (or China's new merchant class) who is envisioned as someone capable of making rapid choices and who is strict, opinionated, and decisive constitutes a new role model that has impacted college educated Chinese. Today, educated males are blending attributes found in the socialist era—notably, homage to the genteel professor persona—with a more aggressive, strong-minded, and in-command business style. In the process, most singleton males strive to present a public persona that is less timid, more decisive, and "cool" in their interactions with their colleagues and their dates.

The shift in folk images of what constitutes authentic masculinity is not altogether new. Throughout Chinese history, as Kam Louie (2000) has observed, there have been two essentially different conceptions of what constitutes proper masculinity: these have ranged from *wu*, which embodies an aggressive toughness, to *wen*, which features manners based on politeness, an ethos of gentility, self-control, and tacit forms of aggression. During the Maoist era educated males adopted the image of the scholar official as their masculine ideal. In the 1980s some members of the working class strove to adopt this posture, and many did not. For most youths, the behavior typically expressed had more in common with a *wu* than a *wen* style. By the twenty-first century, educated urban males were no longer adopting the ideal of the scholar official as the preferred cultural ideal. Rather, most young males were blending elements of gentility with a touch of toughness and frank assertiveness. Moreover, as in the case of many contemporary cultures in Papua New Guinea (Mageo 2005), Chinese men's newfound assertiveness was culturally recognized and valued.

The *wu* and *wen* images of masculinity both acknowledge that the ideal man should be confident and in control. Today, many singletons have embraced the western image of coolness or the belief that it is best to "always look cool (*ku*) under pressure" (Moore 2005). This does not mean that women cannot also be *ku*. Some are, but *ku* is not regarded as a fundamental component of femininity, while it is for masculinity. Moore's research (2005) found that for Beijing youths *ku* referenced both a degree of flamboyance and emotional distance. This is consistent with an increased celebration of an introspective focus. An individual's ability to display an emotional calmness also makes a statement about his or her own internal psychological development. In contrast with earlier personae that were organized around managing social relationships, *ku* is less about performance of social roles and duty and more about making an individualistic claim on self-independence and mastery of one's social position.

This posture also hides an unvoiced fear of failure. Males feel an enormous responsibility or pressure to succeed as signified through obtaining a respected social position that commands a decent income. Many strive for this ideal and few succeed. Adopting a *ku* demeanor enables everyone, especially the more fragile males, to make a claim they are in charge of their lives when, for many, the exact opposite is closer to the truth. A risk economy promotes and, at times, rewards a social persona based more on deceit than fact. In the case of contemporary Chinese young males, their ongoing concerns with social success in a market society, as opposed to the communist redistributive economy, have made Chow Yun-fat, Jet Li, and Jackie Chan—rather than the Confucian sage—their new ideal of proper masculinity. The image of the more assertive male is consistent with the new economy where decisions have to be made and the bold often gain the advantage. The emergence of the new image is also taking place with the arrival of so many bright, talented, and ambitious females who are challenging men for similar jobs. Significantly, outside of the work arena there is a corresponding shift whereby women have embraced a more "feminine" or sexually provocative demeanor designed to attract a male's gaze. In the work context women actively compete with men, but within the domain of sexual encounter, women and men continue to emphasize what they think the other sex most wants to experience.

There appears to be an underlying cultural logic present here: men, on the one hand, continue to value the work arena as the primary domain within which to express and define the self. Most women, on the other hand, although valuing work (often very highly) continue to attend to family as well as other personal activities and outlets. With a few notable exceptions—for instance, women with a Ph.D. or wealthy businesswomen (Southwell-Lee 2009)—for most women work is not the exclusive domain by which they define their identity. For most women, other considerations are just as important as their work identity. For example, a twenty-five-year-old medical doctor admits that "having a happy strong family is more important to me than having an amazing career." She further acknowledges that she likes her job a lot and enjoys learning new things, but her job is not her life. In talking with young women we have found that this woman's opinion is fairly typical. The "mother's problem" is really a female dilemma that was as prevalent in the 1980s as it is today. It arises from women being pushed to achieve in the professional world while also being expected to serve as the primary caretaker of their child.

College students are acutely aware of this. A twenty-year-old woman admitted: "We talk about it all the time in the dorm. For baby or for the career."

This is a real dilemma for contemporary Chinese women. A married woman who decides to raise her child often discovers that she has shifted her orientation from valuing work as an end in itself to valuing the child. This does not mean that women do not enjoy working or that they do not do it very well. This is clearly not the case. But it does mean that women's fundamental sense of self worth is not as intertwined with their professional standing as appears to be the case for men. This is also the reason why young college-educated women have more difficulty in finding a good job in a Chinese, as opposed to multinational, corporation. Chinese male CEOs continue to assume that a young woman who is married will soon become pregnant and will consequently want to reduce her working hours or even quit her job. This cultural conviction that women are less reliable than men has resulted in looser standards being applied to male applicants which makes it easier for a less qualified male to be hired ahead of a more qualified female (Hewitt 2009). Today, Chinese men who have a white-collar job earn, on average, over $2,000.00 (U.S.) dollars a year more than women.

In this way, the "glass ceiling" is a continuing reality in most mainland (but not Hong Kong) companies. It is a cultural model that favors men who are primarily in elite white-collar professions. For uneducated men, however, the marketplace is not as favorable. Among the uneducated, women are preferred over men in unskilled, light, and service industry employment. These women tend to speak standard Chinese, which makes them excellent hires in a variety of service work jobs (e.g., waitress, shop attendant, hotel employee) that involve meeting the public. Shifting dress and language skills enable many migrant female workers to develop marriage strategies to marry a local youth, thus enabling them to go beyond the confines of their regional/native place identities. In contrast, young uneducated men who do not have a decent job tend to be more marginalized and have a lower value as a potential marriage mate in the urban setting. Because rural migrant women are culturally assimilating faster, they are not only able to find urban jobs faster than their rural migrant male counterparts, but also to integrate more successfully into the urban society. This expands their social horizons, while semi-employed rural males are less successful and thus have a more restricted pool of marriage possibilities. Many male youths worry about whether they will ever be able to attract a mate. Women, on the other hand, seldom talk about this.

In sum, the shift from a command economy to a market economy has transformed China into a risk society. Today, there are more winners as well as losers. This is especially so in the case of rural males (but not rural females) as well as less educated urban men and women.

Gender, Class, and Emerging Adulthood

China's shift from a command economy to a market driven society has impacted the sexes differently. It has created unequal opportunities and placed profound pressures on young males and mature females in ways that were not apparent under the era of classic Chinese socialism. Moreover, it has impacted rural youths differently than urban youths. Rural youths have been impacted by the cultural bias toward males that has resulted in a skewed sex ratio of enormous proportions. This social fact has created problems for youths to find a mate and start a family. It has further been compounded by urbanization, which has undermined the conventional expectation that rural youths will eat bitterness and work at any job, even those that are least esteemed. Today rural youths will accept some jobs while refusing others. The jobs they are most likely to refuse are increasingly situated in the construction industry. This has had repercussions for their ability to find work, for the emergence of a full-blown service economy has favored the employment of female service workers over males and thereby further undermined a rural youth's ability to establish a mature social identity and become an attractive potential mate. The migration of females into the city has further reduced the pool of potential mates in the countryside. Rural females who master standard Mandarin are able to quickly adopt the dress and manners of the ordinary urbanite which makes them more appealing mates in the cities, especially in those cities that no longer require a residence permit.

In urban China, male youths are faced with a different, although no less daunting, dilemma: the single child policy has enhanced female opportunities for personal achievement. No longer defined entirely by marriage or motherhood, many urban females are, as has already been noted, focusing on education and outperforming males in the classroom. Many urban-born females have been able to take their formal educational success and obtain very good jobs and thus higher incomes. This is apparent in multinational corporations where it is assumed that females, like males, can be both a parent and a productive loyal employee. This shift in cultural expectations has enabled females to compete effectively against males in a number of different economic spheres, including sales, accounting, marketing, and human resources management.

College-educated men and women, especially those from the elite schools, continue to find good job prospects. This is less the case for uneducated male and female urbanites, who have less attractive job prospects. The end result is that many urban males are not able to find an "attractive" job, which compels many to live with their parents. This is not unique to China. It has often been characteristic of the low socioeconomic classes around the world. What is unusual in the Chinese case is that this orientation now applies to children of the urban working class who do not have clear career paths or who are disinterested in those employment opportunities that are available. The socialist era's association of physical labor with a peasant's life of drudgery ensures that many urban youths will reject any and all forms of strenuous physical labor. For most, it is not cool (ku). Moreover, without stable, decent-paying job prospects, youths are rendered unable to leave the stage of adolescence and become fully responsible adults.

Denied immediate access to social status, many urban and rural males are responding in a remarkably similar fashion: they are delaying adulthood, preferring instead to remain youths who define themselves in opposition to adults. In this way, playing video games all night and extended bouts of "hanging out" not only contribute to but also signify their increasing social marginality (Moore 2005; Moore and Rizor 2008). This pattern of male resistance first emerged among youths who had been privileged during the Cultural Revolution but whose loss of status left them marginalized in the reform era (Yao 2004).

In China, social marginality is most evident among the male offspring of the new super rich as well as migrant poor males. In contrast, Chinese females seem to be active in their pursuit of an alternative path that involves embracing, earlier than their male counterparts, indices that signify the obtainment of adulthood. Much earlier than men, women tend to be employed, self-sufficient, and ready to marry and become a parent. The clash between males and females is now over the timing of when to embrace marriage and parenthood. Many Chinese women want to embrace identities of wife and mother or, in the case of the wealthy, just motherhood earlier than their male counterparts. Singleton educated males, for their part, prefer to delay and focus on their careers, themselves, and personal adventure. These gender differences lie at the heart of the ongoing psychological tensions that shape and are shaping each gender's perception of the other.

Conclusion

According to the 2000 census, some 23 percent of the People's Republic of China's 1.295 billion people are under the age of fifteen. This means that, in the PRC alone, about 300 million Chinese youths are gradually becoming style-conscious participants in an increasingly privatized economy. This new generation, rising like a cultural tsunami, will surge into its own in the decades ahead. The reform era of Deng Xiaoping officially began in 1979. However, the reform's full impact was not felt until the late 1990s when China's work-enterprise *(danwei)* system was completely transformed away from the insular focus of the command economy toward a more vibrant market exchange. The shift in economic organization has given way to an increasingly unpredictable milieu where social and economic interests will compete for China's youths as laborers, consumers, and agents of cultural production. Young people, especially those who have some economic capacity, will be able to transform individualistic modes of expression through their economic decisions into newly created cultural habits. This ongoing and future transformation is a demonstration of the manner in which youths often serve less as agents of cultural reproduction than as catalysts for cultural innovation. Given such historical trends, we can expect that many dramatic developments are in store for the PRC and, ultimately, for China as a whole.

Economic development makes possible the period of independent identity exploration that is at the heart of emerging adulthood (Arnett 2004: 24). More affluent young people have a greater opportunity for an extended moratorium from becoming a full-fledged adult. Popular folklore holds that wealthy Chinese children are slower to take on social responsibilities because they are engaged in a search for more and more opportunities for personal adventure. In contrast, youths from less prosperous homes are more serious and focused on their careers, management of self, and expectation of personal achievement and thus fulfillment. Still, everyone agrees that full adulthood means much the same thing in urban China as it has come to mean in U.S.: being able to take responsibility for your actions, to make independent decisions about your life, and, lastly, to become financially independent (Arnett 2004: 209). However, youths continue to define themselves in opposition to adults and do so while engaged in a variety of activities that often enhance cognitive skills and social ability to navigate the challenges of uneasy transition, fluid careers, and changes in life-orientation (Gerson 2009a).

There appear to be gender differences in the speed with which males and females wish to emerge out of this youthful stage into adulthood. Females seem more mature earlier than their male counterparts and thus want to begin a family earlier, whereas males from similar social classes have invested everything into their careers and want to wait longer before beginning a family. The new sexual ethos enables men to delay marriage as their sexual needs can easily be met via prostitution outlets or just having a series of girlfriends. Women, on the other hand, prefer not to engage in anonymous sex with strangers or to have a series of boyfriends. Consequently, women are often more impatient and, at times, angry at the shift in cultural norms. This presents something of a paradox for women. On one hand, they have benefited from the opportunity to explore their inner life and achieve perhaps a deeper sense of fulfillment; on the other hand, they also remain anxious over their inability to find a viable mate who can fulfill their image of creating the "happy family." Their search for a life partner who is also a soul mate rather than simply a spouse is a strong cultural fantasy constantly articulated in the private and public discourses of young Chinese women in ways that are not paralleled in men's discourses.

The shift away from an exclusive reliance on specific social markers (e.g., marriage and parenthood) has resulted in pushing psychological factors to the forefront. China's first generation of "emerging adults" has transformed and continues to reshape the parent-child bond. In the past, youths made token gifts of money to their parents and, in the case of the onset of parental enfeeblement, actively assisted them. Today, singletons expect their parents to support or at least care for them regularly, or, at least, in a crisis. China's singletons also continue to feel a strong obligation to reciprocate, but this is based on their parents' actual needs and not on sustaining gestures to an ancient symbolic order that has, for most, all but retreated into history (Fong 2007; Hansen 2007). Urban parents are more accepting of the individualistic striving of their offspring as this does not threaten their economic wellbeing. Unlike their rural counterparts, urban parents' wellbeing is not dependent upon inheritance of property but rather on their child's success in finding stable, decent-paying employment (Moore 2005).

In the end, China's embrace of a market economy, combined with the arrival of the singleton generation, has transformed the society away from predictability and boredom into a full-fledged risk society organized around talent, knowledge, money, and bureaucratic power. This has also simultaneously created the conditions necessary for sustaining a vibrant youth stage whose aesthetic and conceptual dimensions we are only beginning to evaluate, understand, and thus appreciate.

Notes

We would like to thank the following people for their suggestions, encouragement, and editorial insight: Vered Amit, Noel Dyck, Shanshan Du, Vanessa Fong, Mette Halskov Hansen, Sadie Hinson, Alice Schlegel, and Lihong Shi.

1. Some of the same features that typified the 1989 demonstrations, along with the 1986/87 democracy demonstrations that preceded them, were student-centered, having much in common with those of the earlier May Fourth Movement. The 1989 demonstration arose from the widespread belief that China's government was corrupt and its leaders had not been serving the country well, as did, in part, the May Fourth Movement. Furthermore, the young student intellectuals in the demonstrations of the late 1980s openly discussed "foreign" ideas, including several pertaining to Western democracy. The philosophical link between the 1989 protesters and those of 1919 was highlighted in a number of ways, perhaps most dramatically in the renewed energy shown by the 1989 protesters on the anniversary date of May 4th.

2. Chinese of all ages were disappointed with their lives as the opportunities to excel remained restricted. We repeatedly found urbanities yearning for the opportunity to achieve and find a future that was open to possibilities. For example, a young woman acknowledged that her life was a failure, as she never had an opportunity to pick her job: "I was told to be a clerk. I never had a choice." The yearning of youths for a kind of self-fulfillment through testing and developing their abilities is evident in a letter to the editor published in 1980 in a popular magazine, China Youth (Zhongguo Qingren). It reads in part: "Dear Editors: I am 23-years-old this year, I should say that I am just beginning life, but already all of life's mystery and charm are gone for me. I feel as if I have reached the end. Looking back on the road I have traveled, I see that I was on a journey from crimson to gray—from hope to disappointment and despair... . I used to have beautiful illusions about life... . Now they are all gone." (Xu 2002: 52–53). People in other age cohorts shared this young woman's negative outlook. A sense of societal anomie can be found in a twenty-nine-year-old mother's reflection on her motivation for having a child: "In China most women have a child because life is so boring that it gives us something to do." Throughout the 1980s deep-seated psychological negativity was something understood and shared across generations. The lack of mobility and economic opportunity also contributed to delaying the creation of a distinct youth culture with its own linguistic expressions, manners, dress, and outlooks.

Bibliography

Anderson, Eugene N. 1970. "Lineage Atrophy in Chinese Society." *American Anthropologist* (72): 363–65.

Arnett Jeffery. 2004. *Emerging Adulthood: The Winding Road from the Late Teens through the Twenties*. New York: Oxford University Press.

Bailey, Beth. 1988. *From Front Porch to Back Seat: Courtship in Twentieth-Century America*. Baltimore: John Hopkins University Press.

Barme, Geremie. 1992. "Wang Shuo and Liumang ('Hooligan') Culture." *The Australian Journal of Chinese Affairs*, 28: 23–64

———. 1999. *In the Red: Contemporary Chinese Culture*. New York: Columbia University Press.

Blum, Susan. 1997. "Naming Practices and the Power of Words in China." *Language in Society*, 26: 357–379.

Brownell, Susan. 1995. *Training the Body for China: Sports in the Moral Order of the People's Republic.* Chicago: University of Chicago Press.

Cohen, Myron. 1976. *House United, House Divided: The Chinese Family in Taiwan.* New York: Columbia University Press.

Csikszentmihalyi, Michael. 1990. *Flow: The Psychology of Optimal Experience.* New York: Harper Perennial.

Daubier, Jean. 1974. *A History of the Chinese Cultural Revolution.* Translated by Richard Seaver. New York: Random House.

Davis, Deborah and Stevan Harrell. 1993. *Chinese Families in the Post-Mao Era.* Berkeley: University of California Press.

Du, Shanshan. 2006. Personal communication with William Jankowiak, May 2006.

Ebrey, Patricia Buckley. 1988. *The Inner Quarters: Marriage and the lives of Chinese Women in the Sung Period.* Berkeley: University of California Press.

Fass, Paula. 1977. *The Damned and the Beautiful: American Youth in the 1920s.* New York: Oxford University Press.

Fong, Vanessa. 2004. *Only Hope: Coming of Age Under China's One-Child Policy.* Stanford: Stanford University Press.

———. 2007. Personal communication with William Jankowiak, August 2007.

Gao, Yuan. 1987. *Born Red: A Chronicle of the Cultural Revolution.* Stanford: Stanford University Press.

Gerson, Kathleen. 2009a. "Adulthood Redefined." *New York Times*, 28 October 2009. Available from: http://roomfordebate.blogs.nytimes.com/2009/10/28/the-40-something-dependent-child/ [Accessed 28 October 2009].

———. 2009b. *The Unfinished Revolution: How a New Generation is Reshaping Family, Work, and Gender in America.* New York: Oxford University Press.

Golding, William. 1954. *The Lord of the Flies.* New York: Perigee.

Goldscheider, Francis and Calvin Goldscheider. 1993. *Leaving Home Before Marriage: Ethnicity, Familism, and Generational Relationships.* Madison: The University of Wisconsin Press.

Hansen, Mette Halskov and Cuiping Pan. 2008. "Me and My Family: Perceptions of Individual and Collective among Young, Rural Chinese." Conference on Trends in Contemporary China, UCLA.

Hewitt, Duncan. 2009. "They're Not Going to Take it: China's Women, Facing Pervasive Discrimination, Decide to Fight for Their Rights." *Newsweek,* 17 August: 19–23.

Honig, Emily and Gail Hershatter. 1988. *Personal Voices: Chinese Women in the 1980s.* Stanford: Stanford University Press.

Ikels, Charlotte. 1993. "Settling Accounts: the Intergenerational Contract in an Age of Reform." In *Chinese Families in the Post-Mao Era*, eds. Deborah Davis and Stevan Harrell. Berkeley: University of California Press.

Jankowiak, William. 1993. *Sex, Death and Hierarchy in a Chinese City.* New York: Columbia University Press.

———. ed. 1995a. *Romantic Passion: A Universal Experience?* New York: Columbia University Press.

———. 1995b. "Romantic Passion in the People's Republic of China." In *Romantic Passion: A Universal Experience?* ed. William Jankowiak. New York: Columbia University Press: 166–186.

Jing, Jun, ed. 2000. *Feeding China's Little Emperors: Food, Children and Social Change.* Stanford: Stanford University Press.

Jones, Andrew F. 1992. *Like a Knife: Ideology and Genre in Contemporary Chinese Popular Music*. Ithaca: Cornell University Press.

Lane, Robert. 2000. *The Loss of Happiness in Market Democracies*. New Haven: Yale University Press.

Liang, Heng and Judith Shapiro. 1983. *Son of the Revolution*. New York: Random House.

Louie, Kam. 2000. *Chinese Masculinity: Society and Gender in China*. Cambridge: Cambridge University Press.

Lu, Xiaobo. 2000. *Cadres and Corruption*. Stanford: Stanford University Press.

Mageo, J.M. 2005. "Male Gender Instability and War." *Journal of Social Justice*, 17: 73–80.

Mines, Mattison. 1994. *Public Faces, Private Voices: Community and Individuality in South India*. Berkeley: University of California Press.

Moore, Robert. 2005. "Generation Ku: Individualism and China's Millennial Youth." *Ethnology*, 44 (4): 357–376.

———. 1998. "Love and Limerence with Chinese Characteristics: Student Romance in the PRC." In *Romantic Love and Sexual Behavior: Perspectives from the Social Sciences*, ed. V. De Munck. Westport, CN: Praeger.

Moore, Robert and James Rizor. 2008. "Confucian and Cool: China's Youth in Transition." *Education about Asia*, 13 (3): 30–37

Pan, Tianshu. 2002. "Neighborhood Shanghai: Community Building in Five Mile Bridge." Ph.D. diss., Harvard University.

Parish, William and Martin King Whyte. 1978. *Village and Family in Contemporary China*. Chicago: University of Chicago Press.

Parish, William and Wenfang Tang. 2000. *Chinese Urban Life Under Reform: The Changing Social Contract*. Cambridge: Cambridge University Press.

Perry, Elizabeth and Xun Li. 1997. *Proletarian Power: Shanghai in the Cultural Revolution*. Boulder: Westview Press.

Putnam, Robert. 2000. *Bowling Alone: The Collapse and Revival of American Community*. New York: Simon and Schuster.

Schlegel, Alice and Herbert Barry. 1991. *Adolescence: An Anthropological Inquiry*. New York: Free Press.

Schlegel, Alice. 2009. Personal correspondence with William Jankowiak, November 2009.

Schoenhals, Michael, ed. 1996. *China's Cultural Revolution, 1966–1969: Not a Dinner Party*. Armonk, New York: M. E. Sharpe.

Shaw, Thomas. 1994. "'We Like to Have Fun' Leisure and the Discovery of the Self in Taiwan's 'New' Middle Class." *Modern China* 20 (4): 416–445.

Shen, Tong. 1990. *Almost a Revolution*. Boston: Houghton Mifflin.

Shi, Lihong. 2009 "'Little Quilted Vests to Warm Parents' Hearts': Redefining the Gendered Practice of Filial Piety in Rural Northeastern China." *The China Quarterly*, 198: 348–363

Spence, Jonathan. 1990. *The Search for Modern China*. New York: Norton.

Southwell-Lee, Meiling. 2009. "Women with Money, Women with Minds: Social Status, Gender, and Marriageability in Urban China Today." Ph.D. diss., Australian National University.

Stafford, Charles. 1995. *The Roads of Chinese Childhood: Learning and Identification in Angang*. Cambridge: Cambridge University Press.

Wang, Jing. 1996. *High Culture Fever: Politics, Aesthetics, and Ideology in Deng's China*. Berkeley: University of California Press.

Wasserstrom, J. 1991. *Student Protest in Twentieth Century China: A View from Shanghai.* Stanford: Stanford University Press.

Watson, James L., ed. 1997. *Golden Arches East: McDonald's in East Asia.* Stanford: Stanford University Press.

———. 2000. "Food as Lens: The Past, Present, and Future of Family Life in China." In *Feeding China's Little Emperors: Food, Children and Social Change*, ed. Jun Jing. Stanford: Stanford University Press.

Whiting, John M. 1941. *Becoming a Kwoma: Teaching and Learning in a New Guinea Tribe.* New Haven: Yale University Press.

Whyte, Martin and William Parish. 1984. *Urban Life in Contemporary China.* Chicago: University of Chicago Press.

Williams, Christopher, et al. 2003. *Youth, Risk and Russian Modernity.* Hampshire, England: Ashgate Publishers.

Wolf, Arthur and Huang Chieh-shan. 1980. *Marriage and Adoption in China, 1845–1945.* Stanford: Stanford University Press.

Wolf, Margery. 1972. *Women and the Family in Rural Taiwan.* Stanford: Stanford University Press.

Xu, Luo. 2002. *Searching for Life Meaning: Changes and Tensions in the World Views of Chinese Youth in the 1980s.* Ann Arbor: The University of Michigan Press.

Yan, Yunxiang. 1997. "The Triumph of Conjugality: Structural Transformation of Family Relations in a Chinese Village." *Ethnology* 36 (3): 191–212.

———. 1999. "Rural Youth and Youth Culture in North China." *Culture, Medicine and Psychiatry*, 23 (1): 75–97.

———. 2003. *Private Life Under Socialism.* Stanford: Stanford University Press.

Yao, Yushang. 2004. "The Elite Class Background of Wang Shuo and His Hooligan Characters." *Modern China*, 30 (4): 431–469.

Zheng, Tiantian. 2009. *Ethnographies of Prostitution in Contemporary China.* New York: Macmillan Books.

———. 2004. "From peasant women to bar hostesses: Gender and modernity in post-Mao Dalian." In *On the Move: Women and Rural to Urban Migration in Contemporary China*, eds. Arianne Gaetano and Tamara Jacka. New York: Columbia University Press.

Part II

MAKING DO IN CHANGING TIMES

Chapter 4

Young Men's Struggles for Adulthood in Urban Ethiopia
Unemployment, Masculinity, and Migration

Daniel Mains

In urban Ethiopia young men are often referred to with the Amharic term *"fendata,"* which translates loosely as explosive. In June 2005, following disputes over the results of Ethiopia's first truly contested multi-party national election, thousands of young men took to the streets in Addis Ababa. These young men threw rocks, chanted protests, and clashed with police. The Ethiopian government argued that the volatile nature of this large population of predominantly urban, unemployed young men necessitated intervention for the good of society as a whole. In the months following the election more than ten thousand young men were arrested and held in detention camps outside of the city. Journalists and academics have documented explosions of violence among young men throughout the African continent (Cruise O'Brien 1996; Diouf 2003; Richards 1996).

Seemingly in contrast to the image of stone-throwing young men rioting in urban centers, others have argued that African young men are facing a crisis of masculinity (Masquelier 2005; Silberschmidt 2004). In urban Ethiopia it is common for young men in their twenties and thirties to be unemployed and dependent on their parents. These young men have little hope of reaching social milestones associated with adulthood like marriage and fatherhood. They appear to be terminally stuck in the present, neither child nor adult, with no possibility of change in the future.

Brad Weiss has perceptively described this contrast, noting that in Africa "young men are seen as either unbridled energies destructively disconnected from any large social totality or as mere emasculated dependents, doomed never to achieve full social maturity" (Weiss 2004: 14).

In this chapter I argue that in urban Ethiopia the constructions of young men as both emasculated dependents and sources of explosive destruction are a product of the same set of social processes. I begin by examining the manner in which urbanization, expanding access to education, and contracting economic opportunity have combined to create a large population of unemployed young men who simultaneously appear to be both a social threat and completely lacking in agency. The peculiar situation faced by young men is a result of their inability to take on the normative social responsibilities of adults, especially concerning economic independence, marriage, and fatherhood. Each of these goals is based on enacting a particularly masculine notion of adulthood that is associated with providing material support for others. As young men diverge from a normative life course that involves progressive movement towards adulthood, they are increasingly perceived both as a social threat and as lacking in agency. I argue that young men's migratory practices stand in sharp contrast to both of these characterizations. Young men seek to migrate within Ethiopia to access work that will allow them to strategically shift their position within social relationships. Migration is a means of exerting agency and at least temporarily enacting an ideal masculine adult role. Ultimately, I argue that this process supports a rethinking of age-based social categories such as youth and adult.

This study is based on research conducted in Jimma, a city of 150,000, between 2003 and 2005 and again for brief periods in 2008 and 2009. Jimma is the primary urban center in southwestern Ethiopia. Both of Ethiopia's major cash crops and primary exports, coffee and *chat*,[1] are grown in the area surrounding Jimma. The city has a large university, hospital, cinema, athletic stadium, and many multistoried hotels, one of which boasts a swimming pool. Jimma bustles with economic activity, and international media is accessed at video houses, internet cafes, music shops, and DVD rental houses. The city of Jimma is very diverse. In terms of ethnicity, significant populations of Oromo, Dawro, Amhara, Gurage, Kaffa, Yem, and Tigrean people make their homes there. Nearly all urban residents are fluent in Amharic, and this is the language generally used for most day-to-day social interactions. The city is split almost evenly between Muslims and Orthodox Christians, and there is a small population of Protestants and Catholics as well.

The Emergence of Youth as a Social Category in Urban Ethiopia

The social category of youth is defined in part by the shift from child to adult, and in this sense transition and transformation are intrinsic components of youth. Studies of youth from across Africa have demonstrated that the movement from youth to adult is best conceived of as a process of social repositioning. Whether it is through initiation (Kratz 1994), education (Stambach 2000), marriage, or childbirth (Hutchinson 1996), becoming an adult entails significant shifts in the way a person interacts with others. The duration of youth is highly variable, but there has generally been an expectation that youth is a finite period of transition. However, anthropologists have recently argued that, due to economic shifts associated with neoliberal capitalism, taking on the normative responsibilities of adults has become impossible in much of Africa and the duration of youth may be indefinite (Cole 2004; Hansen 2005; Masquelier 2005).

During the latter half of the twentieth century, youth emerged as a salient social category in Ethiopia. With the growth of permanent cities and the expansion of education, the concept of youth began to enter public discourse, primarily because expanded access to formal schooling and shifts in the urban economic opportunity structure produced an unprecedented population of unemployed youth. A large and publicly visible population of unemployed young men is perceived as both a source of social unrest and as lacking in particularly masculine forms of agency.

The Amharic term for youth, *wättat*, is not new. But in the past a distinct phase of life that could be referred to as "youth" did not exist among the Amhara (Levine 1965: 96–98), who have been the dominant ethnic group in most Ethiopian cities. In rural areas, young men and women gradually took on adult responsibilities until in terms of work their day-to-day life more or less resembled that of their parents. Once this point was reached the next step was marriage. For women this process generally began around the age of seven and ended at thirteen, while young men began providing significant help with plowing fields around the age of fourteen and then married in their late teens or early twenties. This was a continuous process and at no point did young people experience a lapse in which they had to struggle to occupy themselves or determine what they would do in the future. Deference for elders was a major aspect of Amhara culture and young people generally obeyed the directives of their elders with very little questioning. There was no notion that youth represented a distinct phase of life or a social problem. Within the age-grade system known as *gada*, which was traditionally practiced by the Oromo, the most populous ethnicity in Ethiopia and in the area surrounding Jimma, youth clearly did occupy a particular social position (Asmarom 1973). However, among Jimma Oromo the *gada* system has not been practiced since the mid-nineteenth century, and young people transitioned to adulthood in a gradual manner involving marriage and, for men, the inheritance of land from one's father (Hassen 1990; Lewis 2001).

Although Jimma has long been a major center for long distance trade in southwest Ethiopia (Hassan 1990; Lewis 2001), it did not develop a large permanent residential population until 1941, under the reign of Haile Sellasie. It is during this period that the prestige and desirability of government employment as an urban occupation developed in Jimma. The prestige of government work was partially based on the traditional hierarchical relationship between members of the nobility and farmers. As Allan Hoben (1970: 222) notes in describing Addis Ababa under the reign of Haile Sellasie, the authority of the rural landlord was replaced in this period by the government administrator, and education took the place of military activity as a means for accessing social mobility. Owning land and a longer presence in the city increased one's chances of obtaining an education. If a young man could finish his education (the great majority of students were male), a position as an administrator or teacher was virtually guaranteed. An occupational hierarchy between those with government work and those without began to develop. Government workers had both political and economic power while others generally performed the service work and manual labor necessary to maintain life in the city.

It is also during the Haile Sellasie regime that formal, western-styled education became available and became the primary means by which one accessed government employment. Education had a socializing effect, creating a cohesive group of predominantly male students whose experiences and worldviews were distinct from those of previous generations. Levine (1965) and Bahru (2002) claim that these students had a greater interest in Western culture and generally did not want to take on the occupations (usually farming) of their parents. For this generation, education was the key to accessing status through government employment. In contrast to the present, the quality of education was generally high and secondary graduates were virtually guaranteed a government job. While the particularities differ, similar relationships between government employment, education, and class have been described elsewhere in Africa (Berry 1985; Sharp 2002).

These students may be divided into roughly two groups, those who attained secondary education and those (in the much larger group) who did not. During the 1959–60 academic year, for example, twenty-eight thousand students were enrolled in grades five to eight (middle school) compared to approximately eighty-five hundred in secondary or post-secondary institutions (Teshome 1979). Although secondary-educated youth generally found government employment, Levine (1965: 110) explains that the much larger group who did not pass their eighth grade examinations were left with little to do except "live as loiterers on the streets" of the nation's capital.

Under the Marxist Derg regime that ruled Ethiopia from 1974 to 1991, public education continued to expand. The connection between government work and education also increased as most opportunities to accumulate wealth through private enterprise were eliminated. In general, the numerous young people who graduated with secondary school degrees during the Derg were able to find jobs in the expanding government bureaucracy, and unemployment did not increase dramatically among the educated.

It was after the fall of the Derg in 1991 that a dramatic rise in urban unemployment created the population referred to as "youth" today. Under the post-1991 Ethiopian People's Revolutionary Democratic Front (EPRDF), government education continued to expand while opportunities for desirable government employment decreased dramatically. Today's students are very different than the elite group of the past. With the increase in the number of students the quality of education has declined. A typical secondary school classroom contains eighty to ninety students who share books and learn in English, a language that many students do not understand well. In 1994 only around 10 percent of young people between the ages of twenty and twenty-nine had advanced to post-secondary education (Central Statistical Authority 1999). The others leave school having learned very little in the way of practical skills that can be used in securing employment.

At the same time as the educated population expanded, the International Monetary Fund (IMF) imposed structural adjustments which caused a major decrease in public sector employment opportunities (Krishnan 1998). These were the types of positions that secondary school students typically expected to obtain after graduation. This, combined with a lack of local industry and cultural stigmas towards certain types of manual labor, has contributed to massive levels of unemployment among urban youth. Beginning in the mid-1990s unemployment rates among urban youth have been close to 50 percent, and lengths of unemployment average between three and four years. Rates of unemployment are actually highest among urban youth with a secondary education, indicating the connection between education, aspirations, and unemployment (Serneels 2007).

In contrast to the past, "youth" has become a phase in life that is elastic in duration and may occupy many years. Levine claims that in Amhara culture "the three events which more than anything else establish one as an adult are marriage, moving into one's own house, and begetting a child" (1965: 99). In post-1991 Ethiopia, even if a young man is able to get work it is very difficult to move out of his parents' house and start a family of his own. The ability to remain unemployed for a long period of time is a reflection of the relatively privileged social and economic position occupied by most urban young men. The unemployed young men in my study represented a variety of class backgrounds, but all of them were born and raised in the city, which provided a distinct advantage in relation to Ethiopia's predominantly rural population. Even youth from poor families had extended social networks that provided them with the support necessary to remain unemployed for a number of years. As becoming an adult takes more time, the category of "youth" encompasses individuals of increasingly older age. Parents once expected to be supported by their children, but now they complain that they are forced to work into old age or use their meager pensions to feed their twenty-eight year old "children."

Young men in Ethiopia struggle to attain economic independence, marry, and become fathers. Failing to achieve these milestones along the trajectory from youth to adulthood, however, is more typical than not, and young men are perceived as dangerous idlers when they are unable to take on these normative responsibilities. In the following section my analysis turns to the stories of two young men who struggled with these challenges of becoming an adult.

Barriers to Adulthood:
Independence, Marriage, and Fatherhood

During my initial long-term research between 2003 and 2005, Solomon and Kebede were both unemployed and living with their parents.[2] They were heavily dependent on daily handouts from parents and kin. Eventually both young men sought to change their positions of dependence by leaving Jimma to find work with international companies.

At the time of my research Solomon was twenty-nine and had been unemployed for nearly four years. Like many of the unemployed young men in my study, he had graduated from secondary school. After completing twelfth grade, he spent an additional year studying mechanics at a vocational school. He was able to find work in a garage but he quit in order to pursue a government position. He did not get the government position and he did not return to the garage because the pay was too low. When we met in 2004 Solomon still lived with his parents and his days were generally passed by visiting with friends, watching films, chewing *chat* (a mild stimulant), and drinking honey wine.

For Solomon, the passage of time varied little from day to day. He spent as little time at home as possible. He left in the mornings and passed his days talking with friends and chewing *chat* at teahouses. At night he returned home after drinking honey wine and sat quietly watching television, trying not to disturb his family. His continued dependence on his parents was a particular burden. Although living with one's parents until marriage is common among young men, Solomon constantly had to deal with the stress of knowing that at his age he should have been helping his family instead of the reverse. Young men in their early twenties point out men like Solomon, who are approaching thirty and still living at home, relying on daily handouts from their parents, as models to be avoided. This is a critique of both marital status and economic dependence.

Yet the unemployed young men I encountered revealed a strong sense of ambiguity regarding their dependence on their parents. They insisted that their parents appreciated having them in the house. This was true even for older men who were working but living with their parents. Although a man in his forties who had not married was sometimes the subject of derisive gossip, it was generally agreed that he was doing a good thing by living with his parents. Still, despite the culturally accepted model of living with one's parents until marriage, young men nevertheless expressed significant stress regarding their situation. Although direct conflict with their parents was rare, young men explained that "you feel something." The experience of long-term dependence on their parents was described as "difficult" and "stressful." In some cases youths reached a point where their relationship with their parents began to feel strained. This was particularly true for young men who stayed with their parents until their late twenties and spent most of their time and resources on chewing *chat*. It was common for Solomon to receive gifts of two or three *birr* from his parents for small expenses. He also occasionally received money from other family members. Despite receiving consistent economic support (or perhaps because of it), Solomon felt that in recent years his relationship with his family had changed. "They don't need me," he explained. And he was perhaps right: his family was willing to provide enough support for him to get by, but they appeared to be unwilling to make significant investments in his future.

The social nature of marriage makes it a particularly important marker of becoming an adult and experiencing change within one's life. Older men who are not married are often the objects of disdain even if they are otherwise successful. Marriage means participating in community organizations, having children, and, essentially, becoming a full adult. Even if a man is not wealthy, marriage implies that he is supporting a wife and children. Regardless of all other indicators of status, marriage generally brings a certain level of respect that is otherwise unavailable to young men.

Without quality work marriage is thought to be impossible. Solomon explained to me that he wanted to marry but a person must "first pack his bags before setting out on a trip." A man cannot live with his parents and be married. He has to be able to provide money for food, rent, clothing, and all of the other expenses associated with living independently. Even before marriage, money is necessary to attract a potential wife. Young men claim that women are only interested in a romantic partner who is capable of supporting them financially. Young men are not bitter about this and often explain that in the current environment of poverty and unemployment it is only natural that women should seek out wealthier men.

It is worth noting that in interviews young women were highly ambivalent about the value of a wealthy husband, but there was almost universal agreement on the need to have a job of one's own before marriage. For example, in a group discussion with four young women who had been unemployed since finishing their education two or three years previously, one of them joked, "If we can't continue our education we need to find rich husbands." Another quickly responded, "No! A poor husband is much better. A rich husband will always go with other women, but with a poor husband you can work together and make your lives better." This idea was supported by the others, and a different young woman appeared to speak for the group when she explained:

> We don't think seriously about marriage. You should have a job and education before you marry. If not you will never be independent and you will always wait on your husband's hand. Getting married without first being independent is meaningless. Things will probably be good until you have your first child. Then your husband will begin to wander. Eventually he will leave you and you will be left with a child and no money.

Meanwhile, young men complained that, in addition to the difficulty of attracting a wife, hosting a formal wedding requires a significant monetary investment. Like elsewhere in Africa (Masquelier 2005), weddings in urban Ethiopia have become sites for conspicuous consumption and the performance of class differences. It is not uncommon to rent out large hotels and hire musical groups, professional photographers, and numerous cars for transporting guests. On his own initiative, Solomon once wrote for me what was basically a rant concerning marriage and money. He explained that money is necessary to attract a wife and that a wedding is also very expensive. All neighbors must be invited to a lavish feast in order to avoid gossip or "backbiting." In the end, unless a person is wealthy, marriage is impossible.

Young men often expressed the belief that insurmountable financial barriers prevent them from dating, marrying, and having children. They claimed that they will not marry before the age of thirty or thirty-five and then only if they have become wealthy. Children are seen as a natural and desirable result of marriage, but the financial burden of raising children is an additional factor preventing young men from achieving their aspirations. To simply raise children does not involve any great costs, but most young men desire futures for their children that are better than their own lives.

When I first met Kebede in 2004 he was twenty years old and had been unemployed for two years after finishing secondary school. Kebede lived with his parents and four siblings in a small house in the center of the city. He generally passed his time playing soccer and attending the Orthodox Christian Church. During one of our discussions Kebede first explained to me that he would not accept available forms of work like carpentry or waiting tables because they would not allow him to change his life. He then explained:

> Without something big [a source of money] I won't even think about marriage or children. Even if I am rich I will never have more than two children. With two kids I can educate them properly so that they can reach the university. If they don't reach the university I will send them to America. Of course I could get a job and have children now. Even if I was only making 100 birr a month I could feed them *shuro*,[3] but that kind of life is not good for children. They will not learn properly and they will end up shining shoes or something like that. You want your children to have a better life than yourself. You want them to improve and have a good life.

Similar statements were common among young men who worried that if they had children before they were ready, they would be burdening their own parents with one more mouth to feed. In Kebede's statement, education and small families are contrasted with symbols of lower class urban life like *shuro* to construct different future trajectories. One possible future is based on repeating what are seen as the mistakes of one's parents, while in the other it is assumed that fewer children will allow a heavy investment in education and open up more opportunities for higher learning and desirable employment.

In a different conversation I asked Kebede about the qualities of a good father. Like most young men, the first thing he mentioned in response was providing an education. He specifically explained that a free public education would not suffice. A good father must provide his children with a private education and help his children study in the evening until they have surpassed his own ability. He explained, "In order for my children to reach a good place they must have everything: good school, good clothes, and good food. If my father had been a driver, I could have been a doctor."

Many young men claimed that unemployment made dating, marriage, and parenthood impossible, and yet it seems unlikely that these young men were content to remain celibate for the indefinite amount of time needed to secure financial independence. For the most part, young men were reluctant to speak with me about the specifics of dating, sex, and out-of-wedlock parenthood, but a brief sketch of their behavior is possible. There is evidence that urban fertility rates in Ethiopia dropped dramatically during the 1990s, and in Addis Ababa fertility rates even dropped below replacement levels (Kinfu 2001). Among other factors, including women's increasing access to education, young men's desires concerning family size must also have contributed to decreasing rates of childbirth. As one unemployed young man in his early thirties explained to me: "Without work, I must simply sit with my desire." It appears that a lack of access to financial resources may have curtailed young men's sexual activity.

There are, however, a number of ways to get around this problem. Networks of reciprocity are highly developed in Ethiopia and many unemployed young men in my study received significant amounts of money as gifts. This money was often used to invite young women on dates. One unemployed young man explained to me that, although it is rare, "pure love" (nitsu fikir) does exist in Ethiopia. It is possible to establish a long-term relationship with a woman that does not involve significant amounts of gifting.[4] These relationships are kept secret from parents but they often last for many months, even a year. It is interesting that this young man did not believe a pure love relationship could develop into marriage. Although young men claimed that it is culturally inappropriate for a woman to cover the cost of a date, when I tracked the incomes of twenty unemployed young men for a period of a month I came across two cases where this occurred, which demonstrates that the masculine ideal of being the economic provider was not always actualized in practice.

Perhaps, most importantly, not all young men shared the ideals described above concerning marriage and children. Particularly among young men working in the informal economy it was common to live independently from one's parents with a wife and children. These families rarely conformed to the ideals described above. For example, it is highly unlikely that these young men could send their children to a private school. However, many young fathers derived a great deal of satisfaction from their families, indicating that there is a good deal of diversity among young men's conceptions of what it means to be an adult. As Kebede points out, it is not difficult to have children and feed them *shuro*, but this was not a life he aspired to. For others, however, this lifestyle implied the fulfillment of milestones associated with adulthood.

Adulthood as Controlling Flows of Wealth

The cases of working young men who were married with children demonstrate that supporting a family is possible. It is not, however, simply a family that young men like Solomon and Kebede desire. They wish to support a family in which their children will lead modern progressive lives that involve more than "eating and sleeping." In their discussion of marriage and fatherhood, young men conceive of progress in terms of the types of relationships that can be developed with others. To lead a progressive life and to become an adult is to move from a position of dependence to one where it is possible to offer material support to others and provide one's dependents the chance to lead progressive lives.

Unemployment impedes the transformation from childhood to adulthood because each stage in this process requires money. Material wealth is not, however, an end in itself. It is a means of transforming relations of dependence. To first attain independence from one's parents, then to marry and raise children, and finally to offer support to one's extended family and community is to move from being a dependent to a supporter of others. At each stage in this process one's position within relations of reciprocity is transformed.

The dynamics of the relationship that young men strive to form with kin resemble the patron/client model that has generally structured power hierarchies in Ethiopia (Poluha 2004). For example, historically among the Amhara of highland Ethiopia, men sought to develop networks of clients that were important sources of support in legal battles over rights to land (Hoben 1973). Eva Poluha (2004) argues that in contemporary urban Ethiopia the patron-client model structures relations between parents and children, teachers and students, men and women, and political leaders and citizens. The patron provides security to his dependents in exchange for their allegiance. Both in their work and in their family life young men strive to take on the role of the patron.

In the African context the accumulation of dependents as a form of power has been largely confined to men (Berry 1993; Johnson-Hanks

2006). Local notions of masculinity and the ability to provide material support for others are inseparable. The position of women has been largely restricted to that of dependent clients. Although women have provided essential support for men's accumulation of power, in the past they were generally not in a position to accumulate clients of their own, and to do so would have upset what was seen as a natural hierarchy. To some extent this dynamic has changed in urban Ethiopia as women have become more involved in the informal economy or obtained government work, but young men still maintain a particularly intense association between becoming an adult and providing material support to others.[5]

"The Problem of Youth"

It is this existence of a large population of unemployed young men, unable to move through time and take on the normative responsibilities of adults, that sets the stage for discussions of "the problem of youth" (ye wättatoch chiggir) in urban Ethiopia. While unemployed young women spend the bulk of their time doing housework, for young men an abundance of unstructured time and little access to money cause them to spend their days in public areas, hanging out, and passing the time. The physical presence of young men on street corners, in cafes, or under shady trees serves to continually remind others of their existence, and feeds into the notion that they represent a social problem. Adults and many young people claim that young men pass the majority of their time with activities that present a danger to society as a whole, especially substance abuse (usually chat, alcohol, and cigarettes), crime, and casual sex. Many urban residents complain that young men have become generally disrespectful, insulting their elders in the street and behaving in a way that shows disregard for the norms of their community. To some extent an environment of fear has been created, and at the time of my research it was generally felt that anyone venturing out of his or her house after 10:00 p.m. was inviting an assault or robbery. In seeming contrast to these fears adults also describe young men as being "idle" and simply "sitting" or "chewing" (here "chewing" refers to the consumption of chat). They complain about their sons who are approaching the age of thirty and still living at home, unable to find work or start families of their own.

The contrast between youth as social threat and as emasculated idler is captured in the Amharic phrase "adegeña bozeni." Bozeni refers to a person without work or any activity to occupy their time, and adegeña translates as "dangerous." In other words the simple act of being idle and of being stuck within the category of youth is in itself dangerous. It is in some ways their apparent lack of social agency that causes young men to be viewed as threats.

In 2004, state-sponsored interventions targeted young men precisely at this intersection between their construction as social threat and their simultaneous lack of agency. Hanging out on street corners and watching films are both ways in which unemployed young men pass time, and both are perceived as potentially dangerous social threats. In response to the perceived social problems associated with unemployed youth, a "Vagrancy Control Proclamation" was issued by the federal government in 2004.[6] Although the proclamation is vague, it appears to give police the right to arrest anyone spending time on the streets without a visible means of subsistence (Anteneh 2004). Possessing a state-issued youth identity card was a way of avoiding arrest for this offense.

Also in 2004, police in Jimma raided all of the video houses in the city and arrested the owners. A video house is a sort of miniature cinema where customers, predominantly young men, pay a small fee to watch films (usually American or Indian movies) displayed with a DVD player and television. Local officials claimed that video houses are sources of "bad culture" (*metfo bahil*) and that a number of *adegeña bozeni* had been arrested during the raids.[7]

Through state interventions and discourse concerning the problem of youth, the social category of youth has become marked in terms of both gender and urban residence. It is not common for young women to spend time in public, for example, unless they are carrying out a specific task. It is also rare for young women to enter video houses or to chew *chat*, another potentially "dangerous" activity that is associated with being idle. The same is true of rural and working young men who are generally too busy to pass their time with these activities. In this sense a "youth" is discursively constructed as unemployed, young, urban, and *male*, and the problem of youth is the problem of *young men*.

The "problem of youth" is that young men are significantly diverging from a normative life course. State interventions into the lives of young men reflect an expectation that when young men are idle, simply passing time without engaging in activities related to becoming an adult, they will naturally drift towards practices that are disruptive to social order. Vagrancy and the consumption of international films were both associated with crime, irresponsible sex, and disrespect for elders. Yet despite these predominant views, there also exists an alternative perspective to the discourse surrounding the problem of youth. In youth migratory practices, for example, we can observe how young people often exert agency in ways that do not pose a threat to social order. Young people who migrate for work are in some ways deviating from a normative life course, but they do so in a way that upholds values concerning masculinity and relations of reciprocity.

Migrating for Work and Adulthood

In my discussions with young men about their future, the possibility of migration, especially to the United States, was a constant theme. These young men often claimed that the only way that they could attain their goals was by leaving Ethiopia. International migration has been discursively constructed as a potent source of change for three primary reasons (Mains 2007). For these young men, migration facilitates an association with symbols of modernity like technology and western popular culture. It allows young men to escape local stigmas attached to much of the work available in urban Ethiopia that they claimed prevented them from working locally. Migration also provides access to higher wages that would directly shift one's position within relations of reciprocity. Although discussions of international migration were very important for young men's day-to-day lives, my interest in this chapter is in the actual migratory practices of young people. In contrast to young women, it is not common for young men to leave Ethiopia. Instead, young men move within the country, often to find work with international development projects.

Through a brief discussion of the contrast between migratory practices of young women and young men, we can gain insight into the gendered nature of age-based social categories. Most of the young women who leave Ethiopia travel to the Middle East[8] where they work primarily as domestic servants. In 2005 salaries for domestic servants were around $100.00 (U.S.) per month plus room and board. Although workers sometimes had to pay their employers back for the price of transportation, in most cases they were able to consistently send money home. In some cases young women would return home after completing a two-year contract and in others they would continually renew their contract with the apparent intention to stay in the Middle East indefinitely.

Unlike travel to the US or Europe, working in the Middle East was a realistic possibility for many urban young women. Young women on the spatial or economic periphery of the city had more difficulty contacting potential employers, but with persistence it was likely that they could find work. More opportunities were available for Muslim women, but Christians could certainly find work as well. The primary factor preventing young women from seeking work in the Middle East was the potential for abusive (i.e., sexually, physically, and/or mentally) relationships with their employers. Some women reported very positive relationships with their employers, but a woman never knew the character of the family she would be working for until arrival, and abuse was always a serious risk.

Domestic work in the Middle East shifted the social position of young women. The money earned provided a significant amount of support for a young woman's family while she was abroad. I knew of a number of instances in which young women working abroad supported their unemployed brothers. Money earned as a domestic worker, however, is generally not adequate for saving, and after returning to their families many young women enter a state of extended unemployment. Young women explained that temporarily earning an income and supporting their families provide a sense of independence that subsequently makes unemployment particularly difficult.

In contrast to young men, young women are frequently able to use international migration to shift their position within social relations. Through migration to the Middle East young women are repositioning themselves within relations of reciprocity that have historically been highly gendered. They are taking on the valued masculine role of providing material support to others. Young men often remarked that it would be shameful for them to be financially dependent on a wife or girlfriend. This did not, however, prevent them from relying on remittances from their sisters working abroad. It is interesting that I did not observe tensions surrounding this shift in gendered patterns of reciprocity. It appears that gendered norms regarding giving and receiving can be disrupted when they are accompanied by spatial distance. For the most part women are only able to take on the masculine role of the patron if they live outside of Ethiopia. This shift in relations of power does not enter into everyday interactions between young men and women living in Ethiopia. In this sense, migration mediates gendered norms governing social relationships.

Among young men, migrating locally to obtain work on large-scale international development projects was far more common than traveling abroad. In 2005 Solomon became so frustrated with his dependence on others that he left Jimma to go to the Gambella region, near the Sudan border, where it was rumored that well paid work could be had on a Chinese oil-drilling project. Although Gambella was very unstable at the time and outbreaks of violence were common, Solomon explained that it was better to die there instead of only waiting for death in Jimma. This way at least a good story would be told about him, but staying in Jimma would be to continue a life that lacked meaning.

At that time, leaving for work like this was not common, but when I returned to Jimma three years later in 2008 I was surprised to learn that many young men I knew had followed Solomon's path and left town to search out work on different international projects. A World Bank financed hydroelectric project, run by an Italian company, was the most common destination for young men in Jimma. Others worked on a Chinese road construction project. Of the young men I was able to locate in Jimma, many had returned from these projects and were waiting on work with a Korean road construction project that was scheduled to begin soon. The Korean project promised better wages and the work camp was only a few hours from Jimma.

Kebede was one of these young men, back in Jimma waiting for work with the new project. In 2005, after nearly three years of unemployment, Kebede traveled to the work site for the Chinese road construction project. He used money from his family and kin networks to sustain himself while waiting for work. After about one month he was offered a job doing low-skill manual labor. Kebede explained that although the job did not pay well his expenses were also low. Equally important, working on the project instantly placed him within a valuable network of workers from Jimma, many of them earning substantial incomes as drivers or skilled workers. These other workers often invited him for meals or gave him small cash gifts.

After a few months of work, Kebede was able to begin sending small amounts of money home to his parents in Jimma. Although these amounts were not enough to support his family, they marked a symbolic shift in Kebede's status. He had moved from a dependent to a provider. At least for the moment Kebede was taking on some of the responsibilities associated with adult males. This transition was not permanent, however. After almost two years of work, Kebede quit and returned to Jimma. He had saved enough money to obtain a driver's license and he felt that this would significantly increase his pay grade and perhaps provide him with the resources necessary to marry and raise children.

During the few weeks that I spent with Kebede in 2008 his lifestyle appeared to be unchanged from when I had last seen him in 2005. He lived with his parents and spent most of his time at church or playing soccer. He had little money and was once again reliant on friends and family for daily handouts. In terms of his economic relationships, Kebede was once again a youth. Kebede was, however, confident that his current state of dependence would be over soon. He anticipated beginning work on the Korean project within two months and believed that this would provide a significant change in his life.

When I met with Kebede in 2009, he had followed through on his plans and was working as a foreman on the Korean road construction project. He was earning close to 3000 birr per month in addition to an allowance for food and lodging. He was able to send significant sums of money to his family, purchase food for friends who were looking for work, and save money for the future. Although Kebede's current economic situation was quite good, he acknowledged that work for the Korean company would not extend beyond two or three years and the opportunity to work with a similar project after that remains highly uncertain. Ultimately he hopes that he will be able to find work doing construction in the Middle East.

Kebede's path is typical of the many young men in Jimma who have found work with international projects. Through work they temporarily change their positions within relations of reciprocity and take on roles associated with adult men. The support Kebede received from older and more experienced workers on the Chinese project and later gave to others indicates that many men are able to develop networks of dependents that extend beyond their immediate kin. However, when the work is finished these men often become dependents themselves. I knew many young men in Jimma who had previously earned significant incomes working on the Italian hydroelectric project but were once again living with their parents.

A letter from Solomon sums up the fluctuating nature of life for many young men. Solomon is the best letter writer of the youths who participated in my research and for some time I was fortunate to receive regular reports from him. After moving to Gambela he spent a month waiting for work at a Chinese run oil-drilling project. Once again dealing with the problem of excessive time but with no friends to provide companionship, he described long days of anxiously waiting for something that might not arrive. Eventually Solomon was hired as a guard, a dangerous job in the politically unstable territory surrounding the Sudan/Ethiopia border. The work was temporary and when the job finished he returned to Jimma. If the money he earned had changed his standing locally he did not mention it in his letters. Solomon writes, in English:

> Here in Jimma the things are going to the same ways. Young people just like me who are jobless, each day, morning and afternoon chewing *chat* at every small coffee or tea shop. In this ceremony someone thinks about himself, "how to get the job," another one thinks about "how to get satisfaction in my life," and somebody else is doing another investigation about his country: "why is our country backward? How to develop?" In my side everything is difficult for the future because I have no job. So always chewing *chat*. Maybe I will go to Gambela. If the company calls for me I will go there. If they do not call I don't know what I will do.

Conclusion

I have argued that, in the context of unprecedented levels of urban youth unemployment in Ethiopia, young men are perceived as both social threats and emasculated idlers. These seemingly contradictory qualities are based in young men's inability to take on the normative social responsibilities of adults. Unemployment prevents young men from attaining economic independence, marriage, and fatherhood, and transitioning out of the social category of youth. Each of these goals is based on repositioning oneself within relations of reciprocity. Young men seek to enact a valued masculine adult identity by gradually accumulating economic dependents. Working on internationally funded development projects provides a temporary solution to young men's struggles to become adults. Through this kind of work, young men are able, at least in the short-term, to offer support to others, demonstrating their power to exercise agency in a way that does not threaten social stability.

The case of mobile young workers from Jimma demonstrates that it is necessary to rethink the social category of youth. Clearly, as others have argued, the notion of youth as a period of linear change from childhood to adulthood does not makes sense in this context. Young men and women are not becoming adults in a normative sense and there is no reason to believe that this condition will change in the near future. There is, however, an important relationship between transition and age-based social categories. Youth does involve transition, and the ideal endpoints of adulthood and childhood provide a useful framework for understanding this process. Young men in Jimma take on varying positions within relations of reciprocity. With the movement between employment and unemployment, young men shift between being a provider and a dependent. At times they are adults and at other times they are youths. In the Ethiopian case, age-based social categories are useful for tracking one's position with relations of reciprocity.

Such categories, however, are specific to urban young men who conceive of the transition from youth to adult in terms of progressive movement. These young men expect that their education status will support social mobility and allow them to experience progressive changes in their economic relationships with others. It is their particular notion of what it means to transition from a youth to an adult that leads these young men to be so frustrated with their current situation. The importance of migration as a means of becoming an adult is also based on expectations of social mobility. Young men are compelled to migrate in part to fulfill a masculine ideal in which they are able to provide progressively greater economic and social support to their dependents. Young men who are not invested in this ideal are generally less interested in migration because they may lead a satisfactory life by working locally.

In this sense social categories such as youth and adult have analytical utility as markers within a process of transition, but they are also a means of understanding the variation in the aspirations and struggles of different social groups. The young men I have described in this chapter are distinct from others because of their ideals concerning what it means to be an adult male. Their conceptions of youth and adulthood shape the challenges they face within the life course and the strategies they enact to negotiate these challenges. In this chapter we have seen how young men's expectations concerning adulthood are partially responsible for leading them to engage in extended periods of idle unemployment. This in turn causes others to perceive young men as potential sources of danger. The peculiar position of young men as both idler and social threat is, therefore, inseparable from conceptions of the social categories of youth and adult.

Notes

1. *Chat* is a leafy bush that acts as a mild stimulant when chewed. Ethiopian Muslims traditionally used it for religious purposes (Gebissa 2004), but especially in cities it has become popular among Orthodox Christians as well. In popular discourse *chat* is often associated with unemployment and the "problem of youth."
2. All of the names of individuals discussed in this chapter are pseudonyms.
3. *Shuro* is a spicy chick pea paste that is a popular dish with most Ethiopians, and generally eaten daily by poor families.
4. The distinction between "pure love" and a relationship that involves high levels of gifting deserves further exploration. I suspect that this is a very new concept. For the most part relationships in urban Ethiopia were inseparable from the movement of material goods and the notion that gifts contaminate relationships was not often expressed (Mains 2012).
5. See Cole 2004 for an interesting example of how this dynamic has shifted in contemporary urban Madagascar.
6. Proclamation No. 384/2004. "A Proclamation to Provide for Controlling Vagrancy." 27 January 2004.
7. See Mains 2012 for a more detailed discussion of video houses.
8. The Middle East was referred to as *"Arab hager"* ("Arab country") and the most common destinations for migration appeared to have been Saudi Arabia, Dubai, and Lebanon.

Bibliography

Asmarom Legesse. 1973. *Gada: Three Approaches to the Study of an African Society*. New York: Free Press.

Bahru Zewde. 2002. *A History of Modern Ethiopia, 1855–1991*. Oxford: James Curry.

Berry, Sara. 1993. *No Condition is Permanent: The Social Dynamics of Agrarian Change in Sub-Saharan Africa*. Madison: University of Wisconsin Press.

———. 1985. *Fathers Work for Their Sons: Accumulation, Mobility, and Class Formation in an Extended Yoruba Community*. Berkeley: University of California Press

Central Statistical Authority. 1999. *The 1994 Population and Housing Census of Ethiopia*. Addis Ababa: Federal Government of Ethiopia.

Cole, Jennifer. 2005. "The Jaombilo of Tamatve (Madagascar), 1992–2004: Reflections on Youth and Globalization." *Journal of Social History*, 38 (4): 891–914.

———. 2004. "Fresh Contact in Tamatave, Madagascar: Sex, Money, and Intergenerational Transformation." *American Ethnologist*, 31 (4): 573–588.

Cruise O'Brien, Donal. 1996. "A Lost Generation? Youth Identity and State Decay in West Africa." In *Postcolonial Identities in Africa*, eds. R. Werbner and T. Ranger. London: Zed Books

Diof, Mamadou. 2003. "Engaging Postcolonial Cultures: African Youth and Public Space." *African Studies Review*, 46(2): 1–12.

Gebissa, Ezekiel. 2004. *Leaf of Allah: Khat and the Transformation of Agriculture in Harerege, Ethiopia, 1875–1991*. Oxford: James Curry.

Hansen, Karen Tranberg. 2005. "Getting Stuck in the Compound: Some Odds Against Social Adulthood in Lusaka." *Africa Today*, 51 (4): 2–17.

Hassen, Mohammed. 1990. *The Oromo of Ethiopia: A History 1570–1860*. Cambridge: Cambridge University Press.

Hoben, Allan. 1973. *Land Tenure among the Amhara of Ethiopia*. Chicago: University of Chicago Press.

———. 1970. "Social Stratification in Traditional Amhara Society." In *Social Stratification in Africa*, eds. Arthur Tuden and Leonard Plotnicov. New York: The Free Press.

Hutchinson, Sharon. 1996. *Nuer Dilemmas: coping with money, war, and the state*. Berkeley: University of California Press.

Johnson-Hanks, Jennifer. 2006. *Uncertain Honor: Modern Motherhood in an African Crisis*. Berkeley: University of California Press.

Kinfu Y. 2000. "Below Replacement Fertility in Tropical Africa? Some Evidence from Addis Ababa." *Journal of Population Research*, 17 (1): 63–82.

Kratz, Corinne. 1994. *Affecting Performance: Meaning, Movement and Experience in Okiek Women's Initiation*. Washington: Smithsonian Institution Press.

Krishnan, Pramila. 1998. *The Urban Labour Market During Structural Adjustment: Ethiopia 1990–1997*. Oxford: Center for the Study of African Economies.

Levine, Donald. 1965. *Wax and Gold: Tradition and Innovation in Ethiopian Culture*. Chicago: University of Chicago Press.

Lewis, Herbert. 2001. *Jimma Abba Jifar: An Oromo Monarchy, Ethiopia 1830–1932*. Lawrenceville: The Red Sea Press.

Mains, D. 2007. "Neoliberal Times: Progress, Boredom, and Shame among Young Men in Urban Ethiopia." *American Ethnologist*, 34 (4): 659–673.

———. 2012. *Hope is Cut: Youth, Unemployment and the Future in Urban Ethiopia*. Philadelphia: Temple University Press.

Masquelier, Adeline. 2005. "The Scorpion's Sting: Youth, Marriage and the Struggle for Social Maturity in Niger." *Journal of the Royal Anthropological Institute*, 11: 59–83.

Poluha, Eva. 2004. *The Power of Continuity: Ethiopia Through the Eyes of its Children*. Uppsala: Nordiska Afrikainstitutet.

Richards, Paul. 1996. *Fighting for the Rain Forest: War, Youth, and Resources in Sierra Leone*. Portsmouth: Heinemann.

Serneels, Pieter. 2007. "The Nature of Unemployment among Young Men in Urban Ethiopia." *Review of Development Economics*, 11 (1): 170–186.

Sharp, Lesley. 2002. *The Sacrificed Generation: Youth, History, and the Colonized Mind in Madagascar*. Berkeley: University of California Press.

Silberschmidt, Margrethe. 2004. "Masculinities, Sexuality, and Socio-Economic Change in Rural and Urban East Africa." In *Rethinking Sexualities in Africa*, ed. Signe Arnfred. Uppsala: Nordiska Afrikainstitutet.

Stambach, Amy. 2000. *Lessons from Mount Kilimanjaro: Schooling, Community, and Gender in East Africa*. New York: Routledge Press.

Teshome Wagaw. 1979. *Education in Ethiopia: Prospect and Retrospect*. Ann Arbor: The University of Michigan Press

Weiss, Brad. 2004. "Contentious Futures: Past and Present." In *Producing African Futures: Ritual and Reproduction in a Neoliberal Age*, ed. Brad Weiss. Leiden: Brill.

Chapter 5

GENDERED MODERNITIES AND TRADITIONS
Masculinity and Nationalism in the Society Islands

Deborah A. Elliston

Introduction

In the now extensive body of scholarship on gender and nationalism, there is an odd lacuna that motivates this chapter's project: although men, and particularly young men, have been central actors in most, and perhaps all, twentieth-century nationalist movements, this empirical phenomenon has rarely been made the focus of scholarly interrogation. Instead, the significant body of scholarship on gender and nationalism has focused almost exclusively on women.[1] And while that scholarship has produced vital questions and analyses—of the problematic figurations of women within nationalist imaginaries, of their sitings as subjects and objects of nation-building projects, and more—we are left with a substantial and surprising dearth of critical analysis of the relationships between men, masculinity, and nationalism.

The questions pursued in this chapter focus on these relationships by examining dynamics I encountered in the mid-1990s during research in the Society Islands of French Polynesia (an "overseas territory" of France in the Pacific, also known as "Tahiti and its Islands"). There, young men emerged at the center of a revitalized Polynesian movement to gain independence from France, at the frontlines of anti-colonial activism, and at the apex of local narratives charting both the promises and dangers of an independent Polynesian nation.[2] In this chapter, I ask why.[3] A primary goal of this pursuit is to shift the linkages between masculinity and nationalist struggle out of the realm of commonsense and into that of the sociological: to unmoor the naturalized relationship so often assumed to hold between masculinity and revolutionary violence, between men and nationalist projects.

Tahiti's "Black Wednesday"

I begin with an ethnographic moment, dated 6 September 1995. That day, international media reports briefly unbalanced Tahiti's reputation as a tropical paradise. The early morning images coming out of the South Pacific island were set at its international airport, usually a peaceful place where runways and resting planes nestle in between the lush mountains of the island's center and a seemingly infinite expanse of aqua green Pacific Ocean. On this September morning, however, young Polynesian men were facing off with rocks against French military police, launching Molotov cocktails at the airport runways, and setting fire to terminal buildings and cars in the airport parking lot. The protest spread over the day, as the young men left the airport and were joined by others to march the several kilometers to downtown Papeete, the cosmopolitan capital of this "overseas territory" of France. There, protesters began a night of smashing storefront windows, looting, and setting fire to buildings and parked cars.

"Tahiti's Black Wednesday" (Le mercredi noir de Tahiti), or simply "the Riots" (les émeutes), as this protest was doubly christened in the state-run daily newspaper, took place the day after France's locally televised detonation of its first nuclear bomb test in more than three years in French Polynesia (La Dépêche de Tahiti 1995). Young men's centrality in the September "riots" continued their central role in the many anti-nuclear testing and pro-independence protests staged over the three months leading up to France's September nuclear test. Between June and September, those included marches and sit-ins on a dozen different islands across the territory, the erection of a "Peace Village" in front of the Territorial Assembly, three mass protest marches in the capital drawing 10,000 to 15,000 people each (in a territory of about two hundred thousand), and two sieges of Papeete in which protesters blockaded the city's access roads to shut down the capital for several days each time.[4] Young men were by far most numerous among demonstrators at these protests; sporting army fatigues, bandannas that partly concealed their faces, and T-shirts emblazoned with images of fierce Polynesian warriors, they could reliably be found marching alongside the blue and white flag of Tavini Huira'atira, the territory's largest pro-independence political party.

The Tavini nationalist party took a leading role organizing the protests, galvanizing opposition to the resumption of nuclear testing, and linking their calls to end nuclear testing with calls for immediate political independence. On 29 June 1995, for example, a march of almost fifteen thousand people against nuclear testing ended in a siege of Papeete sustained largely by the young men who made up the rank and file of the Tavini nationalist party. Camped out at the junction points of the capital's main roads, protesters closed the city to all but foot and boat traffic for three and a half days. Throughout the siege, Tavini's independent radio station broadcast continuing pleas for calm, with party leaders appealing specifically to young men to stay calm and beseeching adults to maintain peace by watching vigilantly over the youth.

Young men were consistently described as the instigators of Tahiti's "Black Wednesday" of rioting, just as they had been treated as the unpredictable element requiring special monitoring during the sieges of Papeete and just as they had been singled out for blame when prior demonstrations had turned violent. The prevailing local account of the "riots" and young men's central role in them was captured in the words of a dance teacher I knew in the days just after 6 September: "The youth…" she told me, "it's the youth who did everything. They wait for an occasion to revolt. … They're idle, they have nothing to do. … They go and look for work, and they can't find it. They become ferocious."

Nationalism and Social Differences

Why was it young men who disproportionately responded to nationalist leaders' calls to action? How was it that, by the mid-1990s, on both sides of the nationalist debate, young men had come to be situated at the apex of local discourses about nationalism, as exemplars of the best and the worst that independence could mean? Among adult Polynesian men, for example, young men's nationalist activism—including its more violent manifestations—was at times figured as a source of pride. A few days after the September riots, for example, Ranunu, a middle-aged father of five, reflected on the events as we sat around the kitchen table with some of his relatives: "It's the youth who will lead us to independence," he announced smiling. From the other end of the room, his wife, Vaihere, snorted and rolled her eyes. Ranunu laughed: "It's true, Déborah: it's written in the Bible that it's the youth who will lead us to independence. That's what they're doing out there now." Vaihere quickly called out her disagreement: "No, Déborah, it's because they have nothing better to do."

The differences between Ranunu's and Vaihere's evaluations crystallized a broader pattern of gendered differences in Polynesians' interpretations of young men's nationalist activism and the meanings and desirability of independence. In the mid-1990s, almost all of the Polynesian women I worked with were either opposed to the nationalist struggle for independence from France or deeply ambivalent about it. In contrast, the most ardent activists for independence were men, and specifically young men in the life stage Polynesians term *taure'are'a* (between the ages of about fifteen and thirty). In a society that has had no substantive gender hierarchy, in which gender is actively minimized—discounted rather than embellished as a meaningful axis of social difference—young men's support for the nationalist struggle and women's opposition to it each came to the fore as a phenomenon that required an accounting.

Women's critical stances toward independence, for example, were surprising in part because of the rich histories of the many chiefly (*ari'i*) women who, like chiefly men, ruled districts, islands, and even multi-island chiefdoms in the Society Islands until the twentieth century (Newbury 1980). This history indicates that it is not for lack of a model of women's political authority or political agency that Polynesian women disengaged from the nationalist struggle. Moreover, Polynesian women historically have been, and currently are, socially powerful. One of the more interesting features of social life in the Society Islands has been the relatively egalitarian quality of gender relations: the organization of gender and authority support, in the words of anthropologist Robert Levy, "a doctrine of sexual equality" (1973: 236). This is not, then, a society in which gender hierarchy would render women's participation in the nationalist project a site of contention. Indeed, nationalist leaders I interviewed were themselves puzzled about women's disconnection from their struggle for independence.

Rather than examining women's relationships to nationalism, however, this chapter focuses on those of young men. As the foregoing suggests, the particularizing features of Polynesian social history bring into stark relief the problematic status of any unexamined acceptance of men as nationalist activists and the oftentimes presumptive constructions of masculinity on which that depends. In positioning young men's nationalist activism as an object of ethnographic interrogation, I build on critiques of gender foundationalism. Feminist scholars analyzing the category "woman" have mapped the extensive analytical distortions that flow from analyses that assume women as a category "already constituted as sexual-political subjects prior to their entry into the arena of social relations" (Mohanty 1991: 59; Yanagisako and Collier 1987). The present analysis may be read, in part, as a pursuit of what happens when that insight is applied to "men." In the wake of critiques of gender foundationalism, it becomes the task of scholarly analysis to interrogate the very social processes through which gender differences gain the appearance of having a prediscursive fixity that frames the actions expected of "men" and "women."

The project thus becomes one that analyzes how gender differences are produced through social action, rather than precede it. Complicating this, however, is that, among Polynesians, masculinity did not align in any simple way with the oftentimes impassioned commitment to independence. Indeed, adult Polynesian men I knew were far more divided on the issue than were young men in the generational relationships of sons or grandsons to them. Whereas adult men I knew were much more likely than women (of any age) to support the nationalist movement, and tended to be far more generous in evaluating the sometimes violent activism of young *taure'are'a* men, most did not support independence. Rather, the staunchest supporters were defined by the specific conjunction of gender (masculinity) with generation (*taure'are'a*): they were young Polynesian men. Thus, the question I pursue in this analysis is not "Why men?" but "Why young men?"

Following that question, this chapter charts the specifically sociological dynamics that helped to position young men at the frontlines of pro-independence sentiment and mobilization in the Society Islands in the mid-1990s. This charting takes its cue from local explanations of young men's nationalist activism that asserted a direct relationship between their economic marginality ("They have nothing better to do") and their support for independence. At the level of local representations—and, as I detail below, in practice as well—young men's centrality in the mid-1990s nationalist mobilization was bound up with a much deeper problematic: the gendered history and politics of labor practice in the Society Islands.

While labor is not the only social arena in which gender (or generational) differences are produced, it was the one that emerged as most directly relevant to young men's relationships to nationalism. In part, this is due to the ways gender differences are produced through, for example, social constructions of a gendered division of labor. In addition, in the course of their production, such differences are articulated through and bound to the simultaneous production of regimes of value. Because labor concerns both the productive activities in which people engage and the meanings they ascribe to those activities, it is centrally articulated with regimes of value that, in dialectical form, themselves help to structure the ascription of meaning to activity. Thus, labor practices mediate regimes of value at the same time that they produce social differences in relation to those regimes.

The argument I develop in this chapter is that, by the mid-1990s, young men had come to stand at the epicenter of a pitched moral conflict between what I gloss as French colonial and Polynesian systems of value. This conflict took shape through local formulations of "traditional" Polynesian exchange relations and the forms of social organization and value they articulated, on the one hand, and local formulations of the "modern" French colonial and consumer market economy, along with its forms of social organization and value—including the colonial system of rule— on the other.[5] In the context of French colonialism and its quite recent transformation of these Islanders' subsistence economy into one privileging the market, an ethnographic focus on labor reveals the microprocesses through which labor practice animated competing formulations of "tradition" and "modernity," which, in turn, were primary vehicles through which Polynesians' positions on independence were constructed and debated. These microprocesses highlight the central role of households as primary sites at which "tradition" and "modernity" gain experiential meanings, as fundamental social contexts in which differences and hierarchies are (re)produced, and thus as key mediating sites in the production and negotiation of the conflicting regimes of value that "tradition" and "modernity" came to iconify. Through such tracking, then, this chapter details the practices through which "tradition" and "modernity" were discursively constituted and made available—in particular, interested, and contradictory local forms, and in relation to distinctions of gender and generation—by Polynesians who deployed them to debate, contest, and authorize conflicting sociopolitical projects and visions of the future.

By examining young men's positioning at the center of this conflict in regimes of value, I analyze how the meanings of masculinity became bound up with labor practice, such that post-1950s socioeconomic changes in the Islands generated deep challenges to the symbolic regimes through which moral masculinity could be achieved. In the present analysis, then, the utility of interrogating the sociological production of gender and generational differences lies, in part, in how it reveals contradictions and tensions in the performance of manhood and the criteria for successful masculinity. Those contradictions, in turn, were centrally involved in producing the gendered and generationally distinctive profile of the Polynesian nationalist struggle. Thus, resituating the linkages between men and nationalist activism as sites of investigation helps to demonstrate the theoretical productivity of a move away from an analytics of gender foundationalism and toward interrogations of the very social processes through which gender differences, and masculinity specifically, are produced.

A Labored History

In the Society Islands, the horizon of possibility within which labor practices take shape and gain their meanings shifted dramatically between the 1960s and 1990s. In the early 1960s, France relocated its nuclear testing program (Centre d'Expérimentations du Pacifique, or CEP) from Algeria, which was then on the verge of independence, to its "overseas territory" of French Polynesia, specifically to the Tuamotu archipelago atolls of Moruroa and Fangataufa, located about 775 miles from Tahiti island.[6] Along with the decision to base its nuclear testing program in this territory came a significant change in the French state's investments in French Polynesia: in part "to encourage local acquiescence" to nuclear testing, France began cultivating the territory as an economic dependency (Henningham 1992: 127; see also Regnault 1993 and von Strokirch 1993). The intensive development of the French colonial labor market and consumer economy beginning in the 1960s dramatically shifted the geography of Polynesian social life, including labor practices and their meanings, and it did so in gendered ways.

Before the nuclear testing program, the Society Islands economy was largely organized around household subsistence production built largely on men's agricultural and fishing labors. According to labor histories I collected from older men during my research, some cash-income opportunities had been available through raising copra and vanilla, and some men engaged in short-term labor migration to France's mining operations at Makatea (phosphate) and New Caledonia (nickel) (see also Henningham 1992). Statistics on the territory's trade balance in 1960, however, reflect the predominance of subsistence labor practices and the self-sufficiency of most Polynesian households: as a percentage of exports over imports, the 1960 territorial trade balance of 75 percent plummeted to 9 percent by 1965, recovering to a mere 12 percent by 1990 (von Strokirch 1993: 101). Food imports are especially revealing here: from 37 percent in 1960, they leaped to 58 percent by 1968, and skyrocketed to 80 percent by the 1980s (Henningham 1992: 131).

Beginning in the 1960s, monies began pouring into the territory from the French state, creating significant numbers of jobs: for the nuclear testing facilities in the Tuamotus, the research facilities at Tahiti, and the program's infrastructural supports, including expanding Papeete's harbor and construction projects such as an international airport; sewer, electrical, and water systems; roads, bridges, and housing projects; government buildings; and so on. Such labor projects at the time targeted Polynesian men as workers, who responded by migrating to Tahiti in large numbers, oftentimes accompanied by their women partners, children, and other kin.

These migrations were enormous: in 1951 about 55 percent of the total territory's population resided on Tahiti and its neighboring island, Moorea (the Windward Society Islands). By 1967 that figure was 67 percent, and by 1977 it had reached 74 percent where it stabilized (ITSTAT 1991 [2]: 19, ITSTAT 1999: 68). These migrations reflected a major shift "from traditional agriculture and fishing to cash employment" which "transformed the economy... from 'copra to the atom'" (Henningham 1992: 129). And it was not only Polynesians who migrated: upwards of twenty thousand French military and civil personnel also came to Tahiti for the nuclear testing program and its adjacent projects. This influx itself marked a substantial change in the landscape of interactions between Polynesians and the French; from the beginnings of French colonialism in 1842 until this period, the number of metropolitan French in the territory had never exceeded a few thousand (Rallu 1991: 183). (Unlike the case in other French possessions, this territory never became a French settler colony.) And just as most of the migrating Polynesians moved to Tahiti, so too did most of the arriving metropolitans.

By the mid-1970s, however, the construction boom for which Polynesian men migrated in the 1960s had dissipated, and the more drawn-out process of secondary-tier development was underway. Structured in part through French colonial gender ideologies, this expansion of the commerce, communications, banking, and service industries throughout the territory tended to target Polynesian women workers rather than men. While wage work for women developed along a slower curve, then, it has proved longer lasting than wage work for men. By the early 1990s, for example, women predominated over men in a variety of occupations across the territory: in retail services (63 percent), domestic services (77 percent), hotel, café, and restaurant work (57 percent), public sector service provision like health care and support staff (60 percent), public and private education (64 percent), service industries like waitressing and beauty (79 percent), and clerical work in such private-sector industries as tourism, insurance, and finance (70 percent) (ITSTAT 1991 [2]: 169–178). Men, on the other hand, predominated in only a few occupations: agriculture (76 percent), fishing (94 percent), construction (96 percent), skilled and unskilled industrial laboring (97 percent), and chauffeuring (97 percent) (ITSTAT 1991 [1]: 169–178). (The substantial civil service employs about equal numbers of men and women.)

Polynesian women's predominance in more varied work categories reveals that women engaged in a much wider range of wage labor than men. Additionally, the kinds of work in which women predominated produce cash wages more frequently and consistently. In contrast, the kinds of work in which the majority of Polynesian men predominate have not been primarily cash generating. Specifically, the most prevalent labor practices among Polynesian men in the early 1990s (and dating back to much earlier) were agriculture and fishing (ITSTAT 1991 [1]$%: 182; Levy 1973; Oliver 1981). Furthermore, although these kinds of men's labors could and sometimes did include sale for cash—through, for example, the sale of produce at roadside stands, cash cropping or agricultural cooperatives—in the main, these forms of labor and most of their products were directed to the households of the men laborers and their extended kin for subsistence. By the early 1990s, this had led not only to the emergence among many employers of a marked preference for hiring women over men but to the phenomenon of women bringing cash into their households more reliably than men—and this was only intensifying among the younger generation of Polynesians just entering full-time work.

These larger political economic shifts were experienced as inaugurating dramatic changes in the social landscape: virtually all Polynesians I knew marked the period since the 1960s as one of profound social change. Perhaps most telling for the present analysis, the young men who came to stand at the center of mid-1990s debates about independence and the territory's future were also the first generation to come of age within that substantially changed political economy and social geography. Young men's contentious location at the heart of the nationalist struggle was, I suggest, shaped through a deep and dialectical relationship with their central location in the emergent conflict between the values ascribed to the recently institutionalized French colonial market and consumer economy, and those ascribed to the Polynesian subsistence and exchange economy. Both systems of value became morally inflected and pitched, and both became available to Polynesians as discursive resources for adjudicating the meanings and moral standing of everything from labor practice to schooling to land tenure to independence.

Women's Labor Practices

I turn here to give a more detailed accounting of gendered labor practices, beginning with Polynesian women's labors. I begin with the textile craft business of the Tehari'i family headed by Mama Fa'atere, a widowed woman in her mid-fifties whose business operations were sited at the two households she headed: one in a small village on Huahine; the other in a neighborhood of Papeete on Tahiti. Mama Fa'atere had taught most of the children she had borne and fostered—including three natal sons, three natal daughters, one foster son, and one foster daughter—how to make the Polynesian textiles in which she specialized, but it was the young women of the family who produced textiles for her business. Mama Fa'atere herself had partly retired from sewing and most of the work was done by Hehemi, at age twenty-one the youngest of Mama's natal children; by Heikapua, the middle daughter, age twenty-three; and by Hina, the twenty-six-year-old common-law wife of Mama's eldest son (Tahaia), who had also been trained by Mama Fa'atere. The eldest of the Tehari'i sisters, twenty-nine-year-old Rapana, sometimes sewed but was primarily in charge of selling the textile crafts made by the other women at the vending stall she operated in Papeete's central marketplace.

Each of the household complexes at Huahine and Tahiti had a dedicated area for this work that housed bolts of vibrantly colored cloth, spools of brightly colored thread, and industrial sewing machines atop custom-made tables. The women spent between six and nine hours a day, six days a week, at their sewing machines. They were paid by the piece for making the two types of textile products in which Mama Fa'atere specialized: *vehi tūru'a* (decorative covers for the small pillows that ubiquitously adorn beds, couches, and chairs in Polynesian households) and *tīfaifai* (Polynesian quilts). Mama Fa'atere's two households comprised a multi-faceted business producing and selling these Polynesian textiles and, through that, the women of the Tehari'i family made almost all of the money that came into the family. Nor were the women of this kin group exceptional in their business acumen and productivity: craft production has been a widespread labor practice among Polynesian women across French Polynesia, with women's craft cooperatives established on most islands and atolls (Hammond 1986; Jones 1991, 1992). Such cooperatives mediated between individual women producers and the markets for their crafts by, for example, running a local boutique or renting space in Papeete's central marketplace to display and sell their members' crafts, and the cooperatives were further organized into federations that have played important roles in local and territorial politics (Jones 1991).

By the mid-1990s, making Polynesian textiles was among the more lucrative skills a young woman could develop and, like other craft production, it was also valued for its flexibility: a woman could give whatever time she had to it, in and amidst other daily activities like visiting and childcare. The most prevalent mode of entry into craft production among Polynesians I knew was through informal apprenticeships structured between a young woman and a senior woman relative with an established business. During the apprenticeship period, the novice would receive only nominal payment for her work, which would gradually increase over the course of the apprenticeship as the quality of the crafts she made improved. Such nominal payment was related to the common practice of the novice residing in the household of the kinswoman training her, an arrangement that framed the apprenticeship within the locally salient model of exchanging labor for food and "care" (discussed below).

Such informal apprenticeships were used among women to structure apprenticeships in making and selling a wide variety of local crafts and products: for example, *pāreu* (Polynesian sarongs, hand-dyed and imprinted with local flora and fauna), similarly hand-dyed sheets, curtains, and other household textiles; the festively styled dresses women wear to church; coconut oil *(mono'i)*; flower and plant garlands *(hei)*; and the fine hats women plait from pandanus and other fibers. In addition, young women also accessed cash-paying labor at the roadside stands and marketplace stalls at which a kin group's crafts were sold, as well as at grocery stores, boutiques, restaurants, and hotels. While in some cases, such businesses were owned by someone in their extended kin group, in most cases access was mediated through client–patron relations between a Polynesian kin group and the—usually Chinese or French—owners of the businesses. This was ubiquitously the case at hotels, but also structured access at numerous other island enterprises, from car rental agencies to the airport shops and airlines to grocery and other stores.

Men's Labor Practices: Making *fa'a'apu*

In contrast to the oftentimes cash-producing work of Polynesian women, in the early 1990s most Polynesian men worked at subsistence-oriented agriculture or fishing. There were, of course, adult men who engaged in wage labor, particularly if they lived in Papeete. But most Polynesian men—upward of 92 percent on Huahine—worked at agriculture or fishing (ITSTAT 1991 [1]: 175). And while men's predominance in these labor practices both reflected and produced their deeper involvement in a mixed economy, such work was primarily directed towards subsistence: most of the produce men raised and the fish they caught went to feed their households and those of their extended kin. Such was the case not only for men whose primary form of laboring was agriculture or fishing, but also for many men who engaged in wage or salaried labor. On Huahine, for example, as well as in the outer districts of even Tahiti Island, adult men who worked for wages routinely fished after work or on weekends and many cultivated small gardens to bring fish and local produce into their households. Such labors also reflected and reproduced the primary association of adult men with the agricultural and fishing labors locally signified as valued "traditional" men's work, a subject to which I return below.

Men's agricultural work has long taken the form of cultivating gardens (fa'a'apu) usually grown on lands owned by the man's extended kin group or his wife and located in the fertile valleys of an island's interior. Most men I knew on Huahine who worked fa'a'apu also fished in the bays and lagoons around the island. Ranunu, for example, the father of five introduced earlier, cultivated a fa'a'apu in the interior mountains near his village to provide food for his household and relatives. The year I knew him, Ranunu's fa'a'apu was growing several varieties of the staple root crop taro (taro, taruā, and 'ape); yams (ufi) and sweet potatoes ('ūmara); multiple varieties of banana trees (fē'i); coconuts (ha'ari), breadfruit ('uru), papayas ('ī'ītā), avocados ('āvōta), limes (tāporo), and mangos (vī); and wild-growing like Tahitian chestnuts (māpē) and guava (tuava). Like most men who worked fa'a'apu, Ranunu supplemented his cultivated produce with fish he caught every day or two, usually fished with a few other men relatives[7] or friends, and he participated in the periodic net-fishing ventures organized by groups of men. Ranunu supplemented all of these foods with the prized meat from men's periodic pig-hunting expeditions into the interior mountains.

When Ranunu and other men caught a wild pig or were particularly successful at fishing, they divvied up the spoils among themselves and then each subdivided portions to give to kin-related households. Similarly, when Ranunu's fa'a'apu yielded an abundance, which it regularly did, Ranunu made gifts of its produce to households related to his own and his wife's kin groups. Ranunu's wife, Vaihere, was related to Mama Fa'atere through a fosterage relation and, through Vaihere's link to this kin group, Ranunu had become good friends with Mama's eldest son, thirty-year-old Tahaia, and the two men regularly fished together and helped each other with other labor projects.

On the many occasions when Ranunu gave produce from his fa'a'apu to Mama Fa'atere, she would redistribute a portion of the food bounty to other households with which she had kinship ties. Mama Fa'atere would carefully divide the produce, fish, or meat into boxes or coolers and send the containers with Tahaia down to the island's main wharf. There, her eldest son would join dozens of other Islanders, waiting with their cartons and coolers of local foods for the inter-island freighter. The containers Tahaia sent on the freighter would be marked to go, for example, to the Raiatea island household headed by the wife of one of Mama Fa'atere's stepsons, or to a household in the Tuamotus headed by the foster grandmother of another of Mama's stepsons, or to another Tuamotu atoll where Mama's former in-laws lived. And a particularly large carton would always be sent to Rapana (the eldest daughter), who took care of Mama Fa'atere's household in Papeete and who had no access to the very best foods, which, by local definition, were only to be found on the outer islands.

Among the men I knew, cultivating a *fa'a'apu* required intensive labor for a week or so about every three to four months: during those periods the land would be "cleaned" by burning off organic rubbish, and seedlings would be transplanted. The rest of the time, maintaining a *fa'a'apu* involved a day of weeding every week or two, although most men I knew visited their *fa'a'apu* several times a week. During the more intensive labor periods, men relatives and friends would be called upon to help with the work, and the *fa'a'apu* owner would reciprocate in turn. Such informal labor exchanges have been common among men in the Society Islands, sometimes becoming more formal labor exchange associations (Finney 1965: 300–307; Oliver 1981: 106–107). Tahaia and Mama Fa'atere's other sons, for example, usually helped Ranunu during the intensive labor periods at his *fa'a'apu*, and they also helped him in other labor projects, such as when one of his relatives was building a house. In turn, Ranunu helped Mama Fa'atere's sons (most of whom were *taure'are'a* in their twenties) with their labor projects: outside of fishing, the Tehari'i sons' main labor project during my fieldwork was the construction of a half dozen *fare upu*—Polynesian thatched houses—which Mama Fa'atere had directed her sons to build on the mountainside in back of her main household complex on Huahine.

Labor and Exchange

As the foregoing account of men's *fa'a'apu* and fishing labors suggests, Polynesian men who pursued "traditional" labors have been only marginally involved in the market economy. While some men's agricultural and fishing labor has been structured through government-subsidized cash-cropping projects, and others have found informal ways of earning cash from these labors (selling *fa'a'apu* produce at household-run roadside stands or selling fish off their boats at their island's main wharf), most of men's produce and fish were not directed into the market. Rather, in the early 1990s, the produce men raised and the fish they caught went, first, to feed their households and, second, into circuits of exchange between households of kin. Thus, in addition to feeding kin in their households, men's laboring has been fundamentally directed toward and tied into systems of exchange.

Generally, as numerous theorists following Mauss (1967) and Lévi-Strauss (1969) have demonstrated, exchange is a form of social action productive of social differences and deeply implicated in the production of hierarchy (or, alternatively, its negation). Ethnographic studies have demonstrated that the social relations forged between givers and receivers through exchange practices are not necessarily or even primarily organized around reciprocity (Weiner 1992). Rather, food exchanges across Oceania have been the media for a wide variety of social projects concerned with difference and hierarchy: from creating differences between peoples in Melanesian societies (Fajans 1993) to collapsing differences between kin groups in the Hawaiian islands (Linnekin 1985); from articulating (or repressing) differences of authority and autonomy among Australian aboriginal peoples (Myers 1993) to producing kinship identities and kinship itself in most Polynesian societies (Brady 1976; Howard and Kirkpatrick 1989).

In the Society Islands, Polynesians have produced kinship primarily through a specific exchange practice: the giving and receiving of food (mā'a). More broadly across Polynesian societies, food has been fundamental in accounts of relatedness, standing as perhaps the archetypal symbol of and medium for producing kinship specifically and sociality more broadly (Howard and Kirkpatrick 1989: 67–68). The Tahitian-language word for adoption, fa'a'amu, for example, translates as "to feed" because, as that suggests, for Islanders the giving and receiving of food mark a relationship as one of kinship (Hooper 1970). Moreover, although feeding is beneficently coded by Society Islanders as primarily about caring and nurturance, it is also held to entail obligation and debt. As other scholars have noted, Islanders describe the obligations created when one is given food by one's caregivers as a kind of "feeding debt" that children incur when they are young and must repay when they are grown, by providing food and care to the people who raised them (Hanson 1970; Oliver 1981). In this respect, feeding has constituted a primary practice for articulating primary social hierarchies in Polynesian social life.

The expectations of exchange and obligation embedded in these practices of caring and nurturance were made clear to me one day during a conversation in which my own lack of children had been a topic of discussion. Mama Fa'atere looked at me sternly as she began instructing me to correct that: "One must have children," she stated emphatically. "It's true it's very hard when they're young," she said, "but later, like now"—she paused as she waved her arm around the room, gesturing to her sixteen-year-old foster son who was tidying up, her taure'are'a son who was at the table with us, and Vaihere's teenage daughter who was washing dishes. "If you don't have children," she asked me, "who will do everything for you? Who will do this, do that, do this, do that?" I laughed, assuming she was joking in suggesting that the value of children lies in the work they do for their caregivers. She did not laugh with me. "No," she said shaking her head, "No, Déborah, that's what children do after they're grown. My children are grown now, and they do everything for me. That's why one must have children. If one doesn't have children, who will do things for you?"

Polynesians have extended this model of the feeding relationship, deploying it to frame and motivate the terms of relationships at quite a remove from parent-child. In the early 1990s, for example, people used it to frame patron-client relationships in ways that endowed them with both familial and hierarchical shadings. Closer to home, this model was ubiquitously used to frame the incorporation of distant kin and non-kin, usually young *taure'are'a* men, into households as dependent laborers who, for varying periods of time, gave their labor to the household head in exchange for being "fed" or "cared for." Such a model of "caring for" was also used to frame the apprenticeships of young women discussed previously: there it helped to authorize the lowered wages young women received during their apprenticeships when they resided with the senior women training them.

More broadly, then, food exchanges have served not only as the medium through which Polynesians signify kinship identity and define the parameters of kin groups; food exchanges have also served as the vehicle for incorporating non-kin into relations of kinship and sociality and as the template for producing hierarchical relations on the model of parent-child, giver-receiver, and authority-subordinate. As that indicates, food exchanges constitute a fundamental social practice through which Polynesians negotiate and authorize hierarchies both within kin groups and beyond them: at the same time that food exchanges produce relatedness, they create obligations on the part of recipients, structuring and authorizing the recipients' subordination to the givers. Inside the practices and quite powerful meanings of food giving as nurturance and caring, then, lie the terms of, and agreements to abide by, hierarchical relations of authority and subordination.

Of a piece with the primacy of food for producing both relatedness and hierarchy has been the symbolically central role of food in other projects of difference making: for example, food has served as a potent symbolic form for signifying Polynesian cultural identity. In the 1990s, Society Islanders spoke of "true" Polynesians or "true Mā'ohi" as people who ate "traditional" foods collectively identified as the *mā'a tahiti*: properly prepared by being baked in Polynesian earth ovens (*ahimā'a*), these include local fish, pig, breadfruit, *taro*, and *po'e;* a variety of uncooked prepared foods, like raw fish marinated in ocean water (*fāfaru*); and dipping sauces of coconut milk, fermented (*miti hue*) and sweetened (*miti ha'ari*). Moreover, as signifiers of cultural identity, foods and food preferences have been used by Polynesians to differentiate, for example, French people (*farāni*) from Americans: while Americans are credited with enjoying the *mā'a tahiti*, the French are held to be collectively intolerant of it, and not a few people I knew invoked this as the reason why Polynesians liked Americans and have had such difficult relations with the French. As that suggests, food as a symbolic regime may be deployed to think through a wide range of relations of sameness, difference, and hierarchy, and tailored to a variety of meaning-making projects.

In addition, food as a symbolic form also carries moral meanings. Food exchanges between kin-related households, for example, were used to articulate moral claims about the people engaged in both giving and receiving. Gifts of traditional foods like the small clams (*tū'a'i*) dug from the silt bottom of Huahine's saltwater lake or the cooked meat from pigs caught in the mountains were shaded by the givers' self-representations as Polynesians who ate "traditional" foods and engaged in "traditional" labor: claims to be, as Polynesians phrased it, "true Mā'ohi." During my research, such "traditional" foods were regularly sent to kin-related households in Papeete, whose members could not go pig hunting or dig for *tū'a'i* or raise *taro* in the urban context in which they lived. Papeete households, in turn, sent to kin-related outer-island households store-bought foods, like rice, cooking oil, and tinned meat. The meanings of these kinds of foods and the exchanges in which they were embedded were laced with the changes of the prior thirty years, knotted up in moral messages about the shifting meanings of Polynesian labor practices and the moral character of differences between life on the outer islands and in the urban center.

Moralizing Labors

In the mid-1990s, the ways in which Polynesian men's cultivating and fishing labors were directed to feeding their households and into networks of exchange were both different from and more direct than women's labors. It was not only that women's labors more often earned money. Another significant difference was that, while women usually contributed a portion of their cash earnings to the households in which they resided, the money women earned was treated and understood as under their individual control. The products of men's labor, in contrast—not cash, but local foods—were far less under men's individual control: they were normatively required to go not only toward feeding men's households but also into the system of exchange between kin-related households.

This centrality of men's subsistence labor to the operation of the exchange system—one that produced and authorized kinship relations and social hierarchies both within and between households—points to a primary way in which the production of social relations through the system of exchange was fundamentally articulated with gender difference. For men, full adult masculinity was contingent on their success at "feeding" their families and kin, to such an extent that men's moral adulthood was most often evaluated on the basis of whether they provided food for their households and contributed to exchange relationships with extended kin households.

Or, at least, that was the prevailing discourse for signifying moral adult masculinity. By the mid-1990s another discourse was also available, one Mama Fa'atere had occasion one day to invoke. As described earlier, Mama Fa'atere was among the standard recipients of Ranunu's *fa'a'apu* food gifts. She, in turn, regularly gave Ranunu's wife, Vaihere, store-bought foods like rice, sugar, tinned meat, and cooking oil. One day Mama Fa'atere was recounting to me her recent round of attempts to adopt the eldest of Ranunu and Vaihere's five children, their fifteen-year-old daughter, and explaining to me how much better it would be for the girl to live at her household. At the time Mama Fa'atere was frustrated because Vaihere still had not agreed to the adoption—which challenged the hierarchy between the two women—and also because Vaihere had recently come to her for money to pay her household's electric bill. Mama Fa'atere launched her critique:

> It's not right. Ranunu doesn't work for money, and that's not right. Me, I work: I sew. I sell what I sew. I have a nice home. I give them food—when the [five] children come here I feed them. There, at their house, the children don't listen to the parents. The children don't work, and that's not right. The children get up in the morning and they go out: they go play, they go to the beach... . They don't work and that's not right. What's going to happen whey they get married? If they don't learn [to work] now, later on they're going to have some bad habits.

In this speech, Mama Fa'atere chides Ranunu for failing to engage in wage labor and links that to a larger moral failing in parenting, by articulating a competing moral scheme for evaluating labor practice. Instead of interpreting Ranunu as successfully achieving moral manhood by providing for his family from his *fa'a'apu* and fishing, Mama Fa'atere signifies Ranunu's failure to work for wages as seriously compromising his ability to create the proper hierarchical relations within his household. Ranunu's children are presented as failing to recognize the "feeding debt" they owe to their parents—exemplified by their failure to "listen" to their parents and to contribute to household labor. In Mama Fa'atere's critique, the reason the children do not recognize their feeding debt is because Ranunu is not "feeding" or providing for them properly. Thus, not only are the requisite hierarchical relationships within that household undermined, but also in jeopardy is the children's future ability to reproduce appropriate kinship relations and households. Not learning the right ways of working now, the children later on will not be able to work, parent, or reproduce their kin relations properly.

Of particular significance is that Mama Fa'atere aimed her criticisms at Ranunu, even though this drama unfolded in her relationship with Vaihere. Although the request for money to pay the electric bill came from Vaihere, it was Ranunu on whom Mama Fa'atere laid the blame and moral critique for the shortage of money in Vaihere's household. As that suggests, Mama Fa'atere was not holding Vaihere responsible for bringing money into her household—and, indeed, women who had men partners were not held responsible for that. In the competing moral discourse on men's labor that Mama Fa'atere used for her critique, however, men were held responsible not only for "feeding" their families but also for "feeding" their families in ways that were not narrowly about food. In that competing moral scheme for defining proper adult masculinity, the expansive symbolics Polynesians had developed around the meanings (and uses) of food had been melded into a broader notion of "providing": to properly "feed" their families, men must bring money into their households.

Shifting Political Economies of "Feeding"

Such competing moral frameworks for adjudicating the value of different labors and the gendered subjects who engage in them came about over the course of post-1950s changes to the Society Islands' political economy: from one organized around subsistence to one structured through market relations as an economic dependency of France. Between the early 1960s and the mid-1990s, gender differences were reshaped through complex dialogue with the shifting horizon of labor possibilities and the aspirations that attended these changes. Most relevant for the present analysis, these reshaped the regimes through which moral masculinity could be achieved.

In the 1990s, prevailing understandings of Polynesian masculinity still bound the performance of morally responsible manhood to traditional men's labor practices—*fa'a'apu* cultivation and fishing. Indeed, such labor practices continued to be the ones in which young boys were trained by their fathers and other adult men kin. Boys' gaining competence in "real Mā'ohi" (men's) labors was figured as so essential by adult men that it anchored a conflict between parents over boys' school attendance that was all too common: mothers who wanted their sons to attend school struggled with fathers who believed schooling was irrelevant to their sons' future—and who allied with their sons to support them in regularly cutting school to accompany adult men fishing or to the *fa'a'apu* and, eventually, to support their quitting school altogether. Such conflicts formed the backdrop for significant gender disparities in educational success: Polynesian boys dropped out of school at a rate consistently higher than that of Polynesian girls, and with lower-level certificates than girl age-mates as well.[8]

In such conflicts between parents in the mid-1990s, mothers' arguments for their sons' school attendance were founded in the belief that education was necessary for their sons' future ability to secure wage work. That belief, like Mama Fa'atere's critique of Ranunu's "traditional" laboring practice, reflected the emergence of a competing discourse on moral adult masculinity in which participation in the cash economy was deemed necessary for fulfilling that key criterion of morally successful manhood: "feeding" one's family. The metaphoric entailments of "feeding," and men's responsibilities to provide "food" for their families, had expanded such that the metaphor of "feeding" spoke through the larger political-economic shifts—articulating other ways men could, or should, provide for their households. In that competing discourse on moral adult masculinity, it was no longer enough for men to fish or grow local foods for their households: such activities did not pay the electric bill, the phone bill, or for the propane needed for cooking; it would not materialize pots, dishes, or even dish soap; it would not pay for parts to fix the ancient truck household members relied on to get to the health clinic in town; and it certainly would not buy the tinned meat, rice, cooking oil, sugar, and other grocery items that had by then become staples in Islander households.

By the early 1990s, participation in the market economy was not only desirable but also necessary for Society Islanders' household economies, in a French territory that by then had one of the highest costs of living in the Pacific. But while women had found ways to integrate into the market economy, men, and especially young men, had become significantly compromised in their abilities to participate in the French colonial labor market—even though access to cash was something virtually all of them wanted. Indeed, the difficulty of securing wage labor caused some young men to rethink the very trajectories of the life course they grew up expecting to follow. A *taure'are'a* nationalist supporter in his early twenties, for example, offered this poignant response to my asking him when he was going to marry and settle down:

> Right now, you see the work I do: I hang out at the house, I do some work on the house, but there's no money. I don't have any way to make money… To have a wife one must have money … to give food to their wife and children. Me, my belief is that one must wait. Right now I'm not looking for a wife because I have no way to give food to her and the children.

Mediating Households and Structures of Experience

An ethnographic focus on gender and labor practices in the Society Islands brings to light the micropolitics of households as lived contexts in which social differences, their experiential significance, and their political import are produced. As a primary site for constituting gendered relationships to labor and value, households are central in producing the striking gender and generational profile of the nationalist struggle. In Polynesian households, gender and generational differences were made meaningful through, for example, the different expectations adults had of boys and girls and the salience of generational hierarchies. They were also made meaningful through the very organization of household authority. In the mid-1990s, Islanders' households were usually managed by a senior woman—collectively designated "the Mamas"—who orchestrated the exchange relationships in which the household participated, managed household finances, and directed most of the labor projects of subordinate household members, including kin, visitors, and other residents whom the household head was "caring for."

Gender differences in labor practice became clearest when girls and boys became teenagers. During adolescence, girls commonly began contributing economically to their households: they were incorporated into the cash-earning labors of women relatives and kin-group patrons, taking on apprenticeships or otherwise beginning to work in ways that generated money. Sons, however, had a much harder time finding cash-generating work and, when they did find it, tended to hold jobs for only short periods of time. Such gender differences in success have been partially related to boys' compromised educational achievements rendering them less employable in the market economy. But boys also appeared less willing than girls to tolerate the disciplines of wage labor. While autonomy and freedom were often-stated concerns of Polynesians when evaluating labor project prospects, young and adult women had become better able to withstand the disciplines that characterized the French colonial labor market. Adult men, in contrast, regularly lauded their "traditional" labors of *fa'a'apu* work and fishing as providing the autonomy that, as one man told me, means "one is truly free."

By the mid-1990s, these and other factors had combined to encourage among young *taure'are'a* men the prevalent practice of moving between the households of their extended kin living in different villages and islands: a *taure'are'a* would reside in a given household for a few weeks or months before moving on to another relative's household. During such residencies, young men provided largely non-remunerated labor to their kin—contributing to *fa'a'apu* or fishing work, for example, or to home-improvement projects—in exchange for being "cared for" (fed and housed) by their relatives. While such mobility has a long historical association with the *taure'are'a* life stage and has been highly valued by both men and women (Elliston 2000; Oliver 1974: 611–614), by the early 1990s, changes had occurred in the directions of and reasons for travel, as well as in the gender of the travelers: the result was that residential mobility had increasingly become the province of young men. Indeed, *taure'are'a* men rarely stayed at a household for more than a few months and oftentimes for only a few weeks. And increasing numbers of young men headed for the households of relatives living in and around Papeete, in the hope of securing wage work that most were not able to find or, once found, were not able to hold for long.

The result was an emerging discourse on the unreliability, laziness, and even dangerousness of young *taure'are'a* men. While the long-standing meanings of the *taure'are'a* period signify it as "the season of joy, gaiety, and mirth" (Oliver 1974: 611), a celebrated period of the life cycle when one is free of adult responsibilities, by the early 1990s these meanings were deeply shaded in disapprobation: *taure'are'a* men were collectively cast as lazy, thieving, lacking self-control, and, thus, as becoming nationalist agitators only because "they have nothing better to do." Such a damning discourse, I suggest, merits critical interrogation. I follow Bucholtz's argument that anthropologists consider young people's forms of social action as "acts of cultural critique and cultural production" and as "agentic interventions into ongoing sociocultural change" (2002: 535). The ethnographic analyses offered in the preceding sections thus suggest an alternative sociological explanation: that the social dynamics animating the critical discourse about *taure'are'a* men spoke to and through young men's positioning between competing regimes of value, and gained potency through the everyday practices of reproducing household economies in a radically changed political economy. Sons and daughters had increasingly become differentially productive for their households, with daughters contributing some of their cash earnings and sons contributing labor. Sons were also increasingly held to be unreliable contributors to the household labor economy—in no small part because they tended to move around so often. By the mid-1990s, young men's compromised access to wage labor in conjunction with their mobility had come to have serious ramifications for the forms of authority they could exercise in their households: whereas daughters were actively involved in household decision-making and were being trained by senior women to become household heads, sons in their *taure'are'a* years had become increasingly marginal to household authority structures.

Political Economies of Nationalism

Perhaps the most significant finding to emerge from the shifting conjunctions of gender, generation, and labor tracked through this chapter is that, from childhood on, Polynesian boys and men became more invested in and dependent on the "traditional" Polynesian system of exchange and value than did girls and women. From boys' contested relationships to schooling to the subsistence labor practices in which they were trained as children and expected to practice as adults, the Polynesian "traditional" system had more salience in their lives. Girls, in contrast, from childhood on, negotiated between and combined Polynesian "traditional" with French "modern" systems of value: they succeeded at school while contributing productively to their households; they secured apprenticeships that taught them money-earning skills, while accepting lowered wages that reflected their commitments to the "traditional" exchange of labor for "food" and "care," and to the hierarchies that articulated; they gave store-bought foods to their relatives that reproduced exchange relationships and their values, while prioritizing cash labor for themselves and withstanding the disciplines it required.

It is thus not surprising that it would be among young *taure'are'a* men that conflict between these systems of value came to a head in the mid-1990s. *Taure'are'a* men emerged at the center of conflict between an economy of subsistence labor and exchange, on the one hand, and the French market and consumer economy, on the other; between Polynesian forms of exchange labor and autonomy and French forms of wage labor and work discipline; between Polynesians' desires and needs for money, and the difficulties and trade-offs they encountered in trying to acquire it.

That conflict and the various currents within it operated in multiple ways to draw young men to the frontlines of nationalist activism and into the center of the broader debate on independence. Many young men came to find the nationalist struggle a compelling object of commitment in no small part because it gave a legitimizing voice to the frustrations they experienced at the disjuncture between French "modern" and Polynesian "traditional" systems of value. In the nationalist struggle, these frustrations were refined as anger directed at French colonial rule and linked to a political project that had a clear solution: ending French colonialism. In contrast to the prevailing discourse in which young men were represented as a major social problem and blamed for a wide variety of social ills, the nationalist movement offered an alternative and, for many young men, much more compelling analysis: the problem was not them but French colonialism. No less important, the nationalist struggle also offered a solution: Polynesian independence. Thus, as part of its broader critique of French rule over the Society Islands the nationalist movement held out the promise of remedying young men's frustrated positioning.

Within that broader critique, the conflict between the values of a French market and consumer economy and those of a Polynesian subsistence and exchange economy was a complex site of concern lacing across many nationalist arguments for independence. Drawing on discourses of development, progress, and modernity, for example, one frequently heard argument for independence among Tavini Huira'atira nationalists was that French rule created only obstacles to Polynesians' abilities to benefit from the post-1950s economic changes. Specifically, these nationalists critiqued what they saw as the French state's sporadic and half-hearted commitments to developing local commercial fishing and agribusiness: even those tenuous commitments, they argued, were seriously compromised by France's international agreements and metropolitan economic priorities, which resulted in much of the produce sold in local grocery stores being imported from nations with which France had trade agreements or coming from France itself.

Perhaps most poignantly, nationalists highlighted the unbearable irony of the French state licensing Japanese and New Zealand fishing companies to catch prized bonita and other large fish in Polynesian waters while denying such opportunities to Polynesian men and effectively forcing Islanders to buy "their" fish back from foreign enterprises—often in canned form. In such nationalist narratives, the large-scale successful commercial ventures in which foreigners reaped the profits from abundant local marine life were juxtaposed to the ubiquitously small-scale Polynesian fishers who pulled their boats up to their island's wharf each afternoon to sell fish they had caught that day to local residents who knew to seek them out. In nationalist visions, then, independence would void France's monopoly over French Polynesia's extensive Exclusive Economic Zone (an area roughly the size of Europe), as well as France's circumscribing trade agreements, and instead inaugurate the genuine development of Polynesian-run commercial fisheries and agribusinesses.

As such examples suggest, and in contrast to the prevailing positioning of men's traditional laboring on the periphery of the market, nationalist arguments for independence rested on a promise to revise the hierarchies of value—economic, social, and moral—that structured young men's subordination through a fundamental reorganization of the Islands' political economy and whose interests would prevail within it. Nationalist narratives and visions reconfigured the conflict between the "modern" market economy and "traditional" subsistence economy by disaggregating component signifiers of "tradition" and "modernity" and reaggregating them into a new, more encompassing configuration in which they were no longer in conflict. In this reconfiguration, the forms of laboring associated with the market and the subsistence-exchange economies were no longer opposed and mutually exclusive: men no longer needed to abandon *fa'a'apu* work and fishing to make money. Instead, men's "traditional" labors were made the centerpiece of the post-independence nation's "modern" economic success: it was precisely agriculture and fishing that nationalists proposed to remunerate by developing Polynesian commercial fishing and agribusiness. Men's valorized "traditional" labors (the "true *Mā'ohi* life" and its labors) were thus resituated at the center of a post-independence market economy to take their place as the keys to wealth and prosperity in the post-independence Polynesian nation.

Finally, binding their passion to nationalist activism also offered young men a moral legitimacy they were relentlessly represented as lacking. If the damning discourse about *taure'are'a* men cast them as lazy for not finding or keeping wage work, irresponsible for their movements between households, and volatile when they protested, the nationalist movement offered another interpretation of where moral illegitimacy lay, at the same time validating the very practices that were cited as evidence of young men's shortcomings. Rather than young men's alleged failings or inadequacies, the obstacles to Polynesian development, progress, and modernity were now construed as France's self-interest, scheming, and exploitation: in short, France's ongoing rule over the territory. And to the extent that the damning discourse about young men rested on their status as *taure'are'a*, nationalist activism provided them with a further claim to moral legitimacy: precisely because *taure'are'a* were not yet bound to adult responsibilities, they were the ones best able to see the problems created by French colonialism and best positioned to bring about change. Such was the logic behind assertions like Ranunu's, offered just after the September protests: "It's the youth who will lead us to independence." Thus, in nationalist analyses, young men were not irresponsible but heroic; not maladjusted but justifiably angry; not failures because of their economic marginality but modern-day warriors fighting to overthrow the structures of French domination that had failed to serve not only their own interests but those of all Polynesians.

Conclusion

This chapter has sought to demonstrate the value of asking specifically sociological questions about gender and nationalism by, in particular, resituating the widespread phenomenon of young men's nationalist activism as an empirical problem to be studied, analyzed, and explained, rather than viewed as some "natural" state of affairs. "Why men?" and, for the Society Islands, "Why young men?" are questions that move researchers beyond the gender foundationalism of presuming a natural association between masculinity and nationalist struggle and into ethnographic terrain where we can investigate the social formation of gendered (and, in this case, generationally) distinctive political subjectivities and commitments. In the present case study, questioning young men's nationalist activism opens to view a sociological and historically emergent conflict: one between French colonial and Polynesian systems of value that have been shaped in and through gender and labor practices and the social, moral, and political entailments of different labor forms.

By way of concluding, I turn to address some of the comparative implications of the analyses developed in this chapter. First, as detailed in the preceding sections, the centrality of households in the dynamics shaping nationalist support and opposition points to the need for more extended ethnographic investigations into households as sites of and for the production and mediation of conflicts that may have direct ramifications for large-scale social processes and projects. In the Society Islands, the household emerges not only as an institution commonly managed by senior women but also as the central institution for the management of labor, kinship, exchange, money, and social hierarchy. In this case study, then, and likely in others as well, the household is not an institution that may be contained within such constructs as the "domestic" or "private" sphere, feminized constructs that are so often cast as the reproductive domain of tradition and set against the "public" sphere of a masculinized modernity.

Second, the conflict between Polynesian and French regimes of value raises a set of comparative questions about the meanings of "tradition" and "modernity" as these relate to nationalism. In the feminist scholarship on gender and nationalism, for example, scholars have commonly held that the gendered associations of tradition and modernity align women with tradition and its reproduction in a protected domestic sphere while aligning men with a modernity shaped in a public sphere of political and economic activity. These gendered alignments, furthermore, are commonly held to produce a symbolic economy in which women's association with tradition and relative exclusion from modernity underwrite women's exclusion from political agency in the emerging nation.[9] In the Society Islands, however, such gendered associations are substantially reconfigured. Initially it may appear as a reversal of the standard case, tempting us to interpret Polynesian women as more closely associated with "modernity" through their deeper integration with the French market economy, and Polynesian men as more closely associated with "tradition" through their deeper integration with the subsistence and exchange economy. However, I would argue against such an interpretation and instead argue for a critical reevaluation of the very viability of tagging "tradition" and "modernity" with such unequivocal gendered valences, and the viability of analyzing political subjectivities in relation to such unequivocally gendered spheres. The Polynesian case compels a re-analysis of such bifurcated productions as "tradition" and "modernity" as unstable and varying cultural productions and discursive resources that gain their meanings in and through social practices and conflictual negotiations.

Third, and finally, I suggest that conflicts between regimes of value, like the one so apparent in the Society Islands, may be involved not only in the gender dynamics of other nationalist struggles but also in young men's marginality more broadly, a phenomenon that is hardly specific to the Society Islands. The marginality of young Polynesian men has striking parallels with that of young men in societies that are not sites of nationalist struggle but, rather, are deeply engaged in neoliberal processes of globalization. Common characteristics include young men becoming less competitive than young women in the labor market, developing elevated school-leaving rates, and becoming objects of blame in local discourses about social problems (Bucholtz 2002). Such common characteristics suggest that there may be similarities meriting deeper investigation between processes of neoliberal globalization and those through which a colonial power cultivates economic dependency, beyond the obvious similarity of hierarchical economic relations.

One such set of similarities may involve the ways both processes promote regimes of value that privilege wage labor and the market economy and, in so doing, introduce alternative pathways to status. These innovations, in turn, may stand in awkward or even oppositional relationship to the regimes of value that otherwise organize the meanings of labor practices and the trajectories through which labor practices secure moral and social value. In the Society Islands, for example, one of the effects of France's rapid cultivation of the territory as an economic dependency was challenges to the "traditional" bases of moral adult masculinity. Thus the hierarchies of value produced through both neoliberal globalization and economic dependency may more broadly undermine the relationships that structure the moral meanings of labor practice, leading to ambivalence and contestation or even upheaval and rebellion.

Relatedly, the present case study offers cautionary lessons for investigating young men's economic marginality. In the Society Islands, it would be a mistake to explain young men's nationalist activism as a mere reflex response to their economic disenfranchisement, giving no play to the complexities of their positionings, the contradictory discourses in which they are caught up, or the thoughtfulness with which they consider their predicaments and possibilities. As distinct from such simplistic economic determinism, the questions I have pursued here advocate more dynamic and processual theorizations of gender and labor as social practices situated within larger social fields and processes. Thus, scholars might ask not only how young men's marginality is understood but how, precisely, it has been produced and to what it has been bound. It is not, in other words, a matter of seeing young men as "failing to adjust" to the demands or disciplines of a market economy: what counts as "failure" or "success" must itself be critically examined as part of how we apprehend and analyze the processes through which marginality is produced—and through which a nationalist struggle may become a compelling and persuasive solution to it.

Notes

This chapter is a revised and condensed version of an earlier journal article, entitled "A Passion for the Nation: Masculinity, Modernity, and Nationalist Struggle," that was published in 2005 in the *American Ethnologist* 31 (4): 606–630. Research in the Society Islands was generously supported by grants from New York University (1993), and from the Wenner-Gren Foundation and the Social Sciences and Humanities Research Council of Canada (1994–1995). For comments that helped to clarify the analysis here, I especially thank Douglas J. Glick, J. Kehaulani Kauanui, Jane Moulin, Fred Myers, Bill Rodman, and Deborah Thomas.

Note on Orthography. The Tahitian language orthography used in this article follows that of the Tahitian Academy (Académie Tahitienne – Fare V na'a 1999).

1. See, for example, the classic formulations of key questions in the gender and nationalism scholarship in Anthias and Yuval-Davis (1989) and McClintock (1993, 1995); Yuval-Davis (1997) provides a useful overview. While the oftentimes masculinist projects embedded in nationalism and nation building have been a site of analysis in this scholarship, such a focus differs substantively from one turned to masculinities and nationalism.

2. Primary ethnographic research for this chapter was conducted between November 1994 and November 1995 in the Society Islands of French Polynesia, and augmented by shorter periods of fieldwork both before and after. As that suggests, this chapter focuses on the Society Islands (abbreviated as "the Islands" in the text), one of five archipelago groups in French Polynesia but residential home to 83 percent of the territory's total population of about 200,000 (Institute Territorial du Statistique 1991 [2]: 19). In focusing on the Society Islands, this analysis does not speak to the different dynamics that may structure gender and nationalism in the four other archipelagos, given the significant historical, religious, cultural, and linguistic differences between them.

   Relatedly, my use of the term *Polynesians (Polynésiens)* for people of the Society Islands follows local self-naming preferences and practices and does not refer to all peoples of the culture area of Polynesia. The more common term for Society Islanders (also abbreviated as "Islanders" in the text), *Tahitians*, has been an object of indigenous critique (Raapoto 1988), in part because, as I have argued elsewhere (Elliston 2000), the significances of place-based identifications (especially with islands) renders *Tahitians* too specific to Tahiti island.

3. This chapter is not a comprehensive analysis of the gendered and generational dynamics of the Polynesian nationalist struggle. Other key dimensions are treated elsewhere and include, for example, the potency of "place" difference and its gendered dynamics (Elliston 2000); political practice in the Islands and gendered readings of the meanings of "politics" (Elliston 1997); and the historicity of French colonialism, including the practices of French colonial rule in the Islands in the mid-1990s (Elliston 1997).

4. The protests began within a week of the June 1995 announcement by then-newly elected President of France, Jacques Chirac, that France would undertake a new series of nuclear tests at its Tuamotu test sites. Chirac's announcement, in turn, came in the wake of a three-year moratorium on nuclear testing under former French President François Mitterrand and in the context of the impending signing of an international nuclear test ban treaty that had been covered in some depth by local media in the Islands. Although Polynesians had waged periodic protests against the nuclear testing program since it was relocated to the territory in the 1960s, prior to 1995 nuclear testing had not been an issue that had galvanized mass protests for any sustained period (Danielsson and Danielsson 1986).

5. I treat "tradition" and "modernity" as heuristic formulations rather than as descriptive or ontological categories; as heuristics, they index the polarized ends of a spectrum that gained its meanings through distinctions Polynesians made in the everyday practices of social relations.

6. Since the nuclear testing program became operational in 1966, France has detonated more than 170 atmospheric and subterranean nuclear tests on these two atolls. On the history and effects of the nuclear testing program see Barrillot (1996), Chesneaux (1995), Danielsson and Danielsson (1986), Robineau (1984), and de Vries and Seur (1997).

7. I use the term "men" rather than the more common term "male" here and throughout this chapter to foreground the social bases of gender subjectivity and performativity. As that suggests, this representational choice involves a critical rejection of the ways common usage of "male" relies upon formulations and positionings of gender that are biologized rather than socialized.

8. Based on 1991 statistics, of Polynesians age fifteen and older, 68 percent of boys and 58 percent of girls on the academic track finished their education without achieving any school certificate; 25 percent of boys and 30 percent of girls left school with about a sixth-grade education; 7 percent of boys and 12 percent of girls left with about a ninth-grade education; and 0.9 percent of boys and 1.3 percent of girls achieved a high school diploma *(le bac)* (ITSTAT 1991 [2]: 111).

9. Because these are prevailing lines of analysis in feminist scholarship on gender and nationalism and modernity, the relevant works overflow the space of a footnote. See, for example, Yuval-Davis (1997) for an overview; the more widely cited formulations include Anthias and Yuval-Davis (1989), McClintock (1993, 1995), and Chatterjee (1993). Works that focus more specifically on gendered mediations of modernity, setting aside questions of nationalism, have developed along more varied lines of analysis: see, as a small sampling, Adams and Pigg (2005), Hodgson (1999), Mills (1997), and Schein (2000).

Bibliography

Académie Tahitienne – Fare V na'a. 1999. *Dictionnaire Tahitien–Français. Fa'atoro Parau Tahiti/Far ni*. Papeete: Académie Tahitienne–Fare V na'a.

Adams, Vincanne, and Stacy Leigh Pigg, eds. 2005. *Sex in Development: Science, Sexuality, and Morality in Global Perspective*. Durham: Duke University Press.

Anthias, Floya, and Nira Yuval-Davis. 1989. "Introduction." In *Woman-Nation-State*, eds. Nira Yuval-Davis and Flora Anthias. New York: St. Martin's Press.

Barrillot, B. 1996. *Les essais nucléaires français, 1960–1996, conséquences sur l'environnement et la santé*. Lyon: Centre de Documentation et de Recherche sur la Paix et les Conflits.

Brady, Ivan, ed. 1976. *Transactions in Kinship: Adoption and Fosterage in Oceania*. Honolulu: University of Hawai'i Press.

Bucholtz, Mary. 2002. "Youth and Cultural Practice." *Annual Review of Anthropology*, 31:525–552.

Chatterjee, Partha. 1993. *The Nation and Its Fragments: Colonial and Postcolonial Histories*. Princeton: Princeton University Press.

Chesneaux, Jean, ed. 1995. *Tahiti aprés la bombe. Quel avenir pour la Polynésie?* Paris: l'Harmattan.

Danielsson, Bengt, and Marie-Thérèse Danielsson. 1986. *Poisoned Reign: French Nuclear Colonialism in the Pacific*. 2nd edition. Victoria, Australia: Penguin Books.

de Vries, Pieter, and Han Seur. 1997. *Moruroa and Us: Polynesians' Experiences during Thirty Years of Nuclear Testing in the French Pacific*. Lyon: Centre de Documentation et de Recherche sur la Paix et les Conflits.

Elliston, Deborah A. 1997. *En/Gendering Nationalism: Colonialism, Sex, and Independence in French Polynesia*. Ph.D. diss., Department of Anthropology, New York University.

———. 2000. "Geographies of Gender and Politics: The Place of Difference in Polynesian Nationalism." *Cultural Anthropology*, 15 (2): 171–216.

Fajans, Jane. 1993. "The Alimentary Structures of Kinship: Food and Exchange among the Baining of Papua New Guinea." In *Exchanging Products, Producing Exchange*, ed. Jane Fajans. Sydney: Oceania Publications, University of Sydney.

Finney, Ben R. 1965. "Polynesian Peasants and Proletarians: Socio-Economic Change among the Tahitians of French Polynesia." *Journal of the Polynesian Society*, 74 (3): 269-328.

Hammond, Joyce D. 1986. *Tifaifai and Quilts of Polynesia*. Honolulu: University of Hawai'i Press.

Hanson, F. Allan. 1970. *Rapan Lifeways: Society and History on a Polynesian Island*. Boston: Little, Brown.

Henningham, Stephen. 1992. *France and the South Pacific: A Contemporary History*. Honolulu: University of Hawai'i Press.

Hodgson, Dorothy L. 1999. "'Once Intrepid Warriors': Modernity and the Production of Maasai Masculinities." *Ethnology*, 38 (2): 121–150.

Hooper, Antony. 1970. "Adoption in the Society Islands." In *Adoption in Eastern Oceania*, ed. Vern Carroll. Honolulu: University of Hawai'i Press.

Howard, Alan, and John Kirkpatrick. 1989. "Social Organization." In *Developments in Polynesian Ethnology*, eds. Alan Howard and Robert Borofsky. Honolulu: University of Hawai'i Press.

ITSTAT [Institut Territorial de la Statistique]. 1991. *Résultats du recensement général de la population du 6 September 1988*. 2 vols. Papeete: Polytram.

———. 1999. *Résultats du recensement général de la population de la Polynésie française du 3 September 1996*. Papeete: ITSTAT.

Jones, Anna Laura. 1991. "Contemporary Folk Art in French Polynesia." Ph.D. diss., Department of Anthropology, Stanford University.

———. 1992. "Women, Art, and the Crafting of Ethnicity in Contemporary French Polynesia." *Pacific Studies*, 15 (4): 137–154.

La Dépêche de Tahiti. 1995. "Le mercredi noir de Tahiti [Tahiti's black Wednesday]." *La Dépêche de Tahiti*. 9 September: 29-48.

Lévi-Strauss, Claude. 1969[1949]. *The Elementary Structures of Kinship*. Boston: Beacon Press.

Levy, Robert I. 1973. *Tahitians: Mind and Experience in the Society Islands*. Chicago: University of Chicago Press.

Linnekin, Jocelyn. 1985. *Children of the Land: Exchange and Status in a Hawaiian Community*. New Brunswick: Rutgers University Press.

Mauss, Marcel. 1967 [1954]. *The Gift: Forms and Functions of Exchange in Archaic Society*. Translated by Ian Cunnison. New York: W.W. Norton.

McClintock, Anne. 1993. "Family Feuds: Gender, Nationalism and the Family." *Feminist Review*, 44: 61–80.

———. 1995. *Imperial Leather: Race, Gender, and Sexuality in the Colonial Contest*. New York: Routledge.

Mills, Mary Beth. 1997. "Contesting the Margins of Modernity: Women, Migration, and Consumption in Thailand." *American Ethnologist*, 24 (1): 37-61.

Mohanty, Chandra Talpade. 1991. "Under Western Eyes: Feminist Scholarship and Colonial Discourses." In *Third World Women and the Politics of Feminism*, eds. Chandra Talpade Mohanty et al. Bloomington: Indiana University Press.

Myers, Fred R. 1993. "Place, Identity, and Exchange in a Totemic System: Nurturance and the Process of Social Reproduction in Pintupi Society." In *Exchanging Products, Producing Exchange*, ed. Jane Fajans. Sydney, Australia: Oceania Publications, University of Sydney.

Newbury, Colin W. 1980. *Tahiti Nui: Change and Survival in French Polynesia, 1767–1945*. Honolulu: University of Hawai'i Press.

Oliver, Douglas L. 1974. *Ancient Tahitian Society*. 3 vols. Honolulu: University of Hawai'i Press.

———. 1981. *Two Tahitian Villages: A Study in Comparison*. Laie, Hawaii: Institute for Polynesian Studies.

Raapoto, Turo A. 1988. "Maohi: On Being Tahitian." In *French Polynesia,* eds. Nancy J. Pollock and Ron Crocombe. Suva: Institute of Pacific Studies, University of the South Pacific.

Rallu, J.-L. 1991. "Population of the French Overseas Territories in the Pacific, Past, Present, and Projected." *Journal of Pacific History*, 26 (2): 169–186.

Regnault, Jean-Marc. 1993. *La bombe française dans le Pacifique: l'Implantation 1957–1964*. Papeete: Scoop Editions.

Robineau, Claude. 1984. *Du coprah à l'atome*. Paris: ORSTOM.

Schein, Louisa. 2000. *Minority Rules: The Miao and the Feminine in China's Cultural Politics*. Durham: Duke University Press.

von Strokirch, Karin. 1993. "Tahitian Autonomy: Illusion or Reality?" Ph.D. diss., Department of Politics, School of Social Sciences, La Trobe University, Victoria, Australia.

Weiner, Annette B. 1992. *Inalienable Possessions: The Paradox of Keeping-while-Giving*. Berkeley: University of California Press.

Yanagisako, Sylvia Junko, and Jane Fishburne Collier. 1987. "Toward a Unified Analysis of Gender and Kinship." In *Gender and Kinship: Essays toward a Unified Analysis*, eds. Jane Fishburne Collier and Sylvia Junko Yanagisako. Stanford: Stanford University Press.

Yuval-Davis, Nira. 1997. *Gender and Nation*. London: Sage.

Chapter 6

GOOD HEARTS OR BIG BELLIES
Dzmak'atsoba and Images of Masculinity in the Republic of Georgia

Martin Demant Frederiksen

"When a baby is born and the mother gently kisses its forehead the baby cannot feel the kiss, it does not know where it comes from although the love in this kiss is stronger than any other. Years later, when the mother dies and her child kisses her forehead before she is buried, the same strong affection is there, but this time it is the mother who cannot feel the kiss and the love that is given. Still the love is stronger than anything. This is a toast about the love that exists between people, a love that we sometimes cannot immediately sense, but which is still there, stronger maybe, than the love we can physically feel."

It was this man next to me who first told me this toast. I didn't know him that well at the time, but after hearing him propose this toast I realized that he was a good man, with a good heart.

—Gia, twenty years old, giving a toast while speaking about a new acquaintance

Introduction: An Honest Thief

It is around noon when Avto[1] bursts into the room. We are sitting in the living room of Temo's parents where I am conducting an interview with Temo and his younger brother Mamuka. Temo was drinking with some friends last night to the dissatisfaction of his father and mother. As a result they have had an argument in the morning and it was questionable whether we would be able to meet. Temo looks tired. His thick black hair is messy and his voice rusty from cigarettes. The table is set with cakes, hazelnuts, and Turkish coffee. Vanya, my assistant and a close friend of Temo, is also present. We are discussing what it means to be a man in Georgia. The interview is disrupted when Avto enters and throws himself into a chair. His moves are hectic and his eyes are blurred. His clothes look both newer and smarter than those of anybody else present. Around his wrist dangles a large watch covered with white and pink imitation diamonds, a stark contrast to the style of the rest of the room, which is modestly furnished with old chairs and a small table. Temo explains who I am and what we are doing; Avto asks me if I have any questions for him. Out of curiosity I ask him where he bought the watch. "I didn't buy it, I stole it!" Avto promptly answers. His profession, it turns out, is thieving. Sometimes he also smuggles narcotics over the border from Turkey by swallowing it in small plastic bags. It is mainly for himself, though, he assures me; he is not a drug dealer. It seems important for him to highlight this assertion.

Avto joins our discussion of masculinity and the small group soon agrees that Avto's father could be seen as an archetype of a good man as he is honest, clever, respectable, and has a family that he provides for. Only moments before, as Avto was describing his life as a thief, he did so by contrasting himself with his own father and now this contrast suddenly turns Avto into the antithesis of a good man. A sense of ambiguity suddenly surrounds the discussion and the others begin to rework what it means to be a good man in this particular setting. Some home-made wine is brought to the table and in a toast Temo thus reassures Avto that although he is a thief he is first of all a good friend: a man with a good heart and a good soul (kai guli da kai suli).

This and similar events prompted my investigation of how young men in Georgia seek to create alternative and permanent realms in which they can be perceived as morally "good men" during a period of chronic crisis that has severely affected their ability to become good men in a traditional sense.

For young men in present-day Georgia aspirations of masculinity have become complex, as both time-honored capacities of "good men" and newer indexes of financial success have become difficult to achieve. Being able to take care of one's family, being a generous host, and being able to provide an abundance of wine, verses, and toasts has a long history as a key marker of masculinity in the southern Caucasus, epitomized by sturdy men sitting amid their vast family and possessions. A newer version of masculine success is the nouveau-riche businessman with a big chin, a big belly, and a new four-wheel-drive car. Both of these images are based on questions of abundance and display. But sitting in Temo's parent's living room we seem far removed from these images and displays. In the Republic of Georgia, the male role as a provider for one's family has been greatly challenged by the social fragmentation that has been experienced widely across the country in the wake of the civil wars and socio-economic detour arising in the aftermath of independence from the Soviet Union in the early 1990s.

The Post-Soviet Context

With the notable exception of Rebecca Kay's work on fathers in contemporary Russia (2005; 2007), there has been little focus on the frailty of masculinity in the post-Soviet region. Some authors have touched upon the ways in which gender roles have altered in the wake of the Soviet Union, but the focus has been mainly on women (Gal and Kligman 2000; Kay 2007b). David Kideckel, writing about industrial workers in Romania, makes use of Sherry Ortner's (1996) concept of "gender damage" in order to explain how the post-socialist experience has stripped away predictable contents and practices of gender identities (Kideckel 2008: 156). Living in a situation of loss has been the daily fare for numerous groups in the post-Soviet region. Caroline Humphrey calls these groups dispossessed,[2] that is, "people who have been deprived of property, work, and entitlements" (Humphrey 2002: 21).

In this chapter I expand Humphrey's notion of dispossession to include the kind of "gender damage" described by Kideckel. This kind of dispossession I will refer to as emasculation; the sense of having lost formerly well-established ways of proving oneself as a man. The emasculation caused in post-Soviet Georgia by poverty and unemployment has sparked pursuits of manliness through self-destructive endeavors such as heavy drinking and crime. Within anthropology, there have been numerous studies of male youth which focus on how their search for masculinity and respect often entails self-destructive actions such as drug use, violence, or outright engagement in war. For many young men in Georgia this kind of behavior is by no means exceptional, but engagement with self-destructive endeavours is not the road taken by all. My empirical context is the port city Batumi in western Georgia where I have conducted long-term fieldwork[3] among what I term the first post-Soviet generation, that is, those who do not have any personal recollections of the Soviet period and grew up during the social fragmentation of the 1990s. For my informants, many of the aspects noted by Kay were present in their own daily lives as well as in the lives of their fathers. Some were alcoholics or struggling with drug use;[4] others were or had been engaged in various forms of criminal activity. Few had an education that could be put to use, and even those with jobs had difficulty in making ends meet as salaries were low.

In her study of young teenagers in Russia, Fran Markowitz (2000) has argued that, unlike their parents, the young people she followed seemed to handle the post-Soviet chaos better. Having come of age in a society of changes, she writes, they had learned to plan their future in a more pragmatic way as instability for them had become a stability in itself (Markowitz: 217). Although I agree with Markowitz that there is certainly a contrast in the ways different generations have reacted to the post-Soviet crisis, this does not preclude the possibility that many young people view the crisis and its aftermath as a virtually unwinnable struggle. For the young men I followed in Batumi, the social changes of the 1990s did not signify a rupture of an already established life, but a backdrop against which to begin a life. Having little with which to build their lives, creating something new became pertinent for these young men in order to face the difficulties presented by the current situation. This, I argue, is not merely a matter of wanting to be different than one's parents, as is often the case for young people around the world, but rather an imposed *need* to be different from the men of elder generations who were immobilized by the fall of the Soviet Union.

In exploring the above issues, I take as my point of departure the notion of *dzmak'atsoba*,[5] referred to here as brotherhood or brother-men. In doing so, I show how practices of physical, economic, and moral support amid groups of *dzmak'atsebi* are drawn on in creating oneself as a "good-hearted man" in a situation of chronic crisis. The chapter derives from an analytical interest in how the future informs present action, and it explores my informants' attempts to convert changed images of masculinity into a workable set of practices that can lead them into the future as "good Georgian men" whether as thieves, sailors, or bartenders. I show how, in the shadow of unobtainable masculine ideals and images, these young men struggle to create or uphold a valid moral and social world that holds within it a sense of permanency. *Dzmak'atsoba*, I argue, can be seen as a social tool used to tame an otherwise uncertain future in a period of continuous crisis.

After presenting the field more thoroughly, I describe a traditional image of masculinity and the ways in which it has been challenged by social fragmentation. Following this I explore how the *biznes-man* has risen from these fragments, creating an image of masculinity even harder to achieve. I go on to situate the experiences of my informants within this historical and socioeconomic framework of "transitions" in order to show how the role of brotherhood has become an arena in which young men in Georgia can be perceived as morally good men, at least by each other, thus creating both a situation that makes it worthwhile to keep struggling as well as circumstances that—should they get married—would be better for their own future children.

Social Fragmentation and Young Men in Crisis

The city of Batumi is located in the far eastern corner of the Black Sea. It is the capital of the autonomous republic of Adjara and, with around 130,000 inhabitants, is the third largest city in the republic of Georgia. In the summer season, stretching from early August to late September, the city is normally a bustling place hosting thousands of tourists from the southern Caucasus. Local service workers, as well as students coming in from other cities in Georgia, can earn up to a year's wages during the summer season from jobs in cafés, hotels, and bars. But in early August of 2008, just as the tourists had started to arrive, war between Georgia and Russia broke out and everything in Batumi came to a sudden stop. Within days, almost all of the beach cafés closed, thousands of people lost their jobs, and most of them faced an autumn and winter with no savings and almost no chance of finding another job. Hovering over the city at this time was a feeling of a paradise lost and of possibilities once again having been dissolved. In August 2008, the immediate crisis of the war certainly contributed to this sensation, but the ongoing losses and deprivations created by the tumultuous changes of the post-Soviet period were the main backdrop.

As with the capital, Tbilisi, Batumi was a multiethnic and vigorous city at the turn of the twentieth century. In 1921, after having been under Turkish control, Batumi and the rest of the Ajara region was ceded to the Soviet Union and granted status as an autonomous Soviet Socialist Republic. In this period the region grew to become a favored holiday destination for Soviet leaders and others who could afford it, and the tropical climate made it a main area for growing tea, tobacco, and citrus. In 1991, as the Soviet Union collapsed, Ajara became part of the republic of Georgia, although until 2004 the authoritarian leader, Aslan Abashidze, governed it in effect as an independent entity. On an economic level, it was one of the less affected regions in Georgia, yet the post-Soviet period still hit Ajara hard. The lush tea and citrus terraces surrounding the city and spreading into the region became mere vegetation as the processing factories closed down. Further, as the number of holiday-makers from the other Soviet republics dropped dramatically, the tourism infrastructure was allowed to deteriorate, and even though attempts had been made to reverse this process, the skeletons of old tourist structures are still scattered along the coast to this day. Container and cargo ships continued to enter the port to carry away Caspian oil and scrap metal, but with the financial crisis of late 2008 activity in the port diminished.

At the time of my fieldwork the port, seaside-boulevard, and parks were mostly populated by young men walking around in small groups, some with arms around each other's shoulders, smiling, talking confidentially, and stealing glances at girls passing by, others mock-fighting and chasing each other, some in vivid discussion and still others sitting leaning back on benches alone or in groups eating sunflower seeds and smoking cigarettes in silence. The unemployed young men in Batumi were considered a menace; in schools boys were referred to as "lazy" and many local and international NGOs in Georgia were focusing their activities on women while the young men were often considered to be out of reach—a lost generation. Between the summers of 2008 and 2009 I conducted fieldwork among groups of such young men.

My informants were roughly between the ages of eighteen and twenty-five. Although some of them had been born in the Soviet Union, their only memories of this period were derived from the stories of their parents and grandparents. Almost all of them were unemployed or underemployed, many had only basic education, and most were living at home with their parents or grandparents. They all knew each other more or less through various degrees of friendship bonds, and I mainly focused my research on two groups of friends comprising a total of about twenty-five to thirty persons. I met most of them during or immediately after the August 2008 war when they, along with numerous other people in Batumi, lost their jobs as the tourist season came to an abrupt halt. Only a few months later, as the international financial crisis put a stop to most of the foreign investments in the region, the situation became even grimmer in terms of the opportunities available to young men in Batumi. The numerous sailors in the city had difficulty being hired onto container ships, and those who had worked in the construction business found themselves jobless as many building projects were abandoned. Most of the time that I spent together with my informants consisted in *birdja*—hanging out—on the shore, by the port, in parks, or in my or their apartments. On rarer occasions, we made small drinking parties, making toasts[6] in local vodka and wine, or went on picnics outside town. Such occasions were relatively rare as they cost money, but they were highly prized.

All my informants had reached an age when they either wanted to or were expected to begin thinking about starting a family of their own, a task that for the majority of them seemed almost impossible to accomplish. In addition to losing their jobs, many had also lost their girlfriends during the aftermath of war and financial crisis. By virtue of being unemployed they ceased to be prospective husbands, especially in the eyes of possible in-laws. As mentioned in the introduction, the role as a family provider is a key marker of being a man in Georgia. Although this primarily relates to taking care of one's family, it also means being able to host guests. Images of masculinity and traditional expectations of men were issues that were often raised during interviews, as were the difficulties met by young men in achieving these expectations. The following descriptions outline the aspects of the appearance of a typical "successful man" in Georgia that were most commonly mentioned by young men and women alike: a big-bellied man sitting at a richly set table in his home, drinking wine while making elaborate toasts of love and friendship, surrounded by an expansive family and members of a large network of relations. The representation of "the good man" thus combined the roles of a host, an able drinker, and a poetic speaker. This is a stereotype that has a long tradition in the country. "A guest is sent from God," a popular saying goes, and being a host is seen as an honor and has been seen as such for centuries. The status connected to rituals of display, hospitality, and generosity was met with crisis by the poverty that struck the country in the early 1990s.

Becoming a provider and sustaining that position became a difficult task in the wake of the massive unemployment that followed the general socio-economic breakdown in the 1990s and this proved to be a humiliating experience for many men as well as a serious obstacle for boys aspiring to become men—a situation that has remained so until today. The emasculation caused by poverty and unemployment created a pursuit of manliness through self-destructive endeavors such as heavy drinking, turning the traditional rituals of toast-making into an excuse solely for drinking, and leaving aside the conventional connection with food and sociality. In Batumi it is not an unusual sight to see drunken men in the streets or to be invited to have a drink by a man standing alone with a bottle, fumbling with his words, eager to make the move from saying the toast to drinking. Men drinking this way are looked upon by my informants with regret rather than admiration and respect, but several had fathers, uncles, or older brothers who had ended up in this situation, so it was difficult for them to distance themselves from such characters completely. Based on a survey made at the turn of the millennium, Nora Dudwick noted that in Georgia men of all ages were battling with "male" health problems caused by drinking and heavy smoking (Dudwick 2003: 236).

Another outcome of the post-Soviet period was that crime rates had risen considerably since the early 1990s, especially among boys and men between the ages of fifteen and thirty-five, criminal activities becoming one of only a few available economic options (Dudwick 2003: 240). This continued to be the case in Batumi at the time of my fieldwork. In the prison just outside of town inmates were forced to sleep in shifts due to a lack of beds, and stories of criminal networks in the city recurred frequently in the interviews I conducted.

For the young men that I tracked, the emasculation of the post-Soviet period had resulted in a lack of male role models. "I don't really have any adult men to look up to," one of them explained at one point when we were talking about the meaning of being a man, "so I more or less have to try and figure it out on my own." This was a common sentiment usually based on the fact that many of them had experienced the real or de facto absence of an involved father—as a result of death, migration, or alcoholism. Thinking ahead, this was a situation many of these young men felt they needed to change if they were to become very different kinds of fathers themselves.

Strength in Numbers: New Images of Masculinity

Walking around the city, however, revealed that it was not difficult to see men who had achieved substantial success in their lives. In the midst of the abovementioned images of frail masculinity marked by financial and social fragmentation there were also images of financial success. New modes of display appeared not in the shape of a well-set table for guests but rather in the form of numbers, more specifically in automobile number plates. Imported Mercedes and BMWs sped around the city, flashing number plates such as GGG700, WWW222, BUK500, and BAA100. While these number plates might appear insignificant at first glance, the symbolic value inherent in the simplicity of a number plate was much discussed among my informants—the more straightforward the number plate, the wealthier the driver. It was rumored that a personalized number plate could cost as much as $10,000.00 (U.S.). The owners of such cars were often either politicians or businessmen who had achieved financial success in the aftermath of the Soviet period.

According to Joma Nazpary (2001), an anthropologist who has worked in Kazakhstan, the situation of the dispossessed became apparent in the post-Soviet period as a distinction between consumption and consumerism came into being. As he notes, "consumption is orientated toward the use value of the goods due to their physical structure and material substances. Consumerism is related to prestige/sign values inscribed in them by the genres of fashion and the advertisements which form the social practices of 'distinction'" (Nazpary 2001: 140). While these new modes of consuming created a sense of disillusionment among many of those who were unable to partake of it (Creed 2002; Frederiksen 2008; Humphrey 2002; Shevchenko 2002), others were able to take advantage of the situation and use it to display newly acquired wealth. Hence, at the same time as lines appeared in front of bakeries and beggars rose in numbers in the streets, so too did new Mercedes with "straightforward" number plates as well as people wearing designer clothes while going out to new fashionable cafés, casinos, and restaurants. In Batumi, this was the case in the 1990s and continues to be today. New or renovated houses appeared alongside dilapidated buildings and even after the economic detour of late 2008, when even more people started begging door-to-door, bigger and newer black cars began to drive around the city center. The fact that consumerism and the driving of Mercedes became a part of the social landscape is a clear sign that not everyone experienced the post-Soviet era as one of loss and degradation.

As Katherine Verdery (1996) has argued in relation to the general post-Soviet region, this was a period of agency over structure which ignited legal and illegal entrepreneurial activities. The image of the *biznes-man*[7] entered the scene in many former Soviet republics (Lindquist 2006; Louw 2008), not least in Georgia. For the young men in Batumi, however, the image of the successful big-bellied *biznes-man* was in some respects also a negative one. The success of these *biznes-men* was often explained by informants and many others as the result of illicit activities such as drug dealing or corruption. It is possible, of course, that the negative sentiments towards *biznes-men* expressed by my informants were a result of their resentful realization that they would probably never have an opportunity to drive a new car with a fancy number plate, but these young men nonetheless often maintained that they themselves were better men than these *biznes-men*.

In the following section I will situate the everyday lives and histories of some of my informants within the historical framework presented above and describe how *dzmak'atsoba* is used to maneuver within these changing images. For young men in Batumi, coming of age has been marked by the political chaos of the 1990s and the criminal networks that dominated the city during the time of Aslan Abashidze. Many of the big bellied *biznes-men* rose to financial success and gained their big bellies in this period. As will become clear, the fact that the *biznes-men* were often looked upon in terms of a negative image had less to do with the fact that their activities were illegal than with the fact that they were rumored to have forgotten their friends after earning their money. They had big bellies, but not good hearts.

Dzmak'atsoba and Good Hearts

As mentioned earlier, my informants to a large extent all knew each other, either as mere acquaintances or as "brother-men." In the following I will focus mainly on two of them, Vanya and Zviad, and use their stories to describe the role of *dzmak'atsoba* among young men in Batumi.

A Moral Obligation

A few months into my fieldwork my wife had visited me in Batumi. It was during this period that I first met Vanya. He had worked as a waiter at one of the beach cafés but lost his job due to the diminished tourist season. A few hours after my wife had flown back to Denmark, Vanya came to my apartment. Initially I thought that Vanya was responding to my request for help in improving my proficiency in Georgian, but it soon became apparent that Vanya believed there was a more important reason for us to meet. "You have sorrow in your eyes," he stated as I met him by the door, and he immediately suggested that we go down to the beach. Seated by the shore, Vanya explained that he also was feeling lonely. His girlfriend and he had broken up as she had gone to Tbilisi to study. He had only a few relatives in Batumi; his father had died long ago and his mother was visiting friends in a village. But what was worse, he explained, was that two of his closest friends were not in Batumi. One was in Moscow, the other in prison. These were his *dzmak'atsebi*, his brother-men and as they were not around he was at a loss. I invited him to join me for dinner and in the evening we went to a restaurant where he had once been with his two *dzmak'atsebi*, and through a series of toasts Vanya told me stories of love and friendship, and how these two boys had been part of his life since he was a small boy. In a later interview Vanya explained the concept of *dzmak'atsoba* to me:

> *Dzmak'atsoba* means more than friendship … it is very different from that, because a man who is called *dzmak'atsi* is like a brother: *dzma* means brother, *k'atsi* means man. It is a man who is your brother, but it is not a relation by blood; it is a relation of the soul and the heart. And this means … it has a very big meaning in Georgia. If you call a man *dzmak'atsi* you will show him your friendship by doing [so]. It is difficult to explain, but it has a big meaning.

The bond of *dzmak'atsoba* was a very influential factor in Vanya's life. Not only was it difficult for him when his *dzmak'atsebi* were not around, but when they were present or nearby their activities very much directed his. In the following excerpt he describes his early years as ones marked by poverty and loss:

> When I was small, I didn't have a good childhood, I was born when the Soviet Union split, it was bad times. In these times people killed each other because they didn't have bread. My childhood was not good. Not like in America or Europe—it was Georgia! I remember my mother made tea for me over a candle when I was sick, because we had no light; we had no gas, no oil. It was dark times…. Abashidze, when Aslan Abashidze was here people thought he was a good man, me too. People didn't know about him, he was a good man in our eyes. But it was dark times, there was law of thieves. The police didn't function, because if you had stolen something and you got caught you could pay them maybe 100 lari and they would leave you alone. At this time there were very many narcotics and very many drug-users, because Aslan Abashidze was like a … like a narco-baron, a Don, he had a factory for heroin and got it from other countries as well…. If you were a thief it was a good time, and for killers, because there was a dark law. And all the small boys were acting like "I am a gangster" or "I am uh-uh." Then Abashidze went away and all his secrets showed.

Vanya often recounted how Batumi was like a society of wolves. The wolf has long been a symbol of strength and masculinity. That they live in packs that center around a strong leader has made them a preferred image of group solidarity in Georgia. The wolf however is equally an image of criminal networks, *mglebi* being the equivalent of a Sicilian "Don."[8] For the boys in Batumi it was an image of their childhood as well as an aspect of their current everyday life that was tempting but that ought to be avoided. And as in the period of Aslan Abashidze described in the excerpt above, organized criminal activity is not merely an image but commonplace practice, although no longer so much in political life as amid society itself. Vanya had been involved in small-scale crime such as stealing car radios as a boy. In his own words, he was "a really good thief," but he had mainly done it for fun and had left these sorts of activities behind years ago.

When I first met Vanya he was struggling to put an end to a serious use of marijuana. His health had deteriorated immensely during the course of a very short time; he had difficulties remembering things and often lost his train of thought even in simple conversations; he had continuous pains in his lungs; and his hair had started turning grey. In order to cure some of these ailments he started exercising every morning, and after months of searching he managed to get the job as a barman. The pay was quite low but he was desperate for money so he accepted it. But although Vanya had more or less managed to steer away from crime and drugs, his life was still highly affected whenever one of his friends slipped into it. Two interrelated examples illustrate this point.

One day as I was visiting Vanya at his job he complained that he had lost his mobile phone. Knowing that this was one of his most prized possessions, I asked what had happened to it. He explained that it was at a *lombardi*—a pawn shop. He needed some quick money. It turned out that Avto, the thief mentioned in the introduction, had gotten into trouble. He had "found" some money and spent it but shortly after the owner of this money—a known criminal—had shown up at Avto's home and put a gun in his face, asking for the money back. Vanya immediately stepped in and did his best to loan Avto the money. The problem for Vanya was that he himself needed the money as one of his other *dzmak'atsis* was getting married the same week. Knowing that he had made a bet with Beka—a third *dzmak'atsi*—that Beka had lost, I suggested to Vanya that he could ask Beka for the money so that he would have money for the wedding. Vanya was startled at this suggestion. Their bet had concerned Beka's drinking problem. Although Beka had been drinking for many years, his drinking had risen so sharply after the death of his father a few months back that Vanya had worried it was getting out of control. Vanya had thus urged Beka to stop and told him that he would give him 100 lari if he could refrain from drinking for two months. If, on the other hand, Beka drank during this period he was to give Vanya 100 lari. Only a few days after the bet had been made both Vanya and I were quite certain that Beka had already been drinking, hence my suggestion. But Vanya solemnly explained to me that the bet had nothing to do with money: "He will not drink when I'm around, but I know that he is probably drinking whenever I'm not there. But that's ok, I won't ask for the money because of that—he is my friend and all I want is for him to drink less. As long as the bet is on he won't drink in my presence and will then drink less." The entire situation left Vanya without either a mobile phone or a wedding gift, but it also left him with the reassurance that he had done the right thing, both for Avto and Beka.

It was well known among his friends that Vanya's former drug use had affected him in a negative way and that he had lost many opportunities in life because of it. But whomever I met who knew Vanya revered him as an extremely good friend and thus as a good man because of the way he helped his *dzmak'atsebi*.

A Safety Net

When my informants introduced me to their friends there was often a sense of great urgency in stressing that a certain friend was in fact a good man although he had just come out of prison, had been or still was engaged in various degrees of criminal activity, or was using or abusing drugs. The incident with Avto presented in the introduction is an example of this. Although it was known by all of his friends that he sometimes stole and often used drugs, he was still regarded as a friend who could be trusted. Although he was *doing* bad things, he was *being* good. But the practice of *dzmak'atsoba* was not just one of forgiving wrongdoing or abstaining from passing moral judgement over it. It was also a matter of helping friends who were on the verge of getting caught up in self-destructive pursuits, as we have just seen in the case of Vanya. For Zviad the help and support from his *dzmak'atsebi* was a central pillar without which he feared he would be lost. At 24 years of age, Zviad was living in a rundown house on the outskirts of Batumi with his younger brother. The house was usually full of people, a collection of friends that Zviad consistently referred to as "the family". Zviad was a struggling musician hoping to make it big—not in Batumi, as the possibilities for obtaining a career in music in the town were limited, but abroad. For Zviad this was not just a dream but in fact a possibility. He had some contacts in Moscow who were willing to bring him there and help him record an album. Going to Moscow would be a major opportunity for Zviad, but he was fearful of having to leave the security represented by his *dzmak'atsebi* in Batumi. "There are many drugs in the music industry in Russia," he explained, continuing:

> I know some people there who have become addicted, I'm afraid the same might happen to me if I don't have my friends to support me and tell me to do right… . One time there was a guy from Tbilisi, a drug dealer, who had come to this part of town. I had some problems at that time and the guy offered me some things and I accepted them. But when my friends found out they sought him out and beat him up and told him never to sell anything to me again. It was good, they saved me. You know, there are times when you don't really know what is good for you and what is bad for you, in such periods you need friends, good friends.

Zviad had experienced being left by friends once before. His father had held a high position in the period of Aslan Abashidze, and the family had been well off. After Abashidze fell, the economic and social situation of Zviad and his family changed, and many people whom Zviad had thought were his close friends turned their backs on him. The people around him now, his *dzmak'atsebi* or his "family," were the ones who had helped him through this period of loss and he revered them very highly. In Zviad's life temptations such as drugs were all around, and he was not completely clean. But with help from his friends he managed to get by. Zviad explained how he put his faith and trust in his friends. He had periods of depression in which he was reluctant to leave the house, but even then he was almost always surrounded by people who spent days and nights playing cards in the garden or inside, playing music, chain-smoking cigarettes, and drinking coffee. "My friends and I have nothing financial to offer each other," he would often say when I was sitting with them, "only moral support."

Little Birds and Bonds of Trust

Many of my informants were ashamed to be financial burdens on their parents and wanted to take care of themselves. On a higher level this had to do with being able to settle with a family of their own by buying a house or an apartment, but on an everyday level it was a matter of having cigarette money or buying credit for one's mobile phone. As opportunities were few, crime was an easy way out in terms of getting money, and many seemed to have stumbled into it not knowing what else to do. I interviewed several boys who had been, or still were, engaged in various criminal activities. Steering clear of crime or of drug use was a daily struggle for most of the young men I was following. For many, such as Vanya and Zviad, it was their main project. Still, they needed an arena in which they could be or become men, more importantly *good* men and thus not merely as prey for wolves. Although nobody personally knew everyone in the city, the city was small enough for people to know *about* almost everyone. "If I do something in one end of town, people will know about it in the other end of town even before I myself get there," one young man once explained to me.

Hence, if someone made a mistake or did something wrong there was a big chance that everyone he knew would eventually find out through various networks of acquaintances. In a situation where networks and relations played an immense part of daily life, the nature of relations was thus highly important. A man needs to be able to trust his friends regardless of what happens. Sustaining friendship bonds was usually done in practice by giving moral support or standing up for a friend in a fight. But it was also done within the group most often by expressing gratitude through small toasts if someone in the group had managed to get hold of a bottle of vodka or cognac. During one such occasion the following toast was made by Vanya:

> Let me tell you a story, a small tale. There was a little bird that lived in a crater surrounded by high cliffs. It was a moist place where the sun didn't shine, a shadow. When the little bird looked up to the sun he could see eagles flying, and he hoped and dreamed of being like these eagles. And the bird tried and tried to fly up to the eagles and one day he makes it and flies with the eagles. But the little bird also had friends who he had lived with in the shadow, and when he came up into the sun he forgot these friends. After some time the bird wanted to fly even higher and it kept going up and up until it went into atmosphere and suddenly couldn't fly anymore. So it started falling and falling, it fell down to a place where his friend lived and he fell even lower than this place. This is a toast about not forgetting one's friends. If we have some good periods in our lives, if we have money or this or that, we shouldn't forget our friends, because money that you have today you might not have tomorrow.

In Vanya's toast the rise to money was described as a negative as it meant that one's friends were forgotten. Flying with the eagles was a metaphor for flying with *biznes-men*. In his story the shadows represented the difficult conditions he and his friends were living in and their need to stick together in order to survive in these circumstances. The story also reflects Zviad's agony at having been abandoned by his former friends. Materially my informants had little to display, neither big banquet tables for guests nor fancy cars. But they had good hearts. Merab, aged twenty-one, explained it in similar terms:

> *Dzmak'atsebi* know the price of their relationship and they care about it. For example, maybe one of your friends has some problems, you have to help him, even though you had to do something else. To be a good *dzmak'atsi* means that you support your friends in everything and that there is no subject that you won't talk about with each other, and nothing that you don't know about each other, a *dzmak'atsi* knows everything about the problems of his *dzmak'atsebi*. You might get angry with your friend at times, but you will forgive, it is a relationship of respect and a relationship of the hearts.

My first impressions of brotherhood led me to think of it as a moral world appreciated only by the young men involved. However, even though *dzmak'atsoba* is based on recognition within a group, a *dzmak'atsi* is not just valued as a good man by his brother-men but also by people outside the group—including girls. As one girl noted in an interview when asked what kind of man she would like to marry:

> I prefer boys who have good relations with other boys, *dzmak'atsoba*, a boy who is strong in remembering and knowing his place. There may be three or five or six in a group, one boy's *dzmak'atsi* is also another's *dzmak'atsi*, so it is like a clan. He doesn't have to be a leader but he must have a membership in *dzmak'atsoba*, his word must be strong, he must be strong and respectful.

A boy respected and valued among his peers as a *dzmak'atsi* was thus equally held in esteem by girls, making it even more important for the young men to preserve their relations as girls paid attention to what kind of brother-men the boys were. In this sense, brotherhood was not merely a "subculture" beyond which its internal ideals are not held in esteem; it was also a more widely accepted way of ascribing value to a young man.

The Temporary and the Permanent

When interviewing men or women from older generations in Batumi, I was often told that there was a crisis in Georgia in relation to the new generation, that the younger generations were "lost," and that they lacked respect for their parents and older citizens in general. Young men walking along the shore, standing on street corners, or sitting in parks were seen by many Georgians as being delinquents: "no-good" or "lazy." When, on the other hand, I asked a group of young men why they did not respect older people one promptly answered that it was because many of them did not deserve to be respected. War heroes could be looked upon with respect, perhaps; unemployed fathers could not. Although there were assumptions among my young male informants as to what the future—in this case not just societal structures but also roles within society—should ideally be, the assurance of these assumptions turning into reality were greatly challenged by the world around them.

Based on her work in Russia, Fran Markowitz argues that culture is never stable but consists of actions. In every generation there are individuals who test limits and limitations, create experiments and innovations that at times are incorporated into the rest of society (Markowitz 2000: 219). Markowitz's study of youth in Russia suggests that it is no longer fruitful, if it ever has been, to look at social stability as a prerequisite for coming of age (Markowitz 2000: 220). While I agree that stability is not necessarily a prerequisite, I do not believe that coming of age amidst instability is as easy a venture for my informants as for those of their peers in Batumi who benefited from a stable education or a family that was financially secure.[9] Markowitz calls her study a tale of two transitions: that of Russia as a changing society and that of her young informants. Both are fraught with changes and insecurities as to what lies ahead. My field differs in two important ways in terms of such "transitions." Firstly, Markowitz's informants were teenagers going to school which served, she writes, as a "protective cocoon" (Markowitz 2000: 225), a base from which decisions about one's future could be made. Having no such structural backdrop of support, the future for my informants was much more opaque as they did not have and were unlikely to obtain any skills based on education that could be put to use. Secondly, Markowitz's study was carried out in the late 1990s when the phase of transition in which the Soviet Union moved toward a market economy was still seen as something that would probably come to an end, at least in the eyes of her informants. Things would eventually change, they believed, and they were not overwhelmed by fear and doubts despite knowing that their world was one of unpredictability (Markowitz 2000: 204). This was an everyday feature in the lives of my informants in Georgia as well, but a major difference between them and the young Russians Markowitz describes is that the young Georgians I followed were not sure whether things would ever change. Both of the transitions described by Markowitz anticipate a point of culmination, a belief that things at some point would be better. For my informants the current instability held out the prospect of a more unpromising future as there were no certainties that things would eventually improve.

From Transition to Chronicity

The concept of "transition" became a widely used framework for describing the phase that the newly independent nations in Eastern Europe and Central Asia had entered after the fall of the Soviet Union: a phase that was supposedly leading these countries from socialism, a planned economy and totalitarianism to democracy, market economy, and globalization. Over the years, the notion of transition became heavily criticized within anthropology for failing to explain the subtleties of social change taking place in these countries as well as for its neo-evolutionist connotations (see for instance Berdahl 2000; Greenhouse 2002; Humphrey 2002; Lemon 2006; Verdery 1999). To be sure, the situation in many post-Soviet countries today is different than that of the tumultuous mid-1990s, and it is perhaps questionable whether the concept of transition is at all applicable. Hence, in another critique, Dominic Boyer and Alexei Yur-chak (2008) have suggested that "post-Soviet transition" as an analytical framework has a vanishing pay-off as post-socialism is a vanishing object. However, there are still many people who, in the words of Morten Peder-sen and Lars Højer (2008), seem to be lost in transition and who have not yet managed to get on their feet. Although the changes occurring in the post-socialist period proved profitable for some, as has also been shown here, many are still left with nothing and find themselves in a situation of loss up until this day.

Living with the sensation that life ought to have been something else—and something better—was a reality not just for young people but rather for everyone in Batumi. But whereas their parents' lives were changed and disturbed to a degree that made it seem as if it had come to a halt, for the young men I was following life seemed never really to have started. There was often a very strong sense of grievance among my infor-mants about not being able to become what one was ideally supposed to become, a situation leading many of them into trouble. That young men in Georgia are "trouble"—or are in trouble—was not ultimately seen by the rest of society as being the young men's own fault. Rather, they are a symptom of a failed time.

Even though young men in Georgia are facing problems that could be compared to those of young men in many other parts of the world, the specific problems faced by these Georgian youths could not be explained without taking into account the particularities of the post-socialist crisis in Georgia. The difficulties they faced at the time of my fieldwork were not a product of the crisis itself but of the aftermaths and chronic condi-tions that had been created, for instance, in terms of changed images of masculinity. This we could term as a *post* post-Soviet crisis, but, as Henrik Vigh (2008) has noted, the use of "post" in writing about crises obscures the fact that "a great many people find themselves caught in prolonged crisis rather than merely moving through it" (Vigh 2008: 8). Although affected by other, more temporary crises such as the global financial crisis and the war against Russia, it is the particularities—and chronicity—of the post-Soviet crisis in Georgia that young men live and move within. When young men like Vanya and Zviad invest their trust in their broth-erhoods it is thus not a response to a temporary disorder but a more per-manent solution to a chronic crisis. The empirical data presented here suggests that chronic crisis requires something new in order to make sense of it, as expressed for instance in the role of brotherhood as a sphere with-in which acceptable forms of masculinity could be enacted.

Conclusion: Love and Trust Regardless

After almost two decades of regional violence, an outburst of civil war, and the war against Russia, nationalism, and mobilization would presumably be key lenses through which to look at young people in Georgia today. In some cases these factors would probably also be useful in explaining their actions. However, these present only a partial picture. The situation faced by such young men is disturbing, and surely many do turn to violent or criminal means in order to improve their situation. But this is not the whole picture. As I have attempted to show, the expression of masculinity is manifold in Georgia, and although the striving for financial success and the admiration of strength can be found in images, representations, and discourses about what it means to be a good or proper man, other elements also receive expression such as the importance of being good-hearted. In a situation where many have been deprived of former gender practices and roles, what I have referred to as emasculation, the incentive to create new ways to prove oneself as a man has become immanent. As Herzfeld has noted, masculinity can be seen as performative excellence: men are often not just born "a good man," but have to learn "to be good at being a good man" (Herzfeld 1985: 16). This performative excellence could be said to be what has been lost for many young men in contemporary Georgia as the backdrop for this performance has been torn away, creating a situation where having a good heart has become an alternative to a big belly.

For young men in Georgia, coming of age is not a solitary endeavor but a highly social one. The importance of social networks has not diminished but has perhaps become even more important in the post-Soviet world. As shown, the use of networks does not go uncontested, as *biznes* is becoming a more dominant feature in society. But despite this, or maybe because of it, for those without marketable skills, maintaining and creating networks are becoming even more pressing concerns.

The establishment of *dzmak'atsoba*, peers among whom one can be a good man, created a social network of great importance for my informants: one that ensured help both now and in the future. I began this chapter by quoting Gia retelling a toast made by a man who was now his friend: a toast for the love that we cannot feel, that is not directly there, but which we can still count on. As much as being a toast about the love between newborn and mother, this was a toast to the love between friends, the bonds that could be trusted regardless. The deep affection between friends and especially between "brother-men" seems a platform of permanence and morality in a changing society that is not just of importance in the here and now but also holds within it a promise of a future as husbands and fathers who might provide the role-models they themselves have lacked.

Notes

Anne Line Dalsgaard, Rikke Elizabeth Frederiksen, Marie Højlund Bræmer, Katrine Gotfredsen, and the two editors have provided valuable comments, critiques, and suggestions on early drafts of this article.

1. All names have been changed to protect confidentiality.
2. It is worth noting that Humphrey refers to dispossession as having a double meaning: people who have lost something and people who are no longer being possessed by, for instance, quasi-feudal corporations (Humphrey 2002: 21).
3. The fieldwork was conducted during two periods between 1 August 2008 and mid-June 2009 in relation to my PhD, financed by the Danish Research Council for Culture and Communication, and part of the comparative research project "With the future as a space of agency – innovative strategies among marginalized youth in Uganda, Brazil, Georgia and Denmark" based at the Department of Anthropology, University of Aarhus.
4. As long-time users of various drugs, my informants might equally be called drug *abusers*. There are important differences between use and abuse, but as my informants never described themselves as abusers I use the term drug use.
5. Throughout the article I make use of three conjunctions of this word in Georgian; *dzmak'atsoba* (brotherhood), *dzmak'atsi* (brother-man), and *dzmak'atcebi* (brother-men).
6. The toasts presented in this article were all given in such contexts. Helga Kotthoff writes of Georgian toasting that speakers perform activities that the listeners interpret as signs of respect for them and their world, of pleasure in being together, of affiliation and involvement (Kotthoff 1995: 354). Toasting in Georgia, she continues, can be considered as a genre of moral communication as it contains evaluative judgments about people, human activities, and norms (Kotthoff 1995: 357). Many of my informants were trying to drink less but none of them went completely without drinking. Abstinence was equally a key issue, as many in fact attempted to stop drinking and taking drugs. Similar to a situation described by Kay in Russia (2005: 3), complete abstinence was tricky due to the immense social role ascribed to drinking. While sharing a small bottle of vodka, Levan, a twenty-year old, thus seriously explained how he had stopped drinking, which seemed a contradiction as that was what we were in fact doing at that point. But for Levan it was not; we were toasting and getting acquainted which was not drinking per se. Toasting together was a venue for expressing loyalty.
7. The notion of the *biznes-man* in many ways corresponds to that of the "new Russians" as described by Oushakine (2000) and Humphrey (2002: 175ff).
8. Using informal networks was not as such morally wrong but formed the basis of many aspects of Georgian society. Mathijs Pelkmans (2006) describes how it was thus not the use of patronage or informal networks that made the Mafia in Batumi problematic, but the fact that they misused it. As he writes "the 'Mafia' provided concrete reasons that people had not been able to see their dreams fulfilled. At the same time, the Mafia was more than an image, as it very forcefully pointed to actual practices in

the political and economic domain" (Pelkmans 2006: 181). The same could be said about the Mafia—or *mglebi*—today.

9. I conducted interviews with university students in order to compare their lives, thoughts, and ideals with those of my main informants which proved that the students seemed much more at ease with the times to come.

10. Although the transition narrative in some ways might have lost its analytical value, as argued by Boyer and Yurchak, it has not lost its significance in everyday jargon in Georgia; people still talk about "transition" and as the notion seems to have become an emic term it can, I believe, not be completely discarded.

Bibliography

Berdahl, Daphne. 2000. "Introduction: An Anthropology of Postsocialism" In *Altering States: Ethnographies of Transition in Eastern Europe and the Former Soviet Union*, eds. Daphne Berdahl et al. Ann Arbor: University of Michigan Press.

Boyer, Dominic and Alexei Yurchak. 2008. "Post socialist studies, cultures of parody and American stiob." *Anthropology News*, 49 (8): 9–10.

Creed, Gerald W. 2002. "(Consumer) Paradise lost: capitalist dynamics and disenchantment in rural Bulgaria." *Anthropology of East Europe Review*, 20 (2): 119–125.

Dudwick, Nora. 2003. "No guests at our table: social fragmentation in Georgia." In *When things fall apart: Qualitative studies of poverty in the former Soviet Union*, ed. Nora Dudwick et al. Washington, D.C.: The World Bank

Frederiksen, Martin Demant. 2008. "Temporality in participation and observation: Perspectives from Albania and Georgia." *Anthropology Matters*, 10 (2): 1–10.

Gal, Susan and Gail Kligman. 2000. *The politics of gender after socialism: A comparative historical essay*. Princeton: Princeton University Press.

Greenhouse, Carol J. 2002 . "Introduction: Altered States, Altered Lives." In *Ethnography in Unstable Places*, eds. Greenhouse, Carol J, Elisabeth Mertz and Kay B. Warren. Durham: Duke University Press.

Herzfeld, Michael. 1985. *The poetics of manhood: Contest and identity in a Cretan mountain village*. Princeton: Princeton University Press.

Humphrey, Caroline. 2002. *The unmaking of Soviet life: everyday economics after socialism*. Ithaca: Cornell University Press.

Kay, Rebecca. 2007a. "In Our Society it's as if the man is just some kind of stud: Men's Experiences of Fatherhood and Father's Rights in Contemporary Russia." In *Gender, Equality and Difference during and after State Socialism*, ed. Rebecca Kay. Basingstoke: Palgrave Macmillan.

———. 2007b. *Gender, Equality and Difference during and after State Socialism*, ed. Rebecca Kay. Basingstoke: Palgrave Macmillan.

———. 2006. *Men in Contemporary Russia: The Fallen Heroes of Post-Soviet Change?* London: Ashgate.

Kideckel, David A. 2008. *Getting by in post socialist Romania: Labor, the body and working-class culture*. Bloomington and Indianapolis: Indiana University Press.

Kotthoff, Helga. 2001. "Gender, emotion, and poeticity in Georgian mourning rituals." In *Gender in Interaction*, eds. Bettina Baron & Helga Kotthoff. Amsterdam and Philadelphia John Benjamin's Publishing Company.

Kotthoff, Helga 1995. "The social semiotics of Georgian toast performances: Oral genre as cultural activity." *Journal of Pragmatics*, 24: 353–380.

Lemon, Alaina. 2006. "Afterword." In: Svašck (ed). *Postsocialism: Politics and Emotions in Central and Eastern Europe*. New York and Oxford: Berghahn Books.

Lindquist, Galina. 2006. *Conjuring hope: magic and healing in contemporary Russia*. New York and Oxford: Berghahn Books.

Louw, Maria. 2008. *Everyday Islam in Post-Soviet Central Asia*. New York: Routledge.

Markowitz, Fran. 2000. *Coming of age in post-Soviet Russia*. Chicago: University of Illinois Press.

Ortner, Sherry B. 1996. *Making gender: The politics and erotics of culture*. Boston: Beacon Press.

Oushakine, Serguei. A. 2000. "The quantity of style: Imaginary consumption in the new Russia." *Theory, Culture and Society*, 17 (5): 97–120.

Pedersen, M.A and Lars Højer. 2008. "Lost in transition: fuzzy property and leaky selves in Ulaanbaatar." *Ethnos*, 73 (1): 73–96.

Pelkmans, Mathijs. 2006. *Defending the border: identity, religion, and modernity in the Republic of Georgia*. Ithaca: Cornell University Press.

Nazpary, Joma. 2001. *Post-Soviet chaos: violence and dispossession in Kazakhstan*. London: Pluto Press.

Shevchenko, Olga. 2002. "In case of fire emergency: consumption, security, and the meaning of durables in a transforming society." *Journal of consumer culture*, 2 (2): 147–167.

Verdery, Katherine. 1999. *What was socialism and what comes next?* Princeton: Princeton University Press.

Vigh, Henrik 2008. "Crisis and chronicity: anthropological perspectives on continuous conflict and decline." *Ethnos*, 73 (1): 5–24.

Chapter 7

Being "Made" Through Conflict
Masculine Hardening in Northern Ireland

Rosellen Roche

"Aye, fightin', aye? Fightin' just, it's something ye do like. [Laugh]. Look-it, the way it is in here is that ye'll always be a wee lad if ye don't learn to be a hard wan. [You have to be] harder, like, than themins [the Protestants], so you do. A slap [punch] doesn't do no one any harm neither.... Ye better get used to it anyways, the fightin'."

—Joseph, twenty-one, Catholic

Introduction: Everyday Young People Keeping a "Low" Profile

With few exceptions in academic literature concerning violence in Northern Ireland (Bell 1990; Jenkins 1983; Roche 2008; Roche 2007; Roche 2005a; Roche 2003), young people and their violent interplay have not held much appeal for social scientists. This is so even despite the fact that throughout urban, enclaved, and economically deprived working-class housing areas in Northern Ireland, young people, and particularly young men, are reported as consistently participating in "low-level" violent activities. While no formal definition of this notion of "low-level" violence exists, its use in the Northern Irish context is widespread. Thoughts vary on the origin of the expression although it may have stemmed from political expressions relating to the severity of violence in conflicts and the classification of "high-level" and "low-level" violence regarding intervention needs (see, for example, Carment 1993: 137–50; Diel, Reifschneider, and Hensel 1996: 683–700). Regardless of its origins, the expression "low-level" is used pervasively in Northern Ireland by youth workers, the police, and the media alike to describe acts of violence and criminal or deviant destruction associated with youths generally. Although in Northern Ireland the phrase "high-level violence" is usually employed to characterize acts such as bombings and assassinations in Northern Ireland, the distinctions between "low" and "high" are also reflected in the ethnographic literature in relationship to research with "high-level" social actors, such as paramilitaries or security personnel (Feldman 2000; Feldman 1991; Ní Aoláin 2000; Silke 1999; Weitzer 1995). In this sense, "low level" equals "low profile." This is not merely an outcome of access to research subjects. Because Northern Ireland—although described today as a "low-level" conflict—still has "high-level" violence perpetrated by "high-level" or more prominent figures such as paramilitary figures and/or security personnel, it is these kinds of violence that tend to attract attention both inside and outside of Northern Ireland.[1] It is these types of social actors, and their activities, that still most occupy the minds of most researchers and the public alike.

It would, however, be a mistake to exclude all sorts of "low-level" violent happenings and their intrinsic meaning from the totality of the picture of Northern Ireland, both during the height of the "Troubles" and in the contemporary, post-Agreement context. The enculturation into "low-level" violent routines by young males within Northern Ireland that hardens them for full masculinity is part and parcel of growing up in sectarian enclaves. A failure to consider "low-level" violence conducted in such segregated settings and the implications of such violence in the everyday lives of Northern Irish working-class men leads to an exaggerated dichotomization between different "types" of violence in Northern Ireland. Accounts focusing on exclusively "high-level" social actors, such as paramilitaries or police, may overlook or understate the impact of the less dramatic forms of violence that may shape as much, if not more, the everyday lives of working-class young persons generally and young men especially.

This chapter examines some of these "low-level" violent occurrences, particularly focusing upon actual scenarios of cross-religionist peer fighting, in conjunction with the processes of becoming "hard" (or what I refer to as "hardening") among young men in urban Northern Ireland. Here, I utilize ten years of ethnographic research conducted in urban areas of Northern Ireland among young people aged fifteen through thirty-five. I draw upon statistical data, as well as audiotaped and hand-transcribed interviews with young men and women from Nationalist/Republican (Catholic) and Unionist/Loyalist (Protestant) areas from three distinct field projects spanning from 1999 to the present.[2] All of the young people included are what are commonly referred to in the United Kingdom as "school-leavers," those who leave school at or before age sixteen.

The chapter begins by situating Northern Irish young men and providing the reader with a fuller understanding of the prolific deprivation, segregation, and sectarian divisions that continue to plague Northern Ireland in the post-Agreement period. From here I move to consider work that investigates masculinities and how young men grow to be "hard" through various practices of everyday violence (Bell 1990; Brown 1987; Hall 1997; Jenkins 1983; O'Donnell and Sharp 2000; Parker 1992[1974]; Willis 1993[1977]; Willis 1990). This section focuses specifically on research conducted with young men in everyday contexts across the United Kingdom, including Northern Ireland. By focusing specifically upon these works from the United Kingdom, it will be shown that young men's experiences with both "high-" and "low-level" forms of violence predominantly have been missed in studies conducted in Northern Ireland.

The second section of the chapter will focus on the ethnographic and statistical data that highlights engagement in violent activities by young men in working-class areas in urban Northern Ireland. Time will be taken to focus upon the sectarian spatial divisions that continue in Northern Ireland (for example, Feldman 2000; 1991). The most salient aspects of the Northern Irish conflict—sectarianism and the violence that accompanies it—are explored in further detail through the accounts of the young people with whom I have worked. I will illustrate how young people, and particularly young men, come to acquire a nuanced understanding of the use of sectarian cues in peer fighting across sectarian lines. This comprehension and creative use of sectarian markers is then examined in light of the research conducted among young people in the South African context (Marks 2001; Straker 1992). By expanding the comparative dimension beyond urban working-class areas in the United Kingdom and examining violent occurrences in light of the state of emergency and conflict that has endured in Northern Ireland for over four decades, the violence that young men participate in is shown to be specific to this context yet comprehensible within a broader framework of conflict. In this way, it will be shown that drawing from and employing comparative analyses from various contexts serves to increase our understanding of the stressors that young men face in Northern Ireland.

Locating the Young Urban Northern Irish Male

> We were out, on a night out, like. And it started then... . And he jist said: "Yer a hard wan, aren't ye?" An' I jist said: "Fucking right!!"

An' I got right up in his fucking face, like: "Don't fuck with me wee man
or I'll take every wan of them fucking teeth of yours out with this ring
here, so I will [indicating middle finger ring Ranger's football team logo].
Don't you fucking doubt it, wee lad. I'll fucking make you crawl again,
so I will."

—Robbie, twenty-two, Protestant

Since the period of the initial paramilitary ceasefires in 1994, the eventual removal of permanent Army checkpoints and the relative freedom that
came from a reduction of apparent emergency surveillance following the
Belfast/Peace Agreement in 1998, Northern Ireland's social and recreational sector has expanded to accommodate an increase in tourism and
economic investment (*Tribune Business News*, 11 March 2001). Urban
centers, such as Belfast and Derry/Londonderry, the largest urban areas
in Northern Ireland, have gained most from these trends, and Northern
Ireland's large population of youths has also benefited from the decline in
"high-level" violent occurrences and the boost in social, economic, and
service sectors. Certainly, when situating the young urban male in Northern Ireland, it is important to note that this region has the most youthful population in the United Kingdom. Young people who are less than
eighteen years of age make up 27 percent of the population (Save the
Children 2006). The average age of those living in either the Belfast Urban Area or the Derry/Londonderry Urban Area, is just thirty-five. Young
men comprise 48 percent of the male population in these urban centers
(Northern Ireland Statistics and Research Agency [NISRA] 2005a and
2005b).[3]

Nonetheless, Northern Ireland remains poverty-stricken, highly segregated, and divided as it attempts to move away from conflict. Urban
areas, those hit hardest by the Troubles, suffer from high amounts of social
and economic deprivation. Northern Ireland Multiple Deprivation Measures from 2005 indicate that fifty-six of the one hundred most deprived
wards across Northern Ireland are in Belfast, while nineteen are located
in Derry/Londonderry (NISRA 2005c). Northern Ireland is one of the
poorest areas of the European Union with more than a third of all children living in poverty (Save the Children 2006). Schooling in Northern Ireland remains dramatically divided and segregated. Approximately
46 percent of students attend Catholic schools and a further 43 percent
attend state-controlled schools, which have a predominantly Protestant
enrolment. Only 5 percent of students attend integrated schools (Department of Education Northern Ireland [DENI] 2006). Young men remain
the hardest hit in terms of educational attainment, with more young men
(24 percent) than young women (20 percent) between the ages of nine-

teen and twenty-four lacking basic qualifications. Those most lacking basic educational qualifications at age sixteen are young Protestant males at 27 percent (New Policy Institute – The Poverty Site 2007).

Northern Ireland also continues to sustain readily apparent and strong sectarian markers and events. Northern Irish housing remains divided and segregated. Almost 95 percent of Northern Irish housing estates are segregated on ethno-religious and ethno-national grounds (Northern Ireland Housing Executive [NIHE] 2006). Adding prominently to this physical division are forty-two state-erected security barriers, some of which include gates that are opened during the day to allow freedom of movement and closed nightly by state security personnel to constrain feuds between ethno-national communities.[4] These structural divisions, euphemistically and commonly called "peacelines" or "peace walls," stretch over thirteen miles, dividing communities still experiencing violence and hostilities. Furthermore, the number of "peacelines" has increased over the period of ongoing peacemaking, almost doubling between 1995 and 2005 (*New Statesman*, 28 November 2005).

Economic depression and segregated living have taken their toll, most severely impacting young men. Recent figures on stress from the Health Promotion Authority (HPA) state that men continue to be at the highest risk for suicide with 72 percent of suicides being male and with young men in the fifteen through twenty-four age bracket being at three times greater risk of committing suicide than their female counterparts (NISRA 2008).[5] The research also indicates that men are less likely either to recognize the symptoms of mental health problems or to seek help (HPA 2006). Finally, recent work by Harland (2008) for the HPA has revealed that when young men openly express their feelings and discuss the status of their mental wellbeing, other young men tend to interpret this type of personal disclosure and personal revelation among their peers as a demonstration of compromised masculinity.

Portraits of Violence and Comparisons with the United Kingdom

I was all: "What's your problem?"

And he was all: "What did ye say, what did ye say?" Ye know, just actin' a hard man. Just tryin' te be a big lad or something.

And this wee boy was so funny—this wee boy right, and he must've been about a first year or something [aged eleven] … I couldn't believe it like, and me standin' up like this here looking down at him! [Demonstrating].

And him going, "Hm, hm," like that there [demonstrating being ready to flight]. Tryin' te be a hard man or something.

—Columba, seventeen, Catholic

"Hardness" and "being hard," as used throughout this chapter, are thought of as a state that encompasses a masculine sense of self, physical prowess, and a lack of vulnerability. This is a concept that has been explored by many authors working with young men within working-class housing areas across the United Kingdom (e.g., Bell 1990; Coffield, Borrill, and Marshall 1986; S. Cohen 2002 [1972]; Humphries and Gordon 1994; Jenkins 1983; Offer 1999; Parker 1992 [1974]; Pearson 1983; Willis 1993 [1977]). Although these and other accounts of working-class routines and lifestyles among young men may vary somewhat depending upon their location, collectively these authors bring to the fore many of the mundane sides of life for young people living in government-subsidized housing estates across the United Kingdom. Everyday life for young men included in studies such as these has traditionally involved exploration of activities such as courtship, schooling, and progressing from school to employment in the semi-skilled and skilled laboring trades. However, the presence of consistent violence is also stressed in these works, with particular attention given to daily incidents of violent interplay intermingling with forms of typically youthful behavior in daily routines. Incidents involving everything from simple violent verbal exchanges to intensive fighting (where the young men strive to overcome their opponents with blows or weapons) among young men living in working-class housing areas across the United Kingdom have been shown to be part of the hardening process.

In a classic study that focuses on a group of young men in "Hammertown" in the Midlands of England, Paul Willis emphasises that everyday acts of violence that occurred in myriad situations and forms were essential to an "informal status system" where "the fight is the moment you are tested in an alternative culture" (1993 [1977]: 35). In addition, beyond proving oneself as a "lad" within an "in-group," Willis stresses that violent interchanges are also commonplace and expected among "the lads" themselves. Extracting a mild example of violence used by "the lads" in recreational "piss-taking" or joking about as part of the "laff," Willis discusses their experiences of "ribbing" others, such as authority figures, as a form of "machismo" (1993 [1977]). Going on to describe this type of behavior used among "the lads" themselves, Willis explains:

Of course "the lads" do not always look to external stimulants or victims for the "laff." Interaction and conversation in the group frequently take the form of "piss-taking." They are very physical and rough with each other with kicks and punches, karate blows, arm-twisting, kicking, pushing and tripping going on for long periods and directed against particular individuals often almost to the point of tears (Willis 1993 [1977]: 32).

Willis reports the consistent use of violent language and violent interplay among "the lads" and extended by young men toward authority figures. Emphasizing that violence "breaks the conventional tyranny of 'the rule'" by "opposing it with machismo," Willis stresses that, among the young men he studied, "it is the capacity to fight which settles the final pecking order" (1993 [1977]: 34–35) and demonstrates their masculinity to themselves and to one another. Although all "lads" recognize that fighting is dangerous and might prefer to use verbal threats and symbolic violence, having demonstrated an ability to fight is imperative. Willis goes on to note:

> In a more general way the ambience of violence with its connotations of masculinity spread throughout the whole culture. The physicality of all interactions, the mock pushing and fighting, the showing off in front of girls, the demonstrations of superiority and put-downs of the conformists, all borrow from the grammar of the real fight situation. It is difficult to simulate this style unless one has experienced real violence (Willis 1993 [1977]: 36).

Howard Parker, too, in his study among the "boys" in the "Roundhouse" in Liverpool, stresses the understanding among them about the necessity of violence and its use in everyday circumstances to prove their masculinity. Parker illustrates the importance of being readied for violent confrontation and how this works into all sorts of events for the young men. Regarding violent skirmishes and the pervasive confrontation with violence or "trouble" among the boys, Parker states:

> On a very basic level one can get into a fight for almost no apparent reason. An accidental kick or push in a club or the disco leads to a "butt" and a fight. Les for instance came out of "The Cockle" one night to find his girlfriend talking to another man who appeared to be chatting her up. He simply knocked the bloke out with a "flying head butt" only to find out it was his girlfriend's cousin. These situations are not uncommon and their particular "solution" is again based on the "do unto others before they do unto you." Since there are no restrictions on the form of downtown fighting, one "dig" or "butt" can be decisive and must therefore be got in quickly. Trouble then is always a possibility to be contended with (Parker 1992 [1974]: 145).

Illustrating how the "boys" acquire an "alertness to potentially inflammatory situations," Parker notes throughout his work that toughness is not just operationalized in fighting but remains part of a "whole ethos of being 'hard'" (1992 [1974]: 146–147).

Accounts such as those of Willis and Parker which demonstrate how young men engage in both petty and serious violent occurrences, confront violence, and become practitioners of violence have at times been interpreted as offering an overly aggressive assessment of young working-class men. Other authors who have explored violence and class structure among young people, such as Mike O'Donnell and Sue Sharpe (2000), Tom Hall (1997), and Phillip Brown (1987), for example, indicate that among the young people they studied "fights are to be avoided, [and are] rarely if ever, sought for the thrill they offer" (Hall 1997: 80). Attempting to distance themselves from studies such as Willis's where the author stresses a sought-after form of masculinity often acquired through violent means, these authors seek to accentuate differentiations between and among groups of young people, and to show that not all young people share the "lads' aggressive search for excitement" (O'Donnell and Sharpe 2000: 44).[6]

Academic studies conducted across the Irish Sea in Northern Ireland, for the most part, have been inattentive to investigating acts of violence among young people and between young people across ethno-national communities. In addition to my own recent academic work in this field, only social studies by Desmond Bell (1990) and Richard Jenkins (1983) have also explored the complex network of factors that contribute to the everyday life of young, working-class males living in Northern Ireland.[7] Importantly, both Bell and Jenkins seek to move away from pathologizing youth in Northern Ireland; an assumption that "the general population of youth, living in a milieu of civil disorder and violence, might potentially exhibit similar undetected pathological symptoms" (Bell 1990: 46). However, by virtue of not including discussion of the topic of violence among young men in urban areas, particularly when these areas were in the midst of the Troubles and hardest hit by Troubles-related violence, the lack of information regarding such daily interchanges is compounded.[8] While Bell studied an all-male Protestant Loyalist marching band in Derry/Londonderry, investigating in particular Loyalist street youth culture in order to tear down a unilateral version of "Britishness," Jenkins worked within Belfast's "Ballyhightown" youth club to learn about patterned differences among young working-class people and how those patterns are produced and maintained.

Neither Jenkins nor Bell, however, attempt to explore directly the relationship between violence and the young men with whom they worked.

Bell examines youth street rioting, media attention, and frequent misunderstandings of this rioting. He also gives attention to the shift in focus from youth rioting to paramilitary assassination, what he felt was the eventual promotion of an etiology of juvenile delinquency through paramilitary pressure (Bell 1990: 40–43). Significantly, Bell focuses upon and underlines the continuity of youth subcultures in Northern Ireland in contrast to the circumstances of the rest of their United Kingdom counterparts. His focus is on the complexity of the Ulster Protestant young male being "neither Irish nor apparently fully British" and therefore "particularly complex" within the sectarian context. While both Bell's and Jenkins's contributions have been invaluable, their studies of young men are nonetheless conducted in large part through the use of broader British comparisons framed in terms of the then-current United Kingdom youth policy trends, rather than comparatively focusing upon youths reared within the violent contexts of ethno-national conflict. Although young men within the urban working-class Northern Irish context have much in common with their peers in the rest of the United Kingdom in terms of their hardening through routine instances of violence within their daily activities, the specific aspects of the divided Northern Irish context involve young men there with a hardening process that is distinct and very much their own.

"Sectarian stuff mixes in everythin'": Violence, Hardening, and Conflict

> Kids here are chiselled. They're fucking hard, you know? You just know it by looking at them. Hard.... I mean they are as hard as boys at home, but they have this extra thing, coming from here.... They are different, like. You can just tell. It's different here because of all that's gone on here and how they are always showing that.
>
> —Sean, twenty-five-year-old student studying at Queen's University Belfast, originally from Manchester, England

Violent Engagement

Young people in urban areas across Northern Ireland indicate that they are often involved in violent encounters. Recent work (Roche 2005a: 244–248) that I have conducted across all of the economically deprived district council areas in Derry/Londonderry with approximately nine hundred young school-leavers aged sixteen through twenty-five reveals that when young people were asked if they had been involved in threatening or violent incidents, most reported that they had been. The survey question offered options for possible answers that had been gleaned from the most common responses already obtained from young people in discussion groups.[9] These options included: "threatening looks and glances," "threatening words," "pushing and shoving," "fist fighting," "kicking," "using weaponry, such as sticks, bricks or knives," and "other." In addition, a further optional response read: "I have never been involved in threatening or violent incidents like those listed above." Young people who were surveyed were invited to tick off as many responses as they felt applied to them.[10]

Out of the total sample of 486 respondents, only 13 percent reported never having been involved in incidents like those listed in the other options offered on the survey. The remaining responses received were spread between the options listed above. Overall, 47 percent of the remaining sample had engaged in "fist fighting," 39 percent had engaged in acts involving "pushing and shoving," 39 percent had engaged in incidents involving "kicking," and 27 percent had been involved in incidents utilizing "weaponry (such as sticks, bricks or knives)." Equally important, many young people reported having been involved in other types of threatening incidents: 57 percent had been involved in incidents using "threatening words" while 42 percent considered themselves to have been involved in incidents involving "threatening looks and glances."

The remaining "other" category provided young respondents the opportunity to submit more detailed written responses that did not clearly fit into the other proffered categories. The range of their responses varied in degree of threat, violence, and sectarian intent. Some of these included: "I was sent a sectarian text message (on a mobile phone)"; "I was bitten"; "My face was pushed in glass on the street"; "Hit with a petrol bomb"; "I was hit with a heel (of a shoe)"; "Brick broke window of my house"; "Earring pulled through my ear"; "Used a bottle"; "Put on fire"; and "Had bullet in envelope put through the post."

Male and female reporting of threats and contacts were similar in many cases, with the exception of participation in fist fighting and the use of weaponry. Sixty-three percent of males—compared to 31 percent of females—stated that they had been involved in incidents involving "fist fighting," while 39 percent of males (compared to 15 percent of females) reported they had been involved in incidents using "weaponry."

In the peer fighting that occurs in economically deprived urban areas in Northern Ireland, young men engage in violence that involves exchanging threats or actual physical violence with young people from within their own ethno-national community or, more pervasively, violent fights with young men from the other sectarian community. With approximately 95 percent of families living in conditions that are divided by ethno-political and religious affiliation in Northern Ireland, the structural divisions between communities continues to generate scenarios where young people meet across the divide and engage in violent exchanges. These sectarian divisions contribute to continuing fears of the "other" community as well as pervasive segregation of life ways. I (Roche 2005a), for example, found when young people were asked whether they found crossing through housing estates of the opposite community "easy," "neither easy nor uncomfortable." or "uncomfortable," 57 percent of the total respondents stated that this was an "uncomfortable" thing to do. When asked if they found traveling through housing areas of the opposite community "safe," "neither safe nor dangerous," or "dangerous," 53 percent of all respondents felt that this was "dangerous" (2005a: 261).

Working in conjunction with fears of venturing into areas of the "other" community, over 92 percent of all respondents in my sample felt that "a lot" or "some" sectarianism exists in their areas. Only 2 percent felt there was "no sectarianism" in their areas. When asked what young people experienced that was sectarian, 39 percent of those responding reported experiencing something sectarian through the exchange of "threatening words," 26 percent reported that they had experienced sectarianism through "physical contact," and 26 percent felt they had experienced sectarianism through "physical threat" (Roche 2005a: 263–265). A review of survey data from 2000 to 2005 on sectarian harassment and violence estimates that more than one in four young people have experienced sectarian verbal abuse, and more than one in two young people do not feel safe when in areas with a majority representation of the other community (Jarman 2005: 34). A submission by the British Irish Rights Watch (BIRW) to the United Nations Special Rapporteur notes that from 1 April 2005 to 31 December 2005 alone, 1,240 sectarian crimes were reported. BIRW, however, contends these estimates dramatically under-report the actual levels of such crimes. They suggest that almost half of crimes committed in Northern Ireland are related to sectarianism (BIRW 2007). Young men feature heavily in interchanges across the sectarian divide, both as victims and perpetrators of such crimes (Ellison 2001; Roche 2005a: 230–65).

Sectarianism and Hardening Through Conflict

Recent work illustrates that in the post-Agreement setting, young people are experiencing heightened divisions as well as further separation and increased anxiety between communities (Hargie, Dickson, and O'Donnell 2006; Roche 2008). My (Roche 2008) investigation of these divisions, conducted with over one hundred young people across Belfast and Derry/ Londonderry, illustrates the continuing problems of sectarian divisions. Indeed, many young people discussed lifestyles that were so segregated from the other community they were seen to be encased or "wrapped up" by their own community in a "cocoon" (Roche 2008: 69–107). When encased within a cocoon, it takes effort to find a passage out due to the protective coating that surrounds it to ward off any intruders. Nearly two out of three participants in the above-cited study found themselves located in such a setting and indeed spoke of staying within and defending this type of environment that was so demarcated and excluded from the other community.

Ethnographic work by Allen Feldman (1991), discussing this type of extreme ethno-political and spatial division with relation to violence, conceptualizes and emphasizes violence as being spatially connected to "sanctuary/barricades—interface/adversary community" which the author notes as having been "rapid(ly) translated by the paramilitaries into a militarised configuration" of both a performative and a spatial structure.[11] Although as noted earlier, Feldman's work primarily attends to violent interaction between "high" level social actors such as paramilitaries, in a context of cross-religionist peer violence his depiction of the segregated environment for violent occurrences is practicable. Having experienced decades of state emergency apparatus, paramilitary community control, constant and historical troubles with policing standards and personnel, as well as ongoing segregation and sectarianism, young people, and young men in particular, negotiate the residues and practical spatial aspects of these conflicts on a daily basis.[12]

For example, Christopher, a seventeen-year-old Catholic, thinks the fighting where he lives is "miserable." He has been involved in several physical clashes and has found himself chased through the town, getting caught behind the football pitch and being "givin' a wile hidin'." He describes the situation succinctly: "You, just, you fight, like." Later, he states: "It's important to fight, to be hard like. Ye can't be lightly made up, be a big girl's blouse or anythin' like that. Ye can't like." Explaining the importance of the way segregated and divided living leads to the inevitable results of fighting, Christopher states:

> There's no Protestant welcome where I live like. 'Cause it's all mad men up my way just give them a pure keekin'. That's why they wouldn't go near, that's why they wouldn't come near the town either, them ones from [Prot-

estant area] like. 'Cause they'd just walk in te somebody and they'd just probably deck them. "You're a Prod!" *Smack!*

R.Roche: How would they know that though?

Ye had some person mouthin'. "Aw that boy's a Prod there! I heard about him" and all, like.

And he'll go over, "You're a Prod!" *Smack!* "Get away from here." They don't like each other like. So they just fight. Well that's what I think anyway. That's why Catholic and Protestants don't like, 'cause know, they fight like 'cause of their religion. That's the way I think of it anyway.

Many young people, including Christopher, feel that all cross-community battles of any kind are sectarian. The type of interchange that Christopher discusses is an apt description of the sectarian invocations that young people negotiate in their day-to-day activities.

For some young people, however, encounters are more nuanced and about being raised "in it," "in here" and "in this place," and illustrate that while a fight might not be intended to be "pure sectarian" or be the result of unmitigated hatred in intent, it may employ the trappings of a sectarian attack all the same. As Liam, an eighteen-year-old Catholic explained to me regarding the weekly fights in which he engaged: "It's the way this place is. Sectarian stuff mixes in everythin', like. Sometimes fellas mean it and sometimes they don't." Much like Sean's emphasis in the quotation cited at the start of this section that "you can just tell," young men often discussed aspects of "knowing" or understanding how sectarianism works into physical clashes and how this was part of the hardening process in this specific context. Although he feels that he can't adequately explain the importance of hardening in the Northern Irish context, George, a twenty-two-year-old Protestant aptly states:

I dunno. Ye just know, when, I dunno, it's somethin' about being from this estate or the other. It's like, it just is. Even if wans don't mean it [sectarianism], they use it, if you know what I mean? [Pause]

It's hard, difficult, te explain like. Ye come te be a true hard wan like, even if ye can't 'cause ye have to like. Ye get used to it I suppose. I dunno. I can't explain it, like. But ye do do it. You rise to it, like. Say someone says somethin' or other to ye about your mate, like. "Prod" or all that there. 'Cause if ye don't you're just soft, so.... In the end up, ahh ... we see it as something that, ahh, I dunno, that makes us up, like.

"Low-level" peer violence and fights among young people suffer from a tangle of meanings and interpretations in Northern Ireland. Fergal, for example, discusses how aspects of being hard are tied to these nuanced interpretations. An eighteen-year-old from a predominantly Catholic area, Fergal is the oldest of five children. Fergal's father, a launderer in the local shirt factory, recently died from lung cancer and Fergal now finds he pays in over half his £40.00 per week youth training allowance to his mother to help make ends meet. Trying to keep up appearances for his family and community, and thinking that he might look "soft" if he admitted his overwhelming grief, at the time of the interview Fergal had not informed people at his job placement or his training program about the death of his father.

Fergal now has a lot more to worry about than simply fighting in the city where he lives, but he feels there are "that many people after (him) here," and he will inevitably remain involved in the street fighting. In his description of fights that take place outside venues in an area that is considered predominantly Protestant, Fergal feels that the situation is exacerbated both by the ability to readily identify individuals as well as by the identity of the clientele each venue would attract.

> They just know ye, sure all the, it's all the usual goes in te it. There's three bars in the wan street. There's the *Upstairs Downstairs*, *The Gallery*, and … *Laurence's*. There's them three. There's *The Gallery*, that's Protestant, *Laurence's* is mixed, *Upstairs Downstairs* is Catholic. That's the way it is ye see. So and then, after that there when they all come out, there's all a big fight. They're own, so everybody knows their own then.

> They know ye just. They would, I don't know . . . they would just know, they just *know ye*.

> If ye were walkin' up the street they would shout, "There's Friel!" And they would run after ye and just, if you're caught you're beat. Just, if you're a Catholic you're beat, if you're a Protestant you're beat.

He continues by stating: "but they *would* know ye like. People know people here, like."

To help me understand, he recounts a situation that happened the night before one of our conversations:

> My mate was goin' out there last night and he got his car whacked. It's a wee MINI [Cooper]. Did ye ever see the wan wi' the big stripe up the middle of it? We drive about wi' him. He got his car hit wi' a brick last night. Up past Tullyally [Protestant]. He lives in Ardmore [Catholic] ye see.

For Fergal, it was the car that brought on the attack by being an identifying marker for the group he would "run around wi'." Fergal doesn't necessarily always feel there is a "pure" sectarian element or "bitterness" to this type of interchange, but rather that it's part of the context in Northern Ireland. He continues:

> I don't know it's just, it's just the way people's brought up. Say somebody's brought up in Creggan [Catholic area], they're gonny fight wi' Protestants. 'Cause most of the, most of the Creggan's all Sinn Féin and all that kind of a place. They're gonny fight wi' Protestants. Like Gobnascale, Gobnascale's mixed, too, sort of. Ye would get the odd Protestant in it. But nothing's said te them. I don't know. It's just the way you're brought up, just. If you're brought up te fight wi' Catholics, you're gonny fight wi' Catholics. If you're brought up te fight wi' Protestants, you're gonny fight wi' Protestants. Unless ye change or move te a different country, or meet somebody else.

Research conducted recently in Northern Ireland indicates that young people feel that sectarianism is very present in their lives. However, the nuances of many peer confrontations and fights are thought of as not being "pure sectarian" or "pure bitter in nature." Indeed, in cases like these, sectarianism and the markers that come with it are sometimes "just" added into the mix. Like an extra pinch of gunpowder, sectarian cues are often used merely to give a situation a "wee bit more pow." For example, when explaining the use of words like "Fenian" (a slur for Catholics) and "Jaffa" (a slur for Protestants), Emer, a seventeen-year-old Catholic, feels that "at times" these are representative expressions used to engage someone in a fight for reasons that are purely sectarian in intent. At other times, they are used to help along with the starting of a fight. She states:

> A fight on a Friday night would be something like, you went with her I was going with her—bang! And something like you ate my E and I don't have enough of them it—bang! Or you drunk my drink! Or you said that about me! Or otherwise it's you're a Fenian bastard [Catholic slur) and you're a Jaffa cunt [Protestant slur) [laughter)—bang!"

She continues by stating: "Sometimes they are just words. Sometimes they don't mean a fucking thing."

Bridgeen, a nineteen-year-old Catholic woman also spoke of how young men may come to use such cues in various ways by describing a hypothetical situation in a nightclub:

Say I had some wee boy come up to me in the club, like. And he starts chatting me up and all. My fella (boyfriend) might think: "He's a Jaffa," or come up and say, like: "Are ye a Prod or what?"

And like, he could be and all, and no bother to me about it, and really that's not the thingy, like. It's that I'm chatti'n wi' him, but. Like, it's a way of startin' (beginning a fight).

Situations such as Parker's account of Des in the "Roundhouse" (referred to above) can be contrasted and compared with the hypothetical situation of Bridgeen's boyfriend as outlined above. Both young men make assessments and strive to get the "first hit," yet Bridgeen's boyfriend has an additional "starting" tool in his "kit." He can strike verbally with a sectarian-based insult, and, whether his target is Catholic or Protestant, he will most assuredly succeed in insulting. A verbal exchange ensues and the die is cast. Long-standing cues can be used to provoke, to hurt, and to retaliate, melding into the contextual structure of separated sectarian agendas and helping to cement a young man's sense of selfhood in relation to his own community. In sum, it is how and when such markers can be used that help to "make the man" when protecting or defending himself, his family, his friends, or his property.

Such markers continually align the young man to a particular ethno-national agenda. Used as an extra tool in a fighting kit, aligning with a particular "side" helps a young man to position himself in an oncoming clash, providing him not only with practical back-up from his own community members if needs be but also a kind of emotional back-up, strengthening him through a connection to a larger group.

Importantly, the use of what are ostensibly "just words" to ignite confrontation are well recognized, and *to not use them* would render a person *not clever enough* to truly harden himself in this context and therefore may complicate acceptance of the young man within his own ethno-national community. In the Northern Ireland setting, incidents often mix sectarianism or sectarian markers in ways that are particular to the context in which these occur and in ways that are only identifiable to and definable by those who live within the context itself (Brewer 1992: 352; Roche 2008: 40–68). It is the use of sectarian and conflict-based markers and cues that assist a young man in presenting himself to those whom he is challenging and that connect him to other members of his ethno-national community. In addition to this, it is the adversarial use of these cues that can help to "set up" a confrontation, and when in the midst of hardening, is a process that all young men come to learn about. If a young person does not grasp the importance of such indicators and cues, the end result can be fatal. This is not unlike Paul Willis's later analysis of symbolic creativity and activity among young people, which examines the "dramatic permutations of 'hardness'" and the complexities of "hardness" in social interaction (Willis 1990: 103–09). Emphasizing that hardness is both an "inner" and an "outer" quality, he states that the space between these two qualities is "worked through in what can be thought of as a dramatic grounded aesthetic: acting out your own performance and interpreting the performance of others" (Willis 1990: 104). Significantly, he finishes by pointing out:

> None of this works, however, unless you are prepared to fight *in extremis*. The shadow and the substance intertwine. The performance and the inner reality overlap... . There is a tight moral and dramatic economy here. But it can easily break down. External appearances are not a good guide to the reality of danger (Willis 1990: 105).

In Northern Ireland the skilled deduction of external cues can literally "make" or "break" the man. Indeed, if young people in the Northern Irish context do not have a nuanced, firm, and mature grasp of the many ways in which sectarian cues can be used, and how to tacitly "just know" the differences between them, the results can be severe or deadly. When Graeme, a seventeen-year-old Protestant living in a mixed housing area, described an incident that started over a local greeting and the indicator of a "Protestant name," he aptly recounted to me the consequences of being aligned with one community or another and how this helped to define his overall loyalty to his ethno-national community:

> It started last, the last time it started was there was a young fella I knew and he was walking down through the Triangle and a boy stabbed him in the back... .
>
> He was walking down through the Triangle to go to the bar and ahhh, he seen this fella and he thought it was a boy he knew. And he says: "Alright" to him. [A form of greeting].
>
> The boy that stabbed him turned round and says to him: "What's your name?" [Indicating that he would have a "Catholic" or "Protestant" name].
>
> And the young fella told him his name and he turned round and stabbed him in the back.

Then a big riot started then between Bond Street and the Triangle, like, so. He got eight stitches in his back and his lung collapsed. [The knife] hit him just right there [indicating the back of the lung] it went just clean through. Just round the back and it went down in a slit, went down straight into his lung. That wasn't too good, like... . So, we like really fought, hard, true, like.

That fightin' like that there, that's pure kickin' [hard beatings], so it is. Everyone comes out and shows what they, how hard they can be for their own [ethno-national community] and fight to the ground like. Honestly, to death. Everyone's all over. Fellas really want te hurt each other. They do, like. It's a mess, like. I mean, that comes from a bitter place, so it does. That *is* hate, like. Hating the other side.

Beyond merely locating oneself within a peer "in-group," a threatening display and eventual violent follow-through is part of a historical and ethno-national tradition that must be upheld. In Graeme's example, sectarian cues were used both to validate the initial incident (receiving a "Protestant name" to initiate the fight) and to endorse further fighting between the two groups ("everyone comes out and shows what they, how hard they can be for their own"). While some incidents may be seen to use such cues for bluster or for less extreme purposes, such as merely instigating a verbal argument or light fist fight between two young men over a young woman, it must be remembered that such indicators also have a heady historical significance and meaning and, in an instant, can slip into extreme ethno-national violence.

It is this tie to the overarching and more significant experience of living within ethno-national enclaves that has withstood Troubles-related violence, both "high" and "low," and that has for decades helped young men harden when fighting across communities. Furthermore, it is with the members of the young person's community that young men feel most closely aligned when fighting across religious lines. Not just a desire to be part of a peer "in-group," this type of alliance is far larger and connects one young man to the whole of his community. Describing their links to and loyalty for their individual communities, young men discuss being buoyed-up by this sense of belonging and protection. It is, as Gary, an eighteen-year-old Protestant, noted:

When I feel like, threatened, like, I just think: "No, you're a fucking Loyalist," ye see. No one beats the Loyalists like. I feel like, no matter what happens around there, there are boys I'm connected to in my estate that hear about it and make sure I'm right [alright] like.

Sectarian Fighting in Context

Juxtaposing the circumstances of young men in Northern Ireland with other British examples of urban youth violence and the formation of masculinities—as in Parker's exploration of the young members of the "Roundhouse" in Liverpool (1992 [1974]) or Willis's treatments of both class and creative culture (1993 [1977]; 1990)—can be informative as a means for comparing some dimensions of the violence that young men experience in working-class environments. Yet to limit comparisons of Northern Irish youth exclusively to their counterparts in the United Kingdom would be less productive in certain crucial senses. Given the centrality of conflict and the sectarian factors and cues that accompany it within the lives of young people within Northern Ireland, a broader comparative range may provide a fuller scope of insights.

It is not, in practice, easy for either young people themselves or researchers to disentangle tacit understandings of "knowing" differences in the nuance that distinguishes between "just using" sectarian threats from those acts that have a "pure" or "bitter" sectarian intent. Indeed, the skill in knowing the difference becomes part of "low-level" violent peer interchanges across communities through which young men grow and harden. All interchanges, to one degree or another, are bluntly or creatively tied to a broader scenario where an allegiance to a political community that has long endured conflict is required. Frank Burton's discussion of the social relations of pervasive division and sectarianism in Northern Ireland is crucial in explaining the long-term effects of an ethno-politically divided society. Burton speaks of sectarianism as a normal process of thinking through what he terms as "telling" (Burton 1978: 37–67), which develops from living within a segregated conflict environment. For Burton, "telling is the pattern of signs and cues by which religious ascription is arrived in everyday interactions," and he suggests that telling "furnishes an insight into the nature and depth of a riven society by illustrating the centrality of difference as a typical mode of thought" (Burton 1978: 37). Burton ties the "weighty sentiment of history" (Burton 1978: 67) to telling and states that "telling is a central process in creating and sustaining the coherence of a sectarian cosmology" (Burton 1978: 38).

If we want to consider the Northern Irish case in the context of youth and conflict elsewhere, it is helpful to turn, for example, to investigations into youth violence in South Africa. Gill Straker's (1992) psychologically oriented discussion of youth and violence at the time of anti-apartheid political upheaval in the mid-1980s seeks to address both the communal and personal consequences of political violence. Focusing on youths aged twelve through twenty-two years who fled from Leandra township, Straker separates the young people that she came to know into distinct categories of "leaders," "followers," and "casualties." By separating young people into these categories, Straker is able to draw out some of the personal characteristics that enabled or disabled young people in the struggle.

What is most interesting for the purposes of this discussion is the discovery that many of the young people who were most stress-resistant had the ability to represent outer reality realistically and, thereby, to be active within it (1992: 35). Straker's work lends insight into aspects of the resiliency, capacity, and creativity of youths who are exposed to political violence. Indeed, she found through group work that while some observations regarding aspects of conformity and rebellion of adolescents were applicable to adolescents in the West, in the Leandra group, developmental conflicts "were intensified by their interaction with predictable group processes springing from the social and political context" (1992: 87). Although adults and community leaders disapproved of some "low-level" violent incidents and anti-social behavior, young people nonetheless felt confident about many of their actions precisely because many adults had participated in these events as well. Not unlike the Northern Irish young men's sense of the broader ethno-national group providing emotional support and back-up, young people in Straker's group noted similar feelings of connection to a broader purpose for violence in their context. She states:

> Furthermore, many found reassurance in the fact that adults and community leaders had been involved in these events too. They felt that this lent a moral legitimacy to their actions … the more they believe an act of violence is necessary within the context of transcendent values, such as the notion of a just war, the better they are able to deal with it. In sum, the less guilty they feel about the act, the less distressed they are (Straker 1992: 103–104).

Straker's investigation of the effects of violence on the individual and group psyche is important. Her work shows that, even in cases where civil breakdown has not occurred, exposure to the workings and mechanisms of such community violence changes an individual's consciousness in fundamental ways, producing sharp divisions between those who are seen as friends and those who are seen as foes. In addition to stressing the effects coming from exposure to civil violence, she also notes that many residues remain. Such residues include the fact that young people have acquired skills that equip them to understand how all forms of authority can be challenged, disobeyed, and coerced. Equally, Straker notes the practical consequences of political conflict resulting in increased division and creating limitations for young people to access skills and career paths that would be more appropriate to the development of youths in times of peace (1992: 135–136).

Similarly, recent research conducted by Monique Marks (2001), working with young people who participated politically and violently in the social Charterist anti-apartheid movement in Diepkloof, South Africa, addresses broader questions concerning youth involvement in less politically motivated criminal violence in subsequent years. Marks maintains that the connection of being a "comrade" with being a "youth" in the Charterist movement during the period of anti-apartheid South Africa led youths raised within the ambit of these movements to see themselves as being embedded within their communities in purposeful ways. "Because youth saw themselves as 'energetic,' 'flexible,' 'agile,' and 'adaptable,' they were positioned to defend the community against perceived outside dangers and threats" (Marks 2001: 123). Marks asks whether "yesterday's comrades have become today's bandits" (Marks 2001: 133). Attempting to redefine what is commonly termed the "lost generation" in South Africa, Marks examines and questions causes for current violence, its connection to previous insurrection, as well as its current form. Echoing Straker, Marks concludes there are myriad factors in addition to and coupled with exposure to conflict, such as broken homes, poverty, and a lack of initiation into manhood, that are propelling young men to new forms of criminality and further violence.

Amid speculations that Northern Irish youths who have been exposed to long-term conflict may comprise a "lost generation" themselves,[13] I propose taking account of projects such as those of Straker and Marks and suggest that young people in Northern Ireland should be considered within the historical context of ethno-political conflict and violence that has surrounded them throughout their lives. The lifestyles of Northern Irish young people are not only influenced by urban issues that youths in any urban area may face but also feature an established tradition among youths, and particularly young men, of being involved in a variety of types of ethno-national violence. This involvement represents both the maturation process of young men and the particular ways they harden within this context. Equally, the sectarian conflict has allowed violence, and the sectarian cues that often accompany it, to become a strategizing mechanism as well as a means of coping within this context. The convenience of using a sectarian cue to ignite an argument, an extreme sectarian fight instigated because of "hate," and the ability to trust that others from your community will make sure you are "right" are all part of the unique historical and conflict-laden dimension.

Of course, the contemporary ethno-political climate of Northern Ireland differs in important respects from the political violence that occurred in South Africa as part of anti-apartheid rioting. That being said, similar forms of necessary creativity, active participation, and strategizing that figured in South Africa are no less pertinent to young people within segregated ethno-national enclaves in the post-Agreement setting within Northern Ireland. Conditioned as they are to the regular features of state of emergency that are still in place today, continuing paramilitary control of areas, and abiding youth fighting across communities, young people in Northern Ireland are realistically aware of how these factors influence their lives. Young Irish people themselves often make comparisons between Northern Ireland and other areas experiencing ethnic or racial divisions. For example, Mickey, a sixteen-year-old Catholic, makes passing reference to black South Africans and African-Americans with the comment: "Sure, it was like all them black people, Mandela, all themins in America. Know, we got treated the same." Marty, a seventeen-year-old Protestant, upon having a friend suggest a trip to South Africa, responded that "(He) fuckin' wouldn't go near anywhere like here, like." And Margaret, a twenty-one-year-old Catholic, reflecting upon a tolerance and understanding of violence within specific contexts, states:

> See until like recently, there wasn't a lot of tourism in Northern Ireland. Definitely not. But, just of late there's been a bit. Not much like, but a bit. Ye know, but it'll probably, I do think when, there wouldn't be a wile lot of people keen te come.

> I know if it was me, comin' te somewhere like that Lebanon, or Sierra Leone, like I wouldn't fuckin' go out there. Know what I mean? It would put ye off.

> It's the same thing. Naw, it's not the same thing. Naw it's not, but I mean it's a war. Ye know what I mean? It's fightin'. Pretty much the same like. But obviously it's not religion related like. So if it put me off goin' there. It would put people off comin' here.

> But, I mean the people, take Sierra Leone, for the example. They're livin' there. We're used te this, they're used te that. Ye know what I mean? It's the same. It is comparable like. It is. In a way. On an ongoin' thing like.

In addition to drawing parallels between Northern Ireland and other conflict areas, young people in Northern Ireland often speak of Northern Ireland and, indeed themselves, as definitionally "tougher than" other places and people. These analogous discussions are about comparing elements between themselves and others, as well as deducing levels and degrees of toughness. It is, as George summed up: "In the end up, ahh … we see it as something that, ahh, I dunno, that makes us up, like." By examining the many factors that the young people feel are important to *their* understanding, erroneous ideas that young people, and particularly young men, may be exhibiting an "ingrained" penchant for violence[14] or alternatively, that the antisocial behaviour and violence in which they find themselves involved is exclusively like that of any of their mainland peers, are both challenged and appropriately made more complicated.

Conclusion

> In Northern Ireland, the effects of Troubles-related violence augment the effects of deprivation, creating a "double penalty." For the most part, intervention programmes have ignored this and their social policies have operated as if they were dealing with "simple" socio-economic deprivation, rather than deprivation which is interlocked with and compounded by the attritional effect of the violence of the Troubles.
>
> —Smyth, *Half the Battle: Understanding the Impact of the Troubles Conflict on Children and Young People in Northern Ireland*, 22

This chapter has illustrated how the process of hardening is connected to the "low-level" violent interplay that young men experience when involved in everyday violent peer fighting across ethno-national lines. In this way, young men living in working-class areas in urban Northern Ireland are shown to have distinct ways in which they harden because they not only experience violence in ways that are similar to their peers living in parallel economic circumstances across the United Kingdom, but also because they are growing up within a distinct and coming-from-conflict environment. Other policy-focused writers, such as Marie Smyth, have stressed this combination of factors that makes Northern Irish young people distinct in some important respects. Continuing in subsequent work on aspects of mixed messages about violence, Smyth states:

> Children and young people are at the receiving end of confusing messages about violence and its legitimacy. The culture of violence is pervasive within the worst affected communities, and the use of force widely accepted as inevitable. On the one hand, children may be told that it is wrong to hit another child, and on the other that it is fine to throw stones at the army or the police, or to be unmoved by the death or injury of certain fellow citizens, particularly if they are from "the other side" (Smyth 2001: 13).

The terrain within which everyday, working-class young men living in an ethno-national enclave in Northern Ireland craft and realize their masculinity is one that is comprised of the many factors that emerge from environments that have historically experienced and which continue to experience political violence. Not only are young people dealing with the practical effects of violence, such as decreased access to education, derelict housing areas, and urban poverty, but they are also growing up and living alongside a form of tit-for-tat violence that is distinctive to this type of arena. Like Marks's interpretation of "energetic," "flexible," "agile," and "adaptable" youth, the fights and violence that young people engage in with peers across the sectarian divide and see as part of the hardening process "in here" can be considered self-made, self-preservative, pre-emptive, and community-preventative (Marks 2001: 123).[15] "Being hard" is therefore a personal process of "becoming hard" in a communal context that is shaped by a dramatically segregated post-Agreement Northern Ireland. Experienced personally, heard about through family and friends, and witnessed first-hand, "hardness," through both "low-" and "high-level" violent experiences and incidents, becomes a thing achieved "in this place." It is wrought sometimes of mere threats, and more often of practical injuries given and sustained as a growing man within a community. "Hardness," as explained to me by the young men themselves, is something elemental to growing up and being part of Northern Ireland. For young men it is most important to gain this essential understanding in this divided context by not being a "big girl's blouse" or a "soft one," or to be thrown backwards and to become a "wee man" who "crawls again." Young men note how they became "harder" through fights with peers in a manner inevitably tied to the segregated context. By becoming "used te it" "in here" young people become part of "it"—the conflict and the place—and thus are hard themselves. Importantly, hardening thus inevitably becomes the result of personal training *and* skill in negotiating and creatively using aspects of this highly segregated context. For the young men I know in Northern Ireland, it is more the product of hailing from "in here," where all sorts of interchanges knowingly "just" happen among "hard" peers and it becomes necessary to both mould to and use the exigencies of the place.

In conclusion, it is important to remember that explicit recognition of hardness is not often mentioned by these young men, although it is readily acknowledged when asked about. It is understood to have accumulated due to the presence of the person within these surroundings, a setting for the unavoidable acquisition of hardness. The hardening of individuals, whether individually or collectively, improvised or programmed, is so foreseeable that they are indeed taken for granted as something that just *is* "in here." Being hard registers on a spectrum that is measured invariably against the situation in which it is needed. It can comprise the growing knowledge of how to protect oneself adequately in a divided housing area, the necessity to take a beating for a mate from one's own community, the ingenuity to be able to lash back with a sectarian slur, or the requirement to be seen as a strong and responsible young man in the community even at times of intense sorrow and grieving. It is measured upon personal indices of expectation and involvement and constitutes a valued communal element in relationships and friendships tied to the "weighty sentiment of history" (Burton 1978: 67).

Hardening among young men in Northern Ireland includes taking pains to avoid Willis's permutation of being "hard on the outside but not on the inside." As Willis explains, "Such a person creates an external persona that is unmatched by bodily force and skill. He is not what he appears to be. He is in danger because of this" (Willis 1990: 104). Interpreting this beyond its physical "permutation," hardening is a process of becoming; when achieved, a person guards against external representations of being "light" or "soft" because the spectrum is not from hard to soft, but rather more importantly from "hard" to "victim." Although a symbolic threat in some instances, a practical and physical one in many other situations, and "bitter" at its extreme, all these aspects of such "low-level" forms of violence add to the hardening process for young men within the Northern Irish context and help them learn the process by which to acquire it. It is only when this nuanced understanding of how to be a "true hard wan" is acquired and exhibited that "wee" men are considered to have grown up.

Notes

1. An immediate case in point is provided with the murder of two soldiers and a police officer in Northern Ireland by dissident Republican paramilitaries in March 2009. These events gained major media attention, as both the Prime Minister of the United Kingdom of Great Britain and Northern Ireland, Gordon Brown, and the President of the United States, Barack Obama, publicly condemned these attacks and urged that the peace process continue to move forward. Following this, at the time of writing, a panel comprising four Members of the Legislative Assembly (MLAs), with representatives from the Social Democratic and Labour Party (SDLP), the Green Party, the Democratic Unionist Party (DUP), and the Ulster Unionist Party (UUP), also addressed these crimes. This panel, formed for a group of visiting students for the Institute of Irish Studies Summer School Session in 2009, notably addressed aspects of dissident paramilitary activities against these security forces but never mentioned any issues of youth rioting and heavy violent disturbance injuring several police personnel and innocent bystanders that continually occurred over several days in July in the Ardoyne in the north of Belfast in the same summer. "It was as if," as one summer

school student later noted, "those riots weren't a threat or anything. Just like they never happened."

2. This article makes use of the findings of fieldwork conducted by the author during three projects and periods. Each project had slightly different age parameters, but all projects included young male and female school-leavers (school exit at age sixteen or before) and the young unemployed in both Catholic and Protestant ethno-national enclaves experiencing high levels of deprivation in the urban cities of Belfast and/or Derry/Londonderry, Northern Ireland. Primary research was conducted between 1999 and 2001, sponsored in the main by generous grants from Peterhouse, Cambridge, and the Guggenheim Foundation (Roche 2003). The second period of fieldwork covers the period of 2003-2005 and incorporated both quantitative and qualitative work. *The Toward Reconciliation and Inclusion Project*, or TRIPROJECT, was funded in the main by the Special EU Programmes Body for Peace and Reconciliation administered by CFNI (Roche 2005a; 2005b; 2006). The final segment of field research included here was conducted from 2006 to 2008. Entitled *Facts Fears and Feelings: The Impact and Role of Sectarianism in Everyday Life*, the project sought to uncover mundane and tacit aspects of sectarianism. This project was sponsored by Special EU Programmes Body for Peace and Reconciliation, administered by the NICRC at Queen's University Belfast (Roche 2008). Please note that all names have been changed. The ages of young people and their ethno-national affiliation at the time of their original field interview are as originally recorded. The reader may note some differences in speech between transcriptions. All conversations were transcribed true to the form of the speech patterns of the youths and to the respective areas from which the young people hailed. These differences of accent account for these minor differences in speech.

3. Statistics averaged by author from NISRA based on 2001 census.

4. This figure comes from a recent assessment from the Northern Ireland Office (NIO) Freedom of Information Team. (This information was provided to the author by J. Byrne in personal correspondence, August 2009; Byrne received the information from the NIO by request in March 2009.) This count is of the barriers recognized by the NIO and erected by the state since 1969.

5. Percentages calculated by author.

6. O'Donnell and Sharpe referring to Brown (1987).

7. Here, I stress academic field projects that have been conducted for and within the academy. Several researchers and authors including Jarman (2005) and Smyth (1998), as noted in this piece, have conducted important projects with a view toward policy change and improvement for young people in Northern Ireland.

8. Both authors are clear about their intentions for research, and their respective foci were not to look at violence exclusively. Reasons for this could be many, such as the research climate at the time across the UK or the danger entailed in researching aspects of violence in the midst of conflict. While I am not criticising this gap, I am highlighting the paucity of research on this subject.

9. *The Toward Reconciliation and Inclusion Project* (TRIPROJECT) was a hallmark project in that it was the first survey project in Northern Ireland to consult school-leavers about issues that they had identified for exploration by means of a questionnaire. For one year young people were consulted through round table discussions and group work to assess what should be the main topics included in the survey and what responses might be most significant. After this initial period, young people were included as consultants on the pilot surveys and oversaw changes to the final question-

naire that was circulated among them. To view the final form of the questionnaire, see Roche (2005a:323-348).

10. Although allowing young people to tick as many responses as they felt applied to them leads to extensive cross-tabulation for the researcher, this type of approach enables the researcher to see if young people participated in multiple types of interchanges.

11. Feldman's structure follows a schema of targeted-targeting community/defensive-offensive violence/ targeting-targeted community in what he depicts as a sanctuary/interface/sanctuary configuration (1991: 35).

12. Here I cover aspects of what are considered daily mundane or everyday interchanges. Elsewhere (Roche 2003), I cover aspects of fighting that occur in and around the summer seasons, as well as other types of violence between youths and the police, and youths with paramilitaries. Fighting in and around parading seasons can include more symbolic exercises in threat and violent exchange. Make no mistake, however, this type of symbolic exchange can quickly deteriorate into very violent fighting and rioting, as large groups of young people usually participate in these exchanges.

13. Cf. Cairns (1987). The author does not believe this but notes previous trends in social policy and psychology that indicated growing fears of ingrained violent behaviors.

14. "Violence is Ingrained in the Northern Character," *Sunday Tribune*, 17 February 2002. Based upon a study by Hayes and McAllister (2001: 901–922) that attempted to deduce statistically the long-term effects of extended support for political violence, the article outlines the authors' argument that widespread exposure to violence tends to enhance public support for paramilitaries and their respective paramilitaries' retention of weaponry.

15. Marks also discusses pre-emptive and preventative violence (Marks 2001: 125). Although in this context, ideas of using violence as a preventative "necessary evil" may be farther removed than from the immediate violence of post-apartheid South Africa, Marks's notions regarding the necessities and adaptabilities of violence are noteworthy here.

Bibliograhy

Bell, Desmond. 1990. *Acts of Union: Youth Sub-Culture and Sectarianism in Northern Ireland*. London: Macmillan.

Brewer, John D. 1992. "Sectarianism and Racism and their Parallels and Differences." *Ethnic and Racial Studies*, 15 (3): 352–64.

British Irish Rights Watch (BIRW). 2007. *BIRW Submissions to UN Special Rapporteur of Freedom of Religion 2007*. Available from: http://www.birw.org/freedom%20of%20religion.html [Accessed 29 February 2008].

Brown, Phillip. 1987. *Schooling Ordinary Kids: Inequality, Unemployment and the New Vocationalism*. London: Tavistock.

Burton, Frank. 1978. *The Politics of Legitimacy: Struggles in a Belfast Community*. London: Routledge and Kegan Paul.

Cairns, Edward. 1987. *Caught in Crossfire: Children and the Northern Ireland Conflict*. Belfast: Appletree.

Carment, David. 1993. "The International Dimensions of Ethnic Conflict: Concepts, Indicators and Theory." *Journal of Peace Research*, 30 (2): 137–50.

Coffield, Frank, Carol Borrill, and Sarah Marshall. 1986. *Growing Up at the Margins: Young Adults in the North East.* Milton Keynes: Open University Press.

Cohen, Stanley. 2002 [1972]. *Folk Devils and Moral Panics: The Creation of Mods and the Rockers.* Oxford: Basil Blackwell.

Department of Education Northern Ireland (DENI). 2006. "Education Minister Decides on New Integrated Schools." March Press Release.

Diehl, Paul F. et al. 1996. "United Nations Intervention and Recurring Conflict." *International Organization,* 50 (4): 683–700.

Ellison, Graham. 2001. *Young People: Crime, Policing and Victimisation in Northern Ireland.* Belfast: Institute of Criminology and Criminal Justice.

Feldman, Allen. 2000. "Violence and Vision: The Prosthetics and Aesthetics of Terror." In *Violence and Subjectivity,* eds. Veena Das et al. Berkley: University of California Press.

———. 1991. *Formations of Violence: The Narrative of the Body of Political Terror in Northern Ireland.* Chicago: University of Chicago Press.

Hall, Tom. 1997. "Accommodating Inequality: An Ethnography of Youth Homelessness and Hostel Provisions in South-East England." Ph.D. diss., University of Cambridge.

Hargie, Owen, David Dickson and Aodheen O'Donnell. 2006. *Breaking Down Barriers: Sectarianism, Unemployment and the Exclusion of Disadvantaged Young People from Northern Ireland Society.* Jordanstown: University of Ulster

Harland, Ken. 2008. *Key Issues in Promoting Mental Health: Masculinity and Mental Health.* Belfast: HPA.

Hayes, Bernadette and Ian McAllister. 2001. "Sowing Dragon's Teeth: Public Support for Political Violence and Paramilitarism in Northern Ireland." *Political Studies,* 49: 901–922.

Health Promotion Agency for Northern Ireland (HPA). 2006. *Public Attitudes, Perceptions and Understanding of Mental Health in Northern Ireland.* Belfast: HPA.

Humphries, Steven, and Pamela Gordon. 1994. *Forbidden Britain.* Bristol: Testimony.

Jarman, Neil. 2005. *No Longer a Problem? Sectarian Violence in Northern Ireland.* Belfast: Institute for Conflict Research.

Jenkins, Richard. 1983. *Lads, Citizens and Ordinary Kids: Working-Class Youth Life-Styles in Belfast.* London: Routledge and Kegan Paul.

Marks, Monique. 2001. *Young Warriors: Youth Politics, Identity and Violence in South Africa.* South Africa: Witwatersrand University Press.

Marsh, Peter, et al., eds. 1978. *The Rules of Disorder.* London: Routledge and Kegan Paul.

New Policy Institute: The Poverty Site. 2007. *Young Adults Without Basic Qualifications.* Available from: www.poverty.org.uk/117/index.shtml [Accessed 12 March 2007].

New Statesman. 2005. "Apartheid." *New Statesman,* 28 November. Available from: www.newstatesman.com/200511280006 [Accessed 30 May 2008].

Ní Aoláin, Fionnuala. 2000. *The Politics of Force: Conflict Management and State Violence in Northern Ireland.* Belfast: Blackstaff Press.

Northern Ireland Housing Executive (NIHE). 2006. *Mixed Housing Scheme is Launched.* Available from: www.nihe.gov.uk/news/news,asp?Id=1221 [Accessed 01 June 2008].

Northern Ireland Statistics and Research Agency (NISRA). 2008. *Statistics Press Notice-Mortality Statistics for Northern Ireland 2007.* Belfast: NISRA.

———. 2007. *Northern Ireland Health and Wellbeing Survey 2005/06: Top Line Results.* Belfast: NISRA.

———. 2005a. *Area Profile of Belfast Metropolitan Urban Area: Based on 2001 Census.* Available from: http://www.ninis.nisra.gov.uk/mapxtreme_towns/report.asp?settlementName=Belfast%20Metropolitan%20Urban%20Area%20(BMUA)&BandName=Belfast%20Metropolitan%20Urban%20Area%20(BMUA) [Accessed 14 May 2008].

————. 2005b. *Area Profile of Derry Urban Area – Based on 2001 Census*. Available from: http://www.ninis.nisra.gov.uk/mapxtreme_towns/report.asp?SettlementName=Londonderry&bandName=Derry [Accessed 14 May 2008].

————. 2005c. *Northern Ireland Multiple Deprivation Measures*. Available from: http://www.nisra.gov.uk/archive/deprivation/NIMDM2005FullReport.pdf [Accessed 12 July 2009].

O'Donnell, Mike, and Sue Sharpe. 2000. *Uncertain Masculinities: Youth, Ethnicity and Class in Contemporary Britain*. London: Routledge.

Offer, John. 1999. *Social Workers, the Community and Social Interaction: Intervention and the Sociology of Welfare*. London: Jessica Kingsley Publishers.

Parker, Howard. 1992 [1974]. *View from the Boys: A Sociology of Down-Town Adolescents*. Hampshire: Gregg Revivals.

Pearson, Geoffrey. 1983. *Hooligan: A History of Respectable Fears*. London: Macmillan.

Roche, Rosellen. 2008. *Sectarianism and Segregation in Urban Northern Ireland: Northern Irish Youth Post-Agreement*. Belfast: Blackstaff Press/CDS.

————. 2007. "'You Know America has Drive-By Shootings? In Creggan, we have Drive-By Beatings': Continuing Intracommunity Vigilantism in Urban Northern Ireland." In *Global Vigilantes: Anthropological Perspectives on Justice and Violence*, eds. David Pratten and Atryee Sen. London: Hurst and Company.

————. 2006. "When They Write What We Write: Young People's Influence on Policy Making in Northern Ireland." *Anthropology in Action*, 1 (1–2), 55–68.

————. 2005a. *Something to Say: The Complete TRIPROJECT Report on the Views of Young School Leavers in the Derry District Council Areas*. Belfast: Blackstaff Press.

————. 2005b. *Something to Say Condensed: A Condensed TRIPROJECT Report on the Views of Young School Leavers in the Derry District Council Areas*. Belfast: Blackstaff Press.

————. 2003. "The Inheritors: An Ethnographic Exploration of Stress, Threat, Violence, Guts, Fear and Fun Among Contemporary Young People in Urban Northern Ireland." Ph.D. diss., University of Cambridge.

Save the Children. 2006. *Country Brief: Northern Ireland*. Belfast: Save the Children Northern Ireland.

Silke, Andrew. 1999. "Ragged Justice: Loyalist Vigilantism in Northern Ireland." *Terrorism and Political Violence*, 1 (3): 1–31.

Smyth, Marie. 2001. *Age and Generational Politics in Northern Ireland's Troubles and Their Consequences for Justice and Peace*. Belfast: British/Irish Social Policy Association Annual Conference (June).

————. 1998. *Half the Battle: Understanding the Impact of the Troubles Conflict on Children and Young People in Northern Ireland*. Londonderry: INCORE, The United Nations University and the University of Ulster.

Straker, Gill. 1992. *Faces in the revolution: the psychological effects of violence on township youth in South Africa*. Cape Town: David Phillip.

Tribune Business News. 2001. "Northern Ireland Enjoys Economic Boom." *Tribune Business News*, 11 March. Available from: http://www.encyclopedia.com/doc/1G1-71584392.html [Accessed 05 July 2009].

Weitzer, Ronald. 1995. *Policing Under Fire: Ethnic Conflict and Police-Community Relation in Northern Ireland*. Albany: New York State University Press.

Willis, Paul. 1993 [1977]. *Learning to Labour: How Working Class Kids Get Working Class Jobs*. Aldershot: Ashgate.

————. 1990. *Common Culture: Symbolic Work at Play in the Everyday Cultures of the Young*. Milton Keynes: Open University Press.

Part III

DEALING WITH BEING "TROUBLE"

Chapter 8

YOUNG MEN, TROUBLE, AND THE LAW
A French Case

Susan J. Terrio

Introduction

In the 1990s, juvenile arrest rates increased in France while overall crime declined. As a result, public attention centered on what was identified as a newly threatening social category, a "delinquency of exclusion." This was a category many experts in the media, law enforcement, the bar, the magistracy, the academy, and the government associated with disadvantaged Muslim males, both French citizens and immigrants, living in the stigmatized urban space of the *cités* or housing projects. They depicted the "new" delinquents as younger, more violent, and irredeemable. They came to view the offender "from an immigrant background" through the lens of a cultural ecology model and as the product of deficient social milieus shaped by cultural pathologies and economic deprivation. Because of media coverage on troubled "youth of immigrant ancestry" and new books on urban violence, the figure of the delinquent began to assume monstrous proportions. His offenses were depicted as an unprecedented crisis of public order and as an unacceptable assault on French values.

Jurists, politicians, academics, and public intellectuals on the left and the right reached a consensus on the "new" delinquents as radically different from the juvenile offenders of the past. In the immediate post-World War II period, professionals viewed delinquency as the product of coming-of-age risk-taking, individual pathology, or flawed parenting. French juvenile law reflected this understanding by granting special dispensations and protections to troubled teenagers for exposure to bad influences at an impressionable age or for the developmental immaturity that leads to risky behavior. This consensus on the need to excuse certain behaviors and to prioritize rehabilitation ended as "immigrant" minors came to be over-represented in police custody, the courts, and in prison. Many politicians, police, and court personnel came to view this population differently and to assign conscious intention, bad character, or even total responsibility to them for offending. Such views worked to separate them from French children and, in the interests of public order, to hold them more accountable before the law. Beginning in the 1990s this view became institutionalized in both national legislation and court practice.

Successive governments instituted aggressive modes of policing and enhanced control of minors who were deemed dangerous based on their origin. They constructed a new category of violent youth crime through legislative reform that created new public order violations and heavier penalties for existing infractions. They extended the coercive force and reach of the state through the justice system by enhancing prosecutorial and police power and by accelerating the adjudication process to permit swifter prosecutions, investigations, and trials for juveniles. They reexamined the very notion of penal irresponsibility for minors and, in a dramatic reversal of postwar philosophy, lowered the age at which children could be held responsible for their actions and given "rehabilitative" punishments from thirteen to ten (Law No. 2002-1138).[1] Legislators also changed the rules for preventive detention, permitting a new "flexible incarceration" regime for minors aged thirteen to sixteen.[2] In early August 2007 a new law on recidivism went into effect. It created minimum sentences for the first time in modern French history, suspended the automatic reduction of sentences for youths aged sixteen to eighteen, and mandated prison for a range of offenses (Law No. 2007-1198). These reforms have produced more arrests, more prosecutions, more incarceration, longer prison sentences, and more tension between youth and the police (Wacquant 2004).

The youth riots that erupted in 2005 focused unwelcome international attention on France's "immigrant" problem. They also renewed acrimonious debates on the merits of retribution versus rehabilitation as responses to youth crime. Conservative legislators blamed the urban violence on insufficient controls over illegal immigration and on youth from polygamous Muslim families (*Le Monde*, 16 November 2005). Members of the government depicted the riots as dangerous threats to the republic, vilified the perpetrators as members of organized gangs, and demanded mass arrests (*Le Monde*, 8 November 2005). In fact, the vast majority (75 percent) of those tried for insulting public authorities, resisting arrest, or damaging property were minors who were enrolled in public school and had no police records. One third of them were under sixteen years of age and two thirds were aged sixteen to eighteen. All of them were born in France. There were no groups of criminal instigators at work. Nonetheless, the courts were harsh and heeded then Justice Minister Pascal Clément's instructions "not to hesitate to impose firm prison sentences." The average sentence was five weeks in prison and eight hundred young people served time (Bouarkra 2006). Since 2007, President Nicholas Sarkozy and his Justice Minister Rachida Dati have pursued more accountability and repression in treating delinquency. In 2008 Justice Minister Dati formed a commission to initiate a complete overhaul of juvenile law, insisting that "punishment is a part of socialization" and youth need to internalize the "meaning and importance of a legal sanction." One of her primary objectives was to reconsider "at what age minors could be tried for a crime versus a misdemeanor" (Refondation de l'ordonnance du 2.2 1945).

The growing violent unrest of young men who feel excluded and the increasing penalization of the French legal system beg a number of questions. How do young men view the legal system and how do they understand its role in facilitating or hindering the coming-of-age process? A state's capacity to legitimize its political authority, to rationalize its use of force, and to maintain the consent of the dominated within an unequal social order finds its limits, particularly when it engages in or tolerates discrimination against a particular group.

The French state has been successful in asserting its political hegemony through the power and prestige of national public institutions, the civil service, and laws that claim to be color-blind. It has been far less successful in ensuring its ideological hegemony among disadvantaged minority youth in the face of unequal opportunity, socio-economic polarization, and anti-immigrant bias within public and private institutions. Those who suffer discrimination have little reason to accord legitimacy to French institutions, whether in the public schools or the juvenile court, because, despite vigorous official denials, many know they have been tracked on the basis of collective origin and their rights have been denied or restricted. The ways in which French authorities have used the law and the legal system to control and contain politically disaffected minorities have in turn shaped the ways youth in public schools, neighborhood areas, and judicial proceedings see themselves as legal subjects, make sense of the choices they have, and view (or not view) the law as a counter-hegemonic tool available to protect their interests.

This chapter centers on the interface between young men and the law in a context marked by tension, mistrust, and growing violence. It focuses primarily on exchanges among young men and legal professionals in court proceedings based on my observations of penal proceedings in the Paris juvenile courts from 2000 to 2005 and on published accounts by judges and youth. The growing French interest in repression begs the question of what the late Paul Ricoeur (1995) has called "the just" in the process of accusation and judging, the application of sanctions, the use of rehabilitation, and the question of rights grounded in individual notions of agency and responsibility. It investigates to what extent young men recognize themselves as political subjects with the same rights and obligations before the law. It asks how their encounters with public authorities such as the police, judges, teachers, or social workers affect their understanding of the law. Do they view the justice system as a site where they can mount a credible defense and expect equal treatment under the law?

The French Criminal Justice System

The modern juvenile justice system in France dates back to 1945. At that time, legislators implemented a progressive approach that makes no distinction between endangered and delinquent children. According to this philosophy, a minor is a work in progress and can be successfully re-socialized. The 1945 law established a focus on the child rather than the act and mandated deferred judgments, individualized sentences, national sentencing guidelines that automatically reduce penalties by half for minors, and the separation of adult and minor jurisdictions regardless of the severity of the offense. It created a specialized corps of juvenile judges for the first time and gave them exceptional powers. They examine charges and issue indictments as well as conduct trials and render judgment.

The modern juvenile court bears the imprint of a centuries-old inquisitorial legacy in France. Despite postwar reforms, French trials, in minor and adult jurisdictions, combine elements of inquisitorial and adversarial procedures. They begin with a discovery phase that is secret and written and remains more concerned with the protection of the social order than with the individual rights of the accused, witnesses, or victims (Herzog-Evans 2000). The trial phase is oral and public and, to a very limited degree, adversarial, because it accords primacy to a written archive of evidence over the oral testimony heard in court. In adversarial systems such as in the United States the facts of the case emerge from a strategic confrontation between the prosecution and defense attorneys in which the presiding judge is primarily a neutral arbiter. Such systems assume broad equality between the prosecution and the defense. Each side gathers evidence and presents arguments in oral proceedings intended to establish the facts of the case. In the French system, no such equality is presumed between the parties. The facts are established by the examining magistrate or the prosecutor and presented by the state in the person of the trial judge, not by the individual parties to the case. They are premised on a conception of the truth that is established independently of the prosecution and the defense and puts the onus on the accused to prove his innocence (Garapon, 1997: 169–170; Herzog-Evans, 2000: 20).

Despite official guarantees of the presumption of innocence in the Universal Declaration of the Rights of Man, the Civil Code, and in recent legislation the process of discovery in the French system cannot in practice presume innocence. The state has a monopoly on the facts and the "objective truth" that provide the basis for the decision to prosecute as well as on the act of accusation itself. The French understanding of legal truth explains the concentration of power in the hands of the trial judge as well as the unequal exchanges between the judge and the accused. The French judge, in contrast to her American and British peers, takes an expansive role in the trial. She presides over and controls the exchanges in court and all parties address her, not one another. Her function is to conduct inquiries into the case, not simply to judge the evidence as presented. The trial judge actively questions the accused, witnesses, and victims and will request more information if needed.

Because the French trial is understood as the symbolic affirmation of legal order over social disorder and of the collective will over individual transgression, the accused must be ritually isolated and stripped of his individuality. He stands alone at the bar, and responds directly, without advice from counsel, to an aggressive stream of questions controlled by the presiding judge. French courts intrude authoritatively into the personalities and private lives of the accused because one of the paramount goals is to reintegrate the "bad" citizen through the internalization of legal norms. In inquisitorial systems the accused is expected to contribute to the process of finding the truth in contrast to adversarial systems where guilt or innocence is established on the basis of evidence external to the defendant (Hodgson, 2005: 19–21). The active participation of the accused both before and during the French trial is crucial, particularly in juvenile court proceedings. The confession reins supreme as proof of guilt because French law is not interested in external behavior alone. Rather, it has a pedagogical role and a structuring dimension.

Juvenile Court Proceedings

After arrest, the decision to prosecute an offense, and the designation of the minor as a formal suspect under investigation (*mis en examen*), the next step is the penal hearing before a juvenile judge. Hearings for minor infractions may be scheduled in the judge's chambers or referred to the formal juvenile court in cases involving more serious offenses and/or repeat offenders.[3] Hearings begin when the suspect hears, confronts, and responds to the charges against him. Beyond this, normal legal procedures are routinely suspended in the juvenile court. For example, the right to remain silent is never invoked. Rather, it is deemed antithetical to the establishment of a rehabilitative bond between the youth and "his" judge.

In the hearings I observed, the basis of the charges and, thus, the facts of the case depended greatly on statements obtained by the police during questioning of young men in police custody. Judges relied heavily on statements signed by the accused, victims, and witnesses and referred to them repeatedly. They resisted attempts by the youths to re-frame or retract these statements, even when youths complained that they were told to sign statements without reading or understanding them. Judges likewise refused attempts to undermine the credibility or integrity of police and court personnel. They tended to reject youths' accounts of police malfeasance, as this constituted an unacceptable attack on the moral authority of the legal system. In comparing the words of victims to those of the accused and lacking other proof, judges privileged the testimony of victims over the accused. This is all the more significant in the wake of legislation in 2004 mandating that penal convictions may no longer be erased automatically from the police records of minors upon their majority at eighteen.[4]

The briefings I attended before court hearings suggested that judges had already formed opinions about the nature of the child accused of wrongdoing based on reports in the court filed by school counselors, social workers, and child psychologists. Although judges emphasized that their role was to focus on children rather than families and to avoid judging lifestyle, the disciplinary system of the court included not only penal infractions but also unwritten class-based norms of behavior. Children who did not master the mainstream codes of politeness, demeanor, responsiveness, or oral expression were corrected in court. They were admonished to sit up, to speak clearly, to not interrupt their parents, to control their feelings, to be courteous, and to use the proper salutations.

The hearing consisted of two unequal parts. The first was a confrontation of the "facts" recorded in the written depositions with the oral testimony produced in court. The second part began after the facts were confirmed and the minor admitted his guilt and showed remorse. Judges directed a series of rapid and direct questions at the accused regarding disputed circumstances or inconsistencies in their stories. Judges frequently interspersed sarcastic comments and moralizing questions such as: "So when the police found you behind the wheel of the car, you were just passing the time of day?" and "And you are telling the court that this Tunisian guy from the neighborhood forced you to steal the cell phone? So if he told you to commit murder would you do that?" Judges tended to view claims of innocence, implausible excuses, and the denial of responsibility negatively. They considered the acknowledgment of the wrong done and the acceptance of guilt as a precondition of clemency and rehabilitation. Cases that resulted in verdicts of not guilty or acquittals were relatively rare in the courtrooms I observed.

In the next section I focus on hearings in chambers and in the formal juvenile court. I center on cases where young men admitted their guilt as well as cases where they refused to accept the facts as given and offered a different version of what happened or communicated strong messages by disrupting court proceedings. French judges and defense attorneys have portrayed the behavior of young male defendants in court as passive, intimidated, or disaffected. In my analysis, however, I prioritize the voices and actions of young men who demonstrated mental agility and creative thinking in challenging French law. They insisted on their innocence and constructed alternate narratives, accepted responsibility for lesser charges, shifted the blame from themselves to their peers, parents, or other adults, demanded their right to have cases retried when the penalty was severe, or through their silence refused to participate in and thereby legitimate the court proceedings.

"I Accept Responsibility"

The vast majority of the cases I observed between 2000 and 2005 involved cases where the accused affirmed their guilt by accepting the facts as given by the court. Although this admission fulfilled an important goal for the accused "to assume responsibility for their actions," many of these young men insisted on modifying the expected script. They explained their motivations, invoked extenuating circumstances, and emphasized the personal factors that influenced their behaviors.

One such case came before the Paris juvenile court in April 2001 and involved charges of aggravated theft in a group that resulted in a severe injury. The incident in question had occurred three years before when the accused, Thomas, a Malian male, was sixteen-years old.[5] He was charged with orchestrating the beating and robbery of a teenager who lived near him in a nineteenth arrondissement housing project in Paris. The victim of the beating had been tried and convicted of a grisly attack that had permanently disabled a buddy of Thomas. Thomas was in court because he had requested a re-trial after his conviction in absentia to a five-month prison sentence. He argued that he had re-made his life and deserved the court's clemency.

The judge reviewed the long police record of Thomas that included three previous convictions and prison sentences ranging from one to three months. She invited Thomas to justify his request:

Thomas: We had a friend who was attacked and who was handicapped by kids from this neighborhood.

Judge: So that means that you can act the same way? Do you feel better as a result?

Thomas: No, I am sorry for what I did. I was under age at the time (*mineur*). I have taken stock of my actions. I learned a lesson. I work now. I am not involved in that stuff anymore. I am no longer at risk (*en danger*).

The juvenile prosecutor disputed his account and emphasized the extremely serious nature of the offense:

Prosecutor: It was a reprisal attack carried out by more than ten youths from the projects. Their victim was beaten, robbed, stripped, and left naked in the street…the wrong done to Thomas's buddy in no way justifies a brutal retaliation for the sole reason that the victim lives in the same neighborhood. Justice was done. His friend's attackers were [convicted and] sentenced to five months in prison. Now he (Thomas) tracks down the victim and exacts revenge. It is only fair that he receive the same sentence.

When the judge asked if Thomas would accept an alternate sentence of community service instead of prison, he readily agreed. His *éducatrice* (French equivalent of probation officer) assured her that a Parisian NGO had agreed to work with him. She insisted that he had "evolved."

Thomas: I am sorry for what I did. I want to start all over again.

His attorney took up the same theme:

Attorney: It is very serious to exorcise one's suffering through an act of revenge but after three years this case cannot be tried in the same way. He is no longer the same person. He was in a vicious cycle of retaliation, fights, and hate for society. That's over. He served eighteen months in prison (pretrial detention). He has accepted his responsibility. An alternate sentence would permit his integration, restore the qualities needed for citizenship, and allow him to repay his debt to society. A return to prison would jeopardize that.

The judge ended by remanding the case back to the sentencing judge and recommended community service. Despite the serious nature of the offense and the allusions to territorialized violence in the projects, the court was lenient. Thomas admitted his guilt, recognized the facts, and accepted his responsibility. In doing so, he reinforced the authority of the court and the fairness of its decisions. He also claimed the rights and obligations that are the legal entitlement of French political subjects. He demonstrated that he had "evolved" and matured. His respectful demeanor and meek acquiescence allowed Thomas to isolate a serious offense from his immigrant background without challenging the social and moral order the court must defend. The probation officer and judge, if not the prosecutor, could interpret his delinquency as a temporary lapse on the road to a normal adulthood.

Guilty but ...

Increasingly since the late twentieth century, many court cases have originated from strained relations between police and young men "hanging out" in the street or in apartment building stairwells. Police used repeated ID checks on the same youths in bad neighborhoods that degenerated into confrontations and arrests for public order offenses. The number of these cases tried in adult and juvenile courts increased beginning in the mid-1990s as did the severity of the sentences. Between 1994 and 2006 the percentage of prison sentences doubled, the length of prison terms increased, and heavier fines were imposed. Of the three most common public order offenses—resisting police orders, insulting, and assaulting authorities—resisting the police, the least objectively verifiable offense, increased the most. A new phenomenon emerged, namely civil damage awards made to police who claimed the status of victims and joined the prosecution's case as civil plaintiffs. This practice was virtually non-existent fifteen years ago (Jobard and Zimolag 2005).

The following case was heard in June 2003 in the chambers of the eighteenth arrondissement south courtroom. Abdel, a fourteen-year-old Moroccan male, was accused of assaulting a police officer and ultimately accepted the facts as presented in the police report. Nonetheless, he insisted that the arresting officer used excessive and unlawful force in the encounter. Although the judge supported the police officer, she dissuaded him from joining the prosecution as a civil plaintiff and from seeking damages. She emphasized the minor's family circumstances and clean record. The young man had arrived in France just three years earlier with a widowed mother and did well in school, and this was his first offense. The police officer had come to testify at the hearing. The judge heard the young man first and read from his police statement: "I admit that we were in the subway and a buddy threw a battery at a girl. He was trying to pick her up and she ignored him. When she didn't answer, I slapped her—not hard. I was just fooling around." When the judge asked if that was the right way to get a girl's attention, the young man said nothing but added, "He [police officer] jumped me, grabbed me by the collar, I fought back, he wouldn't let me go, I couldn't breathe, it was Ramadan and I hadn't eaten. I tried to tell him but he held on. I didn't know he was a policeman until he put on the handcuffs."

The judge discounted this version by reading from his signed statement, "A man came, grabbed me by the jacket, pushed me and said, 'it's the police.'" In his own deposition the policeman said that he was not in uniform but had clearly identified himself. This was an important clarification because if the teenager had defended himself against a mere passerby he might not have landed in court at all. Confronted with this discrepancy, the young man accepted the charge of assault but insisted he was the victim of police brutality: "O.K. it's true he did say he was a policeman but the rest is true too. We were near the [subway] public restrooms, and after he cuffed me, he pushed me inside and punched me over and over. I couldn't breathe, I was weak, he wouldn't let go."

When the judge brought in the policeman and asked if he had struck the teenager, the officer adamantly denied it. He complained that the young man was refusing to admit his guilt and warned that this was "the same group phenomenon of violent kids." He admitted being mollified by the boy's mother who apologized for her son. "I will not ask for much, only one hundred euros for losing a day of work. He needs to help her, he never has any pocket money." When the boy's mother broke down and begged him not to seek monetary damages because she was unemployed, alone, and poor, the boy looked at her in disgust and hissed, "shut up." The judge reminded the police officer that fourteen-year-olds could not work. She argued for a reparation measure instead of a court conviction because it was an isolated incident. She prevailed upon the policeman to drop his demand for damages on the condition that the boy could show that "he understands that his action was wrong and that he writes a formal letter of apology."

Not Guilty

In most of the cases I observed judges usually upheld the authority of the police and punished juvenile offenders. One 2001 case in the eighteenth arrondissement south courtroom resulted from an ID check after the police spotted a "known" Algerian youth riding a motor scooter without a helmet. They accused him of refusing to stop and of insulting them. He retorted: "They never ordered me to stop. I was going along and all of a sudden I saw their van directly in front of me. It had no lights. I couldn't stop and the bike fell." He insisted that he was struggling to get up when two officers lunged at him. He admitted defending himself and calling them "dirty pigs." Although the judge noted significant discrepancies in the depositions of the two police officers, she supported them, indicted him, and sent the case for trial to the formal juvenile court. She admonished the defendant: "You cannot refuse an order to stop. The police must be respected. They have a job to do."

In another 2001 hearing in chambers, a seventeen-year-old male of Tunisian ancestry was arrested on the same charges. Because he had no police record, his case was heard outside of court in a special diversion program. It ended up back in the nineteenth arrondissement east courtroom because the judicial officer at the hearing, a former police officer, was outraged that the accused had "refused to accept his guilt" and had been "insolent." The police report indicated that the youth had been "speeding" and, when confronted, "he accelerated, took off in the opposite direction, lost his balance, hit the police vehicle, and fell." The teenager was bruised in the fall, his passenger's leg was broken in three places, and a pedestrian was also hurt. The inspector's report as well as witness statements suggested that the position of the police van itself made it impossible for the youth to stop. The accused insisted, "I never saw the police until their van was in front of me. It had no light. I had only five seconds to react. It was too late." In an uncharacteristically indignant tone, the defense attorney argued that "the police had deliberately positioned their van in front of the scooter and blocked its path" making a collision inevitable, a strategy, she added, that "they were known to use." Although the judge admonished the defendant to respect and obey public authorities, she acquitted him. After the hearing she remarked, "It appears that the police provoke incidents to get themselves insulted or attacked just to ask for damages."

In an April 2001 hearing, a Senegalese male, Albert, who had been convicted in 1997 on drug possession and resisting arrest and given community service instead of a prison sentence, was back in court, this time before the juvenile court, for violating the terms of his alternate sentence. When the hearing began, the judge read a long list of his past convictions and commented sarcastically, "You have a strong attraction to prison." He retorted, "On the contrary, Madame, I like my freedom." When she asked if he worked, he replied, "I restocked shelves in a store. I didn't like it at all. Now I work for myself. I run a booth at the flea market. I have my own place and money." He added, "I never had the chance to tell my side of the story in my trial." But the judge cut him off and the conversation changed tone:

Judge: We are not here to retry this case. You were convicted of possession of marijuana and...

Albert (cutting her off): I have the right to express myself. It wasn't even ten grams.

Judge: You always insist on putting on a show, don't you? You were tried and found guilty.

Albert (interrupting again): I was on a motorcycle when I got pulled over. I didn't resist. The police jumped me. I tried to explain but it happened too fast. There were ten of them on me. When they got me in the van, they punched me and slapped me. Why aren't the police ever held responsible?

Judge (angry): We are NOT retrying this case. What you need to do is to convince me not to send you to prison.

Albert: The facts of the case are four years old. I have changed. I work, I have a good salary. I take responsibility for my actions, I have plans to get some professional skills. I have been taking a remedial class in the seventeenth arrondissement.

The judge asked for proof of both his attendance in class and his income from the flea market but he had none. When the judge invited the prosecutor to speak, she painted a very different picture:

Prosecutor: I say that there is no guarantee of integration...

Albert (standing up and calling out of turn): I have a right to speak.

Prosecutor (loudly to him): You will be quiet when I speak. (To the judge) He displays a hostile attitude, disrupts everything (here she used an Arabic slang expression *faire le souk* that refers to a noisy, disorderly place).

Albert stood again and walked toward the judge's bench, prompting her to thunder:

Judge (motioning to the uniformed guards at the back of the courtroom who came forward): You will sit down and be quiet!

Albert returned to his seat and the prosecutor continued:

Prosecutor: He has no regular work, Madame Judge, he is giving you the run-around. He hasn't completed his community service. I urge you to send this case back for sentencing.

As the judge and her two assessors deliberated behind closed doors, I overheard a side conversation between the juvenile prosecutor and Albert's defense attorney who tried to explain his behavior in court:

Attorney: He is really paranoid and constantly feels persecuted. I can assure you that he is very smart but can act like a real jerk (*d'une manière hyperconne*).

Prosecutor: Smart, you say? I'd say he is a real masochist.

The judge ruled that his case be sent back to the sentencing judge, noting that there was no proof that Albert had completed his community service. In contrast to the case of Thomas, Albert's assertiveness, refusal to respect court protocols, criticism of the police, and accusation of injustice made it impossible for the court personnel to accept his claim of new maturity and desire to avoid prison. He conformed to their view of a "bad" teenager who repeatedly tests the limits, challenges authority, and continues to break rules. In their view his offensive behavior showed the gaps in his upbringing and an improperly structured personality. Adolescents such as Albert refuse to acknowledge the facts and resist the attempts of social professionals to put them on the right path. Bad youths such as Albert are deemed to be at risk to offend again and to end up in prison.

He's Guilty, Not Me!

The next case I examine was widely viewed as another instance of esca-lating violence in public schools by delinquents of immigrant ancestry. The incident speaks to increased tensions surrounding social class, family origin, and cultural difference as critical factors in deciding what consti-tutes delinquent behavior and who is held accountable. It was publicized in the national media as an anti-Semitic hate crime in a Paris middle school in which "seven assailants gang[ed] up on a fourteen-year-old who [was] kicked repeatedly, to the cries of 'die, dirty Jew' and suffers a bro-ken shoulder blade" (*Le Figaro*, 6 December 2003). The newspaper report made no mention of the fact that the victim and the accused were the same age or that the incident occurred during gym class when students were rehearsing sequences from popular combat sports that their teacher had choreographed. The report did not identify the assailants' ethnic-ity, but the school's location in a multiethnic district with a bad repu-tation—the nineteenth arrondissement—suggested their immigrant or foreign ancestry.

The association with "immigrant youth" worked also on another level. Considerable public attention has centered on the rise of anti-Semitic incidents targeting the French Jewish community, the largest in Europe. Since the beginning of the second Palestinian Intifada in September 2000, anti-Semitic attacks have been widely attributed to North African Arab youth. In his 2003 report, the president of the public watchdog group, the National Consultative Commission on Human Rights, described the mounting racist and anti-Semitic violence in public schools and called upon the government to implement a "forceful and coherent policy to fight against it" (*Le Monde*, 29 March 2003). Despite a slight decrease in hate crimes in 2003, heads of the Paris district of the National Education Ministry, the Office of Judicial Protection of Juveniles within the Justice Ministry, and the Juvenile Prosecutor's Office at the Paris court responded by instituting a zero tolerance plan mandating the investigation of all anti-Semitic incidents ranging from graffiti, threats, and vandalism to as-sault. Despite ongoing anti-Muslim racism, the Justice Ministry instituted no such zero tolerance policy to protect the Muslim community.

On 20 October, ten days after the incident, the principal's superiors contacted the juvenile prosecutor's office at the Paris juvenile court. All seven of the boys were picked up and taken into police custody for ques-tioning. They vociferously refuted the Jewish victim's accusation that their anti-Semitism motivated his injury. As a result, the juvenile judge scheduled a hearing in early December 2003 to allow all parties to press their respective cases. For their part, school authorities suspended six of the seven boys for a week. Despite reports that a "group of assailants" was responsible for both the assault and the racist speech, the school disciplinary council held only one individual responsible for the injury and disciplined only one student for hate speech. It turned out that the latter was not even present when the injury occurred. This prompted expressions of outrage by the students' parents, who appealed the principal's decision to the superintendent of Paris schools.

The case drew a well-known attorney to represent the Jewish plaintiff and involved the usual suspects in penal cases at Paris juvenile court, boys from working class families: one from the mainstream French population and the remainder from immigrant (North and West African) and foreign (Turkish) backgrounds. The police and the juvenile prosecutor's office filed charges under a new statute that added racist speech as an aggravating circumstance to the offense of physical assault against a minor. In this case, "racist speech" was grouped with "assault" under articles 222-11 and 12 of the penal code.[6] The stakes were high because the boys were accused of perpetrating a hate-crime and of having acted together (*en réunion*) on a fourteen-year-old—two aggravating circumstances—carrying a maximum adult sentence of seven years in prison and a €100,000.00 fine. National juvenile sentencing guidelines cut the sentences in half, resulting in a maximum penalty of three and a half years in prison and a €50,000.00 fine.

I begin with the victim's account in court testimony because his responses foreground the class, ethnic, racial, and cultural differences that play a central role in the disciplining and control of youth of immigrant and foreign ancestry in public school. It is important to note that the victim, Joel, was represented by a prominent Jewish attorney whose fees were paid by a well-known Jewish organization.[7] When I interviewed that attorney in May 2005, he described his young client's mother as a woman with an "extremely limited education." All of the other boys were from working-class and underprivileged backgrounds and had court-appointed attorneys. In his testimony, Joel deftly contrasted his own class and ethnic background (lower middle-class and Jewish) to his classmates, even as he portrayed them as behavior problems, poor achievers, and racist aggressors.

Judge: Tell us what happened in your own words?

Joel: A group of guys were not doing what the teacher had said but were goofing off and hitting me. I protected my head and arms and couldn't see who they were. One tackled me and I fell down. I tried to protect myself. I managed to get up by hanging on to Nassir. We fell down, he landed on top of me. I heard my shoulder crack, felt pain, and I cried. He didn't realize I was hurt because I got hit again. I got kicked in the throat. Then they stopped. And the guys must have told the teacher that I was crying because she left to get the firefighters [first responders in France]. Slimane came over [this young man was not present until after the injury occurred] and as a joke offered to give me chewing gum to fix my shoulder. Then he left saying, "die, dirty Jew." One other kid, who was not part of the attack, heard Slimane say that. I didn't. He told me later. It was Slimane. I am the only Jew in the class and I felt it. I asked to change classes. They can tell I am Jewish because I am well dressed. The others see it like that.

Both the judge and the defense attorneys questioned Joel about ethnic diversity at his middle school. He spontaneously identified French, Arab, Ivorian, Ethiopian, Turkish, and Chinese teenagers using color hypergamy to distinguish among Sub-Saharan, East African, Sri-Lankan, and mixed-race teenagers. He also used religious markers and cultural practices to surmise that one student wasn't Muslim because he didn't observe Ramadan while another was Christian because he wore a cross. When defense attorneys asked why, given the ethnic and racial diversity in school, there were no other school incidents, no harassment or hazing, Joel insisted that his attackers were "rowdy," were not "hard working," had "repeated grades" in school, and had "taken advantage of the teacher's absence to cause trouble." Another attorney focused on the racist slur, noting that it was normal for teenagers in middle schools with multiethnic populations to exchange insults in a joking way:

> Attorney (for suspects): Don't you say, "dirty black" or "dirty Arab" to one another? Don't you constantly refer to physical traits based on race?
>
> Joel: Other students exchanged insults. Not me.

Nonetheless, as the hearing continued, a competing version of the facts emerged from the suspects' testimony that repeated their October statements to the police. The school gym teacher also supported their account. One of the accused explained:

> Abdel: The class broke up into smaller groups and we were all fooling around, shoving and kicking each other. Joel too. At one point Joel got knocked over and the others jumped on him, and one boy was kicking him. When Joel looked up and saw Nassir, Joel jumped on him and grabbed him from behind. They fell over, Nassir on top, Joel underneath. Then Joel cried out in pain.

The judge next heard from Slimane, a fourteen-year-old born in Gambia whose family circumstances were the most precarious. His parents were separated. His father was in Africa, his mother was living in the United States, and, although his official guardian was his uncle, he was staying with his father's sister in a tiny apartment a long way from his school. He maintained his statement to the police, indicating that he had been instructed to remove his earrings and was returning from the locker room when he noticed Joel lying on the mat. He readily admitted calling him a dirty Jew. When asked by his court-appointed attorney if the racist speech was premeditated, he replied:

> Slimane: I just didn't think. It just came out. I don't resent him because he is Jewish. I resent him because he called me a dirty black and insulted my parents. He said, "fuck your mother" (*nique ta mère*) and that hurt me. Of course we use language like that all the time and mostly it doesn't mean anything. At the beginning of the year we got along all right. We joked around... . I'm not proud of myself. I'm sorry. I apologized the day after it happened when I took him his homework. It was a good decision for the principal to have us take turns bringing him his homework.

A four-month investigation of the case resulted in a decision not to pursue an indictment of the suspects. The similar stories told by the accused plus the teacher's insistence that there were no problem students in the class convinced the judge and the deputy juvenile prosecutor. Nonetheless, the head Paris prosecutor who recommended that the case be prosecuted appealed the decision.

The Suspect Remains Silent

In early June 2003 I attended an indictment hearing in the judge's chambers during which, in the absence of oral testimony, the presiding judge noted only that "[t]he suspect remains silent." This case involved a thirteen-year-old Malian male, Mohammed, the youngest of five siblings, who lived with his mother. He had only sporadic contact with his father who divided his time between Paris and Mali. The boy already had three cases before the court and was suspected of stealing a classmate's wallet in the school bathroom and of shoving him against the wall—an aggravated theft (*vol avec violence*) under French law. His *éducatrice*—and defense attorney all provided background for the judge. Identified as slow and unruly by his teachers in pre-school, the boy had repeated the equivalent of first grade and by 2003 had been expelled from six different schools, mostly for disruptive behavior in class. He was asthmatic and obese and suffered constant "ridicule from his classmates" because he was "fat and slow." According to his attorney, as a result of a poor self-image, he had developed a system of defense and was completely withdrawn. He hardly spoke to anyone in school or at home. His "attitude," "behavioral problems," and "refusal to speak" had resulted in "enormous scholastic problems."

The judge repeatedly attempted to elicit Mohammed's version of the facts, at first patiently encouraging him to open up, but the boy simply refused to answer or to speak in his own defense. After forty-five minutes the judge lost her temper, slammed her desk, and demanded that he respond. He looked directly at her but remained silent.

> Judge: This is getting serious. He has a number of penal cases at court. I want to help but he has to show that he understands. I am willing to consider probation and a reparation measure (a letter of apology to the victim). He has to repair his act. It must come from him.

> Attorney: He is under sixteen and has a mother who is very strict and resorts regularly to physical punishment. At least she takes an interest in him. His *éducatrice* thinks we need to work on the family situation. That is the problem.

> Judge: We will give it some time. I'll defer sentence until the fall.

Conclusion

A central theme in this chapter is the critical role played by class, culture, and gender in the determination of who lands in court and how risk is defined. The association of young men of immigrant and foreign ancestry with different types of risk—personal, familial, social, and national—explains in part their disproportionate representation in the child welfare and juvenile justice systems. The determination of risk begs larger questions about the tolerance for cultural difference, understandings of legal responsibility, and the notion of justice. The normative assumptions surrounding the definition of family, the disciplining of children, the passage into adulthood, and the behavioral requirements for adolescents, particularly young men, are all intimately linked to citizenship and belonging (Shweder et al. 2002). The cases examined in this chapter reveal the difficult negotiations and outright disputes among judges, *éducateurs*, law enforcement officials, and members of minority groups over what forms and degrees of cultural diversity are permissible. The limits of tolerance for certain types of cultural difference emerge in the encounters of minority groups with various agents of authority such as police, school officials, and social workers, as well as neighbors and co-workers. On the local level, in the neighborhood, the apartment building, and the school, cultural differences understood as dress, language, gestures, looks, family forms, and public behavior are the primary means for differentiating among the mainstream French and their Others—primarily disadvantaged children of immigrant and foreign ancestry. These are often viewed, like race, as invariable and immutable clusters of traits that are passed from generation to generation.

Once in court, this population is treated according to a paradigm based on social origin and cultural difference. Class, culture, and gender combine to affect the outcome of hearings. Of the hundreds of cases I observed between 2000 and 2005, there were only a handful of middle-class children. Their parents had the economic means, social status, and cultural capital to protect their children from legal sanctions and court supervision. The class proximity of middle-class parents to court personnel and social professionals could give them an advantage in pressing their claims in court. They could pay for private attorneys and were already conversant with the broad tenets of French law. This contrasted sharply with young men of immigrant ancestry who had only partial or faulty knowledge of penal codes but a strong sense of injustice. In meetings with juvenile judges outside of court, they asked prescient questions about the legality of repeated identity checks. They wanted to know what counted as resisting arrest and inciting a riot and whether police claimed they were insulted in order to get large monetary awards from the court (Rosenczveig 2002: 30–35).

A delinquency of exclusion, associated with the troubled children of disadvantaged immigrants, is seen as a pernicious amalgam of chronic poverty, an urban underclass, school failure, and welfare dependency. It is based on a conception of the minor as determined by his socio-cultural milieu. Many law enforcement and court personnel agreed that offenders such as Abdel, Albert, Mohammed, and Nassir were mired in their own cultural codes and territories and seemed resistant, if not impervious, to the redemptive power of both French norms and laws. The trope "gang" or "group" was used frequently by police, prosecutors, and judges to impute criminal intent to groups of young men who spent too much time in the street. Mohammed and Abdel had already been identified by school authorities and social workers as "*turbulent*" (unruly), without bearings (*repères*), and unlikely to integrate well within French society. This argument is all the more striking for Mohammed who was born and schooled in France.

Many civil plaintiffs who claimed to be victims in the cases I examined turned out to be police officers. The majority of those claims for compensation were for minor physical injuries or merely symbolic insults. Their demands for "justice" and damages in court rested on their very power as public authorities to accuse and arrest begging the question, in the wake of violent unrest in 2005, of who would hold them accountable. The confrontations of police with juvenile defendants rested on a set of categorical oppositions that precluded mutual recognition. For the police and prosecutors, the young offender too often represented social chaos, gratuitous violence, and immigrants, in contrast to public order, legitimate defense, and *Français de souche* (the pedigreed or true French). Although some judges rejected police claims as spurious, the majority took the word of the police and of French civil plaintiffs over that of juvenile defendants. To insist that the courts are color-blind, when the majority of defendants in penal hearings are African and Arab, makes a mockery of the status of victim as well as of the accused and ignores the peculiar nature of "republican racism" in historical and contemporary France.

These cases return us to *The Just* by Paul Ricoeur (1995). The legitimacy of the democratic state as maintained by institutions like the courts relies on able subjects whose rights and obligations are grounded in mutual recognition and acceptance of shared rules. But what of the angry youth, outraged victims, misunderstood parents, indignant public officials, and moralizing court personnel in state institutions? Too often in these cases there was no mutual tolerance or recognition between court personnel, law enforcement, and young men. In most of the proceedings I observed in the Paris juvenile court, the voices of court personnel dominated. Those of children, parents, and even their defense attorneys were muted or silent. This had, no doubt, much to do with their sense that the hearings and trials were a formality whose outcomes were largely predetermined. It was a process in which they had much to lose and little to gain. In this chapter I have focused on the voices of young men and examined closely the cases where they refuted the charges and spoke out. By challenging the facts, they challenged the court's attempt to manage doubt and to control the construction of authoritative narratives of "the facts." These young men attempted to use the court as a place to stake their claims, defend their innocence, or justify their offenses, and to exercise their legal rights to demand accountability of law enforcement for unjust or discriminatory behavior. They commented critically on the cultural categories and therefore the social reality on which the law is based. They attempted to alert the court to the contaminating effects of power on the law—racism, intolerance, different normative systems, and class differences. They sought different outcomes from the legal system by highlighting institutional injustices and emphasizing mitigating circumstances. They warned of the hazards of bureaucratic indifference, the dangers of ethno-racial stereotyping, the hostilities born of social inequality, and the costs of economic polarization. These cases tell stories well worth repeating as French legislators continue to amend existing juvenile law.

Notes

1 These sanctions are modeled on the adult penal code. They center on control over young children's spatial movement, social contacts, and personal property.
2 Law 2002-1138 mandated that minors from thirteen to sixteen years old who violate the terms of their probation pending trial could be sent to closed juvenile detention centers.
3 As in the adult system, there are three jurisdictional levels: minor offenses are tried in chambers by one juvenile judge as in the *tribunal de police*; the formal juvenile court (*tribunal correctionnel*) including a judge and two non-judicial assessors hears cases for juveniles between thirteen and sixteen years of age accused of crimes and for all those under eighteen accused of serious misdemeanors; and the *cour d'assises pour mineurs* tries sixteen- to eighteen-year-olds accused of crimes.
4 See article 769-7 of the penal code procedure amended by law 2004-204 of 9 March 2004.
5 All of the names and identifying characteristics have been changed to protect the confidentiality of the accused in proceedings.
6 These articles outline aggravating circumstances such as assault on minors under fifteen years of age; on vulnerable persons by virtue of their age, infirmity, illness, or pregnancy; on family or household members; on public officials; on witnesses or plaintiffs; or on persons targeted on the basis of ethnicity, nationality, race, religion, or sexual orientation (www. legifrance.gouv.fr).
7 This organization is the *Conseil Représentatif des Institutions Juives de France*.

Bibliography

Bouarkra, N. 2006. "Mineurs "dangereux" et juges "laxistes" Available from: http:///www. moned-diplomatique.fr/2006/11/BOUARKRA/14205. [Accessed 5 March 2008]
Garapon, Antoine. 1997. *Bien juger. Essai sur le ritual judiciaire*. Paris: Éditions Odile Jacob.
Hodgson, Jacqueline. 2005. *French Criminal Justice: A Comparative Account of the Investigation and Prosecution of Crime in France*. Portland, OR: Hart Publishing.
Law No. 2002-1198. 2007. 10 August. Avalable from:www.legifrance.gouv.fr.
Law No. 2004-204. 2004. 9 March. Available from: www.legifrance.gouv.fr.
Law No. 2002-1138. 2002. 9 September. Available from: www.legifrance.gouv.fr.
Jobard, Fabien and Marta Zimolag. 2005 "Quand les policiers vont au tribunal. Étude sur les outrages, rébellions et violences." *Questions Pénales*, March XVIII.2: 1–4.

Nye, Robert, A. 1984. *Crime, Madness, and Politics in Modern France: The Medical Concept of National Decline*. Princeton, NJ: Princeton University Press.

Refondation de l'ordonnance du 2.2.1945 sur l'enfance delinquante. 2008. 15 April. Available from: www.justice.gouv.fr/index.php?rubrique=10030&article=14454. [Accessed 18 May 2008].

Rosenczveig, Jean-Pierre. 2002. *Justice, ta mère*. Paris: Robert Laffont.

Shweder, Richard, A., et al. eds. 2002. *Engaging Cultural Differences. The Multicultural Challenge in Liberal Democracies*. New York: Russell Sage Foundation.

Terrio, Susan, J. 2009. *Judging Mohammed. Juvenile delinquency, Immigration, and Exclusion at the Paris Palace of Justice*. Stanford, CA: Stanford University Press.

Wacquant, Loïc. 2004. "Comment sortir du piège sécuritaire?" *Contradictions*, 22:120–133.

Chapter 9

INCARCERABLE SUBJECTS
Working-Class Black and Latino Male Youths in
Two California Cities

Victor M. Rios and Cesar Rodriguez

Oakland, California, U.S.

James[1] is an African-American young man whose story is very similar to that of many young black men in poor urban areas of the United States. He grew up in poverty, was criminalized at school and on the streets, and, despite receiving a high school diploma, has not found any job opportunities. What he has found is constant police harassment beginning in grade school when, at the age of ten, his teacher called in the police because James had called her a "bitch." The police officer showed up in his class, pulled him out, handcuffed him, and gave him a scare: "he told me 'I'm gonna' take you to jail, boy. You better respect that teacher.'" For years, as James walked home from school, this same police officer repeatedly stopped him and searched him for drugs. Eventually James became accustomed to routine police stops, normalizing police harassment, and brutality despite having never committed a crime. "Police are always gonna' be here to make sure you don't get out of place. That's just life. Even if you don't got nothin' on you, you still gotta' deal with it." The same officer who handcuffed James at age ten, and systematically harassed him for seven years, arrested him when he was seventeen. James was walking home from school. The officer stopped him, searched him, and found a rolled up marijuana cigar in his pocket. James was booked, released, and placed on probation. Eventually, the probation process facilitated further arrests that would lead James to felony convictions. From this point on James became "negatively credentialed" (Pager 2003: 942) by the state. This mark of a criminal record would become a central obstacle in James's ability to acquire a job even after receiving a high school diploma. Today, James looks for work but his criminal record limits his ability to obtain one of the few low-wage, low-skill jobs for which many working-class people compete.

Santa Barbara, California, U.S.

Steven is a twenty-year-old Latino male who belongs to the 52 percent of Mexican Americans who never finish high school in the state of California. His parents migrated to the United States from Mexico in 1981 to labor in the strawberry fields of Oxnard, California. In 2009, his parents made $12.00 (U.S.) an hour when they were lucky to find temporary farm work. Steven has worked in the fields with his parents every summer ever since he was eleven years old. He knows what back-breaking hard work is: "We would come home with back pain and messed up hands. We would get sick and still have to go to work for like ten hours a day. If we wanted to go number two [defecate], we had to walk for a long time just to find a tree to hide in." Steven left school in order to help his parents. In addition, he felt that school officials did not support him. He illustrates his reasoning for deciding to never return with the following incident: "The teacher chose on me, and the white guy [fellow student], he said 'Oh he won't know the answer. He's Mexican.' The teacher didn't say anything." "What did you do about it?" one of us asks. He replies: "Just skip school. Go to a friend's house, help my parents with work, do drugs, fucking just go look for fights, just anything rather than school. I hate school."

These stories highlight the crisis that poor racialized young men in the United States face on a daily basis. The collapse of the welfare state and the expansion of the punitive state in the United States over the past forty years have led to a vicious cycle in which young men are pipelined into the criminal justice system. Deindustrialization, the decline of government-sponsored work and social services, and the proliferation of draconian criminal justice policies have led to a process of abandonment and containment. Abandonment "is the rigorously coordinated and organized setting aside of people and resources" (Ruth Wilson Gilmore, as quoted in Gordon 2009: 178). In the United States the processes and conditions of abandonment are uniquely racialized. Given the racialized nature of abandonment, and the fatal results it has, abandonment evokes Ruth Wilson Gilmore's (2007) definition of racism as "the state-sanctioned or extralegal production and exploitation of group-differentiated vulnerability to *premature death*" (Gilmore 2007: 28).

We should understand the premature death delivered by racist abandonment not just in terms of *biological* death but *social* death as well: the socially dead become subjects void of access to political rights, civic participation, and social connectedness (Rodriquez 2006: 35). While racialized social death has been delivered by various manners of exclusionary abandonment throughout history (e.g., see Patterson 1982), the current mode of producing social death is rooted in capitalist globalization (Harvey 2005: 81–85). Neoliberal elites engineered the flight of factories which could have employed the young able-bodied persons who now find themselves incarcerated, while they simultaneously sharpened the knives that butcher social services down to the bone. Rendered as surplus population by a dilapidated education system and a labor market with few employment opportunities, young, able-bodied, working-class men (and, increasingly women) of color experience abandonment that eventually leads many into a draconian punitive system of racialized social control.[2] Examining its effects on a young, poor, male, and racialized population in the United States, we have found that neoliberalism has produced a population abandoned by the left arm of the state (i.e. welfare state programs) and capital that no longer "learns to labour" (Willis 1981), but instead "prepares for prison" (Hirschfield 2008a).

From Learning to Labor to Preparing for Prison

The United States has now reached a point where an average of six hundred juveniles are arrested each day, and where every black boy born in 2001 has a one in three chance of going to prison, while a Latino boy born in the same year has a one in six chance of facing the same fate (Campaign 2008: 1, 3). The work of Ruth Wilson Gilmore holds tremendous explanatory power when explaining the emergence of California's prison-industrial complex, whereby a large number of working-class, black, and brown men (and increasingly women) like James and Steven now find themselves within California's prison population. Highlighting the impact of capitalist globalization, whereby deindustrialization shipped manufacturing jobs away from California, Gilmore (2007) seeks to understand how so many—mostly working-class—people in the prime productive years of their lives find themselves in prison. She demonstrates that

California's prison-industrial complex emerged to absorb four surpluses: surplus agricultural land, surplus municipal funds, surplus state capacity, and, most important to this project, surplus population—those people left unemployed and/or under-employed in the wake of deindustrialization and capitalist globalization. Avery Gordon's (2006) work complements the work of Gilmore by demonstrating reasons for disposing of so many people in their prime years of life, since mass incarceration, in the context of abandoned communities, serves to quarantine the effects of poverty by removing "from civil society potentially active, angry and demanding political subjects to a remote and closed place where they are civically disabled and socially dead" (2006: 52).

Research dating back to the work of David Tyack (1974) argues that mass education[3] ultimately fails to provide working-class students with the credentials necessary to experience upward social mobility and instead operates to reproduce the very class inequalities that it purports to ameliorate (Althusser 1971; Anyon 1981; Anyon 1997; Anyon 2005; Bourdieu 1984; Freire 2000; Willis 1981). Thus, this body of work provides a critical framework for understanding the school as a site of stratified social reproduction. Yet, much of this research took for granted the terrain of public education in a redistributive state where manufacturing jobs were the next logical step for many of the youths they studied. However, as the prior two bodies of work show, the redistributive state has been largely eradicated (with public education being one of its remaining vestiges), manufacturing jobs that working-class children were overtly and subtly prepared for are no longer there, and prisons have become the places where people left unemployed by deindustrialization likely find themselves.

In light of capitalist globalization, many critical education scholars and youth advocates use the term "school-to-prison pipeline" to encapsulate the processes that continue to inequitably reproduce youth along racialized class lines through mass education and pipeline them into the growing prison-industrial complex. Literature on the punitive turn in public education helps us to identify watershed moments in history—such as the shifts in funding away from education and toward incarceration that occurred through the 1990s (Ambrosio and Schiraldi 1997; Campaign 2008; Connolly et al. 1996; Gold 1995; Taqi-Eddin, Macallair, and Schiraldi 1998), and the moral panics through the mid- and late-1990s based on a string of violent school shootings at suburban and rural high schools (Binns and Markow 1999; Brooks, Schiraldi, and Zeidenberg 2000; Donohue et al. 1998; Dwyer, Osher, and Warger 1998; Dycus 2008; Mukherjee and Karpatkin 2007)—that facilitated punitive investments into public education. This research also helps to identify the specific "objective features" of these punitive investments —in the form of zero tolerance polices, school resources officers (SROs), surveillance technologies, and information-sharing linkages between the education system and the criminal justice system—as well as the impacts they have had on rising rates of suspensions and expulsions, drop-out (or "force-out") rates, and school-based arrests.[4] Yet, while outlining the *objective* features and results of a school-to-prison pipeline and demonstrating how these punitive investments into schools lead to higher arrest rates—especially for students of color like James and Steven— this body of literature does not include the kind of rich ethnographic narratives that illustrate the *subjective* features of reproduction, much like the "learning to labor" body of literature provided (albeit in a prior era).

Finally, within academic literature, there has been a debate emerging in recent years over the impacts of these punitive investments into schools on these institutions themselves and on the trajectories of students in mass education. The "convergence" camp asserts that the impulse to heavily invest punitive resources into schools has reached not only schools in poor communities but also middle-class, suburban, and rural schools as well, so that all schools share the similar contours of a securitized terrain—which includes, for example, cameras, full-time school-based police officers, zero-tolerance policies, and normalized law enforcement responses to otherwise non-criminal issues (Kupchik 2009). This camp argues that the dissemination of this institutional surveillance regime will reproduce, on the one hand, a criminalized class that serves to justify the securitization of social trends and, on the other hand, a compliant class accustomed to surveillance techniques and technologies, the presence of law enforcement personnel in daily life, and a law-enforcement response to non-criminal issues (Kupchik and Monahan 2006).

Pointing to the class variation in the vehicles through which administrators and teachers manifest these punitive investments (i.e., in middle-class schools with drug-sniffing dogs and school-based police officers who see themselves as mentors first and officers second, and in schools largely composed of working-class students of color with humiliating and aggressive metal-detector programs and mandatory pat-downs by condescending police officers), P.J. Hirschfield (2008b) states that: "[i]n short, the gated community may be a more apt metaphor to describe the security transformation of affluent schools, while the prison metaphor better suits that of inner-city schools" (2008b: 84). In the latter form of school, administrators, educators, and SROs can label youths of color, like Steven and James, as "animals," "inmates," or "killers," and they can also project criminal futures onto their students as well as lead their students to believe that their teachers don't support them or care about their success (Blum and Woodlee 2001; Ferguson 2000; Fine et al. 2004; Noguera 2003; Nolan and Anyon 2004).

Our work builds on this literature and examines the subject-position of criminalized youth themselves as they navigate through and respond to the junctures of a school-to-prison pipeline and become reproduced as incarcerable subjects. This chapter, based on ethnographic observations and in-depth interviews with youths of color in two very different California cities (Santa Barbara and Oakland), contributes to the literature on social reproduction in the context of abandonment and mass incarceration. Voices which are often left out can help us understand how meanings are generated and structures become embedded in the everyday lives of youths. We examine how this criminalization creates the reproductive disjuncture between the class trajectory of these young people and the class position of their parents, as criminalization tracks them not only away from education but also away from any semblance of formal and/or legitimated employment, particularly the few jobs that can provide them a living wage.

We pay note to the subjective factors of a school-to-prison pipeline and, in doing so, illuminate how the interpellation of youths according to their racialization and gendering plays a pivotal role in ascribing them their negative credentials and facilitating their reproduction as incarcerable subjects. Furthermore, we examine how these youths respond to the criminalization they experience on a daily basis. In order to demonstrate the complexity of this criminalization and illustrate the experience of these institutional regimes from the subject-position of criminalized youth themselves, we examine some of their critical "partial penetrations" as well as illustrate how some of the actions they undertake facilitate their criminalization.[5] Finally, by returning to the objective features, we illustrate how the punitive investments into schools and the negative credentials these youth "earn" in school overlap with the saturation of their communities with policing, which in turn shapes these young peoples' paths toward prisons.

Children of Migration and Immigration

The family backgrounds of the youths in this study illustrate the ways mutually constitutive systems of racism and capitalism conjure up an im/migrant racialized army of reserve labor situated at the more precarious labor rungs within North America. Thus, the black migrant family which can trace its movement through the Great Migration of blacks from the U.S. South to the U.S. North during the World War II era and the Latino immigrant family of today have been included as cheap labor in the lowest, most unstable, and dangerous labor rungs. As a consequence of these larger world capitalist system phenomena, the youths we interviewed could trace their immediate lineage to numerous places, from the U.S. South to the Global South—Texas, reservations in the United States, Mississippi, various cities and states in México (i.e., México City, Guanajuato, Michoacán, Jalisco, Zacatecas, and Puebla), Guatemala, El Salvador, Puerto Rico, Egypt, and Eritrea.

Contributing to the decision to im/migrate, were the conditions of abandonment that our participants' elders experienced themselves as youths in the United States and/or Global South. For example, Lily, a young woman living with her single mother, describes the precarious conditions that her mother struggled with as a young woman while growing up in Michoacan, México: "Like, my mom used to tell me too…that, when she was little, that Mexico used to be hard for them…like they'd be lucky if they had *carne* [meat] to eat ... like, on Sundays was the day when they had their *caldos de pollos* [chicken soup] or something like that...." Jacinto's father similarly describes the precarious conditions his father faced while working on a farm as a child in Puebla, which cost him his ability to go to school and, subsequently, his literacy:

> Like, he'd work in the morning and he basically only had fifteen minutes to come back home and go to school. Like, literally, he would have little time to go to school and he would have no sleep at all so my dad was like, "fuck it" cuz he can't handle it, cuz he like, had work to do and he had school. Now, he doesn't know how to read and write. Like, he'll ask me to read everything for him in Spanish and ask me to translate everything from English.

Young African-American participants could also recount the precariousness their family members experienced as youths in the U.S. South. Paul's family could trace its family roots to the South, specifically to Mississippi, and Paul was very cognizant of the precarious economic and social conditions his grandfather experienced:

> My great uncle was about eleven or twelve and he just dropped [his grandfather and his grandfather's brother] off in the cabin like, with no food, no nothing ... they had to hunt squirrel and ravens and stuff like that, like they ... they lived it hard core, they had to steal man, they had to do a lot and I mean it was kind of hard when you think about that.

These sorts of conditions of precarious abandonment, experienced as tremendous economic hardship, led many of our participants' families to im/migrate. For some other participants, political conditions played an important "push" role in propelling elder generations to im/migrate.

Many im/migrant elders were subsequently incorporated at the lower labor rungs in California. For example, Lauren was a young African-American woman who could trace her lineage back to the U.S. South (Texas). Her grandparents were members of the Great Migration, a generation of black migrants who migrated to the Bay Area to work in the military industries that sprung up during World War II:

> My dad's dad came from Texas, and he doesn't say much about Texas, but I know they said they just had to come out here ... but I know he used to work at the shipyard in Richmond ... they think that's why he has chest pains, cuz of the stuff he was breathin' in when he was working out there.

Our participants from Latin America told us that their parents now work in the lower rungs of the labor market, typically in informal service labor jobs. For example, Jacinto's father also went to work right away in an informal job, as did his mother:

> When my dad got here, he was working at a restaurant, cleaning dishes I think and then, my mom, I think she was just working with my auntie, like cleaning. She would go help clean houses some days just to get some money and then she started babysitting and, what else, like, her babysitting job lasted like thirteen years ... that's how long she lasted there for the same family. The kids were my age.... I kinda grew up with them.

The racialized class-inclusion of these first generations is pivotal in understanding the racialized abandonment and containment of subsequent generations because, while the labor-potential of the first generation was once valued, racial, political and financial elites were able to exploit their labor profitably by legal and extra-juridical systems of racial disenfranchisement (such as Jim Crow segregation and current immigration laws). Yet, it can be argued that subsequent generations have become abandoned by capital and the state by processes of neoliberalism,[6] and consequently contained by the largest incarceration project in human history.

While the first generation worked as precarious laborers, the second generation finds it difficult to find any employment at all. Sachyn tells us, for example, about her own family and where its various generations wind up, if at all, in the labor market:

> Like, the women, they usually be like, babysitting and cleaning houses, and the men, like, they're in *carpinteria* [carpentry], construction, gardening and stuff, and the younger people, like my brother and my cousins, if

they *do* work, they work at Circuit City, Target, Wal-Mart and stuff like that … but some don't work there, they dropped out or whatever, or they get locked up on some stupid shit, or whatever.

Sashyn's quote perhaps best demonstrates the precarious informal work in which her immigrant family's elders have found a niche as well as the sites of precarious part-time employment and/or incarceration in which her generation now finds itself.

In general, youths hear the stories of their families' resiliency amid conditions of abandonment and strive to use those stories as inspiration to excel in school. They are driven to succeed because they know their success can help their families finally escape the indignities of a racialized, precarious working-class livelihood that they have been trying to escape their whole lives. Yet, something is not allowing these youths to fulfill their families' best wishes and hopes. They are being tracked away from a college education and all the living-wage opportunities such an education purportedly provides. By following the life-stories of two youths in our study, James and Steven, we see how this disjuncture occurs between the hope of working-class parents and the actual social position of their children. Further, we can observe the ways in which they are channeled away from education and subsequent living-wage professional jobs, and towards a juvenile criminal justice system and a likely prison-term.

James and Steven: Different Lives, Similar Struggles

As mentioned above, James encountered the long arm of the law relatively early in his life, at the age of ten, when he lost his temper with a teacher and subsequently encountered Officer Johns. James is a young African-American male who can trace his lineage back to the U.S. South (Texas and Oklahoma). While he is not certain what specifically motivated his grandparents to migrate to Berkeley, California, he nonetheless knows that his grandparents were part of a generation of black migrants who migrated from the U.S. South to satisfy a labor shortage in low-wage, dangerous, and impermanent jobs: "My grandfather worked on the railroads out here, and, I'm not sure why, but I know they came during World War II or whatever, but that's how he got blind, because the sparks got him, and that's how he wound up getting blind." While his grandparents expected James's father and his father's siblings to find opportunities for work, they did not manage to find much. His father found work often at the back of restaurants and/or laboring as a busboy. Nonetheless, his father grew up on the waterfront in Berkeley and in West Oakland, as a member of a generation that, following the collapse of the war-time industries that had employed their own parents, became suddenly and swiftly lumpenproletarianized as they were largely excluded from stable and enfranchised forms of employment by de jure and de facto segregation, as well as further deindustrialization.

Before and shortly after James was born, his father struggled with alcoholism. James confided that while his father struggled with his addictions he was not present in James's early years. During that time, James was in the custody of his mother, who struggled with substance abuse herself. As a result, James was taken into foster custody and bounced around a small number of foster homes until, having controlled his addiction through the help of a twelve-step program, his father one day came back to find James. James eventually gave up his hopes of ever finding his mother or any of his siblings and thinks she may have passed away already.

He has since then grown very close to his father, who often told James about the friends he lost to the streets or to the prisons. These sorts of stories prompted James to dedicate himself to graduating from high school, despite the obstacles he faced. For example, James talked about the street wisdom his father passed on to him:

> [L]ike my dad, he's got a lot of friends that are still homeless. Cuz like, a couple of times, me and my dad rolled down his neighborhood, and he's like, he'll tell me everyone who lived in that house, and there'll be that one guy who everybody knew him, he had the nicest shoes, the nicest clothes, everybody acknowledged him all good, and then, you'll see him Saturdays at the flea market, with a cup out, wearing the same old shoes, but they're worn down to the max and he'll wind up seeing one of those guys and he'll be like, "I don't want you to be like that," … you gotta look at that and think about it.

It was this preparation for life that motivated James to focus on school and helped him recognize the unhappy fate of many of his community members. Yet, because James's father explained his own cohort's detriment as a failure of personal responsibility, James believed that his own hard work would pay off. What they both did not take into account was that a racist and bleak job market for African-Americans was an additional component shaping the poor outcomes experienced by his father's cohort, and later, James's own inability to acquire a job. In the meantime, the narrative of personal responsibility motivated James to focus on school. However, a desire to succeed academically does not always provide a positive educational experience. And, indeed, despite his desire to succeed, James reports having tense conflicts with educators and being constantly punished in school.

Steven

We first met Steven in 2007 when we were conducting fieldwork in Santa Barbara, California where we spent time making observations of the daily routines of the student body. Steven was a student at a continuation school, La Mirada, a high school designed to educate those students who have been expelled from the "regular" high school. Steven was forced to return to school as a condition of his probation. The school was located inside a small, dilapidated industrial building with no signs demarcating its function. At the entrance to the school, a security guard and an office administrator greeted the students, who signed in, pulled all of their belongings from their pockets, and handed them over to the security guard. The guard placed each student's belongings into a large plastic freezer bag. The guard then used a portable hand-held metal detector to search students for weapons. For those students who were wearing what the school considered gang clothing or, in the case of girls, revealing clothing, the school provided an "ugly orange t-shirt" that students wore over their clothes. This was especially humiliating for students as they took their daily physical education walk through the business neighborhood in which the school was located. As Steven passed through the routine, I (Rios) got a feeling of déjà vu. "I have been here before," I told myself. Then I realized that the process was almost exactly the same as when I got booked into a juvenile justice facility at the age of fifteen. The school's practice of booking students in as they prepare for their school day was an almost exact replica of the juvenile facility's entry routine. It later came as no surprise to find out that a few of the security guards at the school had night jobs as guards at the local juvenile justice facility. As soon as Steven turned eighteen, he left the school and has not returned. Steven told us that police had harassed him ever since he was a child. Indeed, after a few months of observing Steven on the streets of Santa Barbara, we were able to observe this police treatment first-hand. On five occasions we were present when, for no apparent reason, police stopped Steven, searched him, and sat him on the curb, sometimes for up to forty-five minutes.

Negative Credentials for "At-Risk" Youths

As we described earlier, James had already experienced negative credentialing by the state early on in his life, at the young age of ten. However,
this pivotal event occurred after his teachers had already labeled him
as at-risk, on account of his foster home record and his father's history
of alcoholism, and subsequently monitored him heavily. This created a
very tense and conflict-ridden relationship between James and his educators. For example, the school attempted to help James by assigning him
a mentor from the local university as well as scheduling regular weekly
appointments with the school psychologist, both of whom attempted to
discipline him to "manage his anger" and obey the teacher. Yet, the at-
risk label also made him predisposed to hypervigilance by other authority
figures at the school, such as the principal, teachers, the playground attendant, and the school-based police officer. This in turn frustrated James
because he felt there was nothing he could do right, as they were quick to
notice and lecture or punish him once he deviated from their strict, perhaps even unrealistic, norms of behavior. The hypervigilance and zero-
tolerance policies consequently engendered a great deal of resentment
within James towards the adult authority figures at his school. What made
him feel even more frustrated was that he knew that, once the "at-risk"
label had been imposed on him, the teachers scrutinized him more and
punished him even more severely than his peers who had not been so labeled. Eventually the school-based police officer helped transition James's
at-risk label into a "potential criminal" label.

Steven, meanwhile, had been marked out in a police gang database.
After leaving school for the first time, Steven hung out on the streets
with a group of friends who had also dropped out of school. The police
began to keep track of Steven by taking his picture and labeling him as a
gang member. This information was then entered into a California Gang
Database system which allowed police throughout the state to determine in an instant whether Steven had previously been associated with
a gang. This labeling would later lead Steven to a criminal sentence. A
few months before the writing of this chapter, in April 2009, Steven was
hanging out with friends who decided to steal a car. Steven told them he
did not want to participate in the crime. As his friends broke into the car
and proceeded to steal it, a patrol car pulled up and arrested them. Even
though Steven did not participate, the police also arrested him since he
was a block away and leaving the scene. Steven was sentenced to two
months in county jail for "unlawful taking or driving of a vehicle." The
reason that the prosecutor was able to press these charges on Steven was

because he had been identified as associated with the gang and therefore was assumed to be on the lookout while his friends committed the crime.

Practices of Resistance: Defying Policing

James and Steven resisted punitive treatment at school by shutting down in the classroom and on the street by ignoring police officers.[7] While they didn't always receive the teachers' best attention this way, they at least avoided their worst. James started forging strong alliances with those few teachers who he knew had some commitment to his development. These practices epitomized the sorts of navigating tactics we found common throughout our interviews, as there were often a handful of teachers who were invested in their students. James learned, through one of these "good" teachers about "code-switching."[8] James, in describing code-switching, said, "we just call it having a 'mouth-piece'" (the ability to negotiate for resources in different contexts). After learning that he could use code-switching in school, he talked his way from a B- to a B+ in one of his classes.

Knowing that hanging out in the public sphere made them predisposed to suffer frequent police harassment, stops, and interrogations, James and his friends deployed various tactics to undermine police interrogation efforts, typically feigning ignorance or remaining adamantly silent when informally interrogated by police. Moreover, James learned to keep his own cool when faced with police officers he knew would purposely taunt him and his friends. He described an encounter he had with an Oakland police officer:

> One time this cop rolled up on us when we were kickin' one night and tried to talk shit to us. A few cats would represent their turf, but not all of us were from that block, but he was still trying to call us a gang. He'd be like, "you guys are from so-and-so block," and we just stayed calm and were like, "naw, who's that?" but he tried to turn it and flip it on us, and was, "good, because I heard those guys from so and so block were a bunch of pussies, I heard they were a bunch of bitches and all that," but we knew what he was trying to do, he was trying to get us mad say something stupid back to him or whatever.

On one of the occasions in which we observed an interaction between Steven and a police officer, we noticed that Steven ignored most of the questions directed at him by the officer. The officer asked him, "Where are you going?" And although he was walking to the local community center for a workshop that we were conducting, Steven replied, "No-where...just around the neighborhood." The officer interjected: "You gotta' be going somewhere. Where are you going?" Steven replied, "No-where." The officer then handcuffed Steven and told him, "You are right, you are going nowhere." He sat Steven on the curb. We stood there for forty-five minutes waiting for him to release Steven. After releasing him, the officer told Steven, "Next time just tell me where you are going." Steven replied, "I already told you, nowhere!" Steven's refusal to tell the officer that he was on his way to do something positive, something that would not have incriminated him, provided the officer an excuse to teach Steven a lesson. When we asked Steven why he refused to tell the officer where he was going, he replied, "He ain't my dad, man. He don't need to know what I am up to." In both cities we observed countless interac-tions between young men and police where the boys displayed disrespect towards officers and defied their authority before they could determine if the officer was going to treat them well or badly. These responses seemed to aggravate police officers and maybe even lead them to further harass and mistreat the youths. But these interactions provided young men with a feeling of agency. Once released, the youths described themselves as having won a battle against authority: the officer did not have his way in the interaction; he expected obedience and subordination but the youths gave him resistance. While on many occasions this may have led the of-ficer to arrest the youths, in the end, the young men felt that it was worth being harassed or arrested as long as they could retain some dignity in their interaction with police.

The High Cost of "Earning" Negative Credentials

After being arrested, James's probation status allowed officers to inter-rupt his daily routines. He recounted, for example, how a police officer stopped him once for barely approximating the description of a suspect, making him late to meet his girlfriend:

> [A]nother time, I was on my way to see my girlfriend and her family, who were having a baptism that weekend over in Hayward. So I hopped on BART and was on my way to A street, where they were going to pick up at the store....and a cop rolled up on me. I guess somebody was shooting at some store around there, and the cop was trying to be like, "you fit the description" or whatever. The thing is that the dude who did it had a grey hoodie on, but I was just in a grey jacket but they still pulled me over, even

though I showed them my BART ticket and everything and even though I
was trying to tell them that my girl was gonna pick me up.

These sorts of interruptions by police officers in his daily life led James to
be late on occasion, which either caused his friends and family concern
or even drew their ire. While they eventually came to terms with this
police-induced tardiness, it still caused some emotional flare-ups between
James and his family members.

James's relationship with the police reached a climax one day when he
was walking back from school and Officer Johns stopped him and found
a marijuana-filled cigar in James's pocket. It was on that day that he was
formally booked and entered into the record books of the criminal justice
system and subsequently placed on probation for drug possession. James'
experience contrasts starkly with that of other North Oakland and Berkeley youths, the middle- and upper-class kids with whom his cousins attended school at Berkeley High. Those more privileged youths consumed
the same substances that James occasionally used, but only in the seclud-
ed confines of their parents' homes or cars. James was well aware of these
differences. He also knew that these middle-class youths had racial and
class privileges that shielded them from the kind of routine harassment
that he experienced at the hands of police almost daily—privileges that
came from living in a world in which their personal and cultural styles
were not targeted and criminalized by police, a world in which private
property literally provided them a level of privacy, shielding them from
the prying stops and searches of police officers. James, on the other hand,
lived in a world without any such protection, and, in the end, Officer
Johns delivered on his promise.

A Dream Deferred:
Negative Credentials and Muted Opportunities

At age twenty Steven attempts to find work. He has no high school diploma, and entry-level jobs that do not require an education have been
impossible to find. We have observed Steven as he has applied for twenty-
two jobs. We have even helped him with his applications. He has received no calls or interviews. He has even attempted to return to the
strawberry fields to work with his parents, but employers at the strawberry
farm refuse to hire Steven. "They say I got a record and they don't want
any problems with all the gang stuff they hear I am involved in."

While Steven decided not to finish school and consequently finds himself at such a disadvantage when it comes to gaining employment, James

did graduate. He too had trouble finding a job, however, firstly because his negative credentials, i.e., his conviction for drug possession, precluded the few opportunities he had available to him, but also because, while he certainly received motivation from some teachers who encouraged him to graduate, he did not always receive the best education in Oakland's failing public schools.

James is currently attending a community college that, on paper, provides an avenue to higher education and the kinds of credentials and training required to get a job that will allow for a sustainable living. Yet, James needs to take a year and a half of remedial courses before any of his community college classes will count toward the transfer agreements with California's four-year universities. And, given the economic position of James and his disabled father (his father suffers from chronic diabetes and relies on his social security check to keep him and his son afloat), alongside statutes that deny the granting of financial aid to anyone with a drug conviction, higher education has essentially been rendered a luxury.

Upon graduating, James attempted to become a longshoreman at the docks in Oakland, but this kind of employment has been precluded by new hiring exclusions put into place by the War on Terror.[9] The Transportation Worker's Identity Credential and background searches have been implemented as mandatory for all dock workers by the Transportation Services Authority. The background checks required to get this ID card screen people for a number of convictions, including drug offenses, thereby effectively denying this opportunity to many young black and brown men in the nearby area—many of whom, like James, have been busted for the kind of minor drug possession charges that young men in middle-class suburban communities do not tend to accumulate.

The routine police harassment that James and Steven continue to endure on the streets is converging with their unemployment. In the process, this is also forging them into incarcerable suspects as the frequency with which they are stopped, frisked, and interrogated by police has led them to accumulate more infractions than the rest of us. Moreover, while most people with gainful employment may be able to pay off any citations and fines, James and Steven, young men who remain unemployed because of their negative credentials, cannot, and may easily see the window of opportunity to pay their fines expire, subsequently escalating a normal traffic citation, for example, into a warrant for their arrest. This has happened to both young men in the past year.

Conclusion: Becoming an Incarcerable Subject

James's and Steven's stories illuminate the reproductive trajectory of disenfranchised and racialized working-class communities in two poor neighborhoods in California. Moreover, these stories also highlight the significant historical transition in which immigrant or migrant generations that have been incorporated at the most precarious and lowest rungs of the labor market are now seeing their children transformed into incarcerable subjects by punitive systems of social control. Instead of being reproduced into their parents' labor position, many poor young men who have been marked by the criminal justice system seem to have been changed from working class into a penalized class.

Steven and James are part of an education-to-incarceration pipeline. It is in the junctures between schools and police officers that these young men of color become negatively credentialed by the state, booked, and entangled to varying degrees with the criminal justice system (i.e., entered into a gang database, arrested, placed on probation, or jailed). Despite being negatively credentialed by the state, these youths find the means to negotiate, avoid, de-escalate, and/or subvert the practices of punishment that they experience—in the school as much as in the street. They often pick up methods of resistance by sharing among themselves the wealth of critical knowledge and cultural practices of resiliency found within their community. Once entangled within the criminal justice system and negatively credentialed, these youths continue to experience more vigilant targeting by police officers What is more, the stakes are extremely high as they face routine stops by police and/or subsequent penalties for committing a crime typical of their age group (such as illicit substance use), for, as we've seen, incarceration is practically an inevitability.

While Santa Barbara and Oakland are very different cities with distinct histories, we nonetheless found similar mechanisms for racialized incorporation of disadvantaged im/migrants into precarious labor systems, abandonment, and containment. We found these mechanisms in seemingly different contexts and applied to different racialized groups. In both cases, we found that im/migrant elders were absorbed as precarious laborers who encouraged their children to take their education seriously in order to escape the poverty they faced. Despite this motivation, in both cities, youths of color found themselves abandoned by underfunded schools and overburdened teachers who implicitly used race and gender to help them decide which students were worthwhile investments for their limited resources, which students to abandon, and which students to "push-out" through punitive practices. The punitive surveillance systems that James and Steven experienced led many youths of color to pick up their "negative credential" while still at school. Many were subsequently pipelined out of school (either because their negative credential rendered higher education a luxury, as it did for James, or because they were "forced-out" of school like Steven), either directly into the criminal justice system or onto the streets where they were unlikely to find employment. Moreover, when on the street, the saturation of policing in their communities led them to become further entrenched within the criminal justice system where today, as we write, Steven is incarcerated for two months in county jail for, according to his arresting officer, Officer Jones, "…disrespecting his probation officer." Officer Jones elaborates: "…he called him an ass-hole." The trouble with young men in postindustrial California during an era of mass incarceration is that issues related to young people's class-trajectory, economic foothold, and dignity are interpreted as criminal troubles. The trouble with young men who are supposed to reproduce a working-class life is that they have become mutated into a penalized class; they have been morphed into incarcerable subjects.

Notes

1. In order to protect the anonymity and confidentiality of the participants in this research project, we have used pseudonyms, rather than their given or nick-names, to refer to them and have altered any other identifiers.
2. On the mass production of social death through incarceration, see Harvey 2000: 45–46. See Geoff Ward (2008) for an expansion on the concept of "racialized social control."
3. Paul Willis, in *Learning to Labor*, provides a thorough discussion of the literature on mass education. Willis begins his discussion with John Dewey, an American philosopher and an early major proponent of the social reform potential provided by mass education. John Dewey argued that education could serve as a means to provide "members of the underclasses, especially black and Hispanics" access to "better jobs and a higher standard of living" (Willis 1981: 127). However, implicit in Paul Willis's ethnography is his engagement with John Dewey and his vision of upward social mobility delivered through education. Willis duly notes, through his analysis of working-class British young males, that this is a rhetoric that obfuscates the reality of a class-based society as "the whole nature of Western capitalism is also such that classes are structured and persistent so that even relatively high rates of individual mobility make no difference to the existence or position of the working class… no conceivable number of certificates among the working class will make for a classless society" (Willis 1981: 127).
4. (Allen et al. 2004; Ambrosio and Schiraldi 1997; Bonczar 2003; Bowditch 1993; Brooks, et al. 2000; Campaign 2008; Cantu 2000; Connolly et al. 1996; Dycus 2008; Ekstrom et al. 1986; Figlio 2006; Fine 1986; Harlow 2003; Mukherjee and Karpatkin 2007; Noguera 1995; Noguera 1994; Sanders 2000; Skiba 2000; Skiba and Rausch 2006; Stoneman 2002)
5. Paul Willis (1981) defines partial penetrations in the following passage:

Penetration is meant to designate impulses within a cultural form towards the penetration of the conditions of existence of its members and their position within the social whole but in a way which is not centered, essentialist, or individualist. "Limitation" is meant to designate those blocks, diversions, and ideological effects which confuse and impede the full development and expression of these impulses. The rather clumsy but strictly accurate term, "partial penetration" is meant to designate the interaction of these two terms in a concrete culture... . It is this specific combination of cultural "insight" and partiality which gives the mediated strength of personal validation and identity to individual behavior which leads in the end to entrapment...it is, I would argue, only the contradictory double articulation which allows a class society to exist in liberal and democratic forms: *for an unfree condition to be entered freely* (italics added for emphasis; Willis 1981: 119-20).

6. For example, Vijay Prashad (2006) argues that Neoliberalism allowed political and economic elites to avoid delivering the concessions that African-Americans had wrested away from them through the Civil Rights Movement. As Prashad (2006: 72) states, "the guardians of the state had dismantled the social-wage state, leaving citizens with high-minded norms as it gutted the institutions that could respond to them". Once these institutions that could provide working-class people of color a means to fight for further empowerment were ultimately gutted by Neoliberalism, a new privatized means of reproducing racialized class-privilege emerged—a means that utilized the wealth already accumulated by working- and middle-class whites during the era of Keynesianism to reproduce said privilege (see the concept of a "privatized notion of citizenship" in Shapiro 2004: 13). The reproduction of racialized class-privilege through privatized means and the simultaneous gutting of social services have exacerbated inequality. This is perhaps best illustrated in the example of Hurricane Katrina, where, as Clyde Woods (2005: 1010–1011) argues, African-Americans were already abandoned by the neoliberal creative destruction of the federal government, long before any natural disaster ever hit the shores of Louisiana. Perhaps nothing demonstrates more drastically the forms of abandonment produced by Neoliberalism and imputed upon working-class people of color than the scores of people who were not only left abandoned by an inefficient response by the state amidst this socially produced disaster, but the ways in which they were subsequently criminalized for attempting to survive and summarily executed by legal and extra-legal forces (see Thompson 2009).

7. For an explanation of how students shut down in school and refuse to learn from teachers as a form of resistance, see Kohl 1994.

8. There is an abundance of literature on "code-switching" within the disciplines of education, linguistics, and sociology. Within the discipline of sociology, Elijah Anderson (2000) has made a widely-recognized contribution on code-switching through his book, *Code of the Street: Decency, Violence, and the Moral Life of the Inner City*. In the book, he argues that some black youth in Philadelphia learn how to code-switch while others do not. In other words, "decent" youth know how to code-switch as they "share many of the middle-class values of the wider white society" and "develop a repertoire of behaviors that do provide...security" when on "the street," while "[t]hose strongly associated with the street, who have less exposure to the wider society, may have difficulty code-switching; imbued with the code of the street, they either don't know the rules for decent behavior or may see little value in displaying such knowledge" (Anderson 2000: 36).

Anderson's insights on code-switching certainly resonate with what we have documented in the field, as youth from racialized and abandoned communities must negotiate with the generationally specific subculture of the older members of their racialized class as well as with hegemonic values and practices, all the while authoring their own values and practices that represent their own youth subculture (Clarke et al. 2006).

While certainly the common sense (Gramsci 1971) and hidden transcripts (Scott 1990) of marginalized people create a contradictory and complex cultural terrain, they are also a site where one can find alternative ideologies and practices necessary for creating an alternative vision and structure of society. Thus, while the hidden transcript and common sense of marginalized people may grate against normative values and practices, they are not necessarily deficient when looking at them through a logic of resistance and resiliency (as opposed to a normative stand-point or logic). For example, James, who learned to code-switch on his own but was taught to name the practice by a teacher, knew how to code-switch when on the street, as he recognized that "you can't always put up a front on the street, because there will always be someone a little bit crazier than you who will call you on it and you'll wind up in a bad spot." We see that code-switching may exemplify how criminalized youth from racialized and abandoned communities are aware of the different social contexts they may find themselves in and how they may, or may not, use code-switching according to the different goals they may be pursuing and/or defending.

9. Following the attacks on the World Trade Center on 11 September 2001, the Bush Administration was able to capitalize on the moment by creating a moral panic regarding terrorism and security, which justified some of the heaviest security reforms in history—namely, the Patriot Act. Christian Parenti (2003) describes the Patriot Act as, "introduc[ing] a sweeping arsenal of new federal powers" that "liberalized use of the federal government's four main tools of surveillance: wiretaps, search warrants, subpoenas, and pen/trap orders." Ultimately, the Patriot Act was "just a mopping-up operation that legalized already existing and ongoing, yet illegal, forms of investigation" (Parenti 2003: 200).

Bibliography

Allen, L. et al. 2004. "From the Prison Track to the College Track." Boston: Jobs for the Future. Available from: www.jff.org [Accessed 23 August 2009].

Althusser, L. 1971. *Lenin and Philosophy and Other Essays.* New York: Monthly Review Press.

Ambrosio, T.J. and V Schiraldi. 1997. "From Classrooms to Cellblocks: A National Perspective." Washington, D.C. The Justice Policy Institute. Available from: www.cjcj.org [Accessed 28 August 2009].

Anderson, E. 2000. *Code of the street: Decency, Violence, and The Moral Life Of The Inner City.* New York: W.W. Norton.

Anyon, J. 2005. "Social Class and the Hidden Curriculum of Work." *Journal of Education,* 162 (1), Fall: 67–92.

———. 1981. "Elementary Schooling and Distinctions of Social Class." *Interchange,* 12 (2): 118–132.

———. 1997. *Ghetto Schooling: A Political Economy of Urban Educational Reform.* New York: Teachers College Press.

Binns, K. and D. Markow. 1999. "The Metropolitan Life Survey of the American Teacher, 1999: Violence in America." New York: Metropolitan Life Insurance Company. Available from: www.metlife.com/about/corporate-profile/citizenship/metlife-foundation/metlife-survey-of-the-american-teacher.html [Accessed 28 August 2009].

Blum, J. and Y. Woodlee. 2001. "Tour was for Youths 'Beyond Control': Teacher Requested Prison 'Experience.'" *Washington Post*, 31 May: B1.

Bonczar, T.P. 2003. *Prevalence Of Imprisonment In The US Population, 1974–2001*. Bureau of Justice Statistics Special Report, NCJ17976. Washington, DC: US Department of Justice, Office of Justice Programs.

Bourdieu, P. 1984. *Distinction: A Social Critique of the Judgment of Taste*. Translated by Richard Nice. Cambridge: Harvard University Press.

Bowditch, C. 1993. "Getting Rid of Troublemakers: High School Disciplinary Procedures and the Production of Dropouts." *Social Problems*, 40 (4), November: 493–509.

Brooks, K., et al. 2000. "School House Hype: Two Years Later. Policy Report." The Justice Policy Institute, Washington, D.C. Available from: www.cjcj.org [Accessed 28 August 2009].

California, State of. 1996. "Summary of the 1996/7 State Budget." Legislative Analyst's Office, Sacramento.

Cantu, N. 2000. Statement of Norma Cantu, Assistant Secretary of Education for Civil Rights, *The Civil Rights Implications of Zero Tolerance Programs*. Briefing for the United States Commission on Civil Rights. 17 February 2000. Cited in E. Donahue, et al., 1998.

Clarke, J., et al. 2006. "Subcultures, Cultures and Class." In *Resistance Through Rituals: Youth Subcultures in Post-War Britain*, eds. S. Hall and T. Jefferson. London and New York: Routledge.

Connolly, K., et al. 1996. "From Classrooms to Cell Blocks: How Prison Building Affects Higher Education and African American Enrollment." San Francisco: Center on Juvenile and Criminal Justice. Available from: www.cjcj.org [Accessed 28 August 2009].

Cradle to Prison Pipeline Campaign. 2008. "California Children in the Pipeline." Children's Defense Fund California, Los Angeles. Available from: http://www.cdfca.org/files/CPPFactSheet.pdf [Accessed 29 August 2008].

Donohue, E., et al. 1998. "School house hype: School shootings, and the real risks kids face in America." Washington, DC: The Justice Policy Institute. Available from: www.cjcj.org [Accessed 28 August 2009].

Dwyer, K. 1998. "Early Warning, Timely Response: A Guide to Safe Schools." Washington, D.C.: U.S. Department of Education. Available from: www.ed.gov/offices/OSERS/OSEP/earlywrn.html [Accessed 28 August 2009].

Dycus, J. 2008. "Hard Lessons: School Resource Officer Programs and School-Based Arrests in Three Connecticut Towns." New York: American Civil Liberties Union. Available from: http://www.aclu.org/pdfs/racialjustice/hardlessons_november2008.pdf [Accessed 29 August 2009].

Ekstrom, R., et al. 1986. "Who Drops Out of High School and Why? Findings from a National Study." *The Teachers College Record*, 87 (3): 356–373.

Ewing, K.P. 2008. *Being and Belonging: Muslims in the United States Since 9/11*. New York: Russell Sage Foundation.

Ferguson, A.A. 2000. *Bad Boys: Public Schools in the Making of Black Masculinity*. Ann Arbor: University of Michigan Press.

Figlio, D.N. 2006. "Testing, Crime and Punishment." *Journal of Public Economics*, 90 (4): 837–851.

Fine, M. 1986. "Why Urban Adolescents Drop Into and Out of Public High School." *The Teachers College Record*, 87 (3): 393–409.

Fine, M., et al. 2004. "Civics Lessons: The Color and Class of Betrayal." In *Working Method: Research and Social Justice*, eds. L. Weis and M. Fine. New York: Routledge.

Freire, P. 2000. *Pedagogy of the Oppressed*. New York: Continuum.

Gilmore, R.W. 2007. *Golden Gulag: Prisons, Surplus, Crisis, and Opposition in Globalizing California*. Berkeley: University of California Press.

Gold, S.D. 1995. "State Spending Patterns in the 1990s." Albany: Center for the Study of the States.

Gordon, A.F. 2006. "Abu Ghraib: Imprisonment and the War on Terror." *Race & Class*, 48 (1): 42–59

———. 2009. "The United States Military Prison: The Normalcy of Exceptional Brutality." In *The Violence of Incarceration*, eds. P. Scraton and J. McCulloch. New York: Routledge.

Gramsci, A. 1971. *Selections From the Prison Notebooks of Antonio Gramsci*. eds. Q. Hoare and G. Nowell-Smith. Translated by Q. Hoare and G. Nowell-Smith. London: Lawrence & Wishart.

Harlow, C.W. 2003. "Education and Correctional Populations." Bureau of Justice Statistics Special Report. Washington, D.C.: U.S. Department of Justice. Available from: http://www.ojp.usdoj.gov/bjs/ [Accessed 23 August 2009].

Harvey, D. 2005. *A Brief History of Neoliberalism*. Oxford: Oxford University Press.

Harvey, T. 2000. "Gentrification and West Oakland: Causes, Effects and Best Practices." Madison: Department of Rural Sociology at the University of Wisconsin, Madison, Wisconsin. Available from: http://comm-org.wisc.edu/papers2000/gentrify/gentrify.htm [Accessed 5 August 2007].

Hirschfield, P.J. 2008. "Preparing For Prison? The Criminalization of School Discipline in the USA." *Theoretical Criminology*, 12 (1): 79–101.

Hunt, K. and K. Rygiel. 2006. *(En)gendering the War on Terror: War Stories and Camouflaged Politics*. Burlington: Ashgate.

Kohl, H.R. 1994. *I Won't Learn From You*. Minneapolis: Milkweed Editions.

Kupchik, A. and T. Monahan. 2006. "The New American School: Preparation for Post-Industrial Discipline." *British Journal of Sociology of Education*, 27 (5): 617–631.

Kupchik, A. 2009. "Things are Tough All Over: Race, Ethnicity, Class and School Discipline." *Punishment Society*, 11 (3): 291–317.

Mukherjee, E. and M. Karpatkin. 2007. "Criminalizing the Classroom: The Over-Policing of New York City Schools." New York: New York Civil Liberties Union. Available from: www.aclu.org [Accessed 28 August 2009].

Noguera, P.A. 1995. "Preventing and Producing Violence: A Critical Analysis of Responses to School Violence." *Harvard Educational Review*, 65 (2): 189–212.

———. 1994. "More Democracy Not Less: Confronting the Challenge of Privatization in Public Education." *The Journal of Negro Education*, 63 (2): 237–250.

———. 2003. "The Trouble with Black Boys: The Role and Influence of Environmental and Cultural Factors on the Academic Performance of African American Males." *Urban Education*, 38 (4): 431–459.

Nolan, K. and J. Anyon. 2004. "Learning to Do Time: Willis' Cultural Reproduction Model in an Era of Deindustrialization, Globalization, and the Mass Incarceration of People of Color." In *Learning to Labor in New Times*, eds. N. Dolby et al. New York: Routledge.

Nordstrom, C. 2007. *Global Outlaws: Crime, Money, and Power in the Contemporary World*. Berkeley: University of California Press.

Parenti, C. 2003. *The Soft Cage: Surveillance in America, From Slavery to the War on Terror.* New York: Basic Books.

Patterson, O. 1982. *Slavery and Social Death: A Comparative Study.* Cambridge: Harvard University Press.

Prashad, V. 2006. "Second-Hand Dreams." *Social Analysis,* 49 (2): 191–198.

Sanders, M.G. 2000. *Schooling Students Placed At Risk: Research, Policy, and Practice in the Education of Poor and Minority Adolescents.* Mahwah: L. Erlbaum Associates.

Scott, J.C. 1990. *Domination and the Arts of Resistance: Hidden Transcripts.* New Haven: Yale University Press.

Shapiro, T.M. 2004. *The Hidden Cost of Being African American: How Wealth Perpetuates Inequality.* New York: Oxford University Press.

Skiba, R.J. 2000. "Zero Tolerance, Zero Evidence: An Analysis of School Disciplinary Practice. Policy Research Report." Bloomington: Indiana Education Policy Center, Smith Research Center.

Skiba, R.J and M.K. Rausch. 2006. "Zero tolerance, suspension, and expulsion: Questions of equity and effectiveness." *Handbook of Classroom Management: Research, Practice, and Contemporary Issues.* Bloomington: Indiana Education Policy Center, Smith Research Center

Stoneman, Dorothy. 2002. "Youth Development and the Preparation of Youth for Employment." Washington, D.C.: American Youth Policy Forum.

Taqi-Eddin, K, et al. 1998. "Class Dismissed: Higher Education vs. Corrections During the Wilson Years." San Francisco, CA: The Justice Policy Institute. Available from: www.cjcj.org [Accessed 28 August 2009].

Thompson, A.C. 2009. "New Evidence Surfaces in Post-Katrina Crimes." *ProPublica,* 10 July 2009. Available from: http://www.propublica.org/feature/new-evidence-surfaces-in-post-katrina-crimes-710 [Accessed 23 August 2009].

Tyack, D.B. 1974. *The One Best System: A History of American Urban Education.* Cambridge: Harvard University Press.

Willis, P.E. 1981. *Learning to Labor: How Working Class Kids Get Working Class Jobs.* New York: Columbia University Press.

Woods, C. 2005. "Do You Know What It Means to Miss New Orleans?" *American Quarterly,* 57 (4): 1005–1018.

Chapter 10

Managing Urban Disorder?
"The Street" and its Malcontents in the London Borough of Camden

Gary Armstrong and James Rosbrook-Thompson[1]

Introduction

In recent years there has been a renewal of academic and political interest in order and disorder in contemporary cities. Many investigations center on the relationship between levels of deprivation and ethno-racial composition as well as how this relationship shapes perceptions and patterns of disorder in given inner-city areas. The state possesses the right not only to manage immigration into its territories but also to define what is "disorderly" and therefore "inappropriate" conduct. In contrast, teenage boys may have their own notions and experiences of propriety.

The adjective "street," despite being empty of meaning beyond the common-sense signification of an urban passageway, is often called upon to refer to the inhabitants of cities and their various behaviors. In recent British political discourse the term "street" has become loaded with processes that Stuart Hall (1997) would describe as both constructed and produced. When we combine the adjective "street" with the noun "violence," the matter becomes even more political and pejorative: "street violence" is ostensibly a threat to the entire populace, its randomness and unpredictability being a source of fear and hysteria. Thus the issue is about appropriate and, indeed, ideal levels of behavior and the "necessary" power, control, and dominance required to police such zones. Such policing must ensure the safe passage of all users and, in the context of the High Street,[2] the completion of commercial transactions. It raises matters of fundamental significance that touch upon access, visibility, social class, social inclusion, surveillance, and gender relations in cities. This is especially the case when the maintenance of social order is pursued by means of what Andrew Rutherford (2002) has referred to as the "Eliminative Ideal" for dealing with troublesome and disagreeable elements.

In promoting such an "ideal," the majority seeks to rid an area of the problematic minority by lawful means. The Eliminative Ideal contains three key elements: visibility, demonization, and the expulsion of the polluting presence, the latter drawing directly on anthropologist Mary Douglas's notion of "dirt" as "matter out of place" (Douglas 1966; Squires 2008). In contemporary Britain, the youths—primarily young men—who inhabit these contested urban zones are increasingly demonized. A rise in the incidence and coverage of teenage conflict—which sometimes results in fatalities—has seen the issue of teenage violence harden as a social, moral, and hence political priority.

If male teenagers are indeed performing acts of violence and intimidation on the streets of Britain, our task is to reveal the socio-cultural dynamics of these issues and explain how they impact upon the protagonists, be it in terms of challenge, avoidance, or negotiation (Box 1981; Cohen 1980). We might also ask—in the tradition of the Birmingham University Centre for Contemporary Cultural Studies, "what does it all mean" (Hall and Jefferson 1976; Muggleton and Weinzierl 2003)? Accordingly, in this chapter we seek to present the life stories of boys and young men living in the London Borough of Camden. Beyond simply narrating our interviewees' responses, we seek to offer some form of explanation as to why things are as they are in this setting. The methods of exclusion practiced upon teenage boys by agents of the state, be they representatives of national or local government, and commercial interests, go some way to explaining how such exclusion is negotiated and even resisted (Raby 2005). Crucial to both of these issues is the notion of consumption. As British society obsesses about social status and the ability to consume, it also derides and excludes some—notably teenage boys—who pursue the ideals of consumption but manifest them in ways considered inappropriate on account of being aesthetically unpleasing, disruptive, subversive, or disorderly (Cohen 1985; Howard and Majid 2006).

In the North London district of Camden Town, located in the London Borough of Camden, concern over the emergence of teenage gangs has been acute. In November 2008 local police closed the file on the largest multi-ASBO (Anti-Social Behaviour Order) case that the borough has seen, with court orders being imposed which banned twelve members of a teenage gang from Camden Town for two years. The group, of mainly Somali origin and collectively known as "The Money Squad," had reportedly been involved in "fighting, drug-dealing, drinking and vandalism" as well as being part of Camden's "aggressive cannabis market" (Keilthy 2008: 4). According to prosecutors, over the last two years the group had been involved in revenge attacks on other North London gangs, more specifically the "c-town niggas," "North London Somalis," "the Camden Boys," "African Nations Crew," and the "Centric Boyz" (Keilthy 2008: 4). This conflict came to a head in May 2008 when Sharmaarke Hassan, a seventeen-year-old Somali member of the Money Squad, was shot dead (Craig and Brown 2008).

A panoply of legislative, technological, and other interventions has focused on teenage boys in the United Kingdom in the past decade. The New Labour government legislated more against crime after coming to power in 1997 than in the history of any other United Kingdom government. Its most notable—and seemingly non-negotiable—crime initiative saw the United Kingdom become the most "surveilled" population on earth because of the ubiquity of government-funded CCTV cameras.[3] The other notable local crime-prevention measure arrived in 2003 in the form of the Anti-Social Behaviour Act comprised of a battery of provisions aimed to address issues of truancy, crack houses, false reports of emergency, fireworks, public drunkenness, and gang activity. The Act's legislative measures designed to target troublesome young men were the Anti-Social Behaviour Order (ASBO) and Dispersal Zones. An ASBO may be issued in response to conduct which caused or was likely to cause harm, harassment, alarm, or distress, to one or more persons not of the same household as him or herself and where an ASBO is seen as necessary to protect relevant persons from further anti-social acts by the defendant. At bottom, an ASBO is an Order of the Court which dictates to individuals over ten years old how they must not behave. Over 250 ASBOs were issued by Camden's Labour Council before being ousted from power in summer 2009. Contained in Part IV of the 2003 Anti-Social Behaviour Act was legislation on Dispersal Zones. This gave the police powers to disperse groups of two or more persons in any public place if their presence has resulted, or is likely to result, in any members of the public being intimidated, harassed, alarmed, or distressed. Furthermore, it permits a police officer to accompany any unaccompanied person under sixteen years old to their home between the hours of 9 p.m. and 6 a.m. Camden contains a number of these zones. Despite being designed to last just six months, the council extended the status of such areas almost indefinitely; in 2009 some of Camden's neighborhoods, estates, and underground stations were entering their fifth year as dispersal zones (Keilthy 2009). Camden has a specialist anti-graffiti unit. The "grime-buster" mobile units literally take the writing off the wall.

Much to the frustration of academics and liberal social commentators, instances of intra-ethnic conflict have received little in the way of media attention. Before the turn of the Millennium, intra-ethnic violence in the United Kingdom—as opposed to that occurring between ethnic groups, especially if a white youth was on the receiving end—provoked negligible reaction from the press and wider British public. Indeed, quarrels among teenage boys, because of their tender age and general irresponsibility, seemed of little or no significance to the government, press, and police alike. In 2008 a study by researchers at Manchester University's School of Law found "no basis for the popular belief that most street gangs are black" but rather that "a gang's ethnic make-up tended simply to reflect its local area – black, white or mixed – even though the media and police overwhelmingly focus on black gangs" (Davies 2008: 1).

The Times reported that twenty-two teenagers were stabbed to death in London in 2008 (Fresco 2009). Despite the fact that the number of knife- and gun-related incidents has remained constant over the last five years, people have been horrified by another statistic: the age of those involved. Indeed, the perpetrators and victims of knife and gun crime are seemingly getting younger by the year. A 2008 survey commissioned by the children's charity Barnardo's found that "most adults think children 'are feral and a danger to society'" and that "people overestimate by a factor of four crime committed by children" (Frean 2008: 17). However, over the last ten years, England, and more specifically London, has seen an increase in the incidence of violent attacks perpetrated by and inflicted upon youths. The weapons involved in such attacks have invariably been knives or guns. This has captured the imagination of the media as attacks involving dependants, especially when committed across ethnic boundaries, makes for good copy. The subsequent coverage has identified the nation's latest moral scourge with gun- and knife-toting "hoodies"—members of teenage gangs whose ringleaders, typically excluded from a failing state education system, loiter, cause a nuisance, and ask the same of their deputies. In order to conceal their faces from CCTV and other surveillance devices, members of such groups typically come clad in hooded leisure wear. This is a contest that shows no signs of going away.

What follows is an account of a specific urban area and its male teenage inhabitants. Through interviewing four teenage boys who reside in Camden Town, North West London, we seek to identify how everyday processes and economies of disorder feature in the boys' life stories as well as their narratives of everyday existence in the inner city. But before examining these life stories we must give a brief socio-historical account of the inner-city area in question.

Nested Contexts: Camden, London

As Chris Hamnett (2003) shows, distinctive historical trends have influenced the complexion of London's housing stock. These trends have been motored by the phenomenon of gentrification, the gradual sale of council housing along with corresponding policies of stock transfer, the Right to Buy under the 1980 Housing Act,[4] and the curtailment of new council buildings (Watt 2006). The complex and compound effects of these trends caused the demographic profile of London's inner-city council estates to become more heterogeneous in terms of their ethnic and socio-economic composition. As a result of this contraction of council housing stock, however, the city's estates have been identified in some instances as dumping grounds for the marginalized and economically deprived. But the increasing numbers of private homeowners and middle-class and/or "key worker" council tenants make this accusation difficult to uphold (Hamnett & Randolph 1987; Watt 2001). The borough of Camden has been no exception to such processes. In the past, the area was occupied by the white working classes (of mainly English, Irish, Portuguese, and Cypriot origin). In the 1950s migrants arrived in Camden from Cyprus and Portugal, the former working in the burgeoning cafes the area provided, the latter also taking ownership of cafes with co-patriots seeking cleaning and portering jobs in the large National Health Service hospitals that the borough hosts. Since the late 1970s migrants came from the Sylhet region of Bangladesh to open many "Indian" restaurants in the borough, followed by a variety of other businesses. Then, post-1990 following the collapse of the Eastern Bloc, came—mainly—the Polish, this time with equal numbers of women as men, the former to serve in bars and cafes and the latter to work in engineering and construction and supersede the Irish in this occupational culture. The 1990s Balkan conflict saw the arrival of a variety of nationalities from that region. Also fleeing war were people from Afghanistan, Sudan, Congo, Algeria, and Somalia.

As a result of these myriad migrations, Camden's population of two hundred fifty thousand is one of the most ethnically diverse in the United Kingdom. The area has welcomed the distressed and dispossessed in various ways over many generations. It has a proud history of acceptance and accommodation. The North of the borough received the Central European Jewish intellectuals fleeing the Nazis. They were to have a profound effect on the intellectual life of the neighborhood, the borough, the University of London, and the Labour Party, not to mention clinics of psychoanalysis. That said, the established and the outsiders have long contested and continue to contest the rights to a variety of resources and spaces. But this contest means that citizens cannot exist in a monoculture or celebrate their perceived or constructed ethnic isolation. Indeed, for over one hundred years Camden residents have found that straddling worlds and cultures is existentially necessary.

In terms of the socio-economic complexion of the borough itself, Camden's social and topographical landscapes are roughly co-extensive. That is, those who inhabit the heights of Hampstead, Primrose Hill, and to a lesser extent Kentish Town enjoy high (to stratospheric) levels of economic security while the downward slope into Camden Town is marked by a corresponding socio-economic gradient. However, the areas that flank Camden High Street complicate this trend. To its west lie rows of expensive private housing that eventually give onto Regent's Park and the border with Westminster. Within this area council housing is largely concentrated within the sprawling Regent's Park Estate, a labyrinthine network of low- and high-rise blocks bordered by Albany Street and Hampstead Road. To the east of the High Street this trend is reversed, with several small to middle-sized estates outnumbering purpose-built private units. Nudging the border with Islington is an urban redoubt dominated by a tower block but also comprising lower-rise blocks of flats and rows of private small houses.

The southernmost portion of the borough is Bloomsbury, one of London's most affluent postal districts and an area that boasts some of the world's most esteemed universities. However, its schooling system is among the most polarized in the United Kingdom; the nine state secondary schools in the borough have produced good exam results in only a few instances. As a consequence, the demand for secondary school places in the church-sponsored schools has influenced a shift to church worship among the middle classes, as the child prepares for his or her final years at primary school. One massively popular school recently changed the church-attending criteria for parents from a minimum of two years to five in an attempt to thwart opportunistic worship. The other tactic for entry is to move house in order that the new residence lies within the school catchments areas. As a result, the price of property in such boundaries is 20 percent greater than similar properties outside the boundary. Parents can do their own sums to reveal that the price is still a bargain when offset against the possibility of a minimum of £10,500.00 per annum on independent school fees—for a minimum of seven years. Schools in the north of the borough outstrip those in the south in exam performance as the latter struggle to attract good pupils. Such schools have been associated with specific ethnic groups and refugees. At one particular school, the white faces are almost exclusively a product of recent East European migration.

The borough has more graduates residing within its boundaries than any other in the United Kingdom and claims to be the most literate in terms of books per household. The borough has produced many literary figures and politicians. It also has its fair share of those who people the "creative industries" and has produced professional sportsmen in both football and boxing. Despite its wealth, the borough returns Labour members of parliament to the national government and historically has been Labour-led at the local government level. The recent victory of the Liberal Democrats in local government reflects "white working-class" disenchantment with Labour, crucial to which is Labour's perceived softness on illegal immigration and the unfair allocation of council housing in favor of minority ethnic populations and refugees at the expense of the sons and daughters of the "white working class."

The Borough of Camden contains many exemplars of conformity and success. It has also facilitated those seeking better lives who, having fallen on hard times, then live on the street, often in a state of intoxication. The reason people arrive in Camden is because it was and remains a place for the ambitious. It has provided employment opportunities for generations. At one time the three railway termini that line up on the borough's southern border were (literally) the end of the line for the thousands of itinerant laborers—the "navvies"—who laid the line that brought millions of others to London via Camden. Many of those who built these rail-lines settled in the adjoining areas as they sought stability, a settled life, and steady income. Decades before them, navvies digging the Regents Canal linking East London to Birmingham had done the same. Throughout the first half of the twentieth century, the magnet that was "London" drew in many a provincial individual who sought both the bright lights and the employment prospects offered by the department stores and the entertainment industries in the nearby West End. The Metropolitan London bourgeoisie also provided the poor and provincial with work and a roof courtesy of domestic service. Such internal migration never stopped but was supplemented after the Second World War by migrants of a different language and hue. The railway termini—St.Pancras, King's Cross, and Euston—continue to receive the ambitious and dispossessed from the north of England, Scotland, and Ireland. The borough's many institutions for the homeless, along with those dealing with drug use, those deemed "problem-children," and those awaiting trial by the Criminal Justice System, sees a population scaling the gamut of human emotion, from hope to desolation. Street drunkenness and homelessness has been witnessed for decades. Such human tragedy is exacerbated by those addicted to heroin and crack cocaine, who pound the pavement begging and seeking out itinerant drug dealers. A "lighter" face of overconsumption is available every night of the week, as revelers enjoy the area's sixty-plus pubs and bars. Their presence means a concomitant demand for cocaine and hashish that a plethora of mainly young African-born men are willing to supply. Periodic police crackdowns temporarily relieve the populace of such blatant street selling but the traders often return without ever being charged.

All forms of human life are visible in Camden Town; the area's children thus grow up quickly. From one perspective, this might be celebrated as an instance where global citizens gather to share space and showcase their cultural repertoires. But such diversity is also contested, and some of the contesting is being done on a daily basis by teenage boys. As the following life stories reveal, this can cause "trouble." They also reveal that behind indices of socio-economic stability lie tales of global movement and disjunction. For Camden Town's teenage boys, methods of navigating their way through urban space are only effective if subjected to constant negotiation and review. Shifting alliances as well as the arrival of new immigrants—and with them varying signifiers of (dis)order—mean that such continuous updating of highly local and specific conditions and considerations is absolutely imperative for the male teenager of Camden Town. What remains constant is a deep frustration with the responses of the police and the government—at both national and local level.

The Phoney Wars: Tom's Tale

The "number one" haircut,[5] while complementing the spotless and well-ironed designer sportswear, was not one sported by his six regular mates. Tom's[6] style was for many in his peer group passé or even atavistic. But then none were as "hard" as Tom. Despite being the shortest of the group he hung around with, Tom was the best fighter, for only he had ever practiced boxing. Alone among them, at the age of seventeen Tom was learning carpentry and working with men twice his age. In the process of transition from boy to man, he was learning that life now meant pre-7 a.m. journeys across London which preceded a day's physical labor but gave the reward of money in pocket every Friday evening.

The comprehensive school Tom attended was literally across the road from the maisonette he lived in with his parents and two younger sisters. This former council property was now theirs, but the mortgage had to be paid. To that end Tom's father worked as a cab driver. The school, while convenient, held limited appeal, for the fact that Tom was the only local-born white boy in his class meant that he was never with the mates he wanted to be with: their parents sent them to schools three miles away from their home. Local white families considered the school as one for Bangladeshi children and thus considered it low on educational achievement and one wherein their offspring were liable to be attacked if trouble arose and the issue became considered "racial."

Admitting to "hating" school, Tom left at the age of sixteen after spending his final year in a cocoon of the few white boys in the school along with some other students of black African heritage. He remained aloof from the Bangladeshis and kept a distance from the Somalis who had a reputation for gang violence. Tom preferred to annoy teachers and be disruptive in class. As a consequence of such disenchantment, Tom was placed under the supervision of an adult learning mentor in the Learning Support Unit (LSU).

The intervention of the mentor proved crucial to Tom's future not only in talking him through his "issues" but by creating a job opportunity. In what proved to be a six-month interim, Tom was, in his terminology, "chillin' out, doin' nothing." During this time a local government-funded youth club was his second home—when he was not barred from it for disruptive behavior and offensive language. Hyperactive and too willing to create disorder, mainly with male club-goers a few years younger, what Tom considered as "just muckin' about" was a persistent nuisance to staff. It was at this time that Tom returned to the school to see his former mentor who was able to use a contact in the building trade to get Tom fixed up with an apprenticeship.

Disruptive in school team games, Tom found some outlet for his frustrations in a boxing club where his father coached. Training from the age of ten to fifteen, he fought a few bouts but then sustained a broken rib in a match. The subsequent months of enforced rest prompted Tom to think twice about the commitment the fight game required. A newly found liking for marijuana coincided with his convalescence. He admitted to "puffin'" daily from the age of sixteen—until this proved to be incompatible with early morning work requirements. At the time of the interview conducted with him (July 2009), Tom's life consisted of weekdays of work and evenings in the locality—in other words, he spent all his time in the council estate where he lived in the company of his male peers. This was an intensely local existence, all taking place within one square mile. Such localism was enlivened by excursions further afield inspired by consumption and hedonism. The latter saw Tom and his mates frequent a West End bar some two miles from home made famous by the presence every

Thursday evening of young American university students (many of them female) studying for a semester in the United Kingdom. At other times, and in the opposite direction, were two nightclubs less than a mile from home where Tom occasionally visited when the security staff members were prepared to overlook his age. A one-time visit to a club in Brixton some five miles south was memorable for the length of the journey and the perceived danger of stepping into the territory of people of the same age, but "black." Trouble with this latter demographic of sorts was considered an "inevitability."

In being divided between the local/familiar versus the distant/unfamiliar, Tom's everyday world was no different than that of most people in his district. Added to this, however, was Tom's perception of the dangers of what we can term "stations" and "transitions." The stations in this analysis are places shared with the rest of the population but which take on a distinctive resonance for boys in their teens. Such places are seen as appropriate places to enact issues involving hierarchy, intimidation, and sometimes robbery. Such places are, on occasion, virtually unavoidable; bus stops, for instance, are where all people wait to board public transport buses. Others who also stand and wait for buses are not usually the problem. The difficulty that such places pose is that a teenage boy who uses them has to stand still—waiting—and the fact that such bus stops are invariably located on Camden's busiest thoroughfares. Journeys to and from school are occasionally hazardous by virtue of boys from other schools also riding the bus.

Away from school hours the same journey was equally hazardous for a boy like Tom as groups of boys traveled around London, many drawn to Camden by virtue of its thriving street life, market, bars and cafes, and thousands of tourists. Not all came primarily to appreciate the global processes of tourism and capitalism. For some the bus routes offered carte blanche opportunities to engage in intimidation—in the upstairs seating areas, for example—and, while such activities sometimes resulted in the robbery of iPods and mobile telephones, these tended to be outcomes of an enjoyment of power at the expense of a boy of similar age. For Tom, the antagonists were "black boys ... if you're sat on your own they'll come and sit near you and start taking the piss." There was little considered appropriate by way of response. To respond was considered hazardous—buses offer little by way of escape and the fear of a weapon-carrying "gang" was pervasive. In such scenarios one took the insults and alighted the bus at one's destination. A boy could not rely on anyone else traveling on the bus; fellow passengers were either unaware of goings-on or aware and fearful—and hence unwilling—to speak out. In this sense Tom's is a generation of children that cannot rely on adult passers-by for assistance.

Tom's public life presented a series of negotiations and performances. Some peers he sought to avoid while others he deliberately sought out. In his terminology, this was "ethnic" in terms of semantics: "I've got 'Sweet' mates, blacks say 'Safe' we say 'Sweet.'" The crucial factor was the level of hostility the various individuals and groups directed towards Tom and his mates. The estate's main thoroughfare—about half a mile in length—hosted dozens of small shops but had a north-south dimension and a corresponding demographic. In the north end, Tom and his mates gathered and walked about without fear. The south end hosted street gatherings of black African boys who lived in the adjacent council properties. In the middle was a general store, once owned by Turks but now a business run by Polish migrants. People of all ages gathered around this station, and, as a consequence, the local government council, in conjunction with the police, had installed a series of CCTV cameras to watch over them and even installed a boom on the cameras which acted as a listening device for the council-run CCTV control room located around a half-mile away. This street had to be negotiated day and night as the various youth collectives gathered and crisscrossed. Tom explained how the street was navigated in terms of movement and comportment:

> It all depends on who I'm with. I've got seven mates, but in a fight only two would stay. The street though is shit. At the bottom end are all the Somalians—we can't be their friend, they don't want to know anyone. If I'm on my own or on a pedal bike, there's less chance of them saying anything. The good shop down there I'll avoid 'cos they're there and instead go to the High Street to buy something.

There were, in fact, two Somali gatherings in Tom's neighborhood. The one that populated the southern end was a permanent fixture, and there existed an unwritten *modus vivendi* with its members. Other Somalis were more mobile. A group of approximately a dozen strong started to visit Tom's neighborhood area regularly as a consequence of being served ASBOs which banned them from frequenting the High Street. They had not stopped gathering as a group; instead, they convened elsewhere and, despite encroaching on an estate that none of them lived on, did not provoke the ire of Tom and his mates who got on well with them, sharing joints of marijuana. This same group then traveled to the neighboring estate and got involved in prolonged, tit-for-tat revenge attacks with boys from the Congo and Nigeria. Some of the African youth groups adopted names for themselves—and earned notoriety—which negatively impacted Tom's willingness to literally look them in the eye: "The ANC ... African Nations Crew ... I wouldn't give them the eye. The Bangladeshis don't like us and we don't like them."

Elsewhere and in broader perspective, Tom had no particular fears. The adjacent council estate held "no worries" as he knew many of the white and black boys from school. Even the streets heavily populated by Bangladeshis posed no particular concern. Some he would deliberately "screw" [pointedly stare at] when passing on a daily basis. Others of his age whom he recognized from school he would acknowledge with words. The unfamiliar was not ethnically coded but took the form of a consideration based on the name of the council estate. One such entity with a reputation, located two miles north, was not considered problematic to negotiate but dilemmas could present themselves: "We know most of them ... but two came down recently and robbed a pedal bike."

In such a scenario who did Tom turn to for protection and safety? In Tom's case the answer was immediate: family, in the shape of his father, and no one else. "My dad's got mates who'll do anythin'—they can sort things out." This was true, to an extent. His father's pugilistic skills produced a street-smart man who knew others with the same capabilities. That said, he could not be on Tom's shoulder day and night. The uniformed agents of the state were dismissed in a variety of ways. The regular police were considered an irritant to be avoided: "They come up and say, 'what you doin'?' and tell you they've had reports of under-age drinking and noise disturbance... .They never think to ask 'How are you?' or ask us about how we have to deal with 'trouble.'"

Other uniformed personnel tasked with the maintenance of public order were viewed with contempt. These included the voluntary citizens who constituted the Police Community Support Officers and the Community Patrol Officers. The latter were council employees who walked the High Street in red boiler suits and baseball caps in order to ensure that the area's business interests were not disrupted by disorder. In Tom's analysis, the former "Don't do nothin' ... if we got chased down the street by a gang, they'd run faster than us." As for the latter, Tom stated: "They're more likely to be sharin' a joint with the dealers ... they do nothing.'" Other council-employed personnel visited the small council-managed recreation areas where Tom and his peers gathered in the evenings to talk and smoke cannabis. Visits of the mobile units to their occasionally noisy gatherings did not trigger feelings of trepidation: "They might say 'C'mon lads' ... but nothin' more." He and others were thus not too perturbed by the different forms of legislation passed to control and stop people like him from doing precisely what he did:

Dispersal zones don't work. They [police] come around in a car and tell you to go home ... you might ignore it and later when they come again they might chase you—so you go somewhere else. They target the under-sixteens. I'm not sure how it works... . I think if you get caught three times you have to pay something.

Despite a life lived so publicly, Tom had no criminal convictions. On one level this reflected his "street smartness": he avoided being arrested when police were seeking arrests on grounds of "disorder." His only journey in a police vehicle came courtesy of a lift home—for his own safety—when found the worse for wear, having inhaled "skunk" [marijuana] in the stairwell of a council-owned block of flats.

Tom has recently begun to frequent nightclubs and date girls; his horizons are quite literally changing. The dangers and issues remain but are re-contextualized. The night economy sees Tom and his mates enter premises offering music and dance until 4 a.m. It also offers alcohol and with this comes recognized—if forgivable—acts of stupidity and in most cases a concomitant sense of duty. One mate is known to be a nightmare when he has been drinking and must be "babysat," both inside whatever premise he has visited and on the way home to protect him from himself, as he willfully barges into people while inebriated. The late-night kebab shop queue contains the potential for insults, real or perceived, from others seeking sustenance at the end of night. Even a date in South London holds perils as Tom, while once walking with a girl, was approached by two West Indians in their late teens who knew his companion and objected to him being in their neighborhood, and so decided to relieve him of desirables:

They ask you "What you got for me?" Then they try to rob me in front of my girl! That's how despicable they are ... they then pull a knife and then I say have a pound coin and leave me ... they were happy with that! Robbin' [stealing from] a bloke out with a "bird" [girlfriend] for a pound ... that's a tramp's economy, that is.

Tom is fortunate to have access through his father to a resource ne work that will stand him in good stead in the future. The skills he learning will always be in demand in London. He can thus live with the educational system which he ignored. Tom is resourceful and st smart and—unlike many of his white peers that intend to leave the convinced as they are that the streets are too dangerous and thereby feiting the contest about who has the "right" to be where they wa be—Tom intends to stay in the area as an adult. For him the future employment as either a carpenter or a taxi driver: he intends to begin the three-year "Knowledge" accreditation process required for the London Hackney cab license when he turns twenty-one.

Meanwhile Tom's attitude to "blacks" has always been ambiguous. In 2008 he knowingly bought a stolen mobile phone from a Somali boy for a bargain price. The phone had been "appropriated" from a Congo-born boy who was to learn of its full service history and subsequently visit Tom's estate accompanied by twelve mates in pursuit of the object's retrieval. In the meantime Tom had sold the phone at a profit to an adult. There was no way of getting it back. The original owner of the mobile phone sent word that the price of recompense was £40.00, a sum that Tom did not possess. He was spared—by minutes—the consequences of not pay-ing the monies demanded by another set of local boys who intervened on his behalf. Sensing the seriousness of the situation, a Uganda-born youth loaned Tom the money, asking him to repay it when he had it. At the time of writing this chapter the money was still owed, but the debt was acknowledged by daily acts of friendship.

Seeing and Believing? Baru's Story

For the seventeen-year-old Baru, completion of sixth-form college was to ad to university studies in the sciences. For him this was the best way of the Bengali enclave in Camden in which he lived all his life. Baru the eldest of three sons of parents who dreamed of leaving their urban for the assumed tranquility of a suburb some six miles north. Their ion to relocate was motivated by a desire to avoid the "trouble" eir area experienced and that, indeed, eventually enlisted the in-nt of their eldest son. Given that Baru's mother's job as a primary aching assistant meant she had a transferable skill and, what wing purchased their council flat, they thus had the financial ove out of their Camden neighborhood.

in street trouble alongside his Bengali mates, Baru straddled enage worlds. One was intra-Bengali. Born in an area re-dense population of Bengalis, he had lived since his early a mere half-mile away from one with a similar profile. nsibly shared cultural legacy, boys in these respective urse of the previous fifteen years engaged in some par-icts with each other which utilized a variety of weap-umber of casualties. Baru was proud to boast that, t in both worlds, "no one ever touches me, I'm fine plained the intra-Bengali issue in terms of insult and gossip alongside custom and a precarious sense of honor: "It's all 'you said that about me, plus I heard this and that'—it's all words ... and then someone says or does something to someone's sister and it all starts." In such scenarios the rivals gathered mobs of up to fifty a side, with an age range from late teens to mid-twenties. And then, as quickly as it began it subsided. Why? The rationale for such outcomes is both age-specific and based upon increasing articulacy: "It just calms down, everyone makes up; we grow up."

Such local contests are usually enacted without local media awareness. However, some contests, although local in scale, carry the potential and intent to go—literally—global. One such incident occurred in 2008 and, in Baru's logic, demanded immediate retribution for the perpetrators. Baru thus joined a group of Bengali boys who executed a revenge attack on four African-born peers who had been present when a thirteen-year-old Bengali boy walking through an estate adjacent to Baru's place was robbed of his phone by a group of local black and white boys. The instigators of the robbery were Congo- and Somali-born. That boys were relieved of their mobile phones was a daily occurrence in the neighborhood. What made this incident different was not only that the victim was at least two years younger than those perpetrating the robbery, but that he was forced to strip for the thieves' amusement—his humiliation was captured on one of their mobile phones. The incident was then posted on the Internet website "YouTube." Because this incident was then widely viewed, it required urgent avenging: "Everyone saw it; I know thirty boys that looked at it, and at school we bashed up some of the black boys involved."

School for Baru was at one time a three-mile journey east to an institution with a good educational reputation. Here Bengali boys were in a minority and, according to Baru, were regularly robbed and bullied by the black boys who enjoyed a majority presence at the school. The ever-expanding trouble this created saw the recruitment of non-attending Bengali boys to assist in retributions. His parents moved him to the local comprehensive where the Bengali children were the majority. The move made him more familiar to groups of local Bengali boys. His grades suffered, he messed around too much, and he eventually left the school before exam year. Now aged seventeen, his parents send him five miles west daily to study for A-levels at a private school in an affluent area. For this Baru is both appreciative and aware: "It's full of posh kids but it's got me off the streets."

When enjoying too much free time, Baru tended to involve himself in a variety of forms of disorder with white and black boys from the adjacent estate. He now claims to deliberately avoid aggravation—in his terminology the "world of 'rago' [fuck it]"—as he pursues upward mobility via the education system. Articulate and good-looking, Baru has no problem with self-presentation. His problem is with consistency in the re-telling of his tales. Boasting that he has the ability to walk unmolested and without provoking derisory comment from others in the neighborhood, he also claims to have had only one fight at school. In this anomalous instance he says he "head-butted" an opponent; minutes later this is better remembered as "battering" said boy. Though the tensions involved in the YouTube incident have largely subsided, they haven't been forgotten. He is, however, at pains to stress that he can cross arterial roads at any time and walk through shops (where the boys who robbed the thirteen-year-old gather daily) without fear of being mugged and/or ridiculed. The only place he feels unsafe is three miles east, when in the vicinity of his former school. Why? "Black boys. I stood up to them at school and some of them haven't forgotten that."

The ambiguity, contradiction, and selective memory continue as he stresses the solidarity he has with his Bengali peer group and their typical responsiveness: "Our group never gave trouble. We had an area which if boys came into they got battered." And despite his claims to have left such a life behind, he cannot help celebrating his self-sufficiency: "I deal with it, me first, then my boys will come. It's normally them coming to me for help." This prompts him to reveal a scar across the bridge of his nose inflicted by scissors: "came after I got jumped."

Avoidance is not apparently part of Baru's daily routine; he shops at the nearest outlet and eats fast food where he wants. He frequents a youth club founded by a Bengali organization and Camden Council. Nevertheless, he avoids another located a mere quarter of a mile away—in this instance founded by the Council and a local charity—where the presence of black and white boys makes him reluctant to enter. Why? "I know how they roll, they give me screws, you know 'what the fuck you looking at?' Pussies." So what makes a "pussy"? "Someone that's talking too much; someone that won't back up their own boys." One is left to wonder how, with no provocation aside from prolonged staring, issues arise; what is the nature of such issues and why and how do such silent hostilities lead to verbal and physical confrontations? "It's about making a rep [reputation] for the area you're from." How is this best done? "In a fair fight, no weapons. But some use knives, pieces of wood or bottles of beer. But there's no point to fighting, you do it at a certain time of your life."

Baru's claims of freedom to walk where he wants and his insistence on his general peacefulness are contradicted repeatedly in the above statements. Baru has clearly been part of and party to trouble as both a victim and attacker, and although—according to him—never a precipitator of such trouble, he is a stout defender of peer morality. Having a mobile phone stolen by other youths was not unusual for young men of his age. What was unusual was a threat to "juke" [stab] him if he did not hand over his phone. He remembers moments of disorder in the chicken shop when issues from school between black and Bengali boys kicked off at lunch but were prevented from escalating by the counter staff who in hindsight were respected for their actions: "They're blessed. You cause trouble, they dash you out, but they're really nice as well."

There were also other adults to whom Baru might turn. When *his* phone was stolen, he reported it to the police. He was also aware of "toy cops," a dismissive term for the Community Support Officers who regularly patrolled the streets where he lived. While he appreciated them and their "chatting away," he opined that they did not have the power to search an individual but could merely take down personal details. If they wished to proceed with a legal issue, they had to inform police to make the arrest.

Eschewing alcohol, Baru's poison of choice is herbal and smoked. At times, "mersh" (a form of "skunk") is favored but his true preference is for "greeny," which, he explains, contains no chemicals and is therefore "better for you." Minutes after talking of greeny, Baru claims that he neither drinks nor "blazes" (smokes "mersh", "greeny" or other forms of marijuana) and, while he attends the mosque, his worship is occasional. He admits to being a non-practicing Muslim. He is however caught up in the age-old conflict between parental morality and expectations and the need to be different. In his attempt to be a dutiful son, he reasons that he tries hard at home with parents who are practicing Muslims and a father who prays five times a day. Their worldview, however, is not his. His parents do not appreciate either his earrings or his recently acquired "Mohawk" haircut. The hashish he admitted to smoking must be concealed from parents and a younger brother. At the same time, the expense incurred by his parents for his education now prompts him to remain in the family home in the evenings, as opposed to his previous wanderings out on the streets until close to midnight.

His immediate ambition is passing exams; this is fueled by a desire to own designer goods: "anything 3 series."[7] Meanwhile, he also covets a specific mobile phone—"the W995." Baru talks big, talks ambition, and is somewhat inconsistent or confused as to his role in "trouble." He is, however, acutely aware of the power of image. His £200.00 silver neck chain complements his leather jacket, designer jeans, and Gucci shoes. What is authentic or real in this ensemble was not revealed nor, perhaps, fully known. Living in an age immersed in youthful images, who knows what the "true" items are? More importantly, who cares?

Living the Dream? Nael's story

Nael arrived at Heathrow Airport, London, some seven years ago at the age of ten, in the company of a brother older by two years and a man of Pakistani origin who abandoned the boys two days after their arrival. Nael last saw his parents seven years ago when they dispatched their two sons to the care of a stranger who promised to take them on a journey halfway round the world to save them from abduction by Afghanistan's Taliban militia. Nael's parents sold all they possessed and gave the proceeds to a Pakistani-born intermediary who promised the boys they would end up in the West and wealthy.

The intermediary was as good as his word. But for Nael and his brother the journey from Heathrow to Camden Town took a few twists and provoked many tears. Speaking no English, the two newly arrived and abandoned youngsters were placed under the care of social workers that provided a place of safety in a children's hostel. The pair's nightly weeping into pillows out of fear and loss were relieved somewhat by the appearance of an Afghan cousin who had arrived in London months earlier. Relocated to foster care, the brothers absconded after just three nights to take up residence with their cousin. Eventually their fifty-year-old uncle managed to find a solution to the group's woes—a three-bedroom Camden council flat in which the three have lived until this day. This domestic arrangement suited Nael who enjoyed both the culture and kinship of his native land. It also offered respite from the outside world within which he constantly negotiated relations with a plethora of boys who were unlike him in both appearance and work ethic. Since he was fourteen, Nael worked in a neighborhood food outlet, a chicken shop. As a result he knew all the area's teenage boys—good and bad.

Aged seventeen, Nael cut a somewhat incongruous figure. His attempt at fashioning a "street look" at times produced the unworldly fusion of hip-hop baseball hat, hooded top, and the de rigueur 'prison walk'. His clothing ensembles and comportment concealed what was in fact a well-mannered, polite, hard-working boy who did not possess attitude in anything he said or did. His preferred future was legal employment; his aspiration to own his own business, to improve his English, and then to enroll in business college. In pursuit of this he worked until 2 a.m. three nights a week and in the course of serving chicken met every self-proclaimed youthful "gangster" that the area can boast. Nael was aware that his identity straddled many boundaries. Employed by secular Islamic Turks serving *halal* food, his co-workers and managers took no nonsense from the regular teenaged customers and gave them some latitude in their noise-making but did not allow alcoholic drinks on the premises. At lunchtime the chicken shop was packed with black, African-born school children plus Bangladeshis. The shop was frequented by a similar demographic in the few hours after the school day had ended. The customer appeal of this business was the cheapness of its product: for £2.50 a teenager could sate their hunger and buy a soft drink. And while the fare on offer might appall nutritionists, for the low-income parent the shop offered sustenance that their child might not receive at home.

As a consequence of serving such a clientele, Nael knew literally hundreds of teenage boys. The demographic of the shop's customers changed following the entrance of late-night workers along with pub and club goers and thus drunken behavior was not unknown. In his downtime Nael could be found in the immediate locality, usually putting the world to rights with three local barbers—one a Cypriot, one a Bangladeshi, one an Algerian. All spoke good if not perfect English as they moaned about income and the occasional stupidity of their respective customers.

Nael's path from small boy to the chicken shop is worth telling here. Once a conscientious student, Nael received an achievement award at his Camden primary school along with the accolade of "best-behaved pupil." By his early teens, Nael recalls, not all involved in the education system appreciated his presence at school. He remembers being beaten by a group of teenagers twenty strong near the block where he lived. The low-achieving secondary school he attended brought more violence to Nael from the majority Bengali demographic. As a consequence, he stuck close to the eight Afghan boys also studying at the school. In Nael's opinion, trouble was unavoidable; he was suspended for five days after a conflict in the classroom continued out on the playground. He left school at sixteen with no qualifications and feeling frustrated that his English was not good enough to understand the curriculum. His fondest memories were of intra-school cricket matches.

In his early teens he regularly attended a local youth club, enjoying both the snooker and gym facilities. An accommodating and polite boy, he was known and liked by fellow club goers and workers alike. But by age fourteen he was forced to seek gainful employment. His unemployed uncle demanded that he study hard and be ambitious. At the same time, money was tight and Nael sought an income. A fast-food proprietor who recognized Nael as a conscientious boy—with a liking for fried chicken—provided him a job. The long hours, although these brought in money, were not conducive to schooling or domestic harmony. While Nael's income brought with it a degree of independence, his newly acquired clothing, hair and sideburns, and earring also drew his uncle's contempt. The latter rarely left the house and was under the impression that Nael was still at school. Taking account of his uncle's feelings, Nael left more controversial clothing and jewelry at work, thus creating two lives and appearances to suit two different audiences.

The shop improved his English no end. It provided, in effect, a "night out" for which he was paid, hence saving him money. It also got him—in his opinion—nice clothes and allowed him to pursue his favorite pastime of cinema-going in London's West End and to attend "shisha"[8] places in other London neighborhoods. This busy working life also meant that his friends knew his whereabouts at most times. Many Afghan friends visited Nael, even though only a few lived locally. In consequence, Nael was not involved in any claims to "neighborhood nationalism." In local terms, he, as an Afghan, had no ethnically assumed territory; he was by ethnicity and nature a territorial "neutral." When meeting other Afghans, the group's rendezvous and exchanges were always conducted as territorial "strangers"—untethered in terms of their meanderings and meeting places.

The chicken shop was resourced in more ways than one. On occasion mobile phones were offered by some of the shop's African customers who had stolen them from members of another peer group. A sum of £10.00 could buy an item of technology that might on occasion be worth twenty times as much. At the same time Nael also exhibited late-night generosity, when, for example, before closing the remaining food was sometimes given to an African child who had arrived as an unaccompanied minor with learning difficulties and was now living in a local hostel. Nael's rationale for generosity was based on a sense of humanity and empathy: "I feel sorry for such people—it could easily have been me."

After living under the Taliban regime, Camden Town was, in Nael's opinion, a safe place: "I can walk anywhere and know all the people here." He brought to the streets a sense of service, and he believed in both propriety and values: "We never hold weapons. As we say, 'we don't start fights, we finish them'—we don't fight, we fit in." Nael provided a service that was desired by the teenage boys who entered the premises, who were not inclined to insult or infuriate the owners. Indeed, the Turkish owners were respected both as people and businessmen. Anybody throwing food or requesting it in an impertinent manner was refused further service. Any group provoking a fight was ushered out of the doors. And the presence of other Turks in nearby premises puts off the area's most hardened troublemakers. Nael had witnessed much disorder. His job was not for the faint-hearted, yet, in the face of provocation by the drunks and mentally-ill persons that the high street occasionally hosted, he had held his position as a server.

The world he came from, while a distant memory, permeated all that Nael did. He disapproved of arguing with elders, he respected the notion of the family in the absence of his own, and he cautioned others about "getting ahead of themselves." His ambitions were traditional: marriage to an Afghan girl and self-employment. To attain these goals, he was prepared to undertake demanding feats of endurance—two weeks after our conversation he had a new job in a south London kebab shop working six days a week from 11 a.m. until 11 p.m. A full working week paid £260.00 in cash plus tips. For Nael, such a sum was heaven. Though the position's hourly rate was well below the minimum wage, a seventeen-year-old with no qualifications could not afford to be choosy. After journeying home he could be found at midnight at his former workplace in Camden. For him, there was nowhere else to go.

Nael knew from his peer group that better money was available from other sources. One Pakistani-born friend had made nearly £60,000.00 in one year selling drugs—but he was now imprisoned. Another Afghan friend took up robbery. Upon arrest and imprisonment he acquired a deeper interest in Islam and on being released he returned to Afghanistan. Such alternative careers, rather like the pursuit of status through violence, did not appeal to Nael who had an argument to end all: "I'm quiet and peaceful. Look at my country, where did years of fighting get them? Nowhere."

On at least one occasion, however, his homeland legacy brought trouble in London. When visiting a council-run gymnasium with friends, the group came across a group of Kosovan migrants who considered the area to be their turf. After the customary preliminaries of sustained staring, words were exchanged and mobile phones engaged. Within an hour both sides were twenty strong in number. In the ensuing disorder an Afghan boy suffered two wounds from a knife. These were not fatal, but the police became involved, taking statements from Nael and a number of the other young men involved in the altercation. The irony was that while the group of Afghans had ostensibly visited the area to "do physical exercise," their ulterior motive was to confront another Afghan boy who had insulted Nael. Nael was, he explained, duty-bound to respond with action just as he would back in Afghanistan.

Nael was ambitious and serious. His alternative would be that of dependency upon an uncle for accommodation and a little money. Aware of his situation, he reflected on the problem of youth unemployment and predicted that "if they don't change it, there'll be trouble ... all these boys doing nothing ... there'll be years of shit."

Designs for Living: Abdi's Story

Born in Somalia 18 years ago, Abdi's London life began in 2002 when he came with his aunt to join his mother who had arrived there two years previously. The latter had left Ethiopia where the family had sought refuge from the Somali civil war. While his mother's move required merely a visa, Abdi and his companions entered the United Kingdom as refugees. Eleven years old and unable to speak English, Abdi was housed by Camden Council with his mother and given a place in the local state school.

In the seven years since then, Abdi's life might be considered a refugee success story. Studious and able to negotiate the perils of the school playground, Abdi was rarely involved in fights; when these did occur, Abdi and his schoolmates relied on tutorial group loyalties rather than "race" to distinguish counterparts from adversaries. In his teens Abdi became aware of the drug dealers who wandered Camden High Street and noted the chicken shop as a site of potential disorder. In this urban setting Abdi managed to forge his own individual path, not becoming part of any identifiable youth collective. "Black" but hardly identifying with any known "sub-culture" in his choices of clothing, he wore garments that were cheap and functional; his only fashionable gesture was a woolly hat worn whenever possible, even in mid-summer. His clothes thus made no statements in terms of peer-group identification, credibility or solidarity.

Abdi was an individual. However, as a black teenager of Somali origin he knew he was subject to social stigmatization. Although not in trouble with the law or at school, his objection to authority arose out of people "staring at me for no reason." He also knew the Somali protagonists of disorder in his neighborhood, but their world was not his. His teenage years had been dominated by playing football which at times could occupy five hours a day. A knee operation undergone at sixteen closed off this potential career path. Subsequently he pursued dreams of a different type and to this end was studying for a B-Tec national qualification in art and design.

In Abdi's words, many of Camden's other Somalis were "hard to love." Nearly all had arrived with some family members in the status of refugees and had been housed in local government properties. Some of the Somali teenagers whose friendship was based on shared residence decided on a nomenclature to match their respective notoriety in street disorder—for instance, the "Money Squad." Eschewing serious engagement in the education system, the boys of this group, who at times numbered as many as twenty, were a constant feature of two streets in the vicinity of Camden market. To most tourists they were perhaps invisible amid the throngs of people. To those seeking drugs, they provided a ready supply.

Such boys had caused consternation in their neighborhood and were a source of fear for all teenagers in the area. Abdi noted their tendency to steal mobiles and money from other teenage boys. As he put it, this was a group comprised of teenage boys who did not expect to live beyond thirty and were thus taking the world's offerings as quickly as possible. According to Camden's rumor mill, the Metropolitan Police suspected that a large number of the group had traveled to London from Somalia's "war zone areas" but could not voice such suspicions due to a lack of evidence. Large-scale police surveillance of this group revealed that its members were selling drugs and harassing passers-by; the resulting dossier listed the respective criminal records of the group's members, including charges of drug dealing, assault, carrying offensive weapons, and sexual assault. The surveillance operation resulted in the local council issuing ASBOs and demarcating dispersal zones to clear the group from its favored haunts. In Abdi's cynical words: "they stay in the area, but sleep a bit longer." Months later, complaints arose from local people living a mile from one of the dispersal zones that drug dealing had shifted to this locale. The police Divisional Commander denied any causal effect.

Abdi lived in the north of the borough. His bus routes were different than those of Tom, Baru, and Nael, for his neighborhood stood adjacent to another Camden borough district called Kilburn. In Abdi's opinion, Kilburn's streets were more dangerous to walk through than Camden Town. For him, the Kilburn streets were rendered perilous by the presence of Somalis who celebrated their locality and were hostile to outsiders, even if they happened to be phenotypical "Somalis." To complicate matters further, Kilburn's Somalis had their own internal antagonisms with other African-born and black British boys. That said, the process of targeting victims was the same in both neighborhoods: "they rob you ... they want your phone. It all depends on their mood. In the daytime if they don't like you they'll rush you, beat you up. But it's [the same in] every area and every people, isn't it?" At the tender age of seventeen, Abdi had a world-weary consciousness of violence and of being disliked. Aware that members of the general public would not likely intervene in such scenarios, he also held no expectation of uniformed intervention: "Police? They're just looking for knives and guns; they're not interested in boys fighting. The police don't really want to know and you don't want to be called a 'snitch'. If you get beaten up they would be suspicious of why you were in the area in the first place."

For Abdi, the prospects for street violence rested upon timing and recognition. With respect to the latter, he believed that he was spared trouble with Camden's Somalis because "I know them and their families. But I wouldn't enter their homes; they're not my kind of people." However, the issue of identification could be used instrumentally: "it's best to dress in your own way and not like a gangster. I wear football kits and shirts which make it obvious I'm into football—nothing they want to rob."

The Somalis he knew but sought to avoid enjoyed their sense of dominance in the streets. Be it a consequence of limited finances or adherence to the tenets of Islam, boys such as these generally concealed their bodies far more than members of other peer groups in Camden. A coat was often worn. Abdi speculated that these cumbersome garments were donned because of their ability to conceal weapons and disguise the physical inadequacy of those wearing them. What some lacked in sinews they made up for in reputation. The murder of seventeen-year old Somali (and Money Squad member) Sharmaarke Hassan in May 2008 after an intra-Somali dispute was preceded two years earlier by another intra-Somali gang fight that saw a teenage boy stabbed to death in one of the gangs' gathering places. Even as the Somalis had attained notoriety among all peer groups, their biggest threat came from their own countrymen.

For Abdi, nighttime was a source of apprehension, and once again public transport was the most pressing issue. The problem was alcohol related: "drunks can attack you: 'What you looking at?' At times you have to defend yourself." The same bus route was avoided during the daytime because of the presence of boys from another school. Consequently, Abdi would sometimes walk two miles to school rather than board the bus. His other fears issued from occasions that were ostensibly meant for shared celebration. One was the annual Notting Hill Carnival; the other was New Year's Eve. The former attracts two million people and takes place over two days in late August in West London, just two miles from Abdi's house. Trouble ensued as youths passed through Abdi's area on their way to the carnival. In Abdi's analysis these groups were seeking violent encounters in and around the event. The same logic was evident during New Year's Eve celebrations in central London. These alcohol-drenched festivities required Abdi to negotiate the youthful excesses that possessed the potential for violence.

Abdi's world was thus divided into "wrong" and "right" times, with the added stipulation of knowing when to talk and when to walk. In situations of trouble, he believed families should not be involved; if the perpetrator was found, then a one-on-one fight should be the preferred solution after which the issue should be forgotten. Where would this occur? "Council estates you know? Make a circle like *Fight Club*. Problem is there's always someone who jumps in and ruins the one-on-one." In Abdi's opinion such scenarios were contrived: "Everyone gets hyped up, stands in a circle, then it happens. After two punches someone shouts 'Police!' And everyone runs." The peer group penchant for violence was seen by Abdi as too often a ludicrous performance. Sometimes running was, in his view, the best option. Abdi had witnessed Bengalis brandishing knives and baseball bats and knew that small handguns were easily obtainable from certain contacts. In Abdi's opinion these "self-assembly guns" were sported not by street kids but more by the "big gangster who always says it's there for protection."

The Somali population in London is one that is slowly opening small businesses and that is, for the most part—beyond its males under the age of 30—not considered to pose a significant criminal problem to the Metropolis. When there is trouble with boys within Camden's Somali community, the troublesome group consists of no more than two dozen boys. There are, one suspects, generational issues. These boys' employment prospects are bleak to non-existent, and they are willing to pursue criminal avenues to obtain the funds to partake in the life of consumption encouraged by the world around them. By contrast Abdi has chosen the route of education. His tactic is to forgo the membership of any identifiable group and to negotiate his way through Camden's youth-group landscape, constantly aware of the various memberships and the places where they are most likely to congregate.

Conclusion

The issues that permeate this Camden landscape go well beyond the violence we've discussed in this chapter. The conduct of male teenagers is frequently boisterous and potentially intimidating. Incivilities of this nature provoke fear in some and frustration in others. For some, the behaviors manifested and witnessed by the four boys we've introduced here may appear brutish. But such behaviors also demonstrate the frailty of social control (Douglas 1966). The response of the government to teenage boys—at both a national and local level—has to be seen in the political context of twenty-first century Britain, a setting which sees widespread cultural uncertainty, loss of faith in church and state, rising levels of unemployment, and short-term working practices. These societal factors have combined to create an unfounded fear of crime and a context wherein teenagers are anathema to their elders. Memories are short. The United Kingdom has never been free of the revelries and improprieties of young men (Brewer and Style 1980; Davies 2008). Earlier instances of disorderly, disruptive behavior were cut short by the demands of military service and employment patterns that brooked no indiscipline. Those days are gone, however. Male socialization norms bound up in both occupational cultures and neighborhood kinship networks have been replaced by social and geographic mobility, new employment (and unemployment) patterns, and trans-national media influences.

In this context the discredited young male might best be considered as the "fall-guy" for a period in British history once mooted by some pundits as economically progressive. Nevertheless, unemployment figures released by the British government in July 2009 showed that of the nearly 2.4 million claiming "Job-seekers allowance," some 25 percent were aged between sixteen and twenty-five. The future for so many young men is one of social insecurity in a political milieu that has accepted neo-liberal economics. At the same time, recent governments have legislated like no other in history in an attempt to control their citizenry. To this end the UK has permitted predictive profiling of the young and the compilation of databases on its young men, both in terms of images and DNA samples.[9] For these young men, their lives are likely to be subject to the unstinting surveillance of the state, whether through the immediacy of uniformed personnel or the silent lenses of controlling technology.

The occupational cultures sought by Tom, Baru, Nael, and Abdi are becoming increasingly de-regularized. The future looks bleak. The disturbances and incivilities attributed to unemployed young men will remain and with them no doubt an ever-expanding state apparatus that seeks to collate information and images gained through surveillance, a process which in turn allows the state to control and restrict society members and invariably stigmatize teenage subjects. Indeed, for those whose threatening image is repeatedly etched by such "data," possibilities for a more meaningful and fulfilling life look tenuous at best. Because of chronic shortages, the social housing in which they currently reside will likely not be available in the future when they seek to settle and raise a family. Their choice is thus restricted to remaining in the extended-family home until their twenties or seeking privacy in affordable accommodation miles away from both the neighborhoods in which they were raised and the kin and childhood friendship networks that previously bolstered social and familial solidarity. Their future is at the mercy of market forces like never before. The previous Labour government announced itself "extremely at ease" with the super-rich and rampant individualism. At the time of writing, the Liberal Democrats in charge of local government in Camden had plans to reduce the council payroll by up to 40 percent and at the same time to auction off dozens of council-owned properties to the highest bidder for the short-term gain of the council coffers and in defiance of a housing waiting list of tens of thousands. In 2008, at the national level—and seemingly without irony—the then Conservative opposition party stressed the need for a more "caring and considerate" society. Meanwhile the prison population of the United Kingdom stands at an all-time high at over eighty-four thousand (some twenty thousand others were released early from their sentences, thus making the figures artificially low).

Returning to one of the issues discussed at the outset, it would be foolish and naive to gloss the narratives presented here as representative of ethnic harmony. Yet, the complicated stories of enmity, alliance, and contradiction contained therein leave the concept of "race" hopelessly fractured and problematic. Those interviewed for this chapter clearly employ a combination of ethnic, linguistic, and cultural markers to order their movement and conduct. But the tripartite division of "black," "white," and "Asian" is patently superficial when we—and more importantly they—try to make sense of these markers: how does one identify the Irish, Afghan, Albanian, Kosovan, Bengali, Congolese, Somalian, West Indian, or Bissau-Guinean teenager in terms of phenotype? As a result, the boys whose lives were examined above must continually chart a shallow socio-historical inventory of their locale in order to move safely through its streets and estates. This knowledge must be continually updated because of the everyday alliances and enmities struck up by themselves and others. Such constant auditing must occur if these young males are to accurately identify their friends and enemies at any given moment. In this sense nothing is "racial," nor is anything "implicit." The boys' awareness of immigration and its impact on the economy of local (dis)order means that to cleave to any fixed "implicit racial bias" (Sampson 2009) would leave them gravely unequipped and misinformed in relation to signifiers of (dis)order and their shifting social meaning.

Notes

The authors are indebted to the four young men who voluntarily contributed their time and memories for the benefit of this chapter. They are also grateful to a number of youth workers in Camden who shared their experience for the benefit of the inquiry. Our thanks are also due to our academic colleagues in the Centre for Youth Work Studies in the School of Sport and Education, Brunel University, especially Michael Whelan whose ideas on "space" and "street" were crucial in the early part of our research. Our final thanks go to the editors of this text for their invaluable —and impressively prompt—assistance in improving the analysis.

1. The authors are both residents of the London Borough of Camden. Gary Armstrong has seventeen years experience as a youth worker in Camden and coaches a boys' soccer team consisting of the local born. James Rosbrook-Thompson is a soccer and basketball coach in Camden schools.

2. The High Street is the generic name (and frequently the official name) of the primary business street of towns or cities in the United Kingdom.

3. Closed-circuit television (CCTV) involves the use of video cameras to transmit a signal to a specific place, on a limited set of monitors. A doubling of recorded crime incidents in Britain between 1979 and 1992 drove the Conservative governments of Margaret Thatcher and John Major to spend heavily on CCTV. Determined to erase the perception that his Labour government was soft on crime, Tony Blair continued the spread of CCTV after taking power in 1997. Today there is one CCTV camera for every fourteen people in the United Kingdom. A Londoner has his/her image captured by CCTV cameras on average three hundred times a day.

4. Council housing is a form of public or social housing in the United Kingdom. Such accommodation was built and operated by local councils to supply homes on secure tenancies at below-market rents to primarily working-class people. The development of council accommodation began in the late nineteenth century and peaked in the mid-twentieth century. The "right to buy" scheme is a policy—the legislation for which was passed in the 1980 Housing Act—that gives council house tenants the right to buy the home they are living in. Between 1980 and 1998 approximately two million homes in the United Kingdom were sold in this manner.

5. This refers to the number one attachment device used in conjunction with electric hair clippers. This attachment ensures that hair is shaved to a length of 1/8 inch.

6. As with the names given to all interviewees, "Tom" is a pseudonym used to protect the confidentiality of the informant featured in this chapter.

7. Here Baru refers to the BMW 3 Series, a compact executive car manufactured by the German automobile and motorcycle manufacturer BMW since May 1975.

8. Shisha, or a hookah, is a single or multi-stemmed (often glass-based) water pipe for smoking herbal fruits and tobacco. It is gaining popularity in the United Kingdom, the United States, and Canada.

9. In the same week youth unemployment in the United Kingdom topped the one million mark, thus reaching a sixteen-year high, and one in four black boys under the age of eighteen residing in the United Kingdom has their DNA samples held by the state.

Bibliography

Brewer, J. and Styles, J. 1980. *An Ungovernable People: The English and their Law in the Seventeenth and Eighteenth Centuries*. London: Hutchinson.
Box, S. 1981. *Deviance, Reality and Society*. London: Holt, Rinehart and Winston.
Cohen, S. 1980. *Folk-Devils and Moral Panics: The Creation of Mods and Rockers*. New York: St. Martin's.
Cohen, S. 1985. *Visions of social Control: Crime, Punishment and Classification*. Cambridge: Polity.
Craig, J. and J. Brown. 2008. "Teenager killed by shot in head after visit to drug deal hangout." *The Times*, 30 May.
Davies, A. 2008. *The Gangs of Manchester: The Story of the Scuttlers, Britain's First Youth Cult*. Preston, United Kingdom: Milo Books.
Davies. N. 2008. "Tactics against gangs fatally flawed: report." *The Guardian*, 14 July.
Douglas, M. 1966. *Purity and Danger: An Analysis of Concepts of Pollution and Taboo*. New York: Praeger.
Frean, A. 2008. "Most adults think children are feral and a danger to society." *The Times*, 17 November.

Fresco, A. 2009. "Life for gang who stabbed boy, 14, to death." *The Times*, 10 July.

Hall, S. 1997. *Representation: Cultural Representations and Signifying Practices*. London: Sage.

Hall, S. and Jefferson, T. 1976. *Resistance Through Rituals: Youth Sub-Cultures in Post-War Britain*. London: Routledge.

Hamnett, C. 2003. "Gentrification and the Middle-Class remaking of Inner London, 1961–2001." *Urban Studies*, 40 (12): 2401–2426.

Hamnett, C., and B. Randolph. 1987. "Residualisation of Council Housing in Inner London, 1971–1981." In *Public Housing, Current Trends and Future Developments*, eds. D. Clapham and J. English. London: Routledge.

Howard, K and Majid, Y. 2006. "The 'Chav' phenomenon: Consumption, media and the construction of the new underclass." *Crime, Media, Culture*, 2 (1): 9–28.

Keilthy, P. 2008. "'Drug-dealing gang' ordered to stay away." *Camden New Journal*, 12 June.

Keilthy, P. 2009. "Youth dispersal zone close to school is removed by police." *Camden New Journal*, 28 May.

Muggleton, D. and R. Weinzierl. 2003. *The Post-Subcultures reader*. Oxford: Berg.

Raby, R. 2005. "What is Resistance?" *Journal of Youth Studies*, 8 (2): 151–171.

Rutherford, A. 2002. "Criminal Policy and the Eliminative Ideal." *Social Policy and Administration*, 31 (5): 116–135.

Sampson, R. 2009. "Disparity and diversity in the contemporary city: social (dis)order revisited." *British Journal of Sociology*, 60 (1): 1–31.

Squires, P. 2008. *ASBO Nation: The Criminalisation of Nuisance*. Bristol: Policy.

Watt, P. 2001. "The dynamics of social class and housing: a study of local authority tenants in the London Borough of Camden." Ph.D. diss., Department of Geography, King's College, University of London.

———. 2006. "Respectability, Roughness and 'Race': Neighbourhood Place Images and the Making of Working-Class Social Distinctions in London." *International Journal of Urban and Regional Research*, 30 (4): 776–97.

Chapter 11

BIG MAN SYSTEM, SHORT LIFE CULTURE
Working-Class Boys and Street Violence
in Southeast London

Gillian Evans

Most of the males have had to harden up not just 'cos [of] the people that are turnin' to the street but the people that are just walkin' along the streets. 'Cos obviously they don't want people takin' advantage of them, like, everyone's had to man-up, I've had to man-up. Like, if someone says, 'can I have your phone? [to steal it]' It's kind of a struggle to say, 'Yeah take it,' 'cos, obviously, if that person sees you again they'll try the same thing again.

—Richard, seventeen, southeast London, 2009

Nobody [h]ad anything [when we were growing up] so you didn't [h]ave to worry about who [h]ad what, you just got on with life and children made their own entertainment, but not anymore, now they're killin' each other over trainers that cost £100.00.

—Trevor, fifty-two, southeast London, 2000

If a bod[1] has a score to settle, he's got to finish it off good and proper and only a carefully placed knife can do that. If he doesn't take that desperate measure he can be sure the knife will be in his belly before the year is out.

—Trevor, fifty-two, southeast London, 2000

Introduction

Towards the end of the summer holiday in southeast London in 2009, in the week when young people are awaiting their GCSE results, a sixteen-year-old black boy is stabbed five times in broad daylight. An A* student without any reputation for making trouble, the young man was said to be simply on his way home, traveling through his own neighborhood. The incident sent a ripple of terror—another ripple of terror—through the network of concerned parents of teenage boys in Southeast London. The stabbing symbolized fears of a horrifying escalation in violent knife crime on the streets. This was not so much a fear of an increasing quantity of attacks (after all, the government is proud of its statistics which suggest that violent crime in Britain is decreasing[2]) but rather that the assaults are becoming indiscriminate—violence for violence sake—rather than pertaining to robbery or revenge-seeking behavior between rival gangs. How could parents sleep easy at night if innocent, young, aspirational men were not safe on the street in their own neighborhoods in broad daylight?

The incident made me think again about my previous analyzes (Evans 2006a; 2006b) of the relationship between working-class masculinity and "the street" and what it means to be a young man growing up in predominantly working-class areas of southeast London in the United Kingdom. I had predicted, then, on the basis of ethnographic fieldwork conducted between 1999 and 2000, that violent crime on the street would increase in proportion to children's possession of increasingly valuable objects of desire—mobile phones, designer trainers and clothes, iPods etc. These were the objects in relation to which children measured each other's sense of personal value, objects that designated a divided world of haves, have-nots, and have-a-go desperados—thieves who simply took what they wanted from the haves and thereby gained, and learned to trade on, a developing reputation for violent intimidation. Thus, the desperados would come, in time, to exert a cruelly vindictive kind of leveling force in working-class areas, denying those children and young people whose parents could afford to buy them nice things the opportunity to safely enjoy the prestige and relative privilege which derives from being more comfortably off. Here, it seems, the street life lived by a very few keeps everyone in working-class neighborhoods down; it keeps people down and it gets them down.

I showed how this relatively new phenomenon of child-on-child and youth-on-youth violence or "mugging" was a transformation of a pre-existing historical precedent in which the development of an appropriate style of masculinity in working-class neighborhoods depends on having to make sense of "the street" as a place where toughness is forged out of territorial conflict. I explained how what it is to be working-class is inseparable from pride in a sense of place, of coming from somewhere in particular, such that, for certain kinds of young men, "the street" operates as both a territorial anchor, tying them to where they come from and, at the same time, giving them a sense of having a stake in something—a sense of possession—a place in the world and, against the background of generations of poverty and societal disrespect, a reputation worth fighting for. My concern was to show how this way of becoming a man on the street made it unlikely, for some, that they would be able to reconcile this style of masculinity with the way in which education required them to be "good boys" at school. The relevant point here is that, with the escalating incidence of child-on-child or youth-on-youth muggings, issues of reputation and a growing consumer culture collide and intensify in interaction.

Although my focus was on white working-class[3] young men in Bermondsey, southeast London, I emphasized that the challenges facing white working-class boys growing up in post-industrial twenty-first century England were remarkably similar to those facing black working-class boys. I have argued elsewhere (Evans 2010) that to explain educational failure in racial terms without an account of social class is to completely obscure the overwhelming significance of social class (compared to any other indicators—gender, race, ethnicity) when trying to predict the chances of any child's success in England. The same point is to be stressed here with respect to knife crime. The issue has come to seem like one that concerns black parents and black boys only. For example, Tony Blair announced in 2007 that "the spate of knife and gun murders in London was not being caused by poverty, but a distinctive black culture."[4] However, a recent report (2007) on knife crime published by the Centre for Crime and Justice Studies suggests, in contrast, not only that the way statistics are compiled is highly problematic for a multitude of reasons, but that there is a need to account for the disproportionate concentration of black and minority ethnic populations in deprived working-class areas. The report stresses that:

> The link between crime and deeper structural causes of inequality, poverty and social disaffection needs to be fully acknowledged and acted upon if the solutions are to be more than cosmetic and short term. At present the government seems to be acting in response to a problem without knowing the full nature and extent of that problem and while overlooking the fundamental causes. (Eades et al, 2007: 32)

In other words, knife crime has recently been too hastily racialized as a black-on-black issue and my aim here is to argue, and to emphasize again, that when closely analyzed it may turn out to be much more an issue related to social class and, specifically, it carries significant meaning for black, white, and Asian young men growing up in working-class areas of our cities. Racializing the issue, that is, making it seemingly related to race, ethnicity, and culture alone, conceals what we really need to be debating, which is the detrimental effects, on young men in particular, of the constraints of coming of age in post-industrial working-class neighborhoods. Currently, the statistics for the youth justice system do not allow us to make an analysis of the correlation between social class and involvement in crime, but if that were made possible, as it has most recently and controversially been made possible in education (to collate statistics in such a way that the significance of race, ethnicity, class, and gender can be analyzed all at once[5]), what are the bets that the young people who are most likely to end up caught up in the criminal justice system at an early age are working-class young men?

Precisely because the majority of people seem to have the impression that knife crime is a black-on-black issue, an impression which is enhanced by media coverage of violent assaults, there is an urgent need for statistics to be collated and analyzed more precisely and for qualitative research to be commissioned and conducted in such a way that we can appreciate, on a much more localized level, exactly what is going on in different kinds of working-class neighborhoods around the country. What if it turns out that in some neighborhoods, in British cities, the prevalence of knife crime is much more associated with white working-class boys than any other group? My suggestion is not that we need not account for race, ethnicity, and culture, but that to do so without accounting for social class in the United Kingdom is nonsense and a dangerous nonsense at that.

With this in mind, in what follows below I will re-present my earlier research and arguments about working-class masculinity—beginning with the case study of Tom,[6] age ten, at Tenter Ground School in Bermondsey.

Tom at Tenter Ground

Tom is a lively freckle-faced ten-year old boy; he lives with his mom Anne, step-dad, and younger sister in a two-bedroom flat on an old housing association estate just across the road form Tenter Ground primary school. At home, Tom is a complete mommy's boy, often sitting on his mother's lap for a cuddle while she steals a reluctant kiss from him. They share a joking relationship in which he plays teasing games with her, cheeking her back when she tries to give him instructions and corrections, and he knows how to provoke her as far as he dares before Anne starts to chase him with her hand raised; in good humor she threatens to clout him. Laughing loudly, Tom often runs from the room to escape Anne's clutches and when her nagging gets him down he runs freely outside onto the streets which demand from him an entirely different disposition. Described as mean, inner-city streets are the playgrounds where, if they are allowed to play out, children learn to grow up tough. In this respect, Bermondsey is no different. As soon as Tom is on the street his demeanor changes and he begins to bowl: to walk in a way that means business, that shows he cannot be pushed around. The street is a place where tough kids rule and these are usually older guys who move in gangs.

When Tom is out of the room, Anne tells that when they first moved to the estate and did not know anyone, Tom got badly bullied by the older boys to the point that he was often scared to go out. Not being able to stand being cooped up, however, Tom would go back again and again for more punishment. On one occasion someone had run to tell Anne that Tom had been put upside-down in a wheelie bin and could not get out. That same night, after Anne had rescued Tom, Tom's step-father Pete made Tom tell him who had done it and, learning which group of boys was responsible and who the ring leader was—Shane a local fifteen-year old—went out to look for him. Anne explains that when he found him, Pete took Shane by the scruff of the neck and told him, "If anything ever [h]appens to Tom on these streets I'm gonna hold you personally responsible whether you've got anythin' to do with it or not." Anne emphasizes how clearly it was spelled out to the local boys that, if any harm should come to Tom, Pete would go straight out to find Shane and kill him. She stresses that, with that warning issued, Tom never had any trouble on the street again. Here we can begin to appreciate how, on the estates, the threat of violence can be an effective form of peace-keeping.

Knowing that his parents are fiercely protective of him, a Bermondsey boy bowls because his parents' and older siblings' or cousins' reputations stand firmly intact behind him. Tom proudly tells his friends at school one day about what a good fighter his mom is: if she ever lost a fight at school, he says, her big brother would wait until she got home and beat her up again for losing. I imagine that Anne toughened up pretty quickly. She shows me Tom's boxing gear that she and Pete have recently bought for him—leather boots and gloves and shiny shorts—and tells me that the boxing coach above the famous Thomas-a-Beckett pub on the old Kent road has said that Tom has shown promise. Bermondsey boxers are

famous; the tough reputation of the men and the area in general is leg-
endary, and it is in relation to this kind of reputation that Bermondsey
boys, like Tom, must make sense of their developing masculinity. While
the women that men desire for their wives are expected by men to be
more gentle and peaceable, Bermondsey women are nevertheless not
pushovers. Anne admits that she used to fight when she was younger but
explains that once you gain a reputation you do not have to fight anymore. You just walk like you mean business and that's enough. Returning
to the subject of Tom's boxing lessons, Anne laments, "He didn't keep it
up, Tom gets bored easily; he can't settle the anythin'."

Anne tells me that she is much happier now about Tom playing out
because he has made friends with Gary, a boy who is a year older from the
Tanner's Gate estate. Gary is in year six at Tenter Ground; he shares a
class with Tom's Year Five cohorts and has a small "crew" of his own that
he moves with outside school and an older fifteen-year-old brother who
is a "bod" with a bit of a reputation, so he and Tom are less likely to be
bothered when they are out and about. Anne's hope is that Gary will be
a good influence on Tom; she knows that Tom is restless and she wishes
he would settle down a bit because she fears that he is heading for trouble
otherwise. Thinking about it, Anne laughs and explains how she has had
to come down hard on Tom lately because last year he was going too far:
"bowlin' down the road with a fag hangin' out his mouth." When she saw
that, Anne says, she took Tom inside and bruised his pride, making him
feel bad for "diggin' out the family," telling him what an idiot he looked.
She is confident that she humiliated him and managed to convince him
that it is not big for kids to smoke. Despite his young age, however, Tom is
already aiming for manhood: he knows how to hold himself, how to "act
big," and is full of self-confident bravado in the place where his charisma
comes into its own—on the street.

The Difference between Boys and Girls

A boy like Tom needs a firm hand and knows how to put on his best manners when it suits him, but he can also be free of his mother's restraining
influence as often as he pleases. Anne speaks hopefully about the stepfa-
ther of Tom's friend Gary, because sometimes he takes the boys fishing.
The problem, she says, is that there is nothing for the kids to do on the estate and so they easily get into trouble. Despite her best efforts to contain
Tom, Anne does not have the kind of relationship with him in which
finding constructive things for him to do—like boxing—is enough to distract him from the fun he can have—making trouble—with his friends on

the streets. Trying to maintain a consistent vigilance over young boys is a fulltime job for mothers in Bermondsey and the commitment to keeping them "on the straight and narrow" requires unceasing resourcefulness and devotion. At the same time, however, boys are encouraged to be tough; they enjoy a teasing relationship with older boys and men in which mock fighting plays a large part in what is seen as the necessity to toughen a boy up.

In general, things couldn't be more different for girls. Tom's sister Mary isn't allowed to play unless she is safe in the garden square at the back of the flat and she is quieter and more serious than Tom, spending more time at home and playing close to Anne and Pete's company. Immaculately turned out with waist-length, straight brown hair which Anne lovingly tends, Mary is what is called "a nice girl": well mannered, nicely spoken, and extremely feminine. Mary enjoys reading and writing and is at least three years in advance of Tom's reading ability even though she is three years younger. Commenting on the difference between her two children, Anne explains what differentiates them: "Tom's 'common' as muck, he's got a mouth on him no doubt about that, he's like me really, not like Mary, she's gentle like her dad and well spoken."

I ask Anne if Tom's story is true—the one in which he had explained to me how he learnt to swear in the pub when he was little—and she confirms the veracity of his tale. Telling me the story of Tom's christening, Anne goes on to clarify further what kinds of early influences Tom was exposed to. She explains that Tom was already five years old when he was christened; during the ceremony his uncle—the older brother of Tom's biological father—told Tom that he would give him a fiver (£5.00) if he was brave enough to go up to the man in the black dress (the priest) and call him a "fucking cunt." Needless to say, Tom did as he was told and was well paid for it. Just as I would have expected, Tom's uncle's sense of humor exerts a leveling force on any ambitions that Anne and Pete might have for Tom's future—as a good christened child, or for that matter anything else that might make them feel that he is a boy to be valued above others. Anne's story confirms my own observations that being a certain kind of "common" person involves, in part, the cultivation of irreverence for what is supposedly sacred—priests and the innocence of children, for example. I draw attention to this aspect of what it means to be "common" because I want to highlight the discrepancy between the ideas that "common" parents have about their children and what teachers assume should constitute suitable behavior in children. There is nothing to suggest, for example, that "common" children, like Tom, don't grow up in a language-rich environment filled with social interaction, but the way that they learn to talk and what they learn to value as an appropriate contribution in a conversation with adults may be miles away from what "posh" teachers expect of children at school.

Mary, however, is significantly different from Tom. In part, this is because she has a different kind of father than he does, and she has not been "got at"—leveled—and made "common" as much by her mother's friends and sisters and her father's siblings in the way that Tom has been. Anne explains, for example, that her sister teases her when she hears Mary talking nicely saying, "blimey Anne where'd she learn to speak like that?" And Anne emphasizes how she protects Mary from such taunts, telling her that there is nothing wrong with speaking nicely. Mary is proud to be her teacher's favorite at school and often teases Tom at home because she can read better than he can and, while she is a good girl, he is always in trouble at school.

Parental Expectations

Anne and Pete's reaction to Tom's initial progress in reading reinforces what I learned in almost every home that I visited during my research: the majority of working-class parents want more than anything for their children to do well at school because they know only too well that it leads to a better livelihood in the future. Some children are encouraged, whether they want to be or not, to continue with formal learning activities at home. This is especially the case in first- and second-generation families of West African origin. Even in families where the mother speaks little English and has, even in her own language, only a very basic education, which is often the case in the families of working-class Bangladeshi origin, the mothers nevertheless push their children towards education as the source of future opportunities in Britain. The important point to note, however, is that, depending on the level of their own education, rarely are working-class parents actually engaging with their children in activities that would constitute formal learning-type tasks. For example, children may regularly be told to "go and pick up a book!" but parents are not necessarily likely to sit down with their children to show them how to read and enjoy it and to thereby build an intimate relationship with the child on the basis of that shared enjoyment.

In "common" households, like Anne's, then, an appreciation of the value of formal learning is less likely to take the form of shared activity during the early relationship of caring between mother and child in the home. Formal learning and caring are not considered to be synonymous and, therefore, the ability to learn and do well at school is not usually thought to be a social skill that parents can influence and encourage directly. "Cleverness" is more likely to be considered to be a heritable quality; the child is thought of as being either "naturally clever" or not. When, for example, I interview the mother of a particularly able girl who is in Year Five at Tenter Ground, I am intrigued to hear her say of her daughter: "I dunno where she gets them brains from 'cos me and her dad are thick as shit." Nevertheless, the same woman also emphasizes how pivotal a role the girl's grandmother has played in her upbringing; the grandmother constantly played interactive games with the girl when she was little, took her to the park, and often rounded on mothers who did not make time to play and interact with their children. If a working-class child does well at school, parents tend not to take the credit themselves; they are more likely to understate their own abilities and, at the same time, underestimate the extent of their own influence over the child. If a child, like Tom, fails to do well, his parents usually feel that there is little they can do about it except to try their hardest to enforce the value of education and hope for the best.

Gender, School, and the Street

My suggestion, then, is that "common" children, like Tom, are usually well cared for at home but they are not necessarily well prepared there for the kind of participation that formal learning at school requires of them. They are more likely, therefore, to resist it. On the other hand, we also need to be able to account for the fact that there are children, like Tom's sister Mary, who also come from "common" households but who are, nevertheless, doing very well at school. Tentatively, I propose that these children are more likely to be girls because girls, unlike their brothers, do not usually have the same degree of freedom to play on the streets. Girls are less likely, therefore, to participate on the street in peer groups in which being tough, looking for trouble, and resisting authority are ways to gain a respected reputation. Gender differences are, therefore, always going to be educationally significant in schools in areas where boys enjoy a large measure of freedom to compete, often violently, for prestige on the streets.

My proposal is not, however, to suggest that everything that we need to know about boys' educational underachievement will be explained by an analysis of the difference that gender makes. While working-class boys may be very different from their middle class peers, it is also clear that not all working-class boys are the same: some are more protected than others from the influence of the street. By implication, those boys who are not allowed to play out and who are not, therefore, likely to be contenders in the tough boys' rankings are, just like nice girls, more likely to do better at school. This is because they are not so likely to be as torn, as tough boys often are, between the competing ideas—tough boy on the street versus good boy in the classroom—of what it means to become valued as a child. Similarly, those "common" girls, like Tom's mother Anne, are allowed to play out and are more likely, therefore, to develop reputations for fighting. Just like "common" boys who develop a taste for trouble, they are much less likely than nice girls and good boys to do well at school. An adequate analysis of the reasons for school failure must, therefore, account for gendered differences between children but it must also account for how those differences intersect with social class distinction. And it must also take into consideration how, even in one family, each child's attitude towards what it means to be "common" may vary. For example, in a family where all the children are boys and the eldest of them has become a notorious trouble-maker who fails at school and enjoys a tough reputation on the street, there is no inevitability that his younger brothers will follow in his footsteps. Each child's history and how that child comes to be socially positioned in the family is unique and any of the younger boys may well be protected, either at home or at school, from what it means for a boy like Tom to become "common": "givin' it large" (becoming a big man) on the street.

When things go wrong at school for Tom and he fails for various reasons to learn what is appropriate to his age group, his parents worry a great deal but they often lack the confidence in their own education and necessary skills to successfully challenge the school or rectify the problems at home. The kind of intervention that I was able to make with Tom—teaching him to read at home—was possible only because I was prepared to visit him at home. I am doubtful, however, whether the extra reading work that we did could have been achieved at school because, in the eyes of his peer group, Tom would have been shamed by his need and desire for special reading assistance. Even if Tom had been amenable to the idea, the school is rarely in a position to either give or afford the individual assistance which children like Tom require if they are to overcome their learning difficulties. By the time the problem has become chronic, as it has in Tom's case, it is usually too late to do very much about it.

Tenter Ground Primary School: Its reputation, Tom's teacher and fellow pupils

In the mornings, when Tom runs across the road to school, he leaves behind him a loving home where he is apparently safe to be a vulnerable ten-year-old boy. At school, however, he adopts the posture that his developing reputation demands and he bowls into the playground to meet his peer group. Some of these are boys and girls he knows and hangs out with on the street, and others he meets only at school. Here are different sets of boys in relation to whom he can test his mettle, but the school is not like the street: Tom cannot run out of the classroom when he is sick of the teacher nagging him, and so his freedom to seek the street when he pleases is limited. At the same time, however, the peer group counts for a great deal at school, not in the same way that it does on the street but certainly in a way that it never can at home. On the street children quite often form groups of disparate ages within a range of a few years on either side of the average age for each group, but at school classes are formed on the basis of mixed gender and same age-set groups. At Tenter Ground School children begin school in the nursery class at age three and formal school proper starts in the class of five- to six-year-olds who progress together through primary school year by year until, at the age of eleven, they make the transition to secondary school.

At the school gate the care of kinship relations gives way to the camaraderie and competitiveness of the peer groups, the importance of which is mediated now by the teachers' responsibilities for the social organization of school life. Perhaps the most important social difference about school, compared to the home environment, is that the adult-to-child ratio is massively reduced. At home children may relate on a one-to-one, two-to-one, three-to-one, or perhaps four-to-one basis with the principal caregiver, but at school the ratio is more likely to be thirty-to-one. For children who have already embodied an understanding of the kind of participation which is required for formal learning, this ratio may not pose a problem, but for children who have no idea what to expect and who find what is required of them at school massively different compared to what happens at home, this low adult-to-child ratio is more likely to pose a significant problem. In schools where the majority of children are unprepared at home for formal learning, teachers will spend a large proportion of their time trying to instill in the children an understanding of the social skills which are required for school-based learning.

Tom is in Year Five at Tenter Ground primary; he shares a classroom and teacher with the older and less numerous Year Six children. Christine, his teacher, is a woman with local roots who grew up in Peckham and who has Bermondsey connections in her grandparents' generation. Even though she now lives in the leafy streets of Richmond in order to be closer to her partner's workplace and could claim middle-class status if she wanted, she will, she says, always think of herself as a working-class woman. Christine is one of education's success stories, but she refuses to turn her back on the struggles of her parents and grandparents because remaining true to and respectful of their struggles is what being working-class means to Christine. Speaking fondly of the working-class community in which she grew up, Christine explains how much she misses the camaraderie among women and men who, when she was young, all pulled together to support one another and have a laugh in the face of common difficulties. She can recount the history of her family's involvement with the now defunct economy of the docks and associates herself with—and is proud of—the resilience that surviving and overcoming poverty entails. Because of her relationship to her background, teaching in a school where she will encounter the children of working-class families has become a personal commitment. Christine says of the children, "I understand them; I know what they're going through."

Christine explains that Tenter Ground School has a bad reputation: prior to the beginning of my fieldwork, Tenter Ground had been labeled by Her Majesty's inspectors as a school with serious weaknesses. This means that in many respects it is a failing school, what people call a "sink school" where children are, by implication, going down the drain. This does not say much for the prospect of the pupils' education and reinforces the metaphors which associate working-class people with waste products. Because it is a school which does not get good results, Tenter Ground School does not attract any of the more ambitious parents in the local area and for this reason, Christine emphasizes, it is not considered to be a typical Bermondsey school. Most Bermondsey people would not even consider sending their children to Tenter Ground; even though they might not have done well at school themselves, Bermondsey mothers still have high aspirations and want the best for their children. They are more likely, therefore, to favor the stricter church schools which have reputations for better discipline, greater formality, and neat uniforms. Even if they have to attend church once a week out of the instrumental desire to secure places for their children, Bermondsey mothers will do what is necessary to give their children access to available advantages in the competition for success at school.

Tenter Ground pupils live mostly on the surrounding council housing estates but not many of them, with the exception of a few, including Tom and Gary, know much about the legacy of Bermondsey's exclusive past. Anne emphasizes that she does not instil in her children any sense that they "are Bermondsey." "I don't," she says, "put any religion or culture on them. I just let them get on with life." Pete points out that the closely knit community that Bermondsey once was is dead and gone anyway. He suggests that what I see at Tenter Ground is more like the future, more like what Bermondsey is to become, which is "a multicultural place." Al-

though Anne was thoroughly schooled by her parents in what she understands to be the conventionally prejudiced Bermondsey views about not
mixing with "colored children," she was able to mix with them at school
and to make up her own mind up about different kinds of people. She tells
me that if ever she hears the children being "racialist" she comes down
hard on them and she emphasizes how distraught Tom was when he was
forced to leave his old school because he had to leave a boy he was really "tight with" (close to)—his best friend Max—who is a "half-caste"
(mixed race) boy.

Compared to those few who are "born and bred" Bermondsey children,
the majority of Tenter Ground's pupils travel from further afield in south
London—from the Elephant and Castle, Nunhead, or Peckham for example. Many of them are the children of first-, second-, or third-generation non-white immigrant families. This does not include the children
of parents who are first-, second-, or third-generation immigrants from
Ireland, but the point is that white children are clearly in the minority at
Tenter Ground School. Boys also predominate, with a ratio of just over
two boys to one girl. Christine suggests that this is the result of the head
teacher's policy of accepting boys like Tom who have been excluded from
other south London primaries. The head feels that she can hardly turn
boys like this away since she is trying to secure funds for the school, but
because these boys are, for one reason or another, usually troublemakers,
the school has become trapped in a vicious cycle from which it is difficult
to escape. Over the years, parents reluctant to keep their children, and
especially girls, in a deteriorating and increasingly troublesome school environment, find places for them elsewhere—usually in the church schools
to the north of the borough.

Christine explains how badly the school is affected by a lack of confidence among parents in the local area: Bermondsey people would be likely, she stresses, to say that only the children of parents who do not know
any better or who for some reason cannot secure their children places at
other schools are to be found at Tenter Ground. The principal effect of
this bad reputation is that children in Year Five and Six have to share one
teacher and classroom because there simply are not enough children to
make a single age-set class. Because funds are allocated to schools on the
basis of pupil numbers there is not enough money to pay for one teacher
per year group.

So the school that Tom runs to in the mornings is not an easy place
to be. It is blighted by low education standards and has a reputation for
both troublesome boys and a lack of funds, and therefore low teacher/staff
morale. But no matter: Tom knows little of these things; he runs in because this is where he can have fun and find his place in the peer group.

Occasionally he is reluctant to go to school because there has been too much trouble there for him to handle, either with other boys or with the teacher, because of his behavior. Every now and again, for example, he is suspended from school which means that he is forced to stay at home because the head teacher is not prepared to keep him in class while he is misbehaving. This always means that he is then in trouble with his parents too and will probably be grounded (prevented from going out to play on the street).

While Tom certainly has more freedom to do as he pleases at home—where, like most boys of his age, he spends a lot of time on his Sony Playstation— he is nevertheless constrained by having to share a small bedroom with his sister. Like many children, and especially teenagers, who spend a lot of time on the street, Tom does so in part because he is seeking space from overcrowded housing. When he is suspended from school and confined to the flat, a sociable boy like Tom quickly gets bored and lonely; he is always keen to get back to school where his friends are. So why does Tom get into so much trouble at school and how does he fit into the boys' peer group there? To answer these questions it is first important to understand how the classroom is organized socially, to appreciate what values are established for children by the form of participation that adults require of them there, and to gain a sense of the discrepancies between this form of participation and what boys expect of each other in their peer groups.

Children's Comportment

Out of the apparent chaos of playtime, the order of entry into the school buildings is marked by the arrival of teachers who take designated places in the playground, expecting the children to line up in single-file class sets. When the line is orderly and relatively quiet, the teacher leads the way into the classroom through the corridors and up the stairs of the huge and aging Victorian building. From the freedom of play to the relative restriction of orderly conduct, movement and noise are constrained further and further until stillness and silence are achieved under the watchful gaze of the teacher who waits for the children to settle down on the carpet for registration. The surveillance of children's comportment is at its most pronounced when they must gather together like this, under the teacher's eyes, either for registration or instruction in the classroom, or for whole school meetings in the assembly hall. In these moments, by virtue of her ability to hold the children's attention, to keep them still and quiet, the teacher's power and authority to impart knowledge is recreated on a daily, if not hourly, basis.

Those children who fail to attend to what the teacher has to say because they are more interested in interacting with those sitting next to them, or in moving about and making noise, are punished first through verbal admonishment and then by increasing degrees of spatial exclusion from the group. If these measures are insufficient to quell disruptive behavior then the spatial exclusion is further emphasized and a disruptive child will be sent to the deputy or head teacher's office. In extreme cases a child might be suspended from school for the day, which means that his parents will be called to come to school and take their child home. Exclusion from the group is supposed to induce shame and encourage conformist behavior in children. If they want to be part of the group, they have to accept the rules of participation; if they do not learn to do as they are told, they will suffer exclusion and isolation at school and bring shame on themselves and their families. Ideally, when a child misbehaves and is suspended for a day or two, what is brought to the foreground for the child and, by implication, for all the other children is the realization that their parents support the teachers in their disciplining of the children and that parents want their children to learn successfully and do well at school. Apart from the force of the law, which requires children between the ages of five and sixteen to be at school, the permanent background of the school's authority to teach and discipline the child is given by the parents' support for the teachers.

Sometimes, however, a suspension has the opposite effect and serves only to highlight the opposition of the child's parents to the school's authority. Conflict between parents and teachers then ensues and education welfare officials might be called in to remind parents of their legal responsibilities with respect to their children's education. In addition, the necessity to temporarily suspend a child from school can stand, in parents' eyes, for a failure of the school to adequately discipline a child within the school. Compared to parents, however, teachers are limited in the means they have at their disposal to enforce their authority; they can withdraw privileges, but since they are forbidden to use physical force of any kind, exclusion from the group is, in effect, their only weapon of restraint. Having no problem controlling their children at home, parents are often frustrated about teachers' inability to discipline their children at school.

The Pecking Order of Disruption

The opposite of the learned disposition that teachers require of children in the classroom is the playful, rowdy, intimidating, sometimes violent, and frenetic movements of particular boys. During and between lessons such boys assert their presence to each other and to other children in ways that enable the reconstitution, on a daily basis, of the pecking order of their physical, as opposed to academic, dominance. The dynamic of this volatile process works alongside and periodically interferes with the pace of the teacher's rhythm for curriculum delivery. She must then intervene to restore order to the learning process. Each child in the classroom is preoccupied every day with trying to accommodate the demands of the different dispositions required for play, peer group, and classroom interaction. Some boys manage to do well in their work and still take part in the pecking order of disruption while others behave beautifully, drawing no attention to themselves, and still struggle nevertheless with the learning tasks assigned to the class. However, because quiet children pose no disruptive threat to the rhythm of the teacher's timetable for curriculum delivery, they are much less likely to command any of the teacher's attention and their learning difficulties are therefore more likely to be overlooked. The obstacles they face in their learning are, however, often no less serious than the problems facing badly behaved boys.

Meanwhile, a large measure of the teacher's and children's emotional and physical resources is preoccupied with the heightening tension that is caused by the disruptive boys' challenges to adult authority. While Tom's case appears to prove the point that the streaming of ability within school classrooms can cause children to become subversive—children react against the demeaning position ascribed to them—it is also true that the worst offenders among the disruptive boys in Tom's class are some of the most able academically. When the climate among them is one of ruthless domination, it is often the brightest among the tough boys who quickly become peer group leaders. It is not simply a matter of brute force; it has also to do with the combined skills of daring and personal charisma. Tom's friend, Gary, for example, excels in this domain.

Observing Tom's class, it soon becomes clear to me that the really difficult challenge which boys face in schools like Tenter Ground is how to work relatively well in class when it suits them and still be able to demonstrate their subversive edge to peers when need be. In Year Five/Six there are a few of these kinds of boys; they tend to be the boys of West African origin who are trying to strike an acceptable balance between their parents' high educational expectations and what is required of them if they are to be valued in the disruptive boys' peer group at school. Even though they are academically capable, these boys will often not excel at school because, as a result of trying to strike the necessary balance between concentrating in class and disrupting their own and others' learning, they lack the required focus for excellence in learning. They tend, however, to do well enough to get through the system, keeping their parents and teachers reasonably happy.

Other boys, like Gary, who could do well academically if they put their minds to it, appear, from an educational point of view, to self-destruct. They play the game of peer group leader all the way to its final conclusion, spending many days either absent from school to try to avoid trouble or suspended by teachers because of bad behavior. Additional problems then arise because boys like this then have to struggle to catch up with missed work. Because he is one of her favorites, Gary is relatively protected at Tenter Ground by his teacher, Christine. She knows, however, that he will not be cosseted at secondary school where, she says, boys like him are quickly and permanently excluded from school.

Gary is one of her favorites, Christine says, because, like the other disruptive boys, he is a rebel. He stands out as a strong individual who dares to resist conventional expectations; he has charisma and refuses to do only as he is told, but his energies and intelligence are misdirected. Christine feels sure that under different circumstances Gary would be a creative and strong leader and she watches in vain as his leadership skills are put to less constructive uses than she imagines for them. Anxious not to alienate him, Christine is determined to win Gary's respect and confidence in order to try to persuade him of education's possibilities. Meanwhile, Rochelle, who is Christine's assistant in the classroom, is often furious about Christine's soft spot for Gary; she knows that Gary has health problems and she is aware that Christine attributes a lot of Gary's behavioral problems to his struggle to come to terms with his illness, but Rochelle is nevertheless constantly infuriated by Christine's failure to take the hard line with Gary which she feels he deserves. Many of the classroom assistants, who have less authority than teachers and who are therefore less respected by the disruptive boys, bear the brunt of Gary's influence at school, and they have little sympathy for any problem he might be struggling with in or outside of school. This means, in the end, that the hopes Tom's mother carries for Gary as a possible role model for her son will not come to fruition. On the contrary, Gary is more likely than any of the other boys at Tenter Ground to bring Tom closer to trouble.

Understanding Troublemaking

The problem at Tenter Ground, then, is two-fold: if these boys have a genuine special educational need, as teachers and other staff suggest that they do, it is a travesty that the will and the funding are not available to get formal statements of that need prepared on the basis of rigorous assessments at the earliest possible opportunity. Without those statements no relevant support can be put in place before the boys leave primary for secondary school where matters usually only get worse. If, on the other hand, as I suggest, the problem with disruptive boys is a social one, having more to do with peer group formation in a school where adult authority is weak and disruptive boys are allowed to rule, then the focus alters. We need to understand how the school environment offers particular kinds of boys the opportunity—which they may not get at home but to which they are becoming accustomed on the street—to compete for power and influence.

In failing schools, boys like this have the opportunity to establish among themselves a form of participation that is completely at odds with what teachers require of them, and therein lies the source of their subversive and charismatic power. All the other children, and especially other boys, have to learn how to accommodate themselves to this disruptive influence in one way or another and, insofar as their behavior goes unchecked, the disruptive boys dominate. Rather than making their behavior seem pathological, my proposal is for research that might help us begin to understand how it is that young boys in certain kinds of social environments, like on the street and in failing schools, can come to structure their relations with one another in such a way that troublesome, violent, intimidating behavior becomes a social good. Only in this way will we be able to understand how, at schools like Tenter Ground, boys are inadvertently given the opportunity to cultivate an ethical disposition which is embodied as an oppositional, surly, intimidating stance that is entirely contradictory to what didactic practice intends to establish for children.

It is easy to see how thrilling and efficacious the competition is for boys to violently seek prestige in relation to peers and to antagonize teachers, and how they eventually become accustomed to the idea that they are going to disappoint their parents. It is true to say that as boys like Tom begin to feel the pressure of adult opprobrium they begin to suffer because, despite their best intentions, they become caught in the cycle of turn-taking pranks and revenge-seeking scuffles which define not only their daring and their reputation but also their friendship with one another. To strongly resist the form of participation that disruptive boys demand is to risk losing their friendship and, therefore, their protection. Only rarely does a boy find the courage to dare to get on with his work and resist others' ideas of what constitutes an appropriate style of subversive masculinity for boys. The question then is: what kind of boy can a boy be in a school like this if he starts to behave well for teachers and to do well at school?

Because the principal dynamic of group formation among the disruptive boys is aggressive competition, there is little solidarity among them. What friendship there is between the boys at school has, as its background, a tension born of high adrenaline, of antagonistic and potentially intimidating physical exchange. What arises is a competitive system of disruption without formal or written rules, which new boys discover in the classroom and which they must choose to either resist or participate in. If they feel themselves to be contenders, they declare, via their ability to fight back effectively, their eligibility to be incorporated into a peer group which is established on the basis of often violent acts of subversion. Success in this inevitably implies the destruction of a boy's chances of doing well at school and quite often jeopardizes the opportunities that being at school presents to his better-behaved peers. In the end, however, an individual boy's disruptive resistance has no effect on the value system that education establishes for children, because, treated as an individual, the most disruptive boy is usually excluded from school and often claimed by the street. And so, for as long as failing schools are protected from proper scrutiny and disruptive boys are treated as individuals with emotional and behavioral difficulties, the basis of the formation of their peer group is neglected as a social phenomenon and the cycle goes on. It is a bit like Lord of the Flies—only in this case there is no desert island and plenty of adults are looking on in vain as dangers looms everywhere.

Race, Place, and Reputation

On the estate where I live, not far from Tenter Ground, Tom's equivalent is a young white working-class boy called Ian. One day, towards the end of the summer, at the boundary of the space he is allowed to travel in, far beyond the other side of the estate, Ian and his friend Glen encounter a group of black boys who take a liking to Ian and Glen's bikes. These black boys also notice Ian's mobile phone and try to take it from him. Ian and Glen, none the worse for wear but scared by their encounter with a group of older teenage black boys, return quickly to the safety of home to report what has happened. Ian's older brother John is sixteen; he has just left school for good.

A week before this incident I had been chatting with John's mother Alice about how John is doing and we had reminisced together about watching him grow up on the estate. As a boy, John had spent every waking moment, when he was not at school, practicing his football skills in the garden square at the back of the flats. When we were chatting I told Alice about my research and asked her if she thought John would mind doing an interview with me, especially since he seemed to have turned into such a "bod" lately. Alice laughed, saying, "It's true, he is a real Bermondsey bod now, since he's hooked up with a group of white boys from down The Blue."

Alice then explained that, before, because John went to a school near the Walworth Road whose pupils are mainly black boys, he was used to hanging out with black boys. Recently, however, there had been a few incidents in which John had been beaten up badly by black boys on the Walworth Road. As if to clarify something for me, Alice emphasized, "I'm not racialist, I get on with everybody; anyone'll tell you that. I don't let my boys say racialist things in front of me, but I've [h]eard 'em talkin' and I know what goes on." She then explained how worried she was because she felt that John always had to prove his reputation on the street. Whenever she told him not to get involved, advising him to walk away from trouble, he would tell her that she would never be able to understand. He had tried to explain to her that if he walked away from confrontations he would not have a reputation and he then would not be safe on the street. Cheering up somewhat, Alice then changed the subject to tell me about how John now had a lovely girlfriend and how she thanked God because John would now start spending a lot of time with this girl indoors instead of out on the street with the boys where trouble starts. Alice told me with pride that after the summer holidays John was going to start looking for a job.

It is not surprising that, when John heard Ian's story, he made his way, probably against his mother's wishes, straight round to these black boys' area to see if he could find them and teach them a lesson. Nobody in the block knows exactly what happened next, but at dusk the terrible sound of a woman screaming in anguish pierced the peace of the evening. I ran to the front balcony to see what was happening and saw Alice, doubled over, holding her side and crying in pain. Pointing and screaming, she cried out, "They're killin' [h]im, they're killin' [h]im, phone the police!" None of us who came out onto our front balconies could see what or where Alice was pointing to, but, witnessing the look of terror on her face, I ran inside and phoned the police straightaway. My partner, meanwhile, ran down to help Alice and to see if there was anything he could do, but by this time John was long gone. Apparently he was being chased by a gang of twelve black youths. It is said that one of them came into our area, after John's earlier incursion into their area, and hailed John out from the street below his flat in our block. Thinking that he faced a one-on-one confrontation, John presumably went down without a second thought. At least ten more boys were hiding however, waiting for him to come down before they pounced.

Eventually, police arrived in numbers, but they were not able to prevent the assault which happened several blocks away and down a quiet street. It emerges later that the boys managed to corner John and one of them used his mobile phone to call his dad for back-up. The father apparently arrived in his car with a baseball bat and assisted the boys in dragging John out from under a car where he had tried to hide. They then proceeded to beat him within inches of his life. The next day, while his son lay in intensive care, John's father, who had a reputation of his own to defend, issued a warning to the man that he heard was responsible for the attack on his son. It was a warning that everyone in Bermondsey can understand and it was not an idle threat. It is popular knowledge that Bermondsey has its own justice system that runs in parallel to and often against the efforts of local police. The foundation of this justice depends on the understanding that you do not "grass" (tell the police anything) because the people who need to seek revenge will do so on their own terms. If you grass you are implicating yourself in the cycle of revenge-seeking which is an extremely dangerous thing to do. It is against this background that the police struggle to bring people to conventional justice in Bermondsey and, not surprisingly, witnesses are a rare phenomenon.

After some time, the police accused the man who allegedly brandished the baseball bat with attempted murder. Fearing for their lives, his family members were quickly moved (by their housing association) to safe housing and the flat was soon boarded up and empty. Meanwhile, Ian's mother and her family, fearing for their own lives too and disrupted beyond measure, struggled for the next eighteen months to try to secure a housing transfer from the council. That this incident should end up becoming an issue related to how the council manages housing in Bermondsey is poignant. Time and again, white people whom I interview and speak to in Bermondsey accuse the council of mismanagement and incompetence because they feel that the pressing needs of local white people are overlooked for the sake of outsiders who are perceived now to be black people and other kinds of immigrants whose needs seem, to them, to be always given precedence. The question of who owns Bermondsey is thrashed out, then, in the tense dynamic between white people's sense of belonging to their manor and the council's legal responsibility to manage the land

and housing rights according to national governmental legislation about housing those people considered to be in most need.

In an article describing the process of gentrification in Bermondsey, a journalist asserts that the "Old Bermondsey" has finally been tamed. Presumably he has not spent time talking with local people and fails to realize that claiming a space is not just about buying up the land or its properties, which smacks of the arrogance of monetary control. Those people who are born and bred here, their allies, and especially the young men at the warrior stage of their lives still feel that Bermondsey belongs to them and some of them are ready to die defending it.

Male Prestige

To most people it seems outrageous that this level of violence could escalate all because of a mobile phone, but it is about much more than that. In part it is about the way in which male prestige, from the age of eight or ten to about eighteen to twenty years and sometimes beyond, is constituted through the capacity for violence and brutality. This is intimately related to the way in which control and influence are wielded over particular neighborhood areas and how this can sometimes lead to involvement in territorial gangs. This had always been the case in Bermondsey; there is nothing new in it. Young white working-class men from Bermondsey battled against their enemies in adjacent manors in Peckham and Walworth long before immigrants from Africa, the Caribbean, and Asia arrived in numbers. The longstanding dynamic of these territorial conflicts is the historical precedent that governs all present transformations.

When I speak to older men and women about this, they say that all that has changed nowadays is that young men carry knives and guns and take drugs; they also have fewer amenities to distract them and so they get carried away more quickly. In addition, most Bermondsey people are quick to blame the presence of black people for what they see as the demise of Bermondsey in general and for the escalation of violent tension in particular. The story of what happened to John becomes the stuff of legend because it is taken to be the evidence for what white people perceive to be the truth about black people: that black people's violence is far more brutal and indiscriminate than their own. Things are rarely as simple as racial explanations would suggest, however.

Two days after John was ambushed, two gangs of white youths further into Bermondsey were involved in skirmishes which resulted in a fifteen-year-old white youth being stabbed to death. He was stabbed fifteen times. Obviously this was not reported as a racial assault because both gangs of youths were white, but I would argue that to differentiate between the assaults on the basis of race is to miss what the assaults had in common. The point is that all young men in Bermondsey have to contend with a prestige system based partly on their ability to be brutal and to withstand brutality in defense of territorial areas. In this system the means for controlling the space, becoming a man, and developing a particular kind of bodily competence via specific kinds of violent exchanges become mutually specified. Being able to handle yourself on the street where territories are mapped out is what counts.

The increased incidence of young black youths' involvement in violent skirmishes on the streets of Bermondsey simply means that as particular kinds of outsiders they are now confident enough to begin to stick up for themselves and compete violently for prestige in this Bermondsey "big-man" system. Perhaps, as the children of immigrants from particular countries like Jamaica, they are already learning from their fathers about a way of life in which the development of masculinity is inseparable from the capacity for territorial violence. In other words, perhaps some immigrant groups have big-man systems of their own. If so, this does not make these youths much different from Bermondsey bods. The focus on racial difference thus eclipses what white and black youths have in common in working-class areas like Bermondsey: they all have to accommodate themselves to the ways in which masculinity is defined, often violently, on the street.

The pertinent question, if we are at all interested in distracting young men from their involvement in this big-man system is: how to change a value system? Schools are obviously failing to show these boys how to create and transform their sense of self-value in a different way than the working-class neighborhood demands. It would seem, then, that part of the solution might involve increasing the numbers of opportunities available outside school for young men to transpose the territorial conflicts of the street into new and less dangerous but nevertheless still meaningful forms of exchange. Currently, sport and music appear to be the only alternative but still legitimate means that bods have at their disposal to make something of themselves without simultaneously damaging their reputations on the street.

It becomes clear, then, that being a working-class young man—black, white or Asian—means much more than attaining adulthood in a world defined by differentiated kinds of low-status work. Becoming a working-class young man has a lot to do with learning to become a particular kind of person by learning how to belong to a particular place. The development and reproduction of economic and political relations are inseparable from the specific means of gaining prestige. This transforms from one generation to the next and evolves as a developmental cycle over time. A boy is most vulnerable between the ages of eight to twenty; if his mother can see her son to the age of twenty-five without him being stabbed, killed, or imprisoned she is profoundly relieved: all her efforts to keep him safe and alive and on the straight and narrow have paid off. Meanwhile, young men involved in a life of trouble and crime in their late teens and early twenties are much less likely to be so in their late twenties, thirties, and forties, as they are more likely to be tamed by the necessities of trying to provide financial and moral support for family life.

Notes

A version of this material appeared in Gillian Evans (2006) *Educational Failure and Working Class White Children in Britain* (New York and Basingstoke: Palgrave Macmillan), reproduced with permission of Palgrave MacMillan.

1. In Bermondsey a 'bod' is the name given to a young man with a tough street reputation.

2. National crime statistics in Britain are published annually; the figures for 2008/09 suggest a significant decline in violent crime (Walker A. et al. 2009).

3. Social class in Britain is a category of relative and ranked distinction. It situates people in relation to economic and political history, in relation to educational and socio-cultural history, and in relation to a history of housing and health spanning across three generations of family life, which makes grandparents particularly important figures in oral testimonies and which suggests that it takes three generations to completely change the class position of a family up or down the social hierarchy. In other words, social class is a relative and ranked category of distinction that indexes, in a complex way, any person's historical placement in a society defined by a particular kind of moral and political economy. In a nation defined by class relations, we are constantly engaged in reading each other's history and trying to work out what the body and its language can tell us about social class and all of its subtle degrees of distinction. As such, class is a peculiarly British obsession, one that intersects clumsily and continuously with a more recent and, discursively, more prominent preoccupation with notions of equality.

4. *The Guardian*, Thursday 12 April 2007. http://www.guardian.co.uk/politics/2007/apr/12/ukcrime.race downloaded 28 September 2009.

5. See, for example, S. Strand (2008). *Minority ethnic pupils in the Longitudinal Study of Young People in England: Extension report on performance in public examinations at age 16*. DCSF Research Report RR-029. London: Department for Children, Schools and Families.

6. Pseudonyms are used throughout to protect the anonymity of the people who participated in this study.

Bibliography

Eades C., et al., eds. 2007. *Knife Crime: a review of evidence and policy*. London: Centre for Crime and Justice Studies.

Evans G. 2006a. *Educational Failure and Working Class White Children in Britain*. New York and Basingstoke: Palgrave Macmillan.

———. 2006b. "Learning, Violence and the Social Structure of Value." *Social Anthropology*, 14 (2): 247–259.

———. 2010. "'What about White People's History?' Class, Race and Culture Wars in 21st Century Britain." In *Culture Wars: Context, Models, and Anthropologists' Accounts*, eds. D. James et al. New York: Berghahn.

Strand S. 2008. "Minority ethnic pupils in the Longitudinal Study of Young People in England: Extension report on performance in public examinations at age 16." *DCSF Research Report RR-029*. London: Department for Children, Schools and Families.

Walker A., et al., eds. 2009. "Crime in England and Wales 2008/9." Vol. 1: findings from the British Crime Survey and police recorded crime. London: Home Office Statistics: Crown Copyright.

Wintour, Patrick and Vikram Dodd. 2007. "Blair Blames Spate of Murders on Black Culture." *The Guardian*, 12 April. Available from: http://www.guardian.co.uk/politics/2007/apr/12/ukcrime.race, 28 September 2009 [Accessed 13 August 2009].

Notes on Contributors

Vered Amit is a Professor of Anthropology at Concordia University. Her research has focused on a range of circumstances and locales including intra- and inter-ethnic boundaries among Armenians in London, youth cultures, ethnic lobbying, expatriacy in the Cayman Islands, transnational consultants, and international student travel. Running through all of these different projects has been an ongoing preoccupation with the workings of and intersections between different forms of transnational mobility. She is the author or editor of ten books.

Gary Armstrong is Reader in the School of Sport and Education, Brunel University, West London. He has written extensively on issues around football and is currently examining the policing implications of hosting the 2012 Olympic Games. His most recent work, co-authored with Jon Mitchell, is titled *Global and Local Football: Politics and Europeanisation on the fringes of the EU* and was published by Routledge in 2008.

Noel Dyck is Professor of Social Anthropology at Simon Fraser University in British Columbia. The author of several books on relations between Aboriginal peoples and governments, he has subsequently conducted field research on sport, childhood, and youth mobility in Canada. His books include *Sport, Dance and Embodied Identities* (2003) (with Eduardo P. Archetti) and *Games, Sports and Cultures* (2000). He is currently completing studies of the social construction of children's sports.

Deborah A. Elliston is Assistant Professor of Anthropology at Binghamton University, State University of New York. Her work in feminist and queer anthropology has been published in the *American Ethnologist*, *Cultural Anthropology*, *Pacific Studies*, and *Reviews in Anthropology*. Her ethnography of Polynesian nationalism is tentatively entitled *Sites of Struggle: The Politics of Difference in Polynesian Nationalism*. She is currently researching questions of sexuality, gender, desire, and labor through fieldwork with sex-worker *raerae*—male-bodied, femininity-performing, men-desiring Polynesians—in the Society Islands.

Gillian Evans is RCUK Research Fellow in the Centre for the Analysis of Socio-Cultural Change (CRESC) at the University of Manchester. Her research centers around the study of post-industrial working class neighborhoods in London. Her first ethnographic monograph, *Educational Failure and Working Class White Children in Britain*, was published in 2006, creating a controversy about the position of the white working class in contemporary Britain. Evans is currently undertaking a major research project on the transformation of the East End of London as a result of the Olympic Games in 2012.

Martin Demant Frederiksen has recently completed his PhD at the Department of Anthropology, University of Aarhus, Denmark. He has conducted several fieldworks in the Republic of Georgia from 2005 to 2009 and published articles on a range of subjects such as development work in post-conflict settings, temporality and methodology, post-Soviet consumption, and youth and anthropological analysis. He is currently affiliated with a comparative research project on innovation, time, and agency among marginalized youth in Brazil, Uganda, Georgia, and Denmark.

Anne Irwin has recently retired from the University of Calgary where she was an Assistant Professor in the Department of Anthropology and held the first Canadian Defence and Foreign Affairs Institute Chair in Civil-Military Relations. She has been conducting anthropological research with a Canadian infantry battalion since 1992 during training in Canada and during combat operations in Afghanistan. Her research interests include discourse analysis and embodied practice in military institutions.

William Jankowiak is Professor of Anthropology at the University of Nevada, Las Vegas. Besides numerous scientific articles and book chapters, he is the editor of *Intimacies: Love and Sex Across Cultures* (2008), *Romantic Passion* (1995), "Well Being, Family Affections, and Ethical Nationalism in Urban China" (*Journal of Urban Anthropology* 2004), Drugs, Labor and Colonial Expansion (with Dan Bradburd) (2003), and *Sex, Death and Hierarchy in a Chinese City* (1993).

Ritty A. Lukose is Associate Professor in the Gallatin School of Individualized Study at New York University. Working at the intersection of anthropology, women and gender studies, and South Asian Studies, she is the author of a number of articles and a book entitled *Liberalization's Children: Gender, Youth and Consumer Citizenship in Globalizing India* (2009) which examines the contemporary cultural politics of globalization in India.

Daniel Mains is Wick Cary Assistant Professor of Honors at the University of Oklahoma. He has published several articles concerning unemployment, the experience of time, aspirations, and neoliberalism in relation to urban young men in Ethiopia. Recent publications have appeared in the journals *Africa* and *American Ethnologist*. Mains is currently working on a collaborative project that explores the relationship between aspirations for the future and mental health among rural and urban youth in Ethiopia.

Robert Moore is Professor of Anthropology and Coordinator of Asian Studies at Rollins College. His recent publications include a contribution to the *Handbook of Research on Asian Entrepreneurship* (2009) and, with James Rizor, "Confucian and Cool: China's Youth in Transition" in *Education about Asia* (2008). He is currently working on a study of Mandarin slang.

Tianshu Pan is Associate Professor of Anthropology affiliated with the School of Social Development and Public Policy, Fudan University, where he has taught since January 2006. He was educated at Fudan University and Harvard University and, before moving to Fudan, he taught at Georgetown University and SAIS, Johns Hopkins University. He has conducted field research on global/local dynamics, local responses to avian flu threat, neighborhood gentrification, the impact of migration on migrant-sending communities, and "Shanghai nostalgia."

Victor M. Rios is an Associate Professor of Sociology at the University of California, Santa Barbara. His recent publications include "The Consequences of the Criminal Justice Pipeline on Black and Latino Masculinity" in *The Annals of the American Academy of Political and Social Sciences* (2009) and *Punished: The Criminalization of Inner City Boys* (forthcoming). As a teenager, Rios was involved in gangs and incarcerated in the juvenile justice system. He conducts research with these experiences in perspective.

Rosellen Roche is an Assistant Professor and Research Fellow at the Institute of Irish Studies, Queen's University Belfast. Acting as Head of Project for two policy-oriented European initiatives, as well a government consultant for post-Agreement legislation, much of her work has an applied focus. Recent academic work includes a piece on the topic of paramilitary punishment in *Global Vigilantes: Anthropological Perspectives on Justice and Violence*. Roche is currently researching aspects of stress in conflict while completing her monograph on young people and violence.

Cèsar Rodriguez is a doctoral student in the Department of Sociology at the University of California, Santa Barbara. His work examines the criminalization of youth of color within the context of capitalist globalization. Focusing on the abandonment and punitivity they must navigate, he also studies how youths navigate and author their own resistance. He has additionally written about gang-members-turned-organizers. Rodriguez has recently published 'Gangs and Community Empowerment: How Critical Literature and Street Credentials Impact Urban Street Activists' Ability to Access Rival Gangs as Social Capital' (*McNair Scholar's Journal*, 2005).

James Rosbrook-Thompson is Visiting Lecturer in Sport and Development in the School of Sport and Education, Brunel University, West London, and a Ph.D. candidate at London School of Economics and Political Science (LSE). His doctoral thesis examines the role of "race" and raciology in British football.

Susan J. Terrio is Professor of Anthropology and Chair of the Department of Anthropology at Georgetown University in Washington, D.C. She has conducted research on youth, migration, and the law in France and the United States. Her most recent book, *Judging Mohammed: Juvenile delinquency, Immigration, and Exclusion at the Paris Palace of Justice* (2009), examines the identification and treatment of problem youth. Her new research centers on the federal custodial system for unaccompanied, undocumented children in the United States.

INDEX

O'Donnell, Mike and Sue Sharpe, 194, 212n6
Olwig, Karen Fog and Eva Gullov, 27n2, 28n9
Ortner, Sherry, 167
Osella, F. and C. Osella, 44, 55n6n8n10, 56n11
Ossman, Susan and Susan Terrio, 15

paramilitaries, 26, 188, 190, 195, 198, 208, 211n1, 213n12n14
Parenti, Christian, 260n9
Parker, Howard, 193–194, 202, 205
Parish, William and Martin King Whyte, 82
patrilineality, 79, 81–82
patron–client relations, 121, 147
peers, 6, 25, 49, 71, 73, 87, 90, 180–181, 183, 188, 189, 191, 195–196, 198, 200–201, 204–205, 209–210, 223, 225, 252, 272–273, 275–277, 279–280, 284–286, 288, 303–305, 307–308, 310–313
Pelkmans, Mathijs, 184, 185n8
Perlman, Janice, 11
Perry, Elizabeth and Xun Li, 87–88
play, 6, 36, 72, 75, 80, 101, 119, 126, 149, 178, 252, 286, 299, 301, 303, 308, 310–311
police harassment, 241, 253, 256
politeness, 97, 224
poverty, 8, 14, 22, 24, 26, 35, 37, 39, 87, 118, 167, 171, 175, 190, 207, 210, 237, 241, 244, 257, 297, 306
power, 158, 220–223, 237–238, 243, 259n6, 266–267, 274, 281, 293, 309, 312
Prashad, Vijay, 259n6
prestige, 81, 114, 172, 221, 296, 303, 312, 316–317
Prince, Ruth, 7
protests, 104n1, 111–112, 134–135, 156–157, 160n4

reciprocity, 120–121, 124–125, 127–128, 146
remittances, 40–41,125
respectability, 10, 12–14, 16–19, 24, 26, 42–44, 48, 53, 166
Ricoeur, Paul, 222
risk, 14, 16, 25, 36, 45, 49, 63–65, 70, 74–75, 98, 100, 103, 125, 191, 220, 226, 231, 236, 252, 312
rites of passage, 20, 55n6, 60, 66–68, 72, 75
Rushdie, Salman, 36, 55n2
Rutherford, Andrew, 266

Samuels, Karen, 60
Saunders, Doug, 1–3
Sarkozy, Nicholas, 221
school-to-prison pipeline, 244–246
Schostak, John and Barbara Walter, 15
Scott, James C., 260n8
sectarianism, 189, 197–199, 201–202, 205, 212n2
security, 26, 61, 64, 121, 177, 188, 191, 211n1, 245, 251, 256, 259n8, 260n9, 270, 274, 290
Sellasie, Haile, 114
sex, 38, 49, 50–54, 56n16, 66, 70, 74–75, 89, 91–92, 98, 103, 120, 122–124, 136, 239n6, 287
Shaw, Thomas, 84
singing, 75
smoking, 1, 122, 166, 169, 170–171, 178, 276, 281, 293, 293n8, 300
Smyth, Marie, 209, 212n7
sociality, 48–49, 146–147, 171
socialization, 4, 75, 221, 289
  rehabilitation, 220, 222, 225
social mobility, 1, 9, 13, 15, 17–18, 24, 26, 27, 42, 114, 128, 244, 258n3
social movements, 35, 80, 84, 133, 207
Spector–Mersel, Gabriela, 73
sport, 18, 85–86, 190, 198, 232, 271–273, 286, 288, 299–300, 314, 317
stereotypes, young men, 4–6, 10, 53, 75, 171, 239
  good man, 165–166, 171, 175–177, 179, 183
  young men and indolence, 3, 5, 7, 17, 26, 153, 156, 170, 180
  young men and irresponsibility, 5, 220, 268
  young men and social problems, source of, 3, 123, 158
  young men and transparency, 5
  young men and unreliability, 26, 153–154
  see idler
stories, 5, 23–24, 42, 49–50, 55, 94, 116, 170, 172, 174, 225, 235, 239, 242, 249–250, 257, 266, 268–269, 272, 291, 305
Straker, Gill, 205–207
style
  fashion, 44–46, 48–49, 52–54, 56n17, 65, 84, 118, 134, 172–173, 200, 250–251, 281–284, 286, 288

Lightning Source UK Ltd.
Milton Keynes UK
UKOW03f0618040813

214789UK00004B/20/P